PSYCHOLOGY RESEARCH PROGRESS

DIALOGICALITY IN FOCUS: CHALLENGES TO THEORY, METHOD AND APPLICATION

PSYCHOLOGY RESEARCH PROGRESS

Additional books in this series can be found on Nova's website
under the Series tab.

Additional E-books in this series can be found on Nova's website
under the E-book tab.

PSYCHOLOGY RESEARCH PROGRESS

DIALOGICALITY IN FOCUS: CHALLENGES TO THEORY, METHOD AND APPLICATION

MARIANN MÄRTSIN
BRADY WAGONER
EMMA-LOUISE AVELING
IRINI KADIANAKI
AND
LISA WHITTAKER
EDITORS

Nova Science Publishers, Inc.
New York

Copyright © 2011 by Nova Science Publishers, Inc.

For permission to use material from this book please contact us:
Telephone 631-231-7269; Fax 631-231-8175
Web Site: http://www.novapublishers.com

NOTICE TO THE READER

The Publisher has taken reasonable care in the preparation of this book, but makes no expressed or implied warranty of any kind and assumes no responsibility for any errors or omissions. No liability is assumed for incidental or consequential damages in connection with or arising out of information contained in this book. The Publisher shall not be liable for any special, consequential, or exemplary damages resulting, in whole or in part, from the readers' use of, or reliance upon, this material. Any parts of this book based on government reports are so indicated and copyright is claimed for those parts to the extent applicable to compilations of such works.

Independent verification should be sought for any data, advice or recommendations contained in this book. In addition, no responsibility is assumed by the publisher for any injury and/or damage to persons or property arising from any methods, products, instructions, ideas or otherwise contained in this publication.

This publication is designed to provide accurate and authoritative information with regard to the subject matter covered herein. It is sold with the clear understanding that the Publisher is not engaged in rendering legal or any other professional services. If legal or any other expert assistance is required, the services of a competent person should be sought. FROM A DECLARATION OF PARTICIPANTS JOINTLY ADOPTED BY A COMMITTEE OF THE AMERICAN BAR ASSOCIATION AND A COMMITTEE OF PUBLISHERS.

Additional color graphics may be available in the e-book version of this book.

LIBRARY OF CONGRESS CATALOGING-IN-PUBLICATION DATA

Dialogicality in focus : challenges to theory, method and application /
editors, Mariann Märtsin ... [et al.].
    p. cm. -- (Psychology research progress)
 Includes bibliographical references and index.
 ISBN 978-1-61122-817-5 (hardcover : alk. paper)
 1. Human information processing. 2. Abstraction. 3. Critical thinking.
I. Märtsin, Mariann. II. Title. III. Series.
 BF444.D53 2011
 150.19'8--dc22
                        2010046995

Published by Nova Science Publishers, Inc. † *New York*

CONTENTS

FOREWORD

The following chapters exemplify vibrant scholarship on dialogism. How does one assess the vitality of a field of research? Currently bibliographic metrics are in vogue (Nature, 2010). By this measure, dialogism is very healthy. According to the Thomson ISI index of journal articles, in a selected range of journals, there have been a total of 2,507 articles on the topic of dialogicality (search term: dialogic*). Publications began slowly, but have accumulated rapidly in the last two decades. For example, there were no articles in 1969, 6 articles in 1979, 27 articles in 1989, 91 articles in 1999, and 249 articles in 2009. The accumulated publications double every 6 or 7 years.

Of course any statement about an increase in publications has to be tempered against the fact that scholarship in general has 'progressed' from publishing a couple of hundred articles a year in the 1700s, to a few thousand in the 1800s, to hundreds of thousands in the 1900s. Jinha (2010) estimates that we started publishing more than 1 million articles a year in 1996, and in 2009 published 1,477,383 articles. Clearly, there have been a lot of 'contributions' to 'the literature' – over 50 million to be precise. Yet, despite this nauseating increase in academic articles overall (doubling every 24 years), the increase in articles on dialogicality is more rapid, thus indicating, it would seem, a picture of vitality.

But what does an increasing quantity of publications in a field actually indicate? As Farr (1996) has pointed out, in relation to the history of social psychology, the accumulation of publications is as much an indicator of a positivist paradigm as it is of any substantial scientific progress. Indeed, it can even be an indicator of a PROBLEM. Consider experimentation in psychology, as discussed by Shotter in the present volume, drawing upon Newell (1973). Exponentially increasing hair-splitting experiments and resultant publications, in which a primary finding is qualified by secondary findings, and then the qualifications are qualified by tertiary findings might actually be a sign of poor health. One could argue that it arises from searching for trans-contextual statistical 'truths' in a social world which is inherently contextual, and accordingly, the so-called 'truths' have to keep being adjusted in the face of varying contexts. In such a case, increasing publications indicate a failure to make generalisable theory (Valsiner, in press).

Phrenology, structuralism, behaviourism and most recently postmodernism all had rapidly increasing numbers of publications before their respective declines. There are bubbles in academic publishing just like in economics. Borrowing a turn of phrase from the investors, bibliographic metrics assessing a field of research should perhaps come with a warning, 'previous publications in a field are no guarantee of future publications.'

Another way of assessing vitality might be to consider the breadth of the movement: Is the field broad based and externally referenced, or is it narrow and internally referential? Returning to the Thomson ISI index, to analyse the subject areas in which dialogism is being utilised, reveals that the dialogical turn is rooted in psychology, but has a very broad basis. There are more than a hundred articles in each of the fields of literature, communication, linguistics, sociology, education, philosophy, health care, economics, psychiatry, social issues, and anthropology. There are 37 further fields which each have published more than ten articles dealing with dialogicality. Closer analysis of the temporal trajectory of this flowering reveals that the movement has always had a broad interdisciplinary basis. It originated in literature journals, then gained massive impetus in the 1990s from psychology journals (such as *Culture & Psychology, Theory & Psychology,* and *Journal for the Theory of Social Behaviour*), and in the 2000s has increasingly spread out to the wide range of afore mentioned fields.

Examining recent book publishing, which is excluded from the Thomson index, confirms the picture of health, with an evident recent flurry of activity in diverse domains. Recent titles and subtitles include: *The Dialogical Therapist* (Bertrando, 2008), *Dialogical Phenomenology* (Stawarska, 2009), *A Dialogical Approach to Child Development* (Van Nijnatten, 2010), *Ethical Teaching: A Case for Dialogical Resistance* (Foster, 2010), *Dialogical Engagements with Joyce in Beckett's Fiction* (Murphy, 2008), and *Dialogical Community Development* (Dowling, 2009). This small sub-sample of book titles supports the assessment that dialogism is becoming a broad based movement (Gillespie, 2010), with relevancies stretching from therapy to philosophy, from education to literature, and from community development to spirituality. It is testament to the broad and generalizable theoretical relevance of dialogism that it contributes to so many fields of enquiry.

However, a more critical analysis, focusing on the content of these books and articles, reveals little unity beyond the level of nomenclature. Put simply, the terms associated with dialogism are becoming popular. But what authors mean when they invoke the nomenclature of dialogism varies considerably. The terms are stretched from an empirical focus on dialogue on the one hand to quasi-spiritual communion on the other. Heterogeneity of meaning is not a bad thing; it can be creative. But unexamined assumptions and the loose invocation of "umbrella terms" (Marková, 2003; Valsiner & Van der Veer, 1999, p. 34) are not going to progress the field. Peeking under this umbrella term reveals a heterogeneous assemblage of scholars seeking shelter, sometimes more unified by trying to avoid the rain than their choice of umbrella.

Are there more substantial indicators of a field's vitality than bibliographic indices of popularity? What about focusing on the content of the research? Maybe one should assess a research field by asking, not what it contributes to the literature, but what it contributes to social and cultural life beyond the literature? Does the research field provide new, interesting, or useful ways of thinking or acting? Does the research field provide powerful and generalizable theoretical tools which can be productively applied to new domains? In short, we can ask the pragmatist question (Cornish & Gillespie, 2009), does the research field open up new and exciting avenues for action?

The phenomenon which dialogism addresses is human interaction. It enables us to conceptualise human interaction as intersubjective, symbolic, cultural, transformative and conflictual, in short, as complex. The complexity of human interaction is evident in all domains of human life, for example, in therapy, education, health intervention, communication, and coordination at all levels. A dialogical approach starts by acknowledging that the social world is perspectival, that people and groups inhabit different social realities. Moreover, it recognises that people are aware of this perspectivism, and thus that the complexity of human interaction often arises from people orienting to the perspective of the other (Rommetveit, 1974). It is the everyday experience of the obstinate complexity of human interaction, in all contexts and domains, which makes a theory of dialogism vital.

The everyday phenomenon of dialogicality explains why dialogism has a long history. The key texts in this field go back far beyond the Thompson ISI index, to the work of Bakhtin, Vygotsky, Mead and James in the early part of the 20th Century. Going back further, beyond the so-called founding of psychology as a science, key texts were produced by Schelling, Hegel, and Shaftesbury. And going back further still, beyond the Renaissance, key texts on dialogism were produced by the rhetoricians of ancient Greece (Billig, 1987). Thus, one could argue, the vitality of dialogism is not evidenced by the surge of recent publications, but rather by the long standing relevance of dialogism. A long history is probably a better indicator of a long future than an exponential increase in publications.

This is not to say that there has been no progress in understanding dialogicality over the centuries. There are important differences between the writings of Protagoras, Hegel, Bakhtin and the authors in the present volume. Each age adapts dialogism to its own concerns. Each era is historical, with its own matrix of ideas and practices, and within which an understanding of dialogicality has differential consequences. Historically situated understandings of dialogicality changed the art of rhetoric in Ancient Greece, changed the politics of Machiavellian Princes, changed how Shaftesbury tried to think, and how, more recently, changed how therapy and education, amongst other things, are practiced. Each era has the benefit of the understandings which have gone before, yet each era must make its understanding of dialogicality relevant to its own concerns.

So how does the present volume fit into this assessment? How does it contribute to dialogism in our time? The present collection of chapters stands apart from the proliferation of recent books on dialogism, because rather than applying dialogism to this or that domain, the present volume focuses on dialogicality itself to interrogate the concepts and methods which are taken for granted in the burgeoning literature. In this sense, it belongs alongside key texts such as Marková (2003), Jovchelovitch (2007), and Linell (2009). The present volume addresses several established tensions within contemporary research on dialogism: What methodologies are suitable for analysing dialogicality? How can I-positions be empirically identified? How do I-positions relate to one another? How can the relation between self and culture in general and current multiculturalism in particular be conceptualised? What is a suitable minimal unit of analysis for studying dialogicality? And, too often concepts render inert the dynamic phenomena they attempt to describe, how can we develop concepts which preserve dynamic complexity? Anyone interested in fresh approaches to these questions will benefit from the enclosed chapters.

But the present volume, in my view, also occupies a distinctive place in recent literature because of a persistent concern with dialogism as a research practice. It raises questions which have received little discussion, but which nonetheless have the potential to transform the way in which research is done in our present era. Specifically: Does research on dialogicality necessitate a distinctive, perhaps dialogical, style of writing? If researchers of dialogicality are to be consistent in their approach, what does this mean for how they relate to participants? How should scholars of dialogism relate to themselves within their analyses? How can one analyse dialogicality in images? How can one analyse moments of change and innovation? Should analyses of the dialogical be dialogical, for example by being the product of many researchers? If any of these questions pique the interest of a potential reader, then I strongly recommend studying the following chapters.

The present volume is, more than any bibliographic metric, an indicator of dialogism's current vitality. This vitality is evident at multiple levels; in the multi-author chapters, in the big issues addressed, in the critical commentaries, and in the debate between junior and senior authors. There is, as Valsiner points out in his commentary, a healthy lack of coherence which provides the fertile soil for debate. But above all, this vitality is evident in the fact that this collection of chapters raises more questions than answers and thus does what knowledge should do, it expands rather than narrows our collective future. Specifically, the present volume challenges us about how we do do, could do and should do research on dialogicality.

Alex Gillespie, Glasgow, August 2010

REFERENCES

Bertrando, P. (2008). *The dialogical therapist: Dialogue in systemic practice*. London: Karnac Books.

Billig, M. (1987). *Arguing and thinking: A rhetorical approach to social psychology*. Cambridge: Cambridge University Press.

Cornish, F., & Gillespie, A. (2009). A pragmatist approach to the problem of knowledge in health psychology. *Journal of Health Psychology, 14*(6), 800-809.

Dowling, G. (2009). *Dialogical community development: Working with depth, hospitality and solidarity*. Armidale, Australia: Tafina Press.

Farr, R. M. (1996). *The roots of modern social psychology: 1874-1954*. Oxford: Blackwell.

Foster, C. R. (2010). *Ethical teaching: A case for dialogical resistance*. Saarbrücken, Germany: Lambert Academic Publishing.

Gillespie, A. (2010). The dialogical turn: Turning the corner? *Theory & Psychology, 20*, 461-463.

Jinha, A. E. (2010). Article 50 million: An estimate of the number of scholarly articles in existence. *Learned Publishing, 23*, 258-263.

Jovchelovitch, S. (2007). *Knowledge in context: Representations, community, and culture*. London: Routledge.

Linell, P. (2009). *Rethinking language, mind, and world dialogically: Interactional and contetxtual theories of human sense-making*. Charlotte, NC: Information Age Publishing.

Marková, I. (2000). Amedee or how to get rid of it: Social representations from a dialogical perspective. *Culture & Psychology, 6*, 419-460.

Marková, I. (2003). *Dialogicality and social representations: The dynamics of mind*. Cambridge: Cambridge University Press.

Murphy, P. J. (2008). *Beckett's Dedalus: Dialogical engagements with Joyce in Beckett's Fiction*. Toronto: Toronto University Press.

Nature (2010). Assessing assessment. *Nature, 465,* 845.

Newell, A. (1973). You can't play 20 questions with nature and win: Projective comments on the papers of this symposium. In W. G. Chase (Ed.), *Visual information processing.* New York: Academic Press.

Nijnatten, C. V. (2010). *Children's agency, children's welfare: A dialogical approach to child development, policy and practice.* Bristol: Policy Press.

Rommetveit, R. (1974). *On message structure: A framework for the study of language and communication.* London: John Wiley & Sons.

Stawarska, B. (2009). *Between You and I: Dialogical phenomenology.* Ohio: Ohio University Press.

Valsiner, J. (in press). *A guided science: Psychology in the mirror of its making.* New Jersey: Transaction Publishers.

Valsiner, J., & Van der Veer, R. (1999). The encoding of distance: The concept of the" Zone of Proximal Development" and its interpretations. *Lev Vygotsky: Critical assessments, 3,* 3–31.

INTRODUCTION:
OPENING THE DIALOGUE

What does it mean to say that the mind is dialogical? At the most general level it means that human thought and action cannot be understood as belonging simply to the individual; rather they must be conceptualized in relation to others – mind and society are dialectically related as interdependent (rather than independent) opposites in tension. Along these lines, a distinction is often made between *monological* and *dialogical* approaches: the former studies individual minds as self-contained entities, whereas the latter explores interrelationships between individual minds, culture and society. Vygotsky and Mead, for example, critiqued the notion that mind already exists in the womb and showed instead how it develops out of social interaction. As Vygotsky (1978, p. 57) famously put it, "Every function in the child's cultural development appears twice: first, on the social level, and later on the individual level; first, between people (interpsychological), and then inside the child (intrapsychological)". Thought can thus be understood as an inner dramatization of life/conversation with others.

The use of dialogue as a metaphor to conceptualize mind has been used long before these twentieth century theorists. Plato, for instance, saw inner thought as a kind conversation with oneself, similar to conversation with others. His 'dialogues' are illustrative examples of what it means to think, that is 'divide oneself' (see Billig, chapter 1) in order to voice multiple perspectives on an issue and then move beyond them. For Plato, however, Truth is singular, universal and unchanging; dialogue was simply the method of reaching it. By contrast, twentieth century dialogical theories (exemplified by Bakhtin) have been more radical in insisting that truth itself belongs to an unfinalizable dialogue: Bakhtin (1986) says, "Any concrete utterance is a link in a chain of speech communication" (p. 91), implying that it is always a response to previous utterances and will in turn be proceeded by other utterances, which will change its meaning. From this perspective, Bakhtin and his followers celebrated heterogeneity, experimentation and the reversal of opposites in society and the realm of ideas.

In continuity with this notion, the present volume provides the reader with diverse perspectives on dialogical research, and encourages the pursuit of research as a dynamic and heterogeneous dialogue. As Linell (2009) has suggested in his recent book, we cannot talk about 'a' dialogical perspective; instead there are many different ways of doing dialogical research. We take this as our starting point and have tried to put different approaches side-by-side to encourage exchanges between them, and thus open a constructive dialogue on dialogicality. The book is unique in this respect: its chapters challenge current dialogical research practice, experiment with new analytic strategies, research contexts and ways of writing, and offer elaborated critical comments on each others' perspectives.

We deliberately choose not to 'monologise' the contributions by pushing a particular perspective and style; instead, we have purposefully encouraged experimentation and diversity, left some edges rather rough, some ideas rather open-ended, so that readers, and in the first instance the commentators, would have hooks to link their ideas to and thus give a sense of having a dialogue with the text as they read it. Thus, rather than asking the authors to look at their argument from different perspectives within their own discussion, we have extended this invitation to others outside the authors' own argumentative space. In short, we have sought to present the book as a space for friendly and mutually respectful dialogues so as to develop new forms of dialogical science.

PREVIEW OF THE BOOK

As already mentioned, dialogical science is not a settled field of theories and research, but rather it is hetereogeneous and contested. The open nature of this field is reflected not the least in the diversity of terms – dialogical science, dialogism, dialogicality, etc. – that have not yet been crystallized. In dialogical spirit, contributors to the book come from around the world (15 countries are represented in all) to reflect on basic ideas of the subdiscipline, how they are presented, and how they lead to particular empirical approaches. Each section of the book includes a commentary chapter (Part I has two), which highlights convergences and divergences between approaches and expands on them from the author's own perspective. The book is divided into three Parts: I. Challenges to dialogical science, II. Reflections on dialogical methodologies, and III. Dialogicality in social practices.

Part I: Challenges to Dialogical Science

To consistently follow a dialogical framework one must not only use dialogical ideas but also reflect on the broader field of dialogical research practice, including challenging key historical figures (rather than worshipping them as heroes), established ways of writing, concepts, methods, and more generally the very aims of the research enterprise. In Part I the chapters pose various challenges to the field of dialogical science and the notion of dialogality within research practice. In chapter 1, Billig begins by asking whether a dialogical approach requires a different way of writing than a monological approach. In particular, he questions whether dialogical theorists should try to write in specifically dialogical ways, rather than in the standard ways of the social sciences. The question is exemplified historically by discussing the relations between John Locke and the third Earl of Shaftesbury. Locke, as the father of modern cognitive psychology, provides an example of a monological thinker, who advocated clear, plain writing and who wished to sweep away error. By contrast, Shaftesbury proposed a dialogical theory of mind, and wrote in an explicitly self-critical dialogical manner that embodied his principle of contrariety. The lessons of Locke and Shaftesbury, however, are not straightforward. Billig explains why it is unreasonable to expect dialogical scientists today to follow Shaftesbury's rhetorical example. The rhetorical problems for today's dialogical theorists are different from those faced by Locke and Shaftesbury. Today's academic world favours technical writing of the sort that neither Locke nor Shaftesbury favoured. Paradoxically, the standard linguistic practice of the social sciences – 'nominal' style – is less precise, not more precise, when it comes to describing human actions. Moreover, social scientists, in using the nominal style, tend to create 'fictional' or 'metaphorical' things whose reality is taken for granted and who are ascribed the power of action. Billig describes why dialogical theorists should avoid the nominal style where possible and should follow both Locke and Shaftesbury in writing clearly. There are also dangers in dialogical scientists writing technically for readers who share their own perspective. The chapter concludes by suggesting that the relations between Locke and Shaftesbury, rather than the triumph of one over the other, hold the key to writing dialogically.

In chapter 2, Joerchel uses ideas from cultural psychology to show why we need to start with the space between individuals (i.e., with two individuals rather than one) in developing the theory of the dialogical self. She points out that the original authors of dialogical self theory have suggested that their concept of the self is especially useful in today's globalizing world as it is 'culture inclusive': in opposition to a Cartesian notion of self and culture, Hermans et al. also challenge the cross-cultural conception of culture in which it is perceived as geographically localized and as static entity with a singular essence. Whilst describing both self and culture as decentralized, and thereby stressing the spatial nature of the self, the proponents of the dialogical self theory have paid little attention to the space in which both culture and self are manifested. Joerchel's chapter aims to describe culture not as something that 'belongs' to the self, but rather as something that emerges from the interaction between individuals and can thus be located within the space between individuals – the cultural sphere. Once the space within a human sphere is scrutinized, a novel understanding of the relationship between culture and self within the theory of the dialogical self can be developed.

Chapter 3 also sets out to develop an analytic unit of analysis for approaching culture and mind. However, in contrast to Joerchel, Haye and Larraín take Bakhtin's notion of the utterance as their starting point to explicate and extend. Even more, they provide a theoretical clarification of the notions of dialogicality, discourse, and their connection, which is important for orienting any kind of dialogical discourse analysis and, moreover, any dialogical inquiry into both subjective and social processes. They stress that each act of discourse carries out an operation of social bonding, and that the utterance is the unit of discourse because it is the unit of social life. Specifically, they explore the conceptualisation of utterances in terms of position-taking dynamics within interlocution fields, similar to Joerchel's notion of 'cultural spheres' (chapter 2). In developing this conceptual framework, they address relevant theoretical and methodological issues, such as the articulation of the given and the new, which are essential to the discursive process of becoming; the problem posed by multiplicity when determining a dialogical unit of analysis; and the relationship between dialogism and monologism.

In chapter 4, Akkerman and Niessen outline what is distinctive about dialogical theories (as opposed to monological theories) and then show how this novelty is often lost when theory is converted into method. Dialogical theories, they say, are valuable for social scientific research because they theoretically provide a way of accounting for the complexity of social practices, by moving beyond dichotomies such as individual and social, part and whole, mind and matter, past, present and future, and knower and known. They then describe how dialogical theories are naturally bounded by the limited scope of research and concepts, and the concomitant risk that these theories result in fixating the fluidity they aim to preserve. Empirical research is presented to illustrate how dialogical concepts tend to be transformed into fixed categories in investigating specific phenomena, paralleling Billig's (chapter 1) claims about nominalisation in scientific writing. By making this point they intend to raise awareness of the issue and at the same time question their own scientific praxis – a topic followed up in Part II.

Commentaries to Part I, by Marková and Shotter, situate the above chapters in their own broad conceptual frameworks and visions of the subdiscipline. Marková points out that in order to understand what it means to 'challenge' dialogical science we first need to know something about the diverse traditions that make up the heterogeneous subdiscipline. To do this, she explores some of the historical roots of dialogicality (e.g. in Bakhtin, Gadamer and Levinas) and their subsequent influence on European culture and, more specifically, recent dialogical thinkers (such as Billig, Rommetveit, Moscovici, Taylor and Hermans). Marková also warns against the simplistic synthesis of Bakhtin with the pragmaticist's notion of the dialogical, which she sees as inferior, as it does not emphasize the ethical side of dialogicality, that is, responsibility to others. In her explicit comment on the chapters of Part I, she says that the challenges posed there are aimed more at the research surrounding the dialogical self theory than the broader framework of dialogical science, sketched out in the first sections of her commentary.

Shotter critiques the authors of Part I for leaving themselves (as embodied actors in the world) out of their characterisation of the dialogical. Developing a dialogical science is as much a matter of working on oneself – one's own ways of seeing the world – as it is refining theoretical concepts. In fact, concepts often get in the way of understanding when they fixate phenomena and separate it from the living whole. He points to an alternative strategy exemplified by Vygotsky's notion of the 'living cell', in which the properties of the whole (to which it is a part) can be seen. Similarly, Shotter advocates the use of 'descriptive concepts' (like James' 'stream of consciousness'), which make sense from our own experience but elude precise formulation. Embracing the ambiguity and vagueness of phenomena is a far cry from psychology's current strategy of using clear and definite concepts that are shown to have a direct causal influence on some process. Instead, we should be prepared to study mind from within, recognizing and using the background of our close but ambiguous everyday lives in practicing dialogical research.

Part II: Reflections on Dialogical Methodologies

The chapters of Part II focus on developing distinctively dialogical methodologies, which are sensitive to the complexities of the phenomena being studied, including their processual and contextual nature. In Part I, Akkerman and Niessen as well as Billig point out how researchers often fail to resist the temptation to fixate processes, by transforming them into static things in their analyses. Wagoner et al. set out in chapter 5 to overcome this problem by developing new methodological tools adequate to the task of identifying I-positions and their spatial-temporal relationships within the irreversible flow of experience. To do this six researchers were given the task of independently carrying out a dialogical analysis of Angel's (1985) stream-of-consciousness short story *The Guerrillero*. In the story the main character narrates her experience of inner change, from a state of strong panic when thinking of being searched by soldiers after having housed and cared for a rebel fighter, through a recollection of her amorous experiences with him, to a heroic state of great calm and readiness for whatever the future holds for her. The analyses all take on the challenge of innovating methodologies capable of capturing these profound intra-psychological changes from a dialogical perspective. Because all the researchers explore the same text, the different analytic strategies they developed can be directly compared (or dialogued). The chapter concludes with a general reflection on the exercise in the multivocality of analyses and its fruitfulness as a methodological tool to further develop analytic strategies in dialogical research.

Lonchuk and Rosa go on, in chapter 6, to explore the neglected dialogical research domain of graphic images. Specifically, they develop a methodological strategy through semiotics to analyze the interpretation of complex graphic images (such as those capable of producing moral interpellations) as a process of constructing symbolic objects. Such objects result from the dynamics of dialogical and argumentative interactions aiming to solve a dispute or differences of opinion between different outlooks arising from alternative I-positions within the self. Following Bakhtin (1993), such dialogues involve the I as a speaker, an interlocutor I-position, and a third party – the protagonist arising as an object from the uttered argument. The latter can also be personified, and so becomes another voice within the dialogue. This three party dialogue, in which the I moves among different I positions, involves voices which produce interpretants carrying affective and ethical appraisals coming from previous socio-cultural-historical dialogues. This is exemplified with excerpts from an empirical study in which a participant gets involved in the interpretation of a poster with national symbols that provokes her strong moral positioning as a citizen.

Hviid and Beckstead, in chapter 7, take up another important methodological issue for dialogical research practice, the dialogical dynamics of the research encounter, which they illustrate through an interview study with children. They conceptualise the research process in terms of I-positions involved in the interaction between researcher and research participants, and go on to argue that the meeting between researcher and research participant is a partly fuzzy, uncertain and generative phenomenon, which is very far from the dreams and hopes of a controlled experiment. Data of interviews with 12-year-old children demonstrate the development of dialogues of mutually coming to understand and define the research agenda, generating new expectancies for the scope of the research and suggesting improvements for it. Although the approach described enables new alignments of researcher and research participant's I-positions, the authors also discuss some ethical and practical considerations of the research encounter.

The commentary to Part II, highlights and extends core methodological principles from each of the chapters, namely 'intertextuality' and the 'stream of consciousness' (Wagoner et al.), 'visual analysis' (Lonchuk and Rosa) and 'reflexivity' (Hviid and Beckstead). Murakami argues that in order to capture the processual nature of the mind, a different approach to time is required. To that end she introduces the notion of *durée* or the time of living, and the Greek term *kairos* – opportune time or a moment when something special happens. Similarly to Shotter, Murakami emphasises the importance of including researchers as actors with diverse and rich experiences in and of the world to the characterisation of the research encounter. For each chapter, Murakami describes the research process as developing new ways of seeing and relating to the world: the research encounter is understood as 'open and ambiguous', which provides the opportunity for the researcher to transform their self in relation to the otherness they study, whether that be through a literary story, a graphic image or a child. This more general and dialogical understanding of research practice (as an involved relationship) requires researchers to develop new quality assurance criteria akin to hermeneutic inquiry. The three chapters of Part II begin to explore new possibilities for dialogical research practice; it is up to future research to fulfil the need for a fully formed dialogical methodology.

Part III: Dialogicality in Social Practices

Ultimately, dialogical research needs to move beyond the confines of the 'ivory tower' into the complexities of everyday social practices, a point made by Shotter in his commentary to Part I. Full development of theory involves its application to a variety of concrete contexts. The chapters of Part III apply dialogical thinking to psychotherapeutic practice (chapters 8 and 9), conflicts between the genders (chapter 10) and immigration politics (chapter 11).

In chapter 8 Gonçalves et al. present their ongoing research programme on innovative moments, which they define as exceptions to a client's problematic self-narratives in therapeutic dialogue. As such innovative moments constitute opportunities for the development of a new, more flexible, self-narrative. The chapter discusses how a novel methodological tool 'Innovative Moments Coding System' can be used to study the process of change in different samples across several psychotherapeutic modalities. Gonçalves et al.'s findings suggest that the emergence of a specific type of innovative moment – re-conceptualisation innovative moments – plays a pivotal role in the development of a new self-narrative, particularly through the dialogical articulation of the self's contrasting positions. From these findings, a heuristic model of narrative change is presented, as well as a model of narrative stability based on the process of mutual in-feeding.

In chapter 9, Gieser and Hermans also focus on psychotherapy processes, in particular, the place of empathy in psychotherapy. They argue that empathy is an essential aspect of dialogicality and, more specifically, a process of two dialogical selves in communication. By examining Margulies's (1989) famous psychotherapeutic accounts of his empathic experiences with clients, they show how he was able to 'feel into' the inner landscape of his client and experience it as his own. Their interpretation of this process starts with an explication of the link between spoken dialogue, perception and emotion. Gieser and Hermans delineate how the perceived sound of speech evokes emotion-laden 'sensory landscapes' in the listener. In this context, empathy is facilitated by speech and creates a cognitive and affective link between client and therapist in a state of 'first-order phenomenology' (Lambie & Marcel, 2002). They argue, however, that this empathic link does not necessarily result in a sharing of the same emotion. In this case, the client experienced a 'secondary emotion' (Greenberg, 2002) while the therapist experienced the 'primary emotion' that was hiding underneath. They propose that the therapy becomes effective when the therapist can leave his empathetic state of 'first-order phenomenology' to reach a 'second-order awareness' of the 'primary emotion' that can then be communicated back to the client as his/her 'counter-emotion'. In the conclusion, the authors leave the case study to explore the implications of a broader understanding of empathy as a premise for dialogical relationships and for assuming I-positions in general.

Like Gieser and Hermans, Raggatt in chapter 10 explores the relationship between embodied emotion and positioning through the dialogical self theory. He describes how positioning theory first emerged through efforts to analyze discourse in micro-social encounters, and how it has also been adapted to account for the dynamics of conflict in a 'multi-voiced' dialogical self. In Raggatt's approach, a person's repertoire of opposing I-positions is thought to have origins both 'inside' in terms of reflexive personal conflicts (e.g., over esteem or agency needs), and 'outside' in terms of social constructions (e.g., arising from role conflicts and from embedding in power and status hierarchies). In his chapter Raggatt describes findings from a survey of positioning in the dialogical self that focuses on gender differences in positioning conflicts. Males and females were found to differ markedly in positioning styles. In women, esteem, communion, and cross-gender conflicts were the focus, while in men agency and independence issues were more problematic. There were also marked differences in the embodiment of I-positions. Females associated their faces with *positive* I-positions, and their lower bodies (legs and buttocks) with *negative* positions. Conversely, men associated their faces with negative I-positions and their torsos with positive ones. Raggatt interprets these findings as evidence for the disjunction of embodied experience across the genders. He proposes that problems of communication emerge between the genders in part because men and women use quite different modes of embodying self-expression. The results are discussed from the perspectives of dialogical self theory, positioning theory, social role theory, and the embodiment of self esteem.

In chapter 11, Kinnvall and Scuzzarello apply dialogical theory to the context of politics and international relations. In the context of increasingly multicultural societies, majority and minority groups may perceive their sense of collective identity as threatened. This perception may lead both groups to develop cognitive and material strategies to preserve their allegedly unique cultures and community mores. This process, which Kinnvall and Scuzzarello label 'securitization of subjectivity', makes attempts to build commonalities between groups difficult to achieve. To better understand how the securitization of subjectivity can be avoided, the authors advocate the integration of critical security studies within international relations theory with dialogical conceptualizations of the self. They maintain that a dialogical conceptualization of the self can complement critical security studies in understanding not only macro social and cognitive relations, but also how these macroscopic relations impact on the micro level of individual identification. They argue that dialogical conceptualization of the self, as non-static, multiple and relational, enables researchers to understand the social and cognitive processes that lead to the securitization of subjectivity. Drawing upon Marková's conceptualization of dialogicality, which sees the self and other as involved in a mutually constituting relationship, they argue that certain kinds of interactions can foster and introduce new forms of identification that conceive of the other as an integrated part of one's identity, rather than as a perceived threat. In particular, they look at the potential of transformative dialogue between minority and majority groups in local communities for fostering shared identifications between the concerned groups. However, they also maintain that these strategies will have limited practical impact if they are not accompanied by structural changes that alter minority groups' marginal positions in recipient societies.

In his commentary to Part III, Valsiner moves beyond the specific social practices discussed in the target articles and once again returns to the question of the relationship between dialogical theory and dialogical methodologies. While welcoming the variety of conceptual and methodological positions utilised by the authors as an indicator of possible productivity of dialogical perspective, he also laments the lack of innovation at the level of methodology. He warns against moving towards an expert status and argues that only by keeping the tension between diverse positions and thus multivoicedness in both theoretical and empirical efforts alive, can the dialogical perspective retain its appeal and value as a moving and evolving field of research.

In Place of a Conclusion

In his foreword Gillespie asks, how one assesses the vitality of a research field. In their own ways all the commentators in this book (especially Marková, Shotter and Valsiner) have also been concerned with the future of the dialogical perspective vis-à-vis other theoretical traditions in social sciences. In our concluding remarks we return to these questions. In particular, we assert that while focusing on dialogicality may offer a viable alternative for conceptualising human mind and interaction, the question about its value for society, in changing and improving people's lives remains. Building on the themes discussed in the book we call for a radical change in conducting dialogical research, which is considerate and open not only to other competing theoretical positions, but equally legitimises the voices and perspectives of the people and communities who are researched. That is, we call for a research tradition that is fundamentally transformative, where different agents come together in another way for a common reason. We thus conclude the book with the future goal of developing dialogical research that is conceptually solid, but also makes sense, and importantly, makes a difference to the people who it is meant for. The reader is invited to join the dialogue about dialogicality, by critically engaging with the ideas discussed here and appropriating them to their own work, and thus become a contributor to the advancement of dialogical research.

REFERENCES

Angel, A. (1985). The guerillero. In A. Manguel (Ed.), *Other fires: Short fiction by Latin American women* (pp. 119-121). New York: Three Rivers Press.

Bakhtin, M. M. (1986). *Speech genres and other late essays.* Austin: University of Texas Press.

Bakhtin, M. M. (1993). *Toward a philosophy of the act.* (V. Liapunov and M. Holquist, Eds., V. Liapunov Trans.) Austin: University of Texas Press.

Greenberg, L. (2002). *Emotion-focused therapy: Coaching clients to work through feelings.* Washington, DC: American Psychological Association.

Lambie, J., & Marcel, A. (2002). Consciousness and the varieties of emotional experience: A theoretical framework. *Psychological Review, 109,* 219-259.

Linell, P. (2009). *Rethinking language, mind, and world dialogically. Interactional and contextual theories of human sense-making.* Charlotte, NC: Information Age Publishing.

Margulies, A. (1989). *The empathic imagination.* New York: W.W. Norton & Co.

Vygotsky, L.S. (1978) *Mind in society: The development of higher psychological processes.* (M. Cole, V. John-Steiner, S. Scribner, and E. Souberman, Eds.) Cambridge, MA: Harvard University Press.

PART I
CHALLENGES TO DIALOGICAL SCIENCE

In: Dialogicality in Focus   ISBN: 978-1-61122-817-5
Editors: M. Märtsin, B. Wagoner, E.-L. Aveling et al.   © 2011 Nova Science Publishers, Inc.

Chapter 1

DIALOGICAL WRITING AND DIALOGICAL THEORY: REFLECTIONS ON LOCKE, SHAFTESBURY AND FICTIONAL THINGS

Michael Billig

INTRODUCTION

One can ask a deceptively simple question. Should dialogical scientists write in a specifically dialogical way? One would expect dialogical scientists to hold dialogical theories, such as dialogical theories of mind rather than the information processing ones. We might also expect dialogical scientists to advocate dialogical methodologies, claiming, for example, that to study the dialogical mind one should be investigating social practices of conversation and dialogue. An academic discipline is always more than theory and methodology: it must be written down. If a dialogical science needs dialogical theories and methodologies, then one can ask whether it also needs distinctively dialogical practices of writing.

The question might be simple to ask but it is by no means simple to answer – not least because the answer must be written. It is hard for academic writers to stand back from their own writing practices, in order to write critically about those practices. For this reason, I will approach the question indirectly, by discussing a historical example: the differences between Locke and the third Earl of Shaftesbury in their approaches to the study of mind. Whereas Locke formulated an approach to the mind that was to inspire individualist cognitive science, Shaftesbury took a dialogical approach that anticipated many of Bakhtin's ideas. Shaftesbury was not only a dialogical theorist, but, unlike Bakhtin, he also tried to write in a style that matched his dialogical ideas.

I will suggest that if we are to take dialogical ideals seriously, then, like Shaftesbury, we should pay attention to the ways in which we write. Although we need not copy the Shaftesbury's self-consciously dialogical style, we should beware of conventional academic styles of writing. Much academic writing today is rich in technical nominals. We tend to populate our theoretical world with 'metaphorical things' or abstract entities that we treat as the agents of actions. I will argue that this sort of rhetorical style compromises some dialogical ideals, closing down debate just where it should be opened up.

JOHN LOCKE AND THE COGNITIVE APPROACH TO MIND

Debates between the proponents of dialogical and non-dialogical theories of mind have a much longer history than current arguments between cognitive scientists and critical psychologists (see Billig, 2008a, for an extended discussion of the themes outlined in this section and the following one). Cognitive and dialogical psychologists tend to view human thinking in very different terms. Cognitive psychologists will examine how individual subjects extract information from their senses and use that information to solve particular problems. By contrast, critical psychologists, especially discursive psychologists, tend to view human thinking as being rooted in the practical and dialogical use of language. For them, language is not a matter of classifying sensory information with categories – as it is for some cognitive psychologists – but of participating in social activity through the use of language. If today dialogical theorists argue against the cognitive view of the mind, then they are participating in a debate that has a long history. An early version of this debate occurred in the eighteenth century as thinkers such as the third earl of Shaftesbury and Thomas Reid reacted against Locke's analysis of mind.

George Santayana (1933) once described John Locke as the father of modern psychology. In his *Essay Concerning Human Understanding* (1690/1964), Locke took a daring psychological approach to the traditional problems of philosophy. Rather than defining 'truth' in an abstract way and then examining which beliefs matched this definition, Locke examined how we come by those beliefs that we hold to be true. In doing this way, Locke was proposing an empirical approach to transform philosophical problems into psychological ones. He was advocating that we look at the operations of the mind – at the way that people actually think - rather than accepting what religious or philosophical authorities said about 'truth' and 'falsity'.

As Locke wrote in the preface to his great work, he regarded himself as an under-labourer "clearing the ground a little and removing some of the rubbish that lies in the way to knowledge" (1690/1964, p. 58). Today's dialogical theorists would have little difficulty in describing Locke's approach as monological. He focussed on the individual mind, treating it as a self-contained entity. In essentials, he was examining what this self-contained entity has to do in order understand the world as it really exists; and, just as importantly, what the mind must not do, in order to avoid error.

In the eyes of dialogical scientists, Locke's *Essay Concerning Human Understanding* contains some basic flaws. Several can be noted here. First, Locke was claiming that human knowledge was rooted in perceptual processes. He argued that whatever we know of the world comes through our senses: we have no inborn ideas. If we receive knowledge through our senses, and if we are capable of true knowledge, rather than mere belief, then our senses must be capable of providing veridical information. For this reason, Locke argued that our senses operate, or rather they should operate, passively. They receive impressions of things that truly represent those things, and, thus, our simple impressions "agree to the reality of things" (1690/1964, II.xxx.2, p. 233). If perception were held to be an active process, then a sceptic might claim that our impressions of the world reflected the structure of our minds rather than the world as it is. That is why Locke insisted that perception is a passive process – an assumption that is at odds with most modern theories of perception which stress its active nature (see, for instance, Fuster, 2003). For Locke, the active part of thinking only occurs when we reflect upon the information that we passively receive from our senses.

Second, Locke argued that language is the means by which we can transfer ideas from one person to another. No-one else can see the impressions that another person receives. However, if we clearly and distinctly label our ideas, then we can communicate them to others. Errors arise when we use concepts that are not clearly and distinctly related to perceptual ideas. Language should, therefore, be as clear as possible. In rejecting metaphysics, Locke aimed to write simply, avoiding the philosophically complex language of the schoolmen. Certainly, he was the first British major philosopher to write all his main works in English. Hobbes, like Ralph Cudworth, whom Locke was implicitly criticising in the *Essay*, belonged to the earlier generation of philosophers that had written in both English and Latin. Although proficient in Latin, Locke chose to write in plain English. His *Essay*, both in its theoretical argument and in its rhetorical practice, represents a case for the virtues of writing simply in the vernacular.

In the *Essay*, Locke expressed his suspicion of flowery, figurative language: "If we would speak of things as they are, we must allow that all the art of rhetoric, besides order and clearness, all the artificial and figurative application of words eloquence hath invented, are for nothing else but to insinuate wrong ideas, move the passions and thereby mislead the judgment; and so indeed are perfect cheats" (III, xi, 34). Ironically, Locke's denunciation of figurative language is itself a fine piece of figurative writing. He did not discuss the sort of figurative, or metaphorical steps a writer must take in order to call a form of language a 'perfect cheat'. Nor did he consider how 'eloquence' is capable of inventing things: no-one has seen eloquence, rather than eloquent people, engage in the activity of inventing. 'Eloquence', in this sense, is a 'metaphorical thing'; Locke was ascribing powers of action to this thing, metaphorically treating it as a person.

By using simple terms with clear definitions, and avoiding the excesses of rhetoric, Locke hoped to transfer the ideas of his mind to those of his readers. As such, Locke viewed language as an adjunct to individual cognition (which, itself, is an adjunct of individual perception). Roy Harris (1997) has called this view of language as 'telementation', for it sees language as the conduit by which ideas are conveyed from the mind of one individual to that of another. Theorists, who see the mind as essentially dialogical, reject such a view of language. Following Wittgenstein's (1953) insight that all language needs public criteria, they claim that the concepts of a public language cannot be defined solely in terms of private mental events (e.g., Harré, 2002; Harré & Gillett, 1994; Potter, 2001; Potter & te Molder, 2005; Potter & Wetherell, 1987; Shotter, 1993a, 1993b). Those who specifically argue against the theory of 'telementation' might draw inspiration from Wittgenstein's later work, but rhetorically they are not being Wittgensteinian. Nowhere in *Philosophical Investigations* does Wittgenstein use a word like 'telementation'. He developed his arguments with examples, always using non-technical language. He never categorized his examples with a multi-syllabic, technical word ending in the suffix '-ation'.

Locke and Wittgenstein might have proposed very different views of language, but both were in absolute accord that philosophers should use as simple language as possible. Philosophy's metaphorical under-labourers should sweep aside old technical terms and, having done so, they should not invent new ones, such as 'telemenation', to classify the piles of accumulated rubble.

THE EARL OF SHAFTESBURY

During the eighteenth century the third earl of Shaftesbury was considered one of Britain's most important philosophical writers. His *Characteristicks of Men, Manners, Opinions, Times* was reprinted numerous times. Now, he tends to be remembered as a minor philosopher of aesthetics. However, he is arguably a major theorist of the dialogical perspective, formulating a view of the mind that contrasts directly with that of Locke. Moreover, the story of Shaftesbury's personal relations with Locke bears repeating, as it is one of the most evocative tales in the history of philosophy.

John Locke's patron was the first Earl of Shaftesbury, the powerful politician who was involved both in the execution of Charles I and the restoration of his son Charles II. Shaftesbury engaged Locke as his personal assistant during the restoration period. Both men shared a Whiggish suspicion of monarchs and both were strongly anti-catholic protestants. Shaftesbury's only son was mentally and physically a peculiar young man, who would, the family feared, have difficulty in attracting a wife. Shaftesbury commissioned Locke to find a suitable bride for the young heir. This Locke succeeded in doing. As a medical man, Locke was directed by Shaftsbury to look after the young wife during her pregnancy. Having successfully superintended the birth, Locke was asked to direct the education of the young boy.

As a tribute to the power of education over genetics, the child grew up with a love of learning and, in particular, of philosophy. Locke might have written about the powers of education, but he was to learn at first hand their limit. The young heir, who was in time to become the third Earl of Shaftesbury, may have developed philosophical interests, as well as an enduring respect, even love, for his great teacher; but, in virtually every respect he was to reject Locke's philosophy. So great were the conflicting feelings of love and intellectual rebellion, that Shaftesbury waited until Locke's death before publishing his own views. Even during Locke's lifetime, Shaftesbury seems to have avoided discussing philosophical matters with the man he called his 'foster-father' (on the relations between Locke and Shaftesbury, see Billig, 2008a, chapter five).

Shaftesbury took inspiration from the ancient stoics. He was more concerned with moral and aesthetic problem than in specifying the operations of the mind. However, he adhered to a dialogical account of mind. Most famously, he claimed that we should test our opinions by subjecting them to ridicule in open conversation. This entailed a very different view of language than Locke's. Shaftesbury was proposing that dialogue provided the means for assessing views, rather than merely being the means for transmitting them from one person to another. In the essay *Soliloquy or Advice to an Author* in the second volume of *Characteristicks*, Shaftesbury went further. Ostensibly he was advising authors how to improve their writing, but he was also advising them how to think. Before offering views in public, aspiring authors should conduct internal dialogues. They should divide themselves into separate parties. "Divide yourself" was his advice (1714/1999, p. 77); this, he claimed, was "the chief principle" of his philosophy (p. 83). Thus, thinking involved dialogue, whether it be public dialogue in which opinions were subjected to the tests of ridicule, or private dialogue, as the self argues with itself.

In these ideas, we can see a view of the mind that in many respects resembles that of Bakhtin. There is a similar celebration of humour, as well as a linking of thinking with dialogue. Moreover, there is a celebration of division, rather than consistent unity. The thinking person has a divided mentality. The thinking society, in which ideas were debated and freedom practised, likewise was filled with differing opinions. Bakhtin would later champion this ideal as 'heteroglossia', arguing that dialogical diversity was a necessary component of freedom. Shaftesbury also linked debate, freedom and diversity. In imagining the freedoms of ancient Athens as the ideal society (which, of course, meant overlooking slavery and the subjection of women), Shaftesbury praised the "wonderful" temper and harmony that arose from all contrarieties of opinions (p. 11).

It is no coincidence that Bakhtin's views parallel those of Shaftesbury, although there is no evidence that Bakhtin read Shaftesbury's work. Bakhtin certainly read, and was deeply influenced, by Cassirer's *The Philosophy of the Enlightenment* (1951). In that book, Cassirer discussed in detail Shaftesbury's philosophy, particularly those themes that Bakhtin was to adopt as his own. As Poole (2002) has demonstrated, Bakhtin's views, including those about the philosophical importance of mockery, seem to have altered after he read Cassirer's book, although he never paid due acknowledgement to the latter.

Unlike Locke, Shaftesbury did not fear the dangers of rhetoric. He saw eloquence as something to be aspired to, rather than avoided. The eloquent society was, in his view, a civilized society. The growth of persuasion was central to the growth of the arts, sciences and freedoms of ancient Greece (1714/1999, pp. 106ff). Shaftesbury claimed that "the natural and simple manner which conceals and covers art is the most truly artful" form of political rhetoric (p. 399). He took great pains with his own writing, drafting and redrafting – as the differences between the 1711 and 1714 editions of *Characteristicks* illustrate. He might have praised the natural, simple manner of speech but his ideal for prose was not the plain style that Locke commended. Shaftesbury complained about writers with "no real accent or cadency of words, no sound or measure of syllables" (p. 450). Shaftesbury wrote rolling sentences, with fine phrases and extensive metaphors, interposed with short, biting comments. Much of his writing gains from being read aloud, in order to capture its cadence.

One might predict that Shaftesbury would not have liked Bakhtin's style of writing, despite their philosophical affinity. Shaftesbury shared with Locke a dislike of technical vocabulary. In describing the wonderful contrarieties of opinions, Shaftesbury felt no need to invent a new term such as 'heteroglossia'. He conveyed his meaning with the available vocabulary. Bakhtin, by contrast, has bequeathed a number of neologisms. Besides 'heteroglossia', there are 'chronotypes', 'dialogization', 'monologization', 'verbal-ideological decentering', etc. Bakhtin's academic followers now use such terms regularly when they develop their dialogical approach to language. Certainly, in English translations, neither these terms, nor the sentences in which they are routinely placed, ring with the sort of musical cadence that Shaftesbury sought.

The rhetorical practice dividing Shaftesbury from Bakhtin involves more than cadence and neologism. There is the issue of dialogue. Bakhtin stressed that the meaning of an utterance depends upon its dialogical context – again, Shaftesbury would not have disagreed. According to Bakhtin, any utterance typically responds to a previous one and, in its turn, provokes others: "The utterance is related not only to preceding, but also to subsequent links in the chain of communion" (Bakhtin, 1986, p. 94). This idea has become central to conversation analysts, who insist that the meaning of any conversational turn is to be understood in relation not just to the turn before but, most importantly, to subsequent ones.

The idea need not be restricted to the analysis of social interaction. It can be applied to literary and philosophical works. One cannot understand what a philosopher is arguing for, unless one knows whom the philosopher is arguing against. The author does not even have to specify the target of their writing. Shaftesbury's *Characteristicks*, for instance, should be understood, at least in part, as a reaction to the work of Locke, although, apart from some heavy hints in a couple of passages, Shaftesbury does not directly discuss Locke or his works. Nevertheless, the personal and intellectual histories of the two philosophers ensure that the argumentative meaning of *Characteristicks* is a reaction against the sort of philosophy that Locke was producing. In the same way Locke's philosophy was a reaction against earlier metaphysics, including that of the Cambridge Platonists, who were much admired by Shaftesbury. Casssirer, in fact, was to call Shaftesbury the greatest of all the Cambridge Platonists.

Shaftesbury's image of thinking, therefore, belongs to an argumentative context in which he was rebelling against his beloved 'foster-father'. If one believes in the importance of dialogue and its continuity, then one must consider whether it is sufficient merely to place one's writing within a chain of dialogue, or whether one has to write in a specifically dialogical manner. Locke's view of his own writing was not dialogical. As he claimed, his intention was to sweep away the rubble of past philosophizing. He was not proposing a continuing dialogue with the opinions he wished to replace. He was not envisaging a wonderful contrariety, as his own views rubbed against metaphysical prejudices – such as the innate belief in God and the divine right of kings. In this respect, Locke's philosophy of language was at one with his practice of writing – so long as one ignores the rhetoric of his own claims to avoid rhetoric.

From a different perspective, Shaftesbury practised in his writing what he preached. He sought to write in a way that expressed the importance of continuing dialogue. *Characteristicks* does not produce ordered arguments, in numbered paragraphs, advancing from premises to conclusions, as if it seeks to stand alone outside of a chain of rhetorical response and counter-response. *Characteristicks* is a 'pot pourri', comprising different genres of writing, including a philosophical dialogue written in the style of Plato. A couple of the chapters of the first volume are presented as if they are letters to friends, replying to previous letters and awaiting responses.

The full dialogical nature of *Characteristicks* becomes apparent in the final volume. Here Shaftesbury poses as a 'miscellaneous' writer, adopting the conceit that he is a different person from the author of the first two volumes. His miscellaneous reflections comment amusingly and critically on the previous chapters. His sharpest comments are reserved for *An Inquiry Concerning Virtue or Merit*, which was the earliest piece of his writings that Shaftesbury included in *Characteristicks*. The *Inquiry*, which analyses the nature of morality, was the nearest Shaftesbury came to writing conventional philosophy. It sets out premises about the nature of virtue and then proceeds to argue that humans possess an innate moral sense.

During the nineteenth century, philosophers quoted this chapter more than any other chapter of *Characteristicks*. It was written in a serious, ordered style that they could recognize as being proper philosophy. But it is this chapter that Shaftesbury most mocked in his final volume, criticising the "regular demonstrations and deductions of our grave author" (p. 426). He wrote that "there is no knowledge or wisdom to be learned" from abstract philosophizing (p. 427), claiming that these "formal and grave sentiments" contradicted the author's own stated belief in the importance of wit and raillery (p. 433).

Thus Shaftesbury engages in dialogue with himself, ensuring that he does not present his own works as the last word on the subjects that he discusses. As he stated in the final volume of *Characteristicks*, "it is indeed no small absurdity to assert a work or treatise, written in human language, to be above human criticism or censure" (p. 434). Given that Shaftesbury was arguing for the priority of practice over theory, then this insight cannot just be asserted as an abstract principle: it must be delivered practically. Hence, Shaftesbury mocks and criticises his own efforts at theoretical reflection. It would be contradictory to present such a work as if it needed no criticism, as if it were the solution to the problems that it addressed. Shaftesbury had no intention of falling into this trap. Instead, he criticises himself, encouraging the reader to formulate more criticisms, thereby producing a text that is itself rhetorically dialogical.

QUESTION OF MONOLOGICAL OR DIALOGICAL STYLES

The philosophies of Locke and Shaftesbury not only express two different theories of mind but they also represent two different rhetorical styles. Locke puts himself in a battle to sweep away error. By overcoming opposing views, he seeks to produce a consistent, single or monological voice of truth. By contrast, Shaftesbury produces a work that is explicitly multi-vocal and delights in its own contrariety. The author takes on another persona, and argues against his own writing. Thus, the complete text, in common with its advocated theory of mind, is divided.

The contrasting examples of Locke and Shaftesbury, when looked at in this way, pose a question for modern, dialogical theorists. Should we attempt to write in an explicitly dialogical style, as Shaftesbury did? That would mean rejecting the standard genres of contemporary academic writing which are more Locke than Shaftesbury. If we do, then perhaps we should be playing with the sorts of literary forms that some self-consciously reflexive social scientists toyed with a few years ago (e.g., Ashmore, 1989; Ashmore et al., 2002; Pinch & Pinch, 1988) – using forms such as fictional dialogues and playlets, that, it should be noted, I am not using in the present chapter. If this is the implication, then, should we not be criticising dialogical theorists, such as Bakhtin, whose style is entirely conventional?

Certainly, Bakhtin in no way followed the dialogical style of Shaftesbury. He did not indulge in literary conceits, pretending to be a critic of his own work. If Bakhtin did adopt other authorial personae – and some scholars believe that he wrote some works attributed to Volosinov and other Russian linguists – then the reasons were economic and political, not philosophical (Holquist, 2002). The texts of 'Volosinov', that Bakhtin may have written, did not argue against Bakhtin's work, or point to any discrepancy between Bakhtin's dialogical theory of mind and his monological literary practice.

So, is there a contradiction between using a monological style while arguing for a dialogical perspective? And should I, as author of this piece, switch genres, in order to argue with myself – or perhaps even set up an imaginary dialogue between Locke and Shaftesbury in order to do more than argue a dialogical point, but to demonstrate its practice?

Such questions might be appropriate, but, at this point, no simple answer will be offered. The rhetorical form of a text is not a thing-in-itself, but its meaning depends upon the rhetorical context in which the text is being written and read. Thus, if we raise questions about the appropriate dialogical forms for a dialogical science, then we must understand the rhetorical context in which this dialogical science is being pursued. There is always what Clark and Ivanič (1997) have called a politics of writing, incorporating writer, publisher and reader. The examples of Locke and Shaftesbury cannot be transcribed three hundred years, as if they set examples in the abstract. Their dialogical context, it will be suggested, was very different from that facing today's academics, including dialogical theorists. However, to understand why this might be important, it is necessary to take a diversion to examine how and why the language of today's social sciences, including dialogical sciences, might differ both from the plain writing of Locke and from the grand style of Shaftesbury. These differences hold a clue about the ways that dialogical scientists should aspire to write, if they want to match their literary style to their dialogical aims.

ACADEMIC WRITING AND THE NOMINAL STYLE

It has already been stated that social scientists tend to write in very different ways from either Locke or Shaftesbury. However, it is insufficient merely to state this as if it were so obvious that it need not be justified. Quite the contrary, it is necessary to specify some of the linguistic features that characterise the way that academics today tend to write. If we do so, then we will be in a better position to see why today's academic writers might wish to use technical terms like those that have already been mentioned – 'telementation', 'heteroglossia', 'dialogization' etc. And also we will be able to see why the use of such terms in the heavily divided world of academia today may not be propitious dialogically. But to sustain this argument, we must go beyond bemoaning the cadence or aesthetic ugliness of technical neologisms, as Shaftesbury might once have done. Some linguistic details are necessary.

Two linguistic features, above all, mark contemporary academic writing, distinguishing it from other genres of prose, such as journalism or popular writing. Academic authors of research articles heavily use nominals and verbs in the passive tense (Halliday, 2006). This style has developed over the past three hundred years, starting with the scientific writing in the seventeenth century. Since then, natural scientists have increasingly filled their prose with nominals and passives, and today the writing of social scientists does not lag far behind in these respects (Banks, 2003). So distinctive is this style of writing, that some linguists have specifically named it 'the nominal style' (Halliday, 2003).

According to linguists, who follow Halliday's systemic-functional approach to linguistics, we should distinguish between things and processes. Things are objects, such as sticks, stones and people. Processes are events that occur over time, such as people writing or jumping, or species evolving into other species. Systemic-functional linguists claim that there is a different 'congruent' linguistic style for describing objects than for describing processes. Things are congruently described by nouns or nominals, whereas processes (including human actions) are congruently described by clauses with nominal subjects and verbs. Scientists, and other writers using the nominal style, habitually develop nouns, or nominals, to describe processes and actions. Instead of using clauses to describe species evolving into other species, or chemicals becoming wetter, they name these whole processes by a single nominal such as 'species-evolution' or 'hydration' – in this way, they linguistically turn processes into things. Linguists have called the process of creating specialist nominals 'nominalization'. The word 'nominalization' is itself a nominal, which is being used to describe a process rather than a thing – or, rather, to make the process appear as a thing (Billig, 2008b).

Specialists frequently give two justifications for writing in technical styles that are rich in nominals. First, technical terms act as a form of short-hand, enabling academic writers to avoid constantly spelling out in detail exactly what they are referring to. In this way, 'telementation', 'nominalization' and 'hydration' work as a convenient short-hand symbols to readers who share the same background knowledge. Second, it is claimed that technical terms are more precise than those of ordinary language. Therefore, to engage in precise analysis, academics must go beyond ordinary language and devise clearly defined terms for their academic purposes. Both justifications nevertheless are contestable in the human and social sciences.

Halliday has shown that the nominal style is not, in fact, briefer than a more conventional, or 'clausal' style of writing. As he writes, "despite a common belief, the more nominalised constructions are not, in fact, noticeably shorter" (Halliday, 2006, p. 156). Of greater interest are the arguments about the dangers of 'nominalization'. Critical discourse analysts, inspired by the classic work of Fowler et al. (1979) and Fowler (1991), have drawn attention to the dangers of 'nominalization' and 'passivization'. When used to describe human actions, sentences rich in nominals, and/or phrased in the passive tense, typically contain less information than more 'normal' or congruent descriptions of actions. For example, if one says 'jumping occurred', one is not specifying who was doing the jumping. Nominals and passives, according to critical discourse analysts, are an important resource for those who, for ideological reasons, wish to hide who is the agent of actions. Critical discourse analysts have suggested that, by using nominals to describe processes, writers can reify the contingent world, presenting it as being filled with necessary things rather than being created by human actions (see e.g., Fairclough, 2003).

The style, which critical discourse analysts claim to characterise ideological language, is just the style that most academic authors use. If ideological language has the tendency to be imprecise and to reify human actions, then so does academic language with the nominal style. When academic writers describe human actions, the technical style can, in fact, contain less, not more, information than ordinary language. The use of the very word 'nominalization' shows this. It sounds an impressively technical, and thereby precise, term, which is officially described as referring to a process. However, if one looks at the way linguists actually use the word, one can see that they use it in a variety of different, and often mutually inconsistent, ways (Billig, 2008b, 2008c). Linguists often categorize features of a text as 'nominalization' and then use the technical term as if it were unproblematic; however they typically leave unclear who is doing the action of nominalising and, most crucially, how they perform such an action.

Paradoxically, experts in the human and social sciences can use their impressive technical language to avoid specifying what they mean. If technical sentences, using 'nominalization', were rephrased in clauses with subjects and active verbs, then the lack of information would soon become apparent. But a writer, using nominals to describe actions, can rhetorically hide this lack of information. Far from providing precision, such technical language, which treats processes as if they were things, can in practice be less clear than ordinary styles of speaking and writing, especially when it comes to describing what humans do.

METAPHORICAL FICTIONS

The problems with using technical nominals to describe human actions go deeper than just a lack of precision. There is a philosophical dimension. Hans Vaihinger, in his unjustly overlooked book *The Philosophy of 'As If'* (1935), argued science is based on 'fictions'. Scientists often use 'fictional' concepts, such as 'atom' or 'square root of minus one', thereby creating conceptual objects that cannot actually exist. The creation of fictions, Vaihinger suggested, can be productive, enabling scientists to go beyond the obvious. There are few problems if scientists acknowledge the fictional nature of their concepts. Problems arise when they treat their fictional objects as if they were genuinely real.

Vaihinger's basic argument can be related to the current state of the social sciences and, in particular, to the conventional language of the social sciences. The rhetorical tendency to create technical nominals to denote processes – often by converting verbs by the suffix '-ization' – grammatically transforms these processes into things. These are not actual things, but, to adapt Vaihinger, they are 'fictional things'. 'Nominalization', 'dialogization', 'globalisation' do not exist in the same way as rocks and glaciers do. However, analysts often treat them as such.

Academic writers often place such concepts as the subjects of sentences, often as the subjects of active verbs – just as Locke wrote about 'eloquence' in doing things (Billig, 2008b; Master, 2006). We might read about what nominalization, or dialogization, or globalisation 'does' or 'accomplishes' or 'permits'. The writings of social and human scientists are filled with these metaphorical fictions that seem to perform the sort of actions that normally humans, or sometimes higher mammals, are only capable of performing in a literal sense.

Despite what Locke asserted, there is no problem with social or human scientists using metaphors. In fact, as Vaihinger recognized, metaphors can be vital for creative insight. The problem is that the metaphors become so habitual that they are no longer recognized as metaphors. Specialists accept the metaphorical things as real things – they write as if they are providing literal, factual descriptions of the world. Often the expertise of social scientific experts depends, in no small measure, on their treating metaphorical fictions as actual, existing objects.

For example, Freudians will consider 'repression' to be something actual. Freud very early in his writing switched from talking about individual patients 'repressing' to 'repression', as if it were a thing that controlled psychological events (Billig, 2008d). When Freud claimed that patients were repressing, he would need to describe how and when they were accomplishing this act. By talking of 'repression', as if it were an existing thing, he could by-pass the detail, claiming that he was talking of an actual, existing mental phenomenon (see Schafer, 1976, for a criticism of Freud's mechanical language). This switch from process to thing exemplifies a gap right at the heart of psychoanalytic theorising: a lack of detail about how people learn to repress and what they have to do in order to repress

(Billig, 1999). The more that psychoanalytically minded social scientists use the technical terminology of psychoanalysis, the more they can avoid noticing that this gap exists.

Social scientists depict a world that is filled with metaphorical fictions, accomplishing all manner of actions. We learn what discourses 'permit' and 'encourage'; what social representations 'communicate' and 'explain'; what social identification 'allows' and 'achieves' and so on. Hallidayan linguists write of what grammar 'construes' and 'understands'. Different theoretical approaches seem to create their own fictional things that seem to run the social world, controlling the actions of ordinary humans.

There is a problem with these metaphorical or fictional objects. Academic writers write in ways that conveys their existence to be unproblematic. As Halliday and Martin (1993) suggest, nominals can be used to suggest existence; this occurs because a nominal "is less negotiable, since you can argue with a clause but you can't argue with a nominal group" (p. 39). In this regard, writers using heavily nominalised language often reify the concepts they use (for examples related to 'nominalization', see Billig, 2008b). In this way, social scientists, through their heavily technical language, can create a world in which shadowy fictional things exist as entities doing the sorts of things that we expect humans to do.

THE CONTEXT OF SPECIALIST WRITING

Locke and Shaftesbury are not just separated from today's academics by their lack of technical nominals. Their styles belong to a different context of writing. Both Locke and Shaftesbury wrote for general publics. Unlike today's academics, they did not address a particular group of educated readers who would share the same technical vocabulary. From today's perspective Locke may have been a monological thinker, and Shaftesbury a dialogical one, but generally they addressed the same readers. Someone who read Locke was likely to read Shaftesbury and vice versa.

Today, by contrast, academics write for specialist readers. Universities over the last hundred years have become increasingly divided into separate disciplines (Russell, 2002; Waldo, 2004). Academics write with the shared vocabulary and syntactical style of their particular discipline (Bazerman, 2006; Hyland, 2009; Martinez et al., 2009). Cognitive scientists, as heirs of Locke, are likely to publish in journals that dialogical scientists seldom read. Academics need to use the accepted technical terminology of the journals in which they seek to publish: if they use plain, non-technical language, they are liable to have their papers rejected (Garbutt, 2009). This means that articles published in one discipline may be virtually undecipherable to specialists from another discipline. Worse than this, it means that the range of dialogue is diminished, for the authors in specialist journals are unlikely to be questioning the terminology that they must use to publish in the journal. In this respect, communities of like minded scholars are likely to read, and write for, the same journals.

Dialogical scientists are no different. We can expect them to have their favourite metaphorical fictions, whose existence will be taken for granted. An editorial statement on the website of *The International Journal for Dialogical Science* claims that "a central notion is the 'dialogical self' that brings together, in innovative ways, theoretical traditions regarding 'self' and 'dialogue'". Thus, the editors pick out the notion of 'dialogical self' (which itself appears capable of performing the action of 'bringing together' certain things). The dialogical self is the sort of concept that prospective authors might be expected to employ if they seek to publish in the journal. The dialogical self is, of course, a metaphorical object – it cannot be seen, touched, or felt, but its existence is to be taken for granted, as well as its capacity for doing things.

Now, perhaps we can see the problems of writing dialogically more clearly. At present, there is no distinctive dialogical style that dialogical theorists use. The contributors to *International Journal for Dialogical Science* typically use standard academic formats. The advice, which the journal offers to potential contributors, is entirely conventional, instructing them to follow the publication guidelines of the American Psychological Association. One can say that the contributions to dialogical science belong to the same genres of writing as do other contributions in the social sciences, whether or not they are explicitly dialogical in their theoretical perspective (on academic genres see Bhatia, 1993, 2006; Swales, 1990, 2006).

This does not necessarily mean that dialogical scientists are contradicting their theory with their own rhetorical practice and that they should follow Shaftesbury's style of self-criticism. Authors might imagine that their work solves problems once and for all. Locke may have imagined that he was decisively sweeping away the erroneous rubble of past generations, but this was an authorial fantasy. However, critical dialogue does not depend on the author already having performed the task, as Shaftesbury did in his final, self-critical volume. Indeed, authors, who produce their own self-criticism, can be seen as trying to control the basis on which they might be criticised, rather than fully opening up dialogue. It is similar to mocking oneself humorously. At first sight, people, who laugh at themselves, seem to be showing that they are aware of their weaknesses. Yet, by choosing which faults to mock, they can direct attention to unimportant weaknesses, thereby protecting themselves against more damaging ridicule (Billig, 2005; Kotthoff, 2000).

Dialogical authors might hope to open up debate, rather than silencing criticism. Most academic authors, however, are unlikely to silence criticism by phrasing their arguments in an assertive, monological style. Nor are they likely even to join an ongoing dialogue of response and counter-response. The argumentative context for most of us, whatever our theoretical perspective, is more dispiriting.

Most academic articles in the social sciences attract tiny readerships and are generally ignored. The mean number of citations for a social scientific article is one (Adler, Ewing & Taylor, 2008). Given that a small number of articles are disproportionately cited, this means that the modal number of citations per article in the social sciences is zero. Even if an article is cited, it is likely to be a perfunctory citation in passing, as another writer displays their knowledge of the 'field'; or maybe the sole citation will be a self-citation (Hyland, 2001). Even if an author, with dialogical aspirations, hopes to provoke informed debate, this is likely to be an authorial fantasy. The rhetorical reality is likely to be bleaker – neglect rather than critical attention. And, if we wish to be dialogically self-referential, then I should add that, as I write this sentence, I have few expectations (as opposed to fantasies) that these present words might enjoy a happier future.

Even if dialogical theorists do not necessarily need to adopt special dialogically self-referential style, they should pay particular attention to their ways of writing. Dialogical scientists will feel the need to publish dialogically scientific articles. As they do so, they will be writing, in the main, for their fellow dialogical scientists, rather than general readers. Rhetorically, they will use the technical terms that fellow dialogical scientists will use. They are likely to write about 'dialogical selves'. In so doing, they will be displaying their own credentials as credible dialogical scientists. But as they do this, they will be taking for granted the existence of certain metaphorical things, treating them as if they were real things.

The problem is not the use of fictional objects in writing as such. It is the closing down of debate – of dialogue – by using a shared technical language. If a writer were to turn on this language, refusing to use the concept of a 'dialogical self', they might be suspected of being an unfriendly outsider. The paradox for a dialogical science is clear. The more academics succeed in establishing a dialogical science – with journals, international conferences and specialist higher degrees – the more they will be rhetorically privileging certain chosen concepts. And in doing so, they risk treating metaphorical things as real things. Despite all good intentions, they will be closing down dialogue within their own dialogical world. The world of dialogical science will not have that contrariety of opposites that Shaftesbury so praised. It will bear the linguistic characteristics of unified, or monological, speech community.

CONCLUSION

But how can this be avoided? Adopting a dialogical style – composing little dialogical dramas rather than using conventional academic formats – will do little. We will be constructing our dramas for a restricted friendly audience, who will possibly smile and inwardly applaud at the right places. In writing this present chapter, I have not used any special dialogical format. The structure is conventional. On the other hand, I have tried not to use too many passive sentences or hefty technical terms – but I have not succeeded in eliminating them altogether.

This chapter is being written for a book whose readers are likely to be sympathisers of the dialogical project. It is based on a conference which attracted fellow dialogical researchers, helping to maintain a community of like-minded scholars. My own prose is likely to reflect this situation. I have contrasted Shaftesbury with Locke, calling the former dialogical and the latter monological. My dialogically minded readers are likely to recognize the code: Locke is on the outside, while Shaftesbury belongs to 'us'. You will probably have recognized who I am setting up to be cheered and who to be booed. The cheering and the booing, in this context, certainly do not extend dialogue or create the harmony of contrarieties that Shaftesbury sought.

'Divide yourself', Shaftesbury proclaimed. So, there is still more to do. Aristotle in his *Rhetoric*, in quoting Socrates, declared that "it is not hard to praise Athenians to Athenians" (1909, p. 39). It is not hard to praise dialogical theorists to dialogical theorists. To respect the goal of contrariety, I should be doing more: I should be praising the great John Locke. His *Essay* shows such insight into the way that the individual looks upon and thinks about the world. In his politics, he defended the freedom of the individual, leaving a legacy to be respected to this day. It is no wonder that Shaftesbury loved his foster-father. Even when criticising Locke privately, Shaftesbury recommended that students read and study him carefully (Shaftesbury, 1746, p. 32ff). And this perhaps is the hidden message of the story of Locke and Shaftesbury. The foster-son needed his foster-father. And so it is with their respective legacies. Modern dialogical science is the foster-child of monological, or cognitive, science. It could not exist without its foster-parent. Nor perhaps should it try to. Otherwise, we risk offending our own dialogical aspirations.

REFERENCES

Adler, R., Ewing, J., & Taylor, P. (2008). *Citation statistics. International Mathematical Union.* [http://www.mathunion.org/fileadmin/IMU/Report/CitationStatistics.pdf]. Accessed April 30th 2009.

Aristotle (1909). *The rhetoric.* Cambridge: Cambridge University Press.

Ashmore, M. (1989). *The reflexive thesis.* Chicago: Chicago University Press.

Ashmore, M., Myers, G., & Potter, J. (2002). Discourse, rhetoric and reflexivity: Seven days in the library. In S. Jasanoff, G.E. Markle, J. C. Petersen and T. Pinch (Eds.), *Handbook of science and technology studies* (pp. 321-342). London: Sage.

Bakhtin, M.M. (1986). *Speech genres and other late essays.* Austin: University of Texas Press.

Banks, D. (2003). The evolution of grammatical metaphor in scientific writing. In A. M. Simon-Vandenbergen, M. Tzaverniers & L. Ravelli (Eds.), *Grammatical metaphor* (pp. 127-148). Amsterdam: John Benjamins.

Bazerman, C. (2006). Distanced and refined selves: educational tensions in writing with power of knowledge. In M. Hewings (Ed.), *Academic writing in context* (pp. 23-29). London: Continuum.

Bhatia, V. K. (1993). *Analysing genre: Language use in professional settings.* London: Longman.

Bhatia, V. K. (2006). Analysing genre: some conceptual issues. In M. Hewings (Ed.), *Academic writing in context* (pp. 79-92). London: Continuum.

Billig, M. (1999). *Freudian repression.* Cambridge: Cambridge University Press.

Billig, M. (2005). *Laughter and ridicule: Towards a social critique of humour.* London: Sage.

Billig, M. (2008a). *The hidden roots of critical psychology: Understanding the impact of Locke, Shaftesbury and Reid.* London: Sage.

Billig, M. (2008b). The language of critical discourse analysis: The case of nominalization. *Discourse & Society, 19*, 783-800.

Billig, M. (2008c). Nominalizing and de-nominalizing: A reply. *Discourse & Society, 19*, 829-841.

Billig, M. (2008d). Social representations and repression: Examining the first formulations of Freud and Moscovici. *Journal for the Theory of Social Behaviour, 38*, 355-368.

Cassirer, E. (1951). *The philosophy of the enlightenment.* Princeton, N.J.: Princeton University Press.

Clark, R., & Ivanič, R. (1997) *The politics of writing.* London: Routledge.

Fairclough, N. (2003). *Analyzing discourse: Textual analysis for social research.* London: Routledge.

Fowler, R. (1991). *Language in the news.* London: Routledge.

Fowler, R., Hodge, B., Kress, G., & Trew, T. (1979). *Language and social control.* London: Routledge.

Fuster, J. (2003). *Cortex and mind.* Oxford: Oxford University Press.

Garbutt, R. (2009). Is there a place within academic journals for articles presented in an accessible format? *Disability & Society*, *24*, 357-371.

Halliday, M. A. K. (2003). *On language and linguistics*. London: Continuum.

Halliday, M. A. K. (2006). *The language of science*. London: Continuum.

Halliday, M. A. K., & Martin, J. R. (1993). *Writing science*. London: Falmer Press.

Harré, R. (2002). *Cognitive science: A philosophical introduction*. London: Sage.

Harré, R., & Gillett, G. (1994). *The discursive mind*. London: Sage.

Harris, R. (1997). *Landmarks in linguistic thought*. London: Routledge.

Holquist, M. (2002). *Dialogism: Bakhtin and his world*. London: Routledge.

Hyland, K. (2001). Humble servants of the discipline? Self-mention in research articles. *English for Specific Purposes*, *20*, 207-226.

Hyland, K. (2009). *Academic discourse*. London: Continuum.

Kotthoff, H. (2000). Gender and joking: On the complexities of women's image politics in humorous narratives. *Journal of Pragmatics*, *32*, 55-80.

Locke, J. (1690/1964). *An essay concerning human understanding*. London: Fontana.

Martinez, I. A., Beck, S. C., & Panza, C. B. (2009). Academic vocabulary in agriculture research articles: A corpus-based study. *English for Specific Purposes*, *28*, 183-198.

Master, P. (2006). Active verbs with inanimate subjects in scientific research articles. In M. Hewings (Ed.), *Academic writing in context* (pp. 169-181). London: Continuum.

Pinch, T., & Pinch, T. (1988). Reservations about reflexivity and new literary forms: Or why let the devil have all the good tunes. In S. Woolgar (Ed.), *Knowledge and reflexivity*. Chicago: Chicago University Press.

Poole, B. (2002). Bakhtin and Cassirer: The philosophical origins of Bakhtin's carnival messianism. In M. E. Gardiner (Ed.), *Mikhail Bakhtin. Vol. 1*. London: Sage.

Potter, J. (2001). Wittgenstein and Austin. In M. Wetherell, S. Taylor and S. J. Yates (Eds.), *Discourse theory and practice* (pp. 39-46). London: Sage.

Potter, J., & te Molder, H. (2005). Talking cognition: Mapping and making the terrain. In H. te Molder and J. Potter (Eds.), *Conversation and cognition* (pp. 1-54). Cambridge University Press: Cambridge.

Potter, J., & Wetherell, M. (1987). *Discourse and social psychology*. London: Sage.

Russell, D..R. (2002). *Writing in the academic disciplines*. Carbondale, Ill.: Southern Illinois University Press.

Santayana, G. (1933). *Some turns of thought in modern philosophy*. Cambridge: Cambridge University Press.

Schafer, R. (1976). *A new language for psychoanalysis*. New Haven: Yale University Press.

Shaftesbury, Anthony Ashley Cooper, Third Earl of (1714/1999). *Characteristicks of men, manners, opinions, times* (Edited L.E. Klein). Cambridge: Cambridge University Press.

Shaftesbury, Anthony Ashley Cooper, Third Earl of (1746). *The letters of the earl of Shaftesbury, collected into one volume*. No publisher given.

Shotter, J. (1993a). *Conversational realities*. London: Sage.

Shotter, J. (1993b). *Cultural politics of everyday life*. Milton Keynes: Open University Press.

Swales, J. M. (1990). *Genre analysis*. Cambridge: Cambridge University Press.

Swales, J. M. (2006). *Research genres: Explorations and applications*. Cambridge: Cambridge University Press.

Vaihinger, H. (1935). *The philosophy of 'as if'*. London: Routledge and Kegan Paul.

Waldo, M. L. (2004). *Demythologizing language difference in the academy*. Lawrence Erlbaum.

Wittgenstein, L. (1953). *Philosophical investigations*. Oxford: Blackwell.

In: Dialogicality in Focus   ISBN: 978-1-61122-817-5
Editors: M. Märtsin, B. Wagoner, E.-L. Aveling et al.   © 2011 Nova Science Publishers, Inc.

Chapter 2

LOCATING THE DIALOGICAL SELF WITHIN A CULTURAL SPHERE

Amrei C. Joerchel

"Spheres are the spaces where people actually live.
I would like to show that human beings have, till today,
been misunderstood,
because the space where they exist has always been taken for granted,
without ever being made conscious and explicit."
Peter Sloterdijk[1]

INTRODUCTION

The objective of this chapter is to suggest that the theory of the dialogical self adapt a spatial conception of culture – a cultural sphere – for a better theoretical understanding of the dialogical self in relation to culture. In opposition to cross cultural psychology, Hermans and colleagues have stated that culture and the Self should be conceptualized as decentralized, permeable and fluid (e.g., Hermans & Kempen, 1998; Hermans, 2001a, 2001b; Hermans & Dimaggio, 2007). Keeping to these premises this chapter proposes a view of culture which manifests itself within the interrelatedness of individuals and their environment (Boesch, 1991; Valsiner, 2003). This perspective is discussed and elaborated with the concept of a cultural sphere as inspired by Boesch (1991) and Sloterdijk (1998, 1999, 2004).

After briefly pointing to some problematic aspects of the conception of culture within dialogical self literature, the need for a novel understanding of culture within dialogical self theory is sketched. The space in which dialogical interactions are culturally organized is emphasized with the notion of a cultural sphere. This cultural sphere is first introduced with Boesch's (1991) conception of the symbolic action sphere and further discussed with two examples on the intricate interrelatedness of two floating poles within a micro-sphere: two lovers, and a mother with her new born child. The two examples of such intimate

---

[1] http://www.petersloterdijk.net/, retrieved March, 2010.

intersubjectivity illustrate Sloterdijk's (1998, 1999, 2004) contribution to the idea of spheres: the starting point of the human condition necessarily being two human beings. The focus here lies not so much on the symbolic meanings individual actions may carry, but rather on the resonating process within a conjunctional experiential space (Mannheim, 1924/1982). The examples of the two lovers and of the mother and her child are then set into a wider frame of reference – a cultural sphere – and discussed in relation to dialogical self theory. While the overall aim of this chapter is to outline a more solid understanding of the relationship between culture and the self within dialogical self theory, some empirical implications will be pointed to at the end of the chapter. But first, let us turn to the conception of culture within dialogical self theory and why a novel understanding of the Self and culture is needed.

CULTURE WITHIN DIALOGICAL SELF THEORY

The Definition of Culture

Hermans and colleagues have proposed that dialogical self theory is especially useful in today's globalizing world as it is 'culture inclusive' (Hermans & Kempen 1998; Hermans 2001a, 2001b; Hermans & Dimaggio, 2007). More precisely, Hermans and Kempen have challenged the cross-cultural conception of culture as geographically localized. Furthermore, diverging from the Cartesian individual paradigm Hermans and colleagues stress that the relationship between culture and the Self is more complicated than either a reified understanding of culture or Self could account for (e.g., Hermans & Kempen 1998; Hermans 2001a, 2001b). Thus, in accordance with Hannerz's (1992, cited in Hermans & Kempen 1998) developments, Hermans and Kempen propose a cultural flow, which stands in opposition to culture seen as a single essence. The cultural flow can be distinguished as a) ideas and modes of thought, b) forms of externalization of these ideas and modes of thought and as c) the social distribution of these (Hermans & Kempen, 1998, p. 1115).

This conception of culture certainly has no single essence and is more dynamic and fluid than the traditional and reified definition suggests. It nevertheless fails to capture the essential features of human culture. If conceptualized purely by thought modes and ideas, their externalization and distribution, then simple *cultural habits* and *common patterns* which constitute a large proportion of everyday interactions remain neglected. The Spanish 'lisp', for example, is certainly no mode of thought, idea, or an externalization or a distribution of it. It is a simple cultural habit which has evolved over a course of time. And yet, this pronunciation of the z as a *th*, which Spanish people do, is cultural. It is cultural in the sense that this sound has emerged as a symbolic mediation (Valsiner, 2003) out of the interaction between the individual human being and his or her environment (Boesch, 1991).

The Implementation of Culture

The definition of culture as cultural flow, as Hermans and colleagues have suggested, does not account for cultural habits and practices (such as the Spanish 'lisp'), as cultural habits and practices do not necessarily fit the categories of thought mode, idea, or externalisation. Yet, precisely these simple habits and patterns, which are formed within a space between various poles of individuals and objects, between individual and environment, are at once cultural and mediate the Self (Mead, 1934). It is these cultural patterns which call for more attention within dialogical self theory. Cultural patterns and structures, their origination and their implication for the orientation of the dialogical interactions are often neglected in favour for the more traditional and mainstream conception of culture as kind of "geography of the self" (e.g., the Korean self, the Japanese self as mentioned by Valsiner & Han, 2008, p. 5, or the Indian self discussed by Rasmussen, 2008, p. 43).

The implementation of culture as structural process corresponds well with aspirations of the theorists of the dialogical self. Hermans and Kempen (1998) state that the focus of a cultural dialogical self is "on intercultural processes that lead to the recombination of existing forms and practices" (p. 1113). Here the focus on processes, forms, structures and habits is clearly given. And yet, in the same article when discussing further research Hermans and Kempen ask questions such as *"Which voices are introduced as the result of distributive processes* across a population? To what extend are *cultural voices* heterogenous, and *what is the cultural unit or contact zone where they are shared with other individuals and groups?"* (p. 1118, emphasis added). Further, they encourage researchers to pay particular attention to the "mixing of *cultural positions or voices.*" These thoughts are elaborated as follows:

> "When an artist of Arabic origin works in Germany, can this be conceptualized in terms of two separate *cultural positions* (Arabic and German) that are available and between which the person shifts from time to time? Or is a *third position* emerging that can be seen as a mixture of the two original ones?" (Hermans & Kempen, 1998, p. 1118, emphasis added).

More than a decade has passed since Hermans and Kempen have formulated these questions. Since then the theory of the dialogical self has undoubtedly further developed. Nevertheless, the mention of cultural voices, cultural positions, and geographically localized selves has prevailed (e.g., Hermans, 2001; Hermans & Dimaggio, 2007; Gratier, 2008; van Meijl, 2008; Choi & Han, 2008). And yet, revealing and analysing cultural positions or voices (and not the processes between them) implies the same reification of culture that Hermans and colleagues aim to transcend (as has already been pointed out by some authors, e.g., Adams & Markus, 2001; Zabinski, 2008; Ruck & Slunecko, 2008). The habitual processes and intersubjective matrices (Coelho & Figueiredo, 2003) which constitute the Self are thus lost.

If culture is seen as a structural process which automatically takes place whenever humans or their dialogical positions interact – as in a cultural sphere – then all positions and voices are necessarily cultural as the interaction between them has already mediated each voice and each position while coming into existence (Valsiner & Han, 2008). Note that whenever a Spaniard speaks in his mother tongue, regardless of which position or voice momentarily is in the foreground, he or she is speaking with a Spanish 'lisp'. This particular cultural habit can be found in multiple positions and voices; it is not restricted to one. Furthermore, whenever a novel position or voice emerges within the Spanish language, it will always take on the colour the Spanish 'lisp' carries.

Thus, as the authors of dialogical self theory aim to conceptualize culture as a process, a revision of the use of the term culture within the theory is necessary. In the following paragraphs the definition of culture as a structural manifestation of human interaction will be sketched with the further suggestion of a cultural sphere.

INTRODUCING THE CULTURAL SPHERE

Valsiner (2003) argues for a conception of culture as "exemplified through different processes by which persons interact with their worlds" (§7). From such a perspective, culture is understood as an organizing principle of each and every human action. It is at once everywhere, always in action, and yet rarely noticed. The interesting aspect of this action based definition of culture, is that every single action (let it be as trivial as breathing or as pronouncing the z as *th*) never occurs within a void and separated from other actions and meanings. It is the organization of actions within a certain space – a certain cultural sphere – which underlines the more trivial actions with meanings (Boesch, 1991, p. 29-37). Once we leave the comfortable boundaries of our home atmospheres, the immanent nature of various actions becomes apparent. For mountaineers or divers the act of breathing may become something very conscious as it suddenly becomes evident that this seemingly trivial task we perform every minute of our lives is of vital importance. The Spaniard who travels to South America may suddenly notice that he has a very particular way of pronouncing certain words. I would thus like to bring more attention to the space in which mediational actions take place in order to contextualize and situate the dialogical self within a cultural sphere.

THE CULTURAL SPHERE: FROM BOESCH TO SLOTERDIJK

The Cultural Action Sphere

The idea of human action being culturally organized within a specific kind of sphere is not new to cultural psychology. In 1991, Ernest E. Boesch outlined the differentiations of cultural action fields and action spheres. According to Boesch a *cultural action field* embraces the totality of action opportunities. In other words, a cultural action field suggests a range of potential uses of objects along with their symbolic values. Boesch describes *action spheres* as 'centres' around which the individual action fields cluster. These clusters of action fields relate to thematic areas in which various actions converge on common purposes. Action spheres are thus areas of behaviour which group different action – of individuals as well as of groups – serving a common purpose. Examples of such action spheres can be 'family' or 'occupation.' If one looks at the action sphere 'family,' several *action domains* come to mind. A housewife may perceive the action sphere family to be composed out of different task, such as cooking, sewing, cleaning, taking the children to school and to sport activities after school, or organising the family holiday. The husband on the other hand may perceive the action sphere family very differently. His action sphere family may consist of coming home for a family dinner, playing football with his son, or spending the weekend with his family at the lake. It becomes obvious that each member of the family may have a very different perception of what the action sphere family consists of, as each member of the family occupies different tasks revolving around 'family life' (Boesch, 1991, p. 71).

Moving away from individual actions and individual perspectives of action fields to the general structures and patterns within these fields, the following paragraphs will discuss not how individual actions structure the space around them, but how we may begin to understand the space between individuals. This shift of focus, the shift from individual action to the space in which the actions are conducted and in which intersubjectivity is patterned, will help to understand how cultural mediation manifests itself within the space between and so is at the same time a component of the space in which action is conducted, as well as a psychological organizing principle.

THE SPACE BETWEEN

The action sphere 'family' is a psychological space which is arranged according to physical objects as well as psychological goals and constraints. Each particular action space (in this case the action spaces belonging to the sphere 'family') is filled with meanings and arranged according to them (Boesch, 1991, p. 30-31). In addition to the meanings that are created through individual actions, other intersubjective matrices underscore the space between the Self and the other with meaning. These dimensions of meanings are hard to grasp, as they are the social material which is not noticeable and yet which taints the human sphere with particular cultural atmospheres. These cultural atmospheres are generated through resonating with the other in a specific space, which is not explicated by traditional symbolic interactionism (Coelho & Figueiredo, 2003). Sloterdijk thus proposes to focus on describing the qualities within the human sphere instead of the individual actions themselves.

According to Sloterdijk[2] (1998), the human sphere should be understood as an orb filled with sense, meaning and with all that lives. Furthermore, and more pertinent to the problem at hand, the space is also filled with the respective habits and patterns of all interactions taking place within it. It should be conceptualized as an *eigenspace* with atmosphere generating qualities which have emerged through the act of being together. Through the tensions, inspirations and the taking part in a sphere we are always a floating pole in sympathy-spaces, in mood-spaces, and in taking-part-spaces. As it is the *space* that is highlighted in Sloterdijk's conceptions, it is never the isolated entities or objects that seem to be of importance, but rather the *resonance* of our interactional relationship in our intentional worlds (Shweder, 1990). It is what is happening between individuals and their immersion with the other which constitutes them.

Within this atmosphere, the inhabitants always experience the world from a certain perspective and never on a direct basis. The individual human being is seen as an effect of the inspired (*beseelte*) space, which is situated at the same time between us and the other as well as within both of us. It is the space itself which orientates the forms of our reality. Important to note here is that while humans are the products of such spheres, the individual human beings themselves are not the producers, as might be the case from a constructivist

---

[2] Before turning to Sloterdijk a word of caution is to be said. On the one hand the problem of translating Sloterdijk's German terminology into English prevails throughout this text. Furthermore, Sloterdijk has himself, on the other hand, purposely not adopted any scientific jargon as he argues that such a distancing technique would necessarily fail to capture the essence of the human condition (Sloterdijk & Heinrichs, 2001). Thus I would like to invite all scientific readers to leave behind the realm of familiar scientific jargon and, for the following paragraphs, enjoy a more poetic picture of floating beings.

perspective. There is no producer as such. The cultural atmosphere emanates from humans resonating within the same sphere and from actions and interactions with one another. The subtle experience of resonating within the space is highlighted within Sloterdijk's twosome quality of a human sphere and further elaborated in the following paragraphs.

RESONATING WITH THE OTHER

According to Sloterdijk (1998, 1999, 2004), individuals *resonate* within a sphere and are able to flourish only because of their participation within it. Only in taking part in the mediational ongoing act of being together does one develop as a human being. At the same time, this taking part in the goings-on of the space between us and the other is what generates and manifests cultural forms and patterns, just as plants in a greenhouse generate oxygen.

The term resonate can best be comprehended with Mannheim's (1924/1982) notion of *contagion*. In this respect, to resonate with someone is to form a kind of existential relationship, a specific union with the other, the *vis-à-vis*. Humans have the ability, quite in the manner of contagion, to grasp in their immediacy things of the spirit through the spirit, things of the soul through the soul (Mannheim, 1924/1982, p.188-189). It is in this contagious manner humans resonate within spheres. As soon as a human inhabits a certain sphere, he or she directly touches and receives the *vis-à-vis* according to a very specific atmosphere and climate which can be found within the sphere.

Figure 1. *The meeting at the golden gate* by Giotto di Bondone; reprinted with permission from Sloterdijk (1998, p. 148).

Two Lovers Resonating with each other

The importance of the act of being together cannot be stressed enough. Sloterdijk (1998) highlights repeatedly that the 'commune' and the act of being together within the sphere is what constitutes not only the sphere but also the individual human being. To emphasize the interrelatedness within the general cultural sphere, a kind of macro-sphere, Sloterdijk first gives the reader a lengthy description of a kind of micro-sphere and begins his sphereology with the inspired municipality or commune (*gehauchte Kommune*). As an example of such a micro-sphere and the inspired goings-on within it, Sloterdijk soon refers to the perfect twosome: the couple who are deeply in love. Again, the importance here is always the immersion in the other. It is the awesome attention which envelopes the twosome as a combined halo of two holy individuals in face-to-face contact might achieve (see Figure 1). It is what John Donne (1896) celebrates in *The Ecstasy*:

"When love, with one another so
Interanimates two souls
That abler soul, which thence doth flow
Defects of loneliness controls"

Here we have a situation of two human beings entering into a highly intimate micro-sphere. The example of these two lovers simply serves as an illustration of how immanent the immersion with the other is. The micro-sphere, or the inspired commune, of these two lovers clearly takes on a unique characteristic – a unique atmosphere – which develops out of the act of the two souls touching each other, out of the two human beings falling in love. Here one can easily imagine the two floating poles creating a very specific psychological field not only between each other, but also around and within each other, through the immergence of the Self with the *vis-à-vis*. Certain patterns and structures emerge out of the simple act of two souls touching, two spirits 'tasting' (Mannheim, 1924/1982, p. 188) each other. The two lovers represent two poles within their very distinct sympathy-space and mood-space which at once has emerged through their interaction and mediates their actions. It is the very close intimacy of the two lovers which beautifully illustrate the resonating process within the human sphere. A further example of such intimate resonance within a micro-sphere would be the first interactions between a mother and her child.

Intersubjective Intimacy at the Beginning of Life

The personal human sphere emerges very early in an infant's life. If we conceive a cultural sphere as emerging out of interpersonal interaction (Boesch, 1991) and the act of resonating together (Sloterdijk, 1998), of tuning into and resonating within the space of the other (Mannheim, 1924/1982), we can safely assume that this space already begins to form in the uterus (Sloterdijk, 1998). In their review article on infant intersubjectivity, Trevarthen and Aitken (2001) state that "perceiving the mother's rhythmic vocal expressions of motive states from her speech can begin in utero, many weeks before birth" (p. 7). Similarly, Sloterdijk (1998) dedicates many pages to the description of the space between and around the infant and his or her caregiver. Such profound intimacy as the child experiences within the mother's womb will be lost forever once the infant has been born (Sloterdijk, 1998, p. 347-401). This loss, according to Sloterdijk, also explains the infants' craving for social contact from the very beginning of their lives. Indeed, "evidence shows that even new born infants, [...] are specifically motivated, beyond instinctive behaviors that attract parental care for immediate biological needs, to communicate intricately [...] with the interest and feelings displayed by other humans" (Trevarthen & Aitken, 2001, p. 3). The infant's craving for communication animates the initial self-other awareness as well as the reception of motives and emotions in intersubjective meanings.

Important to note here is that the "communicative behaviors displayed by infants shortly after birth are homologous with behaviors that are essential to the elaborate intersubjectivity of all collaborative intentional activity in adult society" (Trevarthen & Aitken, 2001, p. 6). Thus, this intersubjective behaviour is not the antecedent of cultural learning (as for example suggested by Tomasello, Carpenter, Call, Behne & Moll, 2005). Rather, from the very beginning of life humans take part in a cultural sphere in which the self emerges through the relation to the vis-à-vis. The space of the mother and child is from the very beginning structured in a particular manner. The first encounter of mother and child, the first vis-à-vis situation in which mother and child literally face each other (see Figure 2) is something very novel in which two souls touch each other and thereby create a new space for each other. The space between mother and child forms out of their process of tuning into each other, out of touching each other's souls. This resonating process happens immediately, unnoticeably and spontaneously.

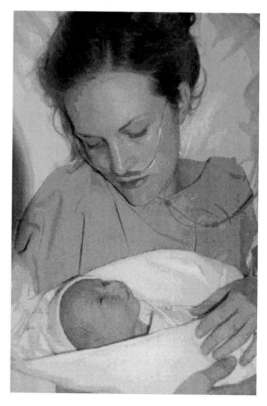

Figure 2. Mother and child facing each other (vis-à-vis) for the first time.

From Micro-Spheres to a Cultural Sphere

The two examples were discussed in order to point to the subtleties of resonating processes within human spheres. The lover touches the soul of his or her partner and instantly begins to resonate with him or her. The actions, feeling, perceptions and, in fact, the whole being is mediated through atmospherical forces which emanate from resonating with one another. Likewise, the mother and the child form a space in which a particular atmosphere is generated and which, in turn, structures and organizes their beings. While these two examples were chosen to illustrate the subtleties of resonating with one another, it is important to keep in mind that these examples represent a kind of micro-sphere, constituted by two floating poles. Yet, just as the individual human being is never isolated from floating in a sympathy-space with another, so is the micro-sphere never cut off from the general ongoing patterns of various clusters of action fields—of the cultural sphere.

The child is never born into a void. The space between the mother and the father, between the mother and the doctor, *ad infinitum*, is already structured before the child enters even the thoughts of the mother. The mother-child sphere into which the child is born already has a particular cultural atmosphere which taints and patterns all interactions that will take place within it. And so also the structural atmosphere which emerges through the resonating process of the two souls of mother and child is structured according to specific patterns and forms which already exist within the cultural atmosphere surrounding both mother and child.

Likewise, returning to the two lovers (Figure 1) it becomes clear that other interlocutors, other micro-spheres are around and intermingle with the lovers' micro-sphere. It is clearly visible that the two lovers are embedded within a greater cultural sphere. Certain cultural rules and structures have evolved out of various interactions and at the same time structure the individual actions. Which kind of clothing is worn by whom and when would be an example (in this case long flowing gowns that drop to the floor). Simple conventions and patterns have emerged which usually go unnoticed or at least un-reflected, but which nevertheless mediate actions (Slunecko, 2008). Acts of being together, which constitute the human sphere (Sloterdijk, 1998) are much more subtle than a baby's cry or the act of nursing a child in order to comfort him. A simple reception of the other is more than enough to spur the resonating processes (Mannheim, 1924/1982). The emphasis must always be brought back to the process of tuning into the mood-space, the meaning-space and the sense-space of the other. This resonating with one another and tuning into the space of the other is what generates a cultural atmosphere, which, in turn, mediates the individuals participating within the particular sphere.

Thus, the singular relationships of the Self and the other are themselves always already embedded within the greater cultural sphere which envelopes both interlocutors. While a very distinct novel space emerges for mother and child or for two lovers due to the resonating processes of one human being with the *vis-à-vis*, this space in turn emerges within a cultural sphere which simultaneously has a history and permanently undergoes restructuring as novel spaces emerge (Sloterdijk, 1999, 2004). Mother and child are never isolated from the general ongoing act of being together within the greater cultural sphere, nor are the lovers who together have created an ellipse with their combined halos. To conclude, in the following paragraphs the approach of culture as structuring processes within a human sphere will be discussed in relation to the theory of the dialogical self.

THE DIALOGICAL SELF RESONATING WITHIN A SPHERE: IMPLICATIONS AND SUGGESTIONS

Theoretical Implications

As humans move within cultural spheres, culture is constitutive of the individual and the individual can never be found outside of culture (Sloterdijk, 1998; Slunecko & Hengl, 2007). Individuals automatically resonate within a particular cultural sphere and cannot escape it. For the dialogical self this would imply that the self, with all of his or her positions and dialogical interactions, should be conceptualized as resonating within a particular sphere. Each sphere in which the dialogical self moves always has a specific cultural atmosphere according to which dialogical interactions, voices and positions are structured. It is thus never the individual position or voice, as suggested by Hermans and Kempen (1998, p. 1118) which culturally influences the rest of the dialogical self system. Rather, as a wind blows though a tree top and leaves subtle traces behind on every branch, so blows the cultural atmosphere through the dialogical self, structuring dialogical interactions in a subtlety which is rarely noticed. Remembering the Spaniard, he rarely thinks about how he pronounces a word, and yet, he does pronounce each singular word in a very particular manner. Further, just as a certain climate allows some trees to grow but not other, so too will some cultural atmospheres allow particular cultural habits to emerge and not others. Turning again to the example of language, the very early consonant-vocal combinations which children produce while learning their mother-tongue already exhibit patterns and characteristics typical of that particular language (see Penner, 2000) and will soon begin to lose the capability of pronouncing and combining vocals typical for other languages. Considering language as one action frame of the cultural sphere in which one grows it becomes evident how cultural spheres at once constrain and present future action possibilities (Boesch, 1991, p. 29-37).

We must then look at the mediational goings-on within particular spheres in order to describe how this particular sphere may simultaneously constitute individual human actions and thus also the Self. Theories that have developed out of the traditional symbolic interactionism school have clearly made a solid contribution to the field of psychology in terms of incorporating the other within psychological theory and within theory of the Self. The elaboration on the space around, between and within two interlocutors served the purpose of emphasizing the cultural structures within particular cultural spheres. Only once the cultural sphere in which particular actions and symbolic mediations take place is described can individual actions and in turn the dialogical interactions of the dialogical self be understood in relation to culture.

Bridging the Gap between Theory and Empirical Studies

In order to leave the realms of an individualistic paradigm I have suggested that the relation between culture and the Self should be conceptualized as a constitutive process, where culture and the Self simultaneously constitute one another. Furthermore, I have suggested that cultural processes emerge out of the act of tuning into the space of the other, simultaneously structuring the space as well as the human beings moving within the space.

Such a conception was chosen in part as it is compatible with the aims and aspirations of dialogical self theory, which emphasise not only the necessity of the other within the origins of dialogical interactions (e.g., Hermans, Kempen & van Loon, 1992), but also the need for cultural structures and patterns to replace a static and localized notion of culture (e.g., Hermans & Kempen, 1998).

The strong emphasis on beginning with two individuals – instead of one – within this chapter is to suggest moving away from the focus on individual positions and their actions (e.g., the Arabic position) to patterns and structures which emerge within the space around and between interlocutors or positions within the dialogical self. This would imply that structural (and for that matter cultural) patterns can be found on the one hand within cultural tools and products (such as media, pictures, narrations etc., see for example Slunecko, 2008) and on the other hand within dialogical interactions (Valsiner & Han, 2008). The goal for empirical research would then be to find specific cultural patterns within cultural artefacts and relate these back to the dialogical self. One notable example of analysing cultural artefacts in relation to the dialogical self is Ruck's and Slunecko's (2008) interpretation of Frida Kahlo's *Tree of Hope*. With the interpretation of a self-portrait of the Mexican painter Ruck and Slunecko successfully show not only how different I-positions may appear in cultural artefacts themselves (the painting), which might not otherwise have come to the foreground (the silent positions). But also how one can find cultural traces within the painting itself as Frida Kahlo make use of typical Mexican symbols and artefacts to express who she is. With the help of image analysis Ruck and Slunecko thus successfully discuss the spatiality of the Self on an empirical level.

CONCLUSION

The aim of this chapter has been to open up the space around, between and within interlocutors and to highlight the conception of culture as structural process which simultaneously organises the space in which positions move as well as the dialogical interactions between positions and thus also the dialogical self. For the theory of the dialogical self this means that it always develops within a cultural atmosphere which constantly, and usually unnoticeably, simultaneously resonates within each individual, structuring and formatting his or her dialogical interactions. The dialogical self, therefore, is also already embedded into the general cultural sphere and resonates with all of his or her resonating fellows. Taking this resonating process seriously, the dialogical self can be viewed from a slightly different angle: the self constructs itself not only through the act of dialogue (as dialogue itself is already inspired by the general cultural atmosphere), but rather, resonating processes govern the dialogical processes and cultural atmospheric forces that inspire them.

REFERENCES

Adams, G., & Markus, H. R. (2001). Culture as patterns: An alternative approach to the problem of reification. *Culture & Psychology, 7*, 283-296.

Boesch, E. E. (1991). *Symbolic action theory and cultural psychology.* Berlin: Springer-Verlag.

Choi, S. C., & Han, G. (2008). *Shimcheong* psychology: A case of emotion state for cultural psychology. *International Journal of Dialogical Science, 3*(1), 205-224.

Coelho, N. E., & Figueiredo, L. C. (2003). Patterns of intersubjectivity in the constitution of subjectivity: Dimensions of otherness. *Culture & Psychology, 9*, 193-208.

Donne, J. (1896) The ecstacy. In E. K. Chambers (Ed.), *Poems of John Donne: Vol. I* (pp. 53-56). London: Lawrence & Bullen.

Gratier, M. (2008). Liminal spaces and narratives of voice and body in infant vocal internchange: Commentary on Morioka. *International Journal of Dialogical Science, 3*(1), 143-154.

Hannerz, U. (1992). *Cultural complexity: Studies in the social organization of meaning.* New York: Columbia University Press.

Hermans, H. J. M. (2001a). The dialogical self: Toward a theory of personal and cultural positioning. *Culture & Psychology, 7*, 243-281.

Hermans, H. J. M. (2001b). Mixing and moving cultures require a dialogical self. *Human Development, 44*, 24-28.

Hermans, H. J. M., & Dimaggio, G. (2007). Self, identity, and globalisation in times of uncertainty: A dialogical analysis. *Review of General Psychology, 11*, 31-61.

Hermans, H. J. M., & Kempen, H. J. G. (1998). Moving cultures: The perilous problems of cultural dichotomies in a globalizing society. *American Psychologist, 53*, 1111-1120.

Hermans, H. J. M., Kempen, H. J. G., & Van Loon, R. J. P. (1992). The dialogical self: Beyond individualism and rationalism. *American Psychologist, 47*, 23-33.

Mannheim, K. (1924/1982). *Structures of thinking* (J. J. Shapiro & S. Weber Nicholsen, Trans.). London: Routledge & Kegan Paul. (Original work published in German 1922-1924).

Mead, G. H. (1934). *Mind, self, & society: From the standpoint of a social behaviorist.* London: University of Chicago Press.

Penner, Z. (2000). Phonologische Entwicklung: Eine Übersicht. [Phonological development: An overview.] In H. Grimm (Ed.), *Sprachentwicklung. Enzyklopädie der psychologie: Themenbereich C. Theorie und forschung: Serie III. Sprache: Vol. 3.* [Language development. Encyclopaedia of psychology: Subject area C. Theory and research: Series III. Language: Vol.3.] (pp. 105-139). Göttingen: Hogrefe.

Rasmussen, S. (2008). Personhood, self, difference, and dialogue. *International Journal for Dialogical Science, 3*, 31-54.

Ruck, N., & Slunecko, T. (2008). Portrait of a dialogical self: Image science and the dialogical self. *International Journal for Dialogical Science, 3*(1), 261-290.

Shweder, R. A. (1990). Cultural psychology – what is it? In J. W. Stigler, R. A. Shweder, & G. Herdt (Eds.), *Cultural psychology: Essays on comparative human development* (pp. 2-43). Cambridge: Cambridge University Press.

Sloterdijk, P. (1998). *Sphären I: Blasen.* [Spheres I: Bubbles.] Frankfurt: Suhrkamp.

Sloterdijk, P. (1999). *Sphären II: Globen.* [Spheres II: Globes.] Frankfurt: Suhrkamp.

Sloterdijk, P. (2004). *Sphären III: Schäume.* [Spheres III: Foams.] Frankfurt: Suhrkamp.

Sloterdijk, P., & Heinrichs, H. (2001). *Die Sonne und der tod: Dialogische untersuchungen* [The sun and the death: Dialogical enquires.] Frankfurt: Suhrkamp.

Slunecko, T. (2008). *Von der Konstruktion zu der dynamischen konstitution: Beobachtungen auf der eigenen spur.* [From construction to the dynamic constitution: Observations in my own tracks.]. Vienna: WUV.

Slunecko, T., & Hengl, S. (2007). Language, cognition, subjectivity: A dynamic constitution. In A. Rosa, & J. Valsiner (Eds.), *Handbook of sociocultural psychology* (pp. 40-61). Cambridge: Cambridge University Press.

Tomasello, M., Carpenter, M., Call, J., Behne, T., & Moll, H. (2005). Understanding and sharing intentions: The origins of cultural cognition. *Behavioral and Brain Science, 28,* 675-738.

Trevarthen, C., & Aitken, K. J. (2001). Infant intersubjectivity: Research, theory and clinical applications. *Journal of Child Psychology and Psychiatry, 42,* 3-48.

Valsiner, J. (2003). Culture and its transfer: Ways of creating general knowledge through the study of cultural particulars. In W. J. Lonner, D.L. Dinnel, S. A. Hayes, & D. N. Sattler (Eds.), *Online readings in psychology and culture* (Unit 2, Chapter 12), (http://www.wwu.edu/~culture), Center for Cross-Cultural Research, Western Washington University, Bellingham, Washington USA.

Valsiner, J., & Han, G. (2008). Where is culture within the dialogical perspectives of the self? *International Journal for Dialogical Science, 3*(1), 1-8.

Van Meijl, T. (2008). Culture and identity in anthropology: Reflections on 'unity' and 'uncertainty' in the dialogical self. *International Journal of Dialogical Science, 3*(1), 165-190.

Zabinski, B. (2008). Anthropology and dialogical theory: Converting the conversation on the processual self: Commentary on van Meijl. *International Journal of Dialogical Science, 3*(1), 191-204.

In: Dialogicality in Focus   ISBN: 978-1-61122-817-5
Editors: M. Märtsin, B. Wagoner, E.-L. Aveling et al.   © 2011 Nova Science Publishers, Inc.

Chapter 3

WHAT IS AN UTTERANCE?

Andrés Haye and Antonia Larraín

"Things grasped together: things whole, things not whole; being brought together, being separated; consonant, dissonant; Out of all things one thing, and out of one thing all things."
(Heraclitus, 1987, fragment 10)

INTRODUCTION

Current developments in dialogical sciences, focused on understanding human mind and behaviour as a semiotic, dynamic, and socially interdependent process, are increasingly concerned with developing appropriate research methods. Recently, several efforts have been made, some of them broadly concerned with methodological issues enabling us to grasp dynamism and dialogicality of human semiotic processes (Gillespie & Zittoun, 2009; Salvatore, Valsiner, Strout-Yagodzinski, & Clegg, 2009; Valsiner & Sato, 2006; Wagoner, 2009; Wagoner & Valsiner, 2005), while others are committed to finding proper analytical tools and procedures (Gillespie & Cornish, 2010; Grossen, 2010; Josephs, Valsiner, & Surgan, 1999; Larraín & Medina, 2007; Linell, 2009; Marková, Linell, Grossen & Salazar-Orvig, 2007; Valsiner, 2005). Motivating these efforts is the idea that the scientific contribution of dialogical approaches to psychology and social sciences depends, to a great extent, on the relevance of their empirical research (Mininni, 2010).

According to Grossen (2010), dialogical approaches to human cognition and communication arise as a new disciplinary field "which takes human interaction as a research object" (p. 5). Consequently, discourse and language should be key elements of those methodological approaches meant to account for dialogicality of human processes (for a discussion on the diversity within dialogical approaches see Linell, 2009). However, although centrality of language and its potentiality for the study of psychological processes has been acknowledged by some dialogical approaches (Marková et al., 2007; Mercer & Littleton, 2007; Billig, 1987; Leitão, 2000; Haye & Larraín, 2009; Mininni, 2010; Larraín & Medina, 2007), others have been more sceptical. Valsiner (2009) argues that in excessively attending to language in contemporary cognitive science "there is danger of losing the complex reality of human phenomena from focus if the primacy of affective processes is downplayed" (p. 10-11). Likewise, Gillespie and Zittoun (2009) highlight the irreducibility of thought to talk. However, as far as we understand, the different emphases among dialogical approaches concerning the role of discourse and language in the study of psychological processes are not rooted in a Scholastic division between those who support and those who are against the idea of reducing experience to language. What explains these different emphases is a diverse and (mainly) vague conceptualisation of language and discourse. The belief that there is a risk of overlooking affective or thinking processes if language is put at the centre, supposes a particular notion of the relation between affective processes and language, or between thought and language, that is neither clear nor shared among dialogical approaches (for a discussion of the notions of thought, discourse and language see Haye & Larraín, 2009; and Larraín & Haye, in press).

In order to have a fruitful discussion about methodological tools capable of grasping the dialogicality of human experience, it is crucial to conceptually elaborate the notions of language and discourse held: to open them up to discussion instead of 'sticking to them' as if they were clear and shared. Bearing in mind that social research always deals with discursive practices as its main data (at least according to Bakhtin, 1986a), the discursive nature of human processes should be made visible. It is neither necessary, nor desirable, to reach an overall agreement about the notion of discourse, but if human experience counts as discourse for other people and for oneself (Voloshinov, 1926/1976), we would not be able to apprehend it without an explicit theorisation of discourse. Thus, the aim of this chapter is to contribute to a theoretical understanding of the dialogical nature of discourse in order to provide insights for the development of proper discourse analytical tools. We attempt to do this by focusing on the *dialogical unit of analysis* in discursive practices.

REVISITING AN OLD PROBLEM

What is discourse? A conversation among two lads is discourse, despite their improper use of language. A written text is discourse, without oral speech. The thought unfolding while reading a text is also discourse, even if it is just an interpretation of the text. A self-dialogue is discourse, even if only one and the same living being is involved. A monological address to the people is discourse, even if there is no immediate response and no turn taking. Workers' silent coordination in a process of production is discourse, without overt words. The charming and enthusiastic chat around the fire is discourse, in spite of being a sort of chaotic crossing of multiple simultaneous conversations with no fixed parties. Given such a diversity of discursive practices, what unity is there to discourse?

In *Discourse in Art and Discourse in Life*, Voloshinov (1926/1976) shows that we do not need overt words to work in language, and that the extra-verbal situation plays an important role in communication. Voloshinov claims that the word as part of the living reality of verbal discourse, is not the same as the word understood as a lexical unit. Likewise, in *Towards a Methodology for the Human Sciences*, Bakhtin (1986b, p. 166) writes: "To a certain degree, one can speak by means of intonations alone, making the verbally expressed part of speech relative and replaceable, almost indifferent." If lexemes and phonemes are not an essential ingredient of discursive activity, then we may ask again: What is the basic unit of language? If both the extra-verbal situation and the affective tones are particularly important aspects of language practices, as suggested by Voloshinov and Bakhtin, then: How should we conceive of discourse? What is to be taken as the minimal whole of discursive communication, such that the extra-verbal situation and the affective tones, as essential ingredients of language, are articulated as a unit?

The relevance of this question about language stems from the need to determine proper units of analysis in dialogical research. Discourse analysts have discussed the issue of the unit of analysis for a long time because of its crucial role in research procedures. This is especially the case for conversation analysts (see Linell, 1998; 2009), whose focus on verbal interaction has pushed them to discuss dynamic and social units of analysis that are different from the formal units of *langue*. Previously, Bakhtin (1981, 1929/1984) addressed the question about the dialogical unit of discursive communication in the context of novelistic discourse research, but also gave hints as to what a dialogical inquiry into any sphere of culture ought to take into account. For Bakhtin, the unit of discourse is the utterance. The specific questions are, then, how to conceptualise utterances so as to highlight their dialogic quality, and how to determine in each case the limits of an utterance so as to take it as a unit of analysis. These seem to be sensible questions not only for us, readers of Bakhtin or discourse analysts, but also for Bakhtin himself, since he dedicated one of his last publications, *The Problem of Speech Genres* (1986c), to discussing these issues. He struggles here with the problem of the unity of discourse and the limits of the utterance, in an effort to clarify why any utterance is crossed by the discourses of others, thus including multiple voices within itself, and at the same time is a response to others' utterance, thus expressing a unitary and singular positioning towards the other. When reading *The Problem of Speech Genres*, more than finding definite answers to these questions, one gets the sense that the author is posing the problem. The fact that Bakhtin did not offer a solution, and that we still discuss the question of the unit of analysis of discursive practices as a fresh issue, are to be taken as clues about the difficulty of the problem of determining a minimal unit of cognition and communication capable of conserving the dialogicality of the whole. In current dialogical sciences, the hard knots of the problems have been discussed in terms of the complexity of *alter–ego* interdependence (Marková, 2006) and of double dialogicality (Bakhtin, 1929/1984; Linell, 2009).

Within the realm of Bakhtin's work one can easily recognise a chain of conceptual links regarding the nature of discursive communication.[1] We read that language and culture are to be understood as living discourse, and not as formal systems (Bakhtin, 1986c); that the living unit of discourse is the utterance, neither the sentence nor the proposition (Bakhtin, 1986c); that each utterance is an unrepeatable event of interaction of different voices (Bakhtin, 1986c); that each utterance is a response to other utterances, so that it has a meaning in the context of other utterances pre-existing one's word, or anticipated in the shaping of one's word (Bakhtin, 1981); that the utterance is not a semiotic composition but the taking of a position of a speaking subject by means of such semiotic composition, so that it essentially implies an evaluative stand towards the other voices involved in the field of interaction (Voloshinov, 1929/1986); and that these other voices, as well as the extra-verbal situation of the interaction,

---

[1] We specially follow Bakhtin *Discourse in the Novel* (1981), *The Problem of Speech Genres* (1986c), and *The Problem of the Text in Human Sciences* (1986a), as well as Volosinov's *Marxism and the Philosophy of Language* (1929/1986), and *Discourse in Life and Discourse in Art* (1926/1976).

participate in any utterance as the social atmosphere that gives every word and position its particular ideological density (Bakhtin, 1981). These connections should sound straightforward to readers acquainted with dialogical sciences, and may sound reasonable for other readers even if not familiar with Bakhtin's work. However, such an account is not free from conceptual difficulties and important ambiguities, which should not be left aside in thinking about fundamental concepts of dialogical sciences such as utterance and discourse. As a matter of fact, Bakhtin's work does not give us a clear and consistent system of well-defined concepts, each with a single and fixed meaning. Rather, it seems to be open in regards to conceptual problems and strongly suggestive concerning a theoretical view of culture and language that creatively responds to the predominant and assumed order of concepts.

In what follows we discuss some key aspects involved in conceptualising discourse and utterances, guided by two sets of questions:

- *What does it mean to highlight the dialogical property of discursive practices?* If we take the notion of utterance to name the dialogical unit of discourse, what is implied in a dialogical conception of the utterance? What is the precise role played by contestability and sociality in a dialogical account of discourse? If any utterance is an active response to other utterances, how do we grasp responsiveness in concrete discourse analysis?

- *What is the relationship between the positioning movements involved in any utterance and the field of other voices populating the utterance?* Is the taking of a position of one speaking subject a part of the whole utterance, linked to other positioning movements and subjects? Is the extra-verbal situation the context that surrounds the utterance, or an inner component of the utterance? Are the other voices with which the utterance interacts, actual voices of the immediate others, of remote others, of imagined others, of oneself? How are these different voices interlaced in an utterance?

Along with exploring these issues, we try to offer a possible framework for answering these questions in an integrated way. In so doing, we directly draw on a number of Bakhtin's ideas, taken here as an opening moment of dialogism, but our elaboration is also in line with important previous ideas within current dialogical sciences (Billig, 1987; Goffman, 1975; Davies & Harré, 1999; Hermans, 2001; Marková, 2006; Marková & Foppa, 1990; Shotter, 1993, 2006; Wertsch, 1991; Valsiner, 2002).

ANALYSING DIALOGICALITY

The starting point of our discussion is Bakhtin's idea that the dialogic unit of discursive life is the utterance. However, this formulation is only a starting point, because even the term 'utterance' is predominantly employed to refer to non-dialogical phenomena. In developing our interpretation of Bakhtin's idea of the utterance, our first task is to differentiate a dialogical conception of the unit of discourse from other, not particularly dialogical approaches.

In dialogical sciences the voice 'utterance' has a special meaning; it is used to highlight, precisely, the dialogical unit of discourse. However, when the time comes to explain the term in this technical meaning, one finds diversity and ambiguity. Surprisingly, the concept of the utterance seems unproblematic for contemporary scholars committed to discourse theory and discourse analysis. The discussion is often focused either on the difference between utterance and sentence (Tannen, 1989; Levinson, 1983; Searle, 1969) or on whether the utterance is the appropriate option as the unit of discourse when compared with other alternatives (see Linell, 1998). It seems that the problem of the utterance appears only as a practical issue when scholars are confronted with the task of analysing concrete discourse, but this task is not accompanied by a theoretical clarification of the concept. Even dialogical linguists such as Linell (1998, 2009) recognise the vague use of the term in language and communication sciences. In this fuzzy context, the basic property implied by the notion of utterance, shared by different formulations, is the *interdependence* of each utterance to another. Such is, then, our basic clue in exploring dialogicality (Marková, 2003). But if we just define the utterance as interdependent acts of discourse we are walking in circles, because it remains to be explained how and why acts of discourse are interdependent.

According to our reading, Bakhtin's notion of the utterance must be distinguished from other notions such as statement, linguistic expression, and speech act, just to mention a few. We will not discuss them all here, but simply point out a general difference. For Bakhtin, the utterance is always a response to other utterances, which are also responses to other utterances. Likewise, for Vygotsky (1934/1999) the word is not possible for one but it is possible for two. In this sense, it is the unit of sociality. To put it differently: The word is an encounter with the other. Here the terms utterance and word are used with the same sense, referring to discourse as an event realising social encounters. Consistent with a dialogical approach, all these references emphasize otherness as central to discourse. On the contrary, notions such as linguistic expression, sentence, proposition, phrase, or speech act, do not imply in themselves an encounter with the other. Even if an expression becomes contestable within a concrete discourse stream, what we need to understand is not the expression in itself but the process of being contested. Hence, these notions do not allow us to account for the *dialogical* unit of discursive activity. Let us analyse this concept by examining three of its critical aspects.

Responsive and Contestable

One could state that utterances are dialogic units of discursive activity in the sense that they are interdependent, such that each utterance offers the *possibility of responding to it* (Bakhtin, 1986c). For instance, in current dialogical sciences it is frequent to see that the notion of utterance is understood as an active response, in opposition to the notions of word or sentence, referring to the minimal lexical and grammatical composition determined by a given language structure (see also Bakhtin, 1986c). Acts of discourse, including the comprehension of any given text, are essentially meant by Bakhtin and Voloshinov as responses to other acts of discourse. With this idea of utterance as active response, the living and creative quality of any act of discourse is fore-grounded. Bakhtin (1986b) talks about the utterance and about the work of art as an active response by a *creative speaking personality*, in contrast to a mechanical reaction by a *voiceless thing*. "Any utterance is a link in the chain of speech communion. It is the active position of the speaker in one referentially semantic sphere or another" (Bakhtin, 1986c, p. 84).

However, one could also state that linguistic expressions, sentences, or speech acts are dialogic units of discursive activity as far as we accept that in discursive activity such units are interdependent because each expression, sentence, etc., offers the *possibility of responding to it* (Bakhtin, 1986c). Despite being a correct conceptual clue for many purposes, we argue that this explanation of utterances as active responses does not yet disclose the distinctly dialogical nature of discourse. For it would again be possible to think that single phrases or verbal expressions that are produced as responses to previous or anticipated phrases, are thus basic acts of discourse. The focus would still be the phrase, the semiotic expression, and not the event of responding-to, not the process of linking one phrase to another. Hence, what we need is to disentangle the dialogic nature of discursive activity from other aspects eventually involved in discourse, as linguistic expressions and speech acts sometimes are. Recall that Bakhtin and Voloshinov have suggested that such kinds of things are not essential to discourse. To be clear, each utterance is a response, but so is the verbal expression articulated in the utterance, the gestures involved in the utterance, the speech act performed, the position taken by the speaker, the emotional tone expressed, and so on. What remains to be explained is the dialogic process that makes a phrase or gesture a responsive expression, because the very responsive and creative movement will not be in focus if analysing expression or speech act, their form or type. What is missing is the perspective of the movement of social encounter that takes place, even if there is no understandable expression or clear speech act. The technical meaning of 'utterance' in dialogical sciences is precisely meant to keep our attention focused on the living process of engagement among responding gestures, phrases, sentences, expressions, or speech acts. Our point here is that this necessary emphasis on responsiveness does not go far enough, because the responsive quality of discourse acts does not illuminate how each utterance becomes a link of an "organised chain of other utterances" (p. 69).

Situated and Unrepeatable

One step further would be to conceive of the utterance as the event of responding to another *in context*. In this way, one may think that the text or linguistic expression, and the context or situation of the expression in relation to other expressions, form the basic unity or minimal whole of discourse. In understanding a simple statement, for instance, one cannot but take into account the context that gives it a meaning. As the quote from Bakhtin below illustrates, the content and form of the linguistic expression, in its responsive character, is inextricably conditioned by the surrounding points of views.

"The word, directed toward its object, enters a dialogically additated and tension-filled environment of alien words, value judgments and accents, waves in and out of complex interrelationships, merges with some, recoils from others, intersects with yet a third group: and all this may crucially shape discourse, may leave a trace in all its semantic layers, may complicate its expression and influence its entire stylistic profile." (Bakhtin, 1981, p. 276)

From a dialogical point of view, though, one must take care not to think of the unit of discursive life as the compound of linguistic expression plus its context, because even the notion of a contextualised responsive statement implies a static quality. In this connection it seems important to recall that Bakhtin (1986b) criticises the static and closed notion of cultural unit that was, or is, typically used to interpret the meaning of the works of art in relation to their immediate context. The dialogical environment of a given utterance is not given as a static surrounding that receives and holds a responsive linguistic expression. Rather, the very context is already a responsive environment.

> "The living utterance, having taken meaning and shape at a particular historical moment in a social specific environment, cannot fail to brush up against thousands of living dialogical threads, woven by socio-ideological consciousness around the given object of an utterance; it cannot fail to become an active participant in social dialogue. After all, the utterance arises out of this dialogue as a continuation and as a rejoinder to it—it does not approach the object from the sidelines." (Bakhtin, 1981, p. 276-7)

It is precisely because of this living and changing nature of the situation to which an utterance is an active response, that each utterance is unrepeatable, historically unique (Bakhtin, 1986a). What is missing in an expression + context compound is the dynamic nature of the relationship between the utterance and its situation, being the former a rejoinder to a sort of ongoing conversation made up from other rejoinders. As such, each utterance modifies the ongoing conversation in which it is situated. The very notion of discourse calls attention to the event-like nature of language, its being a living process, a process of change, of alteration. Discourse and utterance do not refer just to the *use of language*, or the *text in action*, but to language itself as the process of thinking and speaking, as *language practice*. In other words, language is thought of as a movement rather than a thing, as a transit rather than a state, as activity rather than as potentiality.

Dynamic and Embodied

A third step would be to conceive of the utterance, in line with its living condition, as the *event* of responding to another in a given context, in contrast to the semiotic composition – the sentence, the phrase, the gesture – that takes place. As events, utterances are processes of change in themselves, not fixed forms that happen to take place in a particular space-time point. As a matter of fact, the term 'utterance' has the advantage, if any, that it immediately calls to mind the verb 'to utter' and makes one think of the act of uttering a statement or a question, so that we can easily distinguish between the linguistic expression or speech act, on the one hand, and the event of uttering or generating it, on the other. A given concrete utterance is thus said to embody linguistic form. But again, how do the multiple responsive events or occurrences of linguistic forms become a chain of discourse communication? There is nothing in the notions of response and of event in themselves that explain why utterances are interdependent rather than parts that are added to a discursive chain by means of external glue. Rather, from a dialogical point of view each utterance as such is the act of social bonding, of joining one subject with another, one perspective with another, one position with another. When someone answers a question, she is not only articulating an answer-like expression just after the question-like expression, but she is realising the movement of answering to such a question, thus *joining* in a particular way an answer-like expression to a question-like one. Again, it is not enough to conceive of discourse as an event; it is necessary to think of this event as an event of social interaction: "Dialogic interaction is indeed the authentic sphere where language lives" (Bakhtin, 1929/1984, p. 183).

INTERLACING SUBJECTS

In our view, then, the utterance is neither the sign uttered nor the act of uttering the sign, but the *rising* of a new perspective from a previous one, contesting or complementing a given perspective with a response. To put it graphically, one may imagine two statements, one responding to the other, thus generating a chain where each statement counts as a link. It is easy to think that the analytical units of discourse are such links. However, we propose that, consistent with a dialogical approach, the unit of discourse is each engagement among statements, is the point of juncture between the links of the chain, not the links themselves. Indeed, the metaphor of the chain and the links can be understood as representing the fact that, within a course of dialogical responses, an utterance is a bond that ties together the position taken in a previous moment with a new position; and another utterance may bond to the latter position, as it is taken by the speaker, with an even newer position.

This interpretation of Bakhtin's concept of the utterance includes the responsive, contextualised, and dynamic aspects, but emphasises sociality. It finds support in a number of critical ideas posited by Bakhtin about the utterance in *The Problem of Speech Genres*. Note that the first time Bakhtin refers to the utterance as a unit, he writes "a *real unit of speech communion*" (1986c, p. 67; italics in the original). The term 'communion' refers to co-participation, thus emphasising social bonding as the as the nature of discourse. This emphasis is also strongly present in Voloshinov's work.

The Changing of Subjects

Also consider that, with the model of a conversation among two speakers in mind, Bakhtin mentions the change of speaking subjects as one of the crucial determinants of the limits or borders of an utterance. This may be thought of as simply referring to the turn-taking movement in typical conversations that cut discourse into expressions or semiotic compositions that take place between one change of turn and another. What we would like to stress is the idea that the utterance essentially involves a *change* of speaking subjects. The utterance is not strictly what takes place between one change of turn and another, but as the *process* of changing the place of the subjects.

> "The boundaries of each concrete utterance as a unit of speech communication are determined by a change of speaking subjects, that is, a change of speakers. [...] The speaker ends his utterance *in order to relinquish the floor to the other or to make room for the other's active responsive understanding*. The utterance is not a conventional, but a real unit, clearly delimited by the change of speaking subjects, which *ends by relinquishing the floor to the*

other, as if a silent dixi, perceived by the listeners (as a sign) that the speaker has finished." (Bakhtin, 1986c, p. 71-72; emphasis added)

Finally, consider a related idea: The change of speaking subjects does not only refer to a turn-taking shift, but at the same time to a transformation of the listener subject into a speaking subject.

> "The fact is that when the listener perceives and understands the meaning (the language meaning) of speech, he simultaneously takes an active, responsive attitude toward it. [...] And the listener adopts this responsive attitude for the entire duration of the process of listening and understanding, from the very beginning—sometimes literally from the speaker's first word [...] Any understanding is imbued with response and necessarily elicits it in one form or another: the listener becomes the speaker." (Bakhtin, 1986c, p. 68)

Polyphony and Contestability

A surprising implication of the concept of the unity of discourse we are putting forward is that one single utterance may be said to involve several statements, at least two. This is how we understand, following *Problems of Dostoevsky's Poetics* (Bakhtin, 1929/1984), the polyphonic condition of utterances. The utterance is, then, in this view, the articulation of different positions, not just the statement of a single position. For example, when answering a question delivered by a partner, the speaker moves from the position implicated in the question to a new position. The answer is not just the statement of the new position, but the putting together and making a distinction between the two positions involved. As another example, consider the silent reading of a written statement. Bakhtin suggests that the mere understanding of a text involves the initiation of an utterance, because dialogical understanding is a responsive understanding (Bakhtin, 1981). For each comprehension is already a position taken by the reader, within her inner discourse, towards the position expressed in the statement. The crucial role played by the speaker *as* reader or listener can be traced back to Bakhtin's formulations of the very concept of responsiveness, which was our notion of departure:

> "The first and foremost criterion for the finalization of an utterance is *the possibility of responding to it* or, more precisely and broadly, of assuming a responsive attitude to it (for example, executing an order)." (Bakhtin, 1986c, p. 76).

The possibility of responding to an utterance, which is the dialogical core of any utterance, does not belong to the expression or sentence but to the listener or reader. Any utterance takes place as a complete unit firstly in the attitude awakened in the speaker that is listening to it and responding to it. The dialogical idea of responsiveness, then, does not refer just to the possibility that an expression, sign, or gesture may have within a discursive flow, but specifically to the possibility that a speaking subject may actively understand it, taking a position towards it. Only when this happens is the possible utterance completed, thus becoming a unit. Put differently: an utterance is resolved as a unit only by the other (this other being another speaker or the very author of the utterance at a second moment). According to

Bakhtin and Voloshinov, each utterance is the semiotic articulation of an ideological position towards previous and future utterances. This means that an utterance is completed only when it becomes contestable by another utterance, a moment that does not need to coincide with the semiotic finishing performed by the author. The moment of contestability may come even before the articulation begins, as is the case of anticipated utterances. Moreover, it seems reasonable to argue each utterance is never effectively a complete utterance, because every movement towards defining the ending border of another's utterance is also, at some point, contestable.

Utterance as Open Unit

The idea of the utterance as the responsive changing of subjects has some important implications for the dialogical analyst of discourse. Each utterance is an occurrence with no clear limits, no precise beginning, no definite ending – for its boundaries are not determined by itself but are set by the other. Thus, on the one hand, an utterance is only virtually a complete utterance. Another way to put it: an utterance is an *open* unit – a notion that Bakhtin develops regarding the analysis of utterances in distant cultures, and regarding the notion of cultures *as* utterances (Bakhtin, 1986b, 1986d). This idea imposes important demands on any analysis of utterances, particularly in regards to the place the analyst gives to the speaker's process of interlocution. On the other hand, in addition to this virtual totality, each utterance can always be interpreted in its actual occurrence as incomplete, as part of a larger movement, as when Bakhtin asks about the position held by the author of novels along and across his whole literary production, suspecting that each single novel is not properly a complete utterance. Each position that is eventually being taken emerges out of a multiplicity of signs, gestures, movements that are also positioning movements on a different scale. At root, a single gesture, sign, or word, is a matter of discourse as soon as it is a response to another's positioning (including one's own previous or even anticipated positioning movements). In analysing a text, formal aspects of narratives can be interpreted as local expressions or phases of a larger positioning movement, pieces that build with each other, forming a new movement at a higher scale, and then another higher scale, until the speaker trying to understand the text reaches a contestable reconstruction of the narrative. Thus, the utterance in a given narrative was the global positioning movement as it was comprehended as a whole by the other, that is, as it was contestable as a complete utterance. Again, this has important implications for analysis, particularly regarding the attention of the analyst to her own response towards the speaker's positioning effort, for the analyst cannot avoid the role of the other that understands.

The general idea that a single utterance involves at least two statements or positions is, despite its difficulty, consistent with several other theories arguing that the unit of discourse is social interaction (van Dijk, 1997), communicative event (Linell, 1998), or shared activity (Rommetveit, 1992). According to these views, discourse is essentially mediated by otherness. On the one hand, these supporting approaches may help overcome a terminological disadvantage of Bakhtin's notion of the utterance, namely, that the term utterance in plain English does not refer to inter-statement articulation but to single statements. We should bear in mind this atypical meaning of the term within the theory, and lacking a better term, keep it. On the other hand, one advantage of the Bakhtinian notion of the utterance is that it emphasises that the work of the utterance is to put together the positions of *alter* and *ego* and, at the same time, generate the difference that makes the latter a response to the former. To meet and to split as faces of the same event of being. Juncture and diversion. For each utterance is simultaneously the encounter and the difference with the other. We will explore these two facets of the utterance in terms of the complementary notions of position-taking and interlocution field.

POSITIONING

Following Voloshinov's idea in several passages of *Marxism and the Philosophy of Language*, utterances are sometimes said in current dialogical sciences to essentially involve the taking of a position of someone towards something. The notion of *active* response, as different from mechanical response, means that response in discourse is creative positioning. Further, the concept of position-taking is important because it implies that:

- Each utterance involves an attitude, evaluation, and an affective accent. It is neither neutral nor context-free.
- Typically, each utterance expresses one main evaluation on the part of a single speaking subject, so that the semiotic composition of words and gestures can be recognised as a unitary process of positioning, despite the multiplicity of voices or positions called upon.
- A position-taking movement is not a position, a location, but rather an effort towards holding a position. Because efforts are not always absolutely successful, utterances are typically incomplete and erratic, thus demanding the speaker's work and commitment.

However, there are several problems to address regarding the concept of positioning (cf. Davies & Harré, 1999; Hermans, 2001). For instance, it is not clear whether positioning is the same as the utterance, if the latter is the expression of the former, or if positioning is a component part of the utterance. The risk involved in explaining the utterance simply as a positioning is forgetting that every utterance is the engagement among several position-taking movements, and then analysing concrete discursive practices in a sequence of single positioning acts, leaving the unity of social encounter in the background. Another related problem is that, as an evaluative positioning effort, any utterance is not just a judgement about an object, as if it were a definite position taken, but the feeling of a movement and the emotion of that movement in interaction with other voices or positions.

This discussion involves several problems that we will not unpack here. We will only point out that evaluations are not about objects, but about previously evaluated objects, thus, about other evaluations, other positioning movements. Perhaps utterances are emotional events only because they are an encounter with these other position-taking efforts, other subjects. Following our previous discussion, it is possible to argue that neither the position taken nor the event of taking a position fully account for Bakhtin's notion of the utterance as the basic unit of discourse. A position is always to be taken in front of other positioning movements either present as actual voices that one's positioning movement responds to, or anticipated in one's positioning movement as virtual responses to one's movement. In fact, each position-taking movement is not to be analysed as an isolated process but as a process that takes place in a field of interdependent position-taking movements (see above quote of Bakhtin, 1981, p. 276-7). The concept of positioning thus needs to be developed jointly with that of interlocution field.

FIELD OF INTERLOCUTION

The notion of the utterance is typically understood with the model of a positioning movement as responding to a preceding position. To understand the notion of the utterance in all its complexity as the unit of discourse, however, it is important to note that typically utterances do not respond only to a previous utterance but to a web of virtual positions, past or future, that surpass the immediate positions of the actual others. Typically, utterances also respond to more or less distant positioning movements by oneself or another, as well as one's own and another's positions which are merely imagined. All these other positions or voices draw a web that, within a given utterance, plays the role of a discursive environment for one's position-taking effort. Bakhtin describes this environment as "made up of contradictory opinions, points of view and value judgments—that is, precisely that background that, as we see, complicates the path of any word toward its object" (Bakhtin, 1981, p. 281).

This environment, however, is not an external context, but an inner component of one's utterance. According to Voloshinov, the role played by the extra-verbal situation of interlocution is not that of an outer space containing several speaking subjects, but that of a context that operates from within. Voloshinov (1926/1976) and Bakhtin (1986a) emphasize that situational factors do not stay in the exterior, influencing the utterance; rather, the semiotic and rhetorical aspects of the situation enter into the utterance itself, becoming a constituent part of it, determining both its form and content.

Consequently, we conceptualise positioning, as entailed by each utterance, not as an isolated process but as taking place in a field. We employ the term 'field' because of its reference to the notion of a whole constituted by tensions, as in the case of magnetic fields. In the case of the utterance, we argue that positioning is performed within a dynamic constellation of perspectives with which a locutor establishes interlocution. This interlocution process is configured by tension among perspectives, because perspectives are interested ideological stands. In other words, positioning takes place in a tissue of convergent and divergent interests that constitutes a problematic conflict of interests in the here and now of the utterance. The field instigates the speaker to taking a position that may eventually resolve the impasse generated by the crossroads of interests. In this context, every utterance is like an effort towards solving the impasse in one way or another, favouring in different possible ways one interest or another.

The notion of field is meant to account for the assumption that utterances are emergent totalities bonding together a multiplicity of speaking subjects and subjective perspectives, thus essentially involving sociality. In breaking down this social totality, such parts or parties loose their interconnectedness. In this sense, utterances are joints as well as the articulated parts thus joined. Overall, this property means that speaking and understanding ought to be explained in terms of part-whole dynamics, in terms of putting together and mediating the conflicting multiplicity, in terms of union and differing – a kind of dynamic that may also describe the job of *logos* (see epigraph above).

Utterances as Historical Events

As a whole, the discursive field of any utterance consists of a complex audience, part of which is the alien perspective that, in the form of a second party (*alter*), is confronted as a direct, more or less concrete interlocutor. Another part is a tacit audience that, in the form of a third (*alter ego*), plays the role of an 'apperceptive background', either as a generalized other or as an intertwined multiplicity of alternative perspectives. Thus: "Each dialogue takes place as if against the background of the responsive understanding of an invisibly present third party who stands above all the participants in the dialogue (partners)" (Bakhtin, 1986a, p. 126). As suggested by contributions that explore the role of third parties (e.g., Marková, 2006; Marková et al., 2007; Linell, 1998, 2009; Salgado, 2006), the field of interlocution of any given utterance must be analysed not only as a perceptual field, that is, as a scenario within which a second party is disclosed as an object, but also as a complex social *milieu* that gives positioning towards the other a particular ideological density and multivoicedness.

Games, Moves, and Rules

The idea of position already calls for the idea of a space in which to recognise the position. One may even think of a board-game whose possible positions are given by the structure and rules of the game, and the actual positions are taken by players within such possibilities. In the case of utterances, we interpret Bakhtin to be saying that positioning is the discursive construction of a perspective or point of view from which other possible perspectives are appraised. At first glance, one may apply the board-game metaphor to point out that positioning movements, like game moves, are strategic changes in the course of social interaction that respond to previous moves and that, in turn, provoke a next move, all taking place within a field of interlocution. As a matter of fact, every utterance relates to a complex set of conventional discursive resources and shared knowledge, as well as the dispositions of interlocutors, that come from past interactions between perspectives adopted by speakers in a group or in a personal history. These given conditions of the utterance provide a structured platform where a position is to be taken.

Singularity and Emotion

However, the metaphor is limited in the sense that, in the case of utterances, the interlocution field is not fixed, as the rules of a game are. It is extremely important to acknowledge that the interlocution field, where a position is taken, is transformed during the dialogic process of discourse; in other words, the field is re-created, or appropriated, by each utterance. The platform of each positioning is a part of the utterance, as the positioning itself is another part, and as such it does not have stable boundaries nor a rigid structure. If one insists on the metaphor, then discourse would be a game whose rules are modified with each move.[2] Consequently, as a general idea we would like to stress that the utterance re-articulates

---

[2] It is interesting to note that Wittgenstein's notion of *language game* implies that discursive practices can be regarded as games, involving a sequence of moves on the part of interlocutors. The fact we are stressing here,

the field of interlocution given by history and the new position created within this field, thus carrying out a historically singular event of discourse.

Take, for instance, the emotional atmosphere of an utterance. The past experiences of positioning, thanks to a particular work of memory, are carried to the here-and-now of the utterance in a more or less undifferentiated fashion, so that the mass accumulation of such experiences takes presence as the emotional atmosphere of the interlocution field. The locutor is responding with a particular emotional tone within the context of such atmosphere, as if her positioning effort were to produce an affective resonance against the background of the field.

The Topic Dimension of Interlocution Fields

Apart from the emotional atmosphere, other aspects of the interlocution field must be mentioned, especially the stylistic resources such as a *discursive repertoire* (Potter, 1998), the cognitive resources such as *themata* (Marková, 2003), and the rhetoric resources such as *common places* (Billig, 1987). In this context, we understand speech genres (Bakhtin, 1986c) as a set of compositional, representational, and positioning resources that, coming from the past thanks to the work of memory, gives the utterance a specific type of semiotic shape, of semantic possibilities, and of evaluative background. Thus, the field carries a know-how concerning pertinent discursive devices, taking place as the compositional features of the utterance, its form; it carries knowledge about relevant objects that may become thematised, determining the representational content of the utterance, its theme; and, most importantly, carries an heritage of *topoi*, that is, of arguments, viewpoints, stands, types of reasoning, and accumulated conclusions more or less available to the speaker as tactics and strategies for her positioning work. Overall, the field carries a situated, continuously negotiated, and partially shared background of understanding. Heterogeneity of the field is not reduced to the fact that different voices, perspectives, or interests meet. A field is dynamic and heterogeneous also because it is composed by different *topoi* or (common) places, each partially shared with different interlocutors and differentially activated along with a discursive flow.

Both content and form, as well as the emotional tone of the field, are historical products of social interaction. In this sense, the objects thematised or the positions recruited in an utterance are not just things there, independent of the dialogical process, but sedimentation of human practices. According to Bakhtin (1986a), objects are not voiceless things but crystallisations of previous voices and their interaction. Consequently, utterances are not just evaluative positions towards an object but also towards a previously evaluated object.

> "The linguistic significance of a given utterance is understood against the background of language, while its actual meaning is understood against the background of other concrete utterances on the same theme [...]. Only now in its contradictory environment of alien words is present to the speaker not in the object, but rather in the consciousness of the listener, as his apperceptive background, pregnant with responses and objections. And every utterance is oriented toward this apperceptive background of understanding, which is not a linguistic

---

namely, that discursive activities are like games with no fixed rules, is consistent with Wittgenstein's discussion of the (problematic) role of rules in social activities among speakers. See *Philosophical Investigations* (1953/1997).

background but rather one composed of specific objects and emotional expressions."
(Bakhtin, 1981, p. 281)

Summing up, the concept of interlocution field is important because it implies that:

- Each utterance takes place in a situation, in a crossroads with other utterances.
- The situation of each utterance is made up of tension, that is, of multiple interests among which there might be different degrees of correlation and conflict.
- The evaluative attitude and emotional tone of each utterance is recognised against an affective background carried by the other participating positions.
- Each utterance, taking place in a chain of discursive communication, comes with a past, whose fragments are preserved and crystallised by memory processes in the topic structure of the situation and its emotional atmosphere.

The Problem of Multiplicity

This concept of field may solve a paradox that arises when considering positioning alone. On the one hand, as we stated regarding our conceptualisation of positioning, each utterance typically expresses one evaluative position on the part of one speaking subject. On the other, as the very idea of interlocution field implies, in each utterance multiple positions and positioning efforts participate—at least that of *ego,* the author of the utterance, and that of *alter,* the listener or reader, the 'second' in interaction. How is the semiotic composition of words and gestures recognised as a unitary process of positioning, despite the multiplicity of voices called upon? Which of the positions participating in an utterance is the dominant voice, setting the tone of the whole utterance? Our interpretation of Bakhtin is that polyphony, which does not preclude unity, nevertheless poses a problem in understanding multiple voices as giving shape to one global positioning movement. At this point, one could take different theoretical routes. Following Bakhtin's emphasis on the creative nature of utterances, our answer is that the voice that sets the tone among an ongoing conversation of voices is the new one. That is, the position or voice that determines the evaluative stand, the favoured interest, the specific accent of an utterance is the one that is not present in the recent past of the field, the one that produces the "surprise effect". The positioning effort, in contrast to the positions or voices populating an utterance, is an effort towards changing the field of voices given. Of course, a concrete "surprise effect" is only recognised against a background of lasting positions. The field of interlocution brings the past to the utterance; the positioning effort makes the difference. The effect of an utterance is a transformation of the field of interlocution. If the positioning effort is minimally successful, the effect is a recognisable change in a certain direction, either favouring or disfavouring the listener's previous position. Therefore, each utterance is a predominant positioning tendency, even if built up from multiple and incongruous partial positions, as far as a creative re-articulation of these partial positions is recognised by the other.

Together, positioning and field, as two dynamically connected faces of the utterance, account for the idea, stressed by both Bakhtin and Voloshinov, that each utterance is thus unrepeatable, historically unique, a concrete piece of an ongoing discursive chain of replies. Each utterance is a movement within a singular history of replies pertaining to a given group of living beings, a given social environment, a given language, and a given set of ideological possibilities. This singularity is rooted in the historicity of discursive life, that is, in the fact that each utterance, or positioning, necessarily produces a modification of the script being socially constructed. Even if the semiotic composition of a given utterance consists of a silence, the whole field of interlocution is changed so that a further utterance cannot be the same as the one just prior to such speaking silence. The inner dynamics of each utterance among positioning and field is precisely a process of creatively transforming the situation of interaction. Thus, in analysing utterances it is important to focus not on identifying repeatable forms or contents but in discovering their singularity. Likewise, analysing the dynamics of positioning and field in any given concrete utterance may help in discovering its singularity.

CONCLUSION

What is an utterance, then? We have described the utterance as an event of becoming; as an active response; as a position-taking towards other positions; and as an encounter with the other. This means that each act of discourse carries out an operation of social bonding. To stress the importance of a dialogical approach to discourse, we would like to radicalise the idea by stating that the utterance is the basic unit of social life. For each utterance not only articulates different perspectives but also multiple subjects. Discourse joins them and divides them. Hence the utterance is the unit of discourse *because* it is the unit of social life. In other words, the advantage of a dialogical approach to language is that discourse becomes conceptualised not as a marginal, partial, or occasional phenomenon within our life processes, but as a process of becoming that directly imports to concrete social phenomena, radically pertaining to our experience with others.

A theoretical clarification of the notion of discourse is important for orienting any kind of discourse analysis and, moreover, any inquiry into both subjective and social processes if it is assumed that these are discursive in nature. Thus, Bakhtin suggests that any methodology for the human sciences must take into account some fundamental problems stemming from the acknowledgement of culture as discursive communication (Bakhtin, 1986a, 1986b). In this context, we have tried to interpret Bakhtin's notion of discourse, building upon his rather unconventional theory of the utterance as the unit of discourse. In so doing, we went beyond the text of Bakhtin himself, gathering notions from other developments consistent with a dialogical approach, in order to sketch a conceptual account of the components of the utterance and its basic dialogical dynamic. Specifically, we propose to conceptualise utterances in terms position-taking within interlocution fields, thus accounting for the articulation of the given and the new that is essential to the discursive process of becoming.

Grossen (2010) has recently stressed "the difficulty of developing methodological tools that are fully consistent with dialogical assumptions" (p.1), that is, the difficulties of accomplishing the demands related to dynamism and social interdependence that a dialogical theory of discourse imposes on research methods. According to our point of view, such difficulty is also due to the fact that some key theoretical concepts are underdeveloped. For example, in the cited paper the author brought our attention to the apparent contradiction present in Bakhtin's notion of dialogical word, because "from a dialogical stance, we have to assume that some pieces of discourse are 'more' dialogical than others or are even monological" (p. 12). Here, Grossen (2010) points out a crucial theoretical problem that might have an impact on the way we use discourse analysis and other research tools. Accordingly, we have argued at the beginning of this chapter that theoretical problems like this should not be overlooked. We would like to end by illustrating the implications of our approach in terms of this particular problem—showing that it helps understanding how dialogicality does not exclude monologism.

We propose to understand the utterance as the movement of bonding two or more positioning acts, so that the discursive field in which a given position have been taken becomes reorganised. It is a dynamic process. On the one hand, this discursive field, whose configuration changes along with the raising of a position or evaluative stand, is sometimes more open to diversity ("centrifugal force" said Bakhtin), sometimes more homogeneous ("centripetal force"). One may say that fields are not only made up of tension, but also by a sort of "spin" or acceleration factor. On the other, the positioning movement that transforms the interlocution field in one way or another, might favour centrifugal or centripetal forces—to keep Bakhtin's metaphor. This idea allows us to overcome the contradiction between acknowledging dialogicality as the essential property of utterances while, at the same time, recognizing the possibility of a "gradation" of the dialogical condition in an utterance (i.e., from monological utterances to dialogical ones). Yet, within the conceptual framework proposed in this chapter, it is impossible to conceive of utterances as composed by only one stance or perspective; there should be at least two. Rephrasing Vygotsky's claim: The utterance is possible for two, but not for one. However, the configuration of voices within the landscape of an utterance could offer different degrees or levels of inner dialogisation (for this concept, see Bakhtin, 1981). At the extreme, sometimes realised in scientific discourse, an utterance may involve an effort to deny its internal heterogeneity or to push away its addressees towards an infinite distance or future, generating the effect of a seemingly single, pure, unitary voice. In focusing on the dynamic process constituting the utterance, the dialogical analyst would be better prepared to track this kind of discursive strategy, which is frequently involved in 'de-dialogising' accounts (Potter, 1996) and processes (Billig, 2006). For instance, in talking of dialogical science in singular, we might be pushing towards 'monologisation' of a dialogic field (see Billig, 2011; Wagoner et al., 2011).

ACKNOWLEDGMENTS

This work has been supported by the Fondo Nacional de Desarrollo Científico y Tecnológico de Chile (FONDECYT), grant N° 1100067. We would like to thank Ivana Marková for her thoughtful questions and lively comments on our ideas during the first steps of this work.

REFERENCES

Bakhtin, M. (1929/1984). *Problems of Dostoyevsky's poetics* (C. Emerson, Trans.). Minneapolis: University of Minnesota Press.

Bakhtin, M. (1981). *The dialogical imagination* (C. Emerson & M. Holquist, Trans.). Texas: University of Texas Press.

Bakhtin, M. (1986a). The problem of the text in linguistics, philology, and the human sciences: An experiment in philosophical analysis. *Speech genres and others late essays* (pp. 132–158) (V. W. McGee, Trans.). Texas: University of Texas Press.

Bakhtin, M. (1986b). Toward a methodology for the human sciences. *Speech genres and others late essays* (pp. 159–172) (V. W. McGee, Trans.). Texas: University of Texas Press.

Bakhtin, M. (1986c). The problem of speech genres. *Speech genres and others late essays* (pp. 60–102) (V. W. McGee, Trans.). Texas: University of Texas Press.

Bakhtin, M. (1986d). Response to question from the Novy Mir editorial. *Speech genres and others late essays* (pp. 1–9) (V. W. McGee, Trans.). Texas: University of Texas Press.

Billig, M. (1987). *Arguing and thinking: A rhetorical approach to social psychology.* Cambridge, UK: Cambridge University Press.

Billig, M. (2006). The language of critical discourse analysis: the case of nominalization. *Discourse & Society, 19*, 783–800.

Billig, M. (2011). Dialogical writing and dialogical theory: Reflections on Locke, Shaftesbury and fictional things. In M. Märtsin, B. Wagoner, E. L. Aveling, I. Kadianaki, & L. Whittaker (Eds.), *Dialogicality in focus: Challenges to theory, method and application* (pp. 3-18). New York: Nova Science Publishers.

Davies, B., & Harré, R. (1999). Positioning and personhood. In R. Harré & L. van Lagenhove (Eds.), *Positioning theory: Moral contexts of intentional action* (pp. 32–51). Blackwell: Oxford.

Gillespie, A., & Cornish, F. (2010). Intersubjectivity: Towards a dialogical analysis. *Journal for the Theory of Social Behaviour, 40*, 19–46.

Gillespie, A. & Zittoun, T. (2009). Studying the movement of thought. In A. Toomela & J. Valsiner (Eds.), *Methodological thinking in psychology: 60 years gone astray?* (pp. 69-88). Charlotte, N.C.: Information Age Publishing.

Goffman, E. (1975). *Frame analysis: An essay on the organization of experience.* Harmondsworth: Penguin.

Grossen, M. (2010). Interaction analysis in psychology: A dialogical perspective. *Integrative Psychological and Behavioural Science 44*, 1–22.

Haye, A., & Larraín, A. (2009). The notion of discourse: Beyond thought and language. In T. Teo, P. Stenner, A. Rutherford, E. Park, & C. Baerveldt (Eds.), *Varieties of theoretical psychology. Internationa,l philosophical and practical Concerns.* Concord, ON: Captus University Publication.

Heraclitus. (1987). *Heraclitus: Fragments* (T.M. Robinson Ed., Trans.). Toronto: Toronto University Press. (Original work 500 b.c).

Hermans, H. (2001). The dialogical *self*: Toward a theory of personal and cultural positioning. *Culture & Psychology, 7*, 243 – 281.

Josephs, I. E., Valsiner, J., & Surgan, S. E. (1999). The process of meaning construction: Dissecting the flow of semiotic activity. In J. Brandstädter & R.M. Lerner (Eds.), *Action & self-development: Theory and research through the life span.*

Larraín, A., & Haye, A. (in press). The discursive nature of inner speech. *Theory & Psychology.*

Larraín, A., & Medina, L. (2007). Análisis de enunciación: Distinciones operativas para un análisis dialógico del discurso [Utterance analysis: Operative distinctions for a dialogical discourse analysis]. *Estudios de Psicología, 28,* 283–301.

Leitão, S. (2000). The potential of argument of knowledge building. *Human Development, 43,* 332–360.

Levinson, S. C. (1983). *Pragmatics.* Cambridge, UK: Cambridge University.

Linell, P. (1998). *Approaching dialogue. Talk, interaction and contexts in dialogical perspectives.* Amsterdam: John Benjamins.

Linell, P. (2009). *Rethinking language, mind, and world dialogically.* Charlotte, N.C.: Information Age Publishing.

Marková, I. (2003). *Dialogicality and social representations: The dynamics of mind.* Cambridge, UK: Cambridge University Press.

Marková, I. (2006). On the inner alter. *Journal for Dialogical Science, 1,* 125–148.

Marková, I., & Foppa, K. (1990). *The dynamics of dialogue.* New York: Harvester Wheatsheaf.

Marková, I., Linell, P., Grossen, M., & Salazar-Orvig, A. (2007). *Dialogue in focus groups: Exploring socially shared knowledge.* London: Equinox.

Mercer, N., & Littleton, K. (2007) *Dialogue and the development of children's thinking: A sociocultural approach.* London: Routledge.

Mininni, G. (2010). The method of dialogue: Transaction through interaction. *Integrative Psychological and Behavioural Science 44,* 23–29.

Potter, J. (1996). *Representing reality: Discourse, rhetoric and social construction.* London: Sage.

Potter, J. (1998). *Discursive* social psychology: From attitudes to evaluations. *European Review of Social Psychology 9,* 233–66.

Rommetveit, R. (1992). Outlines of dialogically based social-cognitive approach to human cognition and communication. In A. H. Wold (Ed.), *The dialogical alternative: Towards a theory of language and mind* (pp.19–43). Stockholm: Scandinavian University Press.

Salgado, J. (2006). Thought as dialogue: A comment on Marková. *Journal for Dialogical Science, 1,* 149–154.

Salvatore, S., Valsiner, J., Strout-Yagodzinski, S., & Clegg, J (Eds). (2009). *YIS: Yearbook of idiographic science.* Rome: Firera & Liuzzo Group.

Searle, J. (1969). *Speech acts. An essay in the philosophy of language.* Cambridge: Cambridge University Press.

Shotter, J. (1993). Vygotsky: The social negotiation of semiotic mediation. *New Ideas in Psychology, 11,* 61–75.

Shotter, J. (2006). Vygotsky and consciousness as con–scientia, as witnessable knowing along with others. *Theory & Psychology, 16,* 13–36.

Tannen, D. (1989) *Talking voices: Repetition, dialogue, and imagery in conversational discourse.* Cambridge: Cambridge University Press.

Valsiner, J. (2002). *Forms of dialogical relations and semiotic autoregulation within the self.* Theory & Psychology, *12,* 251–265.

Valsiner, J. (2005). Transformations and flexible forms: Where qualitative psychology begins. *Qualitative Research in Psychology, 4,* 39–57.

Valsiner, J. (2009). Integrating psychology within the globalizing world: A requiem to the post modernist experiment with Wissenschaft. *Integrative Psychological & Behavioural Science, 43,* 1–21.

Valsiner, J., & Sato, T. (2006). Historically structured sampling (HSS): How can psychology's methodology become tuned into the reality of the historical nature of cultural psychology? In J. Straub, C. Kölbl, D. Weidemann, & B. Zielke (Eds.), *Pursuit of meaning: Theoretical and methodological advances in cultural and cross-cultural psychology* (pp. 215–251). Bielefeld: Transcript Verlag.

van Dijk, T. (1997). Discourse as interaction in society. In T. *van Dijk* (Ed) *Discourse as social interaction.* London: Sage.

Voloshinov, V. N. (1926/1976). Discourse in life and discourse in art. *Freudanism. A Marxist critique* (I.N. Titunik & N.H. Bruss, Trans.). New York: Acadamic Press.

Voloshinov, V. N. (1929/1986). Marxism and the philosophy of language (L. Matejka, I. I. Titunik, Trans.). Cambridge, MA: Harvard University Press.

Vygotsky, L. S. (1934/1999). Thinking and speech (N. Minick, Trans.). In R. W. Rieber, A. S. Carton, (Eds.), *The collected works of L.S. Vygotsky, V. 1.* London: Kluwer Academic/Plenum Publishers.

Wagoner, B. (2009). The experimental methodology of constructive microgenesis. In J. Valsiner, P. C. M. Molenaar, M. C. D. P., Lyra & N. Chaudhary (Eds). *Dynamic process methodology in the social and developmental sciences* (pp. 99–121). New York: Springer.

Wagoner, B., & Valsiner, J. (2005). Rating tasks in psychology: From a static ontology to a dialogical synthesis of meaning. In A. Gülerçe, I. Steauble, A. Hofmeister, G. Saunders & J. Kaye (Eds), *Contemporary theorizing in psychology: Global perspectives* (pp. 197–213). Toronto: Captus Press.

Wagoner, B., Gillespie, A., Valsiner, J., Zittoun, T., Salgado, J., & Simão, L. (2011). Reparing ruptures: Multivocality of analysis. In M. Märtsin, B. Wagoner, E. L. Aveling, I. Kadianaki, & L. Whittaker (Eds.), *Dialogicality in focus: Challenges to theory, method and application* (pp. 105-128). New York: Nova Science Publishers.

Wertsch, I. V. (1991). *Voices of the mind.* Cambridge, MA: Harvard University Press.

Wittgenstein, L. (1953/1997). *Philosophical investigations.* Oxford: Blackwell.

In: Dialogicality in Focus

ISBN: 978-1-61122-817-5

Editors: M. Märtsin, B. Wagoner, E.-L. Aveling et al.   © 2011 Nova Science Publishers, Inc.

Chapter 4

DIALOGICAL THEORIES AT THE BOUNDARY

Sanne Akkerman and Theo Niessen

"There cannot be a unified (single) contextual meaning. Therefore, there can be neither a first nor a last meaning; it always exists among other meanings as a link in the chain of meaning, which in its totality is the only thing that can be real. In historical life this chain continues infinitely, and therefore each individual link in it is renewed again and again, as though it were being reborn." (Bakhtin, 1986, p. 146)

Within social sciences, ranging from education to psychology, sociology and anthropology, we see theories emerging that are based on the concept that our social world is existentially dialogical. According to Valsiner and Van der Veer (2000), dialogical theories referring to the work of Hermans (1994, 1995, 1996a; Hermans & Kempen, 1993), Josephs (1998), Marková (1990, 1994) and Wertsch (1991, 1997) are strongly influenced by the theories of literature of the 1920s and 1930s, particularly Mikhail Bakhtin's work. We welcome the emergence of dialogical theories because they share a tendency to reject the rigidity imposed on us by linguistic dichotomies and thereby can advance our understanding of the social world as essentially fluid and contingent. In this chapter, we examine how dialogical theories can help us reconcile dichotomies. We will argue that dialogical theories do justice to the complex nature of reality, but at the same time seem incapable of fully realising the potential of this ability because of propositional and linguistic characterization in research practice. By making this point we intend to raise awareness of this phenomenon, and question how to deal with this issue in dialogical science.

DIALOGICAL THEORIES

In the work of Bakhtin (1981, 1986; Morris, 1994; Wertsch, 1991), the notion of dialogicality is one of the basic theoretical constructs. Bakhtin uses this term to refer to the relational nature, or 'multi-voicedness', of language use (as opposed to language as a self-contained sign system). He argues that:

"The expression of an utterance can never be fully understood or explained if its thematic content is all that is taken into account. The expression of an utterance always responds to a greater or lesser degree, that is, it expresses the speaker's attitude toward others' utterances and not just his attitude toward the object of his utterance." (Bakhtin, 1986, p. 92)

Bakhtin points out how utterances are produced by a voice, a speaking personality existing in a certain social milieu, and how they relate to the personality that is being addressed. By addressivity to both previous and future speakers, voices of others become woven into our utterances. By introducing this dialogical perspective on language, Bakhtin centralises the *use* of language, a position that is consistent with a focus on situated action in social, cultural and historical theories (Wertsch, 1991). Hence, dialogical theories expand the scope of our attention to include a fuller complexity. Not only does this affect the study of language, it also enables us to understand social phenomena in terms of their multiplicity. Marková (2006) notes how dialogicality usually refers to some kind of interdependency between the Ego and the Alter. Following her perspective, we look upon dialogicality as being of *ontological* nature[1]. Based on this premise, dialogical theories can help us move beyond dichotomous thinking.

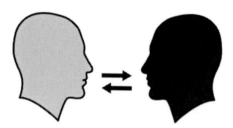

Figure 1. Two people with different nationalities in conversation – meaning-as-fixed.

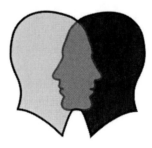

Figure 2. Two people with different nationalities in conversation – meaning-as-motion.

In social scientific research, there are several commonly implied dichotomies, which can be traced back to ancient Greek roots in Plato (Sawada & Caley, 2003), such as individual

---

[1] By contrast, the notion of dialogicality has also been used to refer to dialogue in explicit terms, that is, a situation of dialogue between people is considered dialogical. Besides, people have used the notion of dialogicality in normative terms, pointing to the extent to which people are open to different perspectives. In this latter understanding, a conversation in which a person considers the point of view of the other, and vice versa, is taken to be more dialogical than a conversation in which a person does not really listen or account for the other person (monological conversation). In the ontological sense presented in this chapter, all phenomena are considered dialogical.

versus social, part versus whole, unity versus multiplicity, mind versus matter and knower versus known. Interpreted from a dialogical perspective, the opposites of these dichotomies are defined as coexisting only *in relation to* or *in dialogue with* each other. The danger that is inherent in dichotomous thinking is the type of categorisation where membership of one of two opposing categories of a dichotomous pair precludes membership of the other category. Although analytically very useful, this divisive either/or mode of thinking reinforces the image of the social world as static and circumscribed; a world where something or someone either does or does not fit into a certain category. To highlight the differences between dialogical theories and most theories relying on dichotomous thinking, we will look at the following situation. We are interested in understanding what goes on in a conversation between two persons born and raised in different countries, let's say The Netherlands and Poland. Most social scientific theories from which such a conversation is studied generally start by including the involvement of two different nationalities. Next, these nationalities are attributed as categories to the participants in the conversation: the person from Poland is labelled Polish and the person from The Netherlands is labelled Dutch. Based on this conceptualisation, what is said by the Dutch person can be understood in light of Dutch culture (the way someone talks, what is said, reactions), whereas what the Polish person says can be understood in light of anything subsumed under Polish culture. Such an understanding is pictured in Figure 1. In this figure, each person has a colour representing their nationality and related predefined characteristics.

At first sight this might seem the proper way of taking account of cultural context in studying a microsituation. However, from a dialogical theoretical perspective this point of view is inadequate because it latches onto a definite cultural difference and treats it in a monological and individualistic way. 'Dutchness' and 'Polishness' are considered closed concepts and attributed in their entirety to persons from these countries. In other words, Dutchness is looked upon as an intrinsic property of Dutch persons. It characterises any Dutch person wherever they go and with whomever they talk. In this perspective, meaning is treated as a *fixed* entity. By contrast, from a dialogical point of view the relationship between Dutch and Polish persons resides not only in the words they say to each other but also in the malleable notions of what it means to be Dutch or Polish. In this view, Dutchness depends on how it is different from Polishness and vice versa. Figure 2 shows how this dialogical approach can be pictured. Each person's colour represents the particularity of their nationality as defined in light of that of the other person.

In a dialogical approach, the meaning of the category Dutchness depends on the person to whom the Dutch person is talking as well as that person's nationality. In a conversation with a Chinese person, the meaning of Dutchness would be quite different (e.g. grey would be red and black would be green). In other words, concepts cannot be conceived in isolation from other concepts, because they co-constitute each other. Meaning is *motion*. Leaving open the definitions of the concepts Dutchness and Polishness is the only way in which we can approach (cultural) identity as well as (cultural) difference as functions of a specific context. This point of view does not negate the existence of differences or opposites, but rather emphasises that these emerge only from a dialogical process of coming into being. It is important to perceive this in a temporal dimension. Abbey (2007) discusses how meaning-as-motion (as opposed to meaning-as-fixed) is a necessary perspective to account for the ambiguity and indeterminacy of meaning, allowing constant transformation at the boundary of "the just barely known moment and the unknown future" (p. 364). Such a temporal perspective on meaning as motion moves beyond a pure dialectic understanding of opposites that create tensions and mutually define one another, by including a notion of a continuous emergence. Furthermore, Marková (2003) emphasizes that Bakhtin's understanding of dialogicality makes it possible to see the abstract and formalised notion of dialectic of Hegel itself as a form of thinking, as a communicative existence by means of which we try to understand continuous emergence in the context of how we voice matters.

BOUNDED RESEARCH

Building on Bakhtin's work in our own research, we have come up against barriers in dialogical research despite attempts to overcome dichotomous and thereby monological thinking. One limitation is the scope of research, specifically the desire to account for the "world in its entirety" when studying an object of analysis. This desire can be recognised in a quote from Hermans and Kempen (1993) on the study of microcontext: "the microcontext of concrete dialogical relationships cannot be understood without some concept of macroframes" (p. 73). These authors refer to the organisational and ethnographical context as macroframes. Although they are careful to talk about the need for "some concept of macroframes", they also say the microcontext "cannot be understood without it". This plea for contextualised (social, cultural and historical) understanding can be traced back to Bakhtin's claim that "trying to understand and explain a [literary] work solely in terms of the conditions of its epoch alone, solely in terms of the most immediate time, will never enable us to penetrate into its semantic depths." (Bakhtin, 1986, p. 4). But where does this concept of macroframes or contextualisation end? Inevitably, there must be a limit to the scope of attempts to understand 'semantic depths' of social phenomena. Returning to the example of the Dutch–Polish conversation, it takes little effort to make a long list of issues that are neglected when our efforts to understand the conversation are limited to matters of cultural differences. Typical contextual issues that are the traditional focus of social scientific study are gender and age, which are both assumed to be associated with specific ways of thinking and acting. Additionally, we could point to the importance of these persons' differing life histories, consider specific artefacts mediating the conversation or, for that matter, account for the influence of the weather. But then again it would seem ridiculous if not impossible to strive for an exhaustive anatomy of a microsituation encompassing all social, cultural and historical implications. Such a level of complexity simply eludes us.

A second limitation relates to our use of language to capture phenomena. With reference to phenomena, research continually construes names and applies concepts. This is the primary task of science: to name aspects of the world as we encounter them to enable us to act in the world in a meaningful manner. Owing to our limited capacity for information processing (Miller, 1956), we cannot reinvent the world all of the time so we have to use what we have encountered previously to categorise things and name objects (Bowker & Star, 1999). Sawada and Caley (2003) state how naming is essential to knowing:

"We define others and ourselves and the stuff around us (things) by naming them. Names reify and solidify, embellishing a sense of identity and permanence. Once named, a thing is both known and its properties become specified." (p. 50)

Bakhtin even argues that we have not really experienced an event until we have represented it to ourselves in words. Hence, we might say that conceptual constructions can help us organise experiences into something meaningful. Thus, naming involves signifying what distinguishes one thing from other things; in other words, delineating what it is not, followed by categorising and structuring. For an example of how naming can create meaning consider a government campaign to reduce drink driving conducted nationwide in Belgium and The Netherlands in 1995. In the efforts to reduce the number of accidents involving drink driving, commercials were developed for the general public pointing out that drinking before driving home was a very bad idea indeed. Various commercials disseminated this message in both countries but what stuck in people's minds was the one featuring "Bob", a common Dutch name and an acronym of the Dutch phrase denoting a 'deliberately sober driver'. Catchphrases were introduced such as "Who will be Bob tonight?", or "Do you Bob or do I?", converting Bob into a verb. It was a very clever move of the creators of the commercial to personify the desired behaviour by giving it a name and creating a concrete person who answered to that name. Taking a paternalistic stance and admonishing people to do the right thing always involves the risk of provoking the opposite of the intended response. It is fascinating to contemplate whether Bob, the deliberately sober driver, existed as a phenomenon before the acronym was invented. Obviously, there must have been plenty of occasions where drivers incapacitated by alcohol were driven home by spouses, relatives or friends, but the copywriter who personified this act managed to lodge it in our consciousness as a named phenomenon. It was made coherently visible as a function of the concept where Bob is dually portrayed as the nice guy taking care of his friends as well as the victim cast in the role of the sober driver prohibited from joining in the fun.

The same mechanism is used in science. Language is the vehicle for distinguishing and identifying objects and phenomena and for communicating about them. As Säljö (2002) observed, the world does not come all neatly labelled and it is only through naming that we come to experience it in certain ways. In the case of the Bob messages, the named behaviour became accepted behaviour and it was even considered cool for adolescents to stay sober and be Bob once in a while. Similarly, communicative tools strongly mediate, that is, fundamentally transform, our day-to-day interpretations of the world (Vygotsky, 1934/1986). Obviously, science does not create the world but by reinforcing certain ways of experiencing it, it guides how we act in it and also how we continue to shape it.

By naming the world, we grapple with its meaning. However, the important point to make here is that naming is necessarily accompanied by 'disambiguation', in other words by a reduction in interpretative alternatives and thereby a reduction of complexity (Akkerman, Overdijk, Admiraal & Simons, 2008). And it is here that we come face to face with the problems of dialogical theories. We use language and conceptual constructs to simplify and organise the world. Above we discussed how a conversation between two people from different cultures, Dutch and Polish, can be analysed from a dialogical perspective, enabling the categories of Dutchness and Polishness to remain open to mutual definition and interpretative flexibility, where what is Dutch depends on how it differs from what is Polish and vice versa. By saying this, we imply that it is scientifically possible to name things and at the same time advance contextual understanding including the maximal acknowledgement of aspects of the situation at hand (contextualisation). However, we have found it impossible to adhere consistently and fully to this approach in conducting empirical studies of social phenomena based on dialogical theories. In the following section, we illustrate this problem with an example from dialogical research.

An Empirical Example

First, let me say that conducting empirical research in the dialogical tradition has been a challenging endeavour from the outset. As Valsiner and Van der Veer (2000) stress when discussing Bakhtin's work: "Appropriating his ideas has enriched contemporary social sciences theoretically, while leaving them baffled as to the kind of empirical work that needs to follow" (p. 390). With no concrete methods at their disposal, many contemporary researchers have been looking for ways to study social phenomena dialogically while at the same time striving to firmly ground this theoretical perspective in the empirical traditions of observation.

To illustrate such an ambitious attempt, we now discuss a study by Raggatt (2000), whose intention was to find a 'method of assessment' or a 'mapping' of the dialogical self. Instead of presupposing an integrated, coherent and autonomous 'core self' or 'ego identity', Raggatt considers the self a field of narrative voices, each telling a different story and competing for expression in the individual's lived experience and psychosocial storytelling. In this way, he strives to study the individual in relation to surrounding cultures, historically situated and ecologically faithful. Using a dialogical notion of the self and appropriating the concept of the dialogical self, he builds on the work by Hermans (Hermans, Kempen & Van Loon, 1992; Hermans, Rijks & Kempen, 1993; Hermans & Kempen, 1993; Hermans, 1996b), while also referring to the work of others who elaborated on the multiplicity of the self (e.g. Gergen, 1991, 1992, 1994; Gregg, 1991). The reasoning underlying Raggatt's methodology is as follows:

> "The individual appropriates meaning from the culture in the form of important attachments, including influential people, critical events and narratives, valued objects and environments, and even orientations and attitudes to our bodies, i.e. to our embodied self." (Raggatt, 2000, p. 68)

He argues that the individual develops different narrative identities or 'voices', each with their own constellation of attachments and stories to tell. Next, he points to his special interest in those narrative voices that are oppositional (e.g., the family patriarch versus the servile worker or the independent adult versus the dependent child). What is of interest here is that he places oppositional voices in a dialogical relationship, stating that "each self has another in its shadow" or "a self and its anti-self" (p. 70). This seems very much in line with our earlier account of dialogicality as underlining the co-constitutive nature of possible opposites. But moving onto Raggatt's empirical work, we discern ambiguity in how the relational nature of the multiple voices is examined.

Raggatt uses a semi-structured interview, the so-called 'personality web' or "Personality Web Protocol" (Raggatt, 2011), to reveal the dominant narrative voices by means of their attachments. In interview phase 1, 24 attachments are elicited in four categories: people, objects and places, life events and body orientations (e.g., liked and disliked body parts). During the interview, the history and meaning of each attachment are explored, for example by asking questions about (in the category 'people') which figures are considered positive in a participant's life, the relationship between the participant and these figures, which stories testify to the figures' good qualities and which imaginary conversations could take place with this figure. In phase 2, the participants are asked to group their attachments into clusters according to the strength of their associations, and multidimensional scaling (MDS) is used to map the individual's 'web' of attachments. The individuals are asked to attach a self-relevant descriptive label to each cluster, such as 'dominant me', 'religious voice' or 'adventurer'. Subsequently, the participants are asked to look at each cluster and at each of the 24 original attachments and try to identify relevant pairs. The results of this sorting become the input for creating a triangular similarity ratings matrix, containing 24 attachments and four self-relevant cluster labels. Both the text-based interviews and MDS solution are input for 'mapping' the dialogical self.

Raggatt goes on to present two case studies based on this methodology. In the case descriptions, he first typifies which voices and corresponding attachments emerge from the mapping procedure. Supported by an MDS figure representing the voices and their statistical relationships (based on proximity), he states which voices are found to be oppositional to each other. For example, in one case featuring a man named Mark, he presents the contrast between a 'deceitful' and a 'social–relational' voice. However, in a further narrative elaboration of Mark's case, Raggatt initially confines the description to the life narrative of the deceitful voice and explains how this voice is attached to, for example, selling oranges aged eight, to Mark's father reneging on a deal, which taught Mark that the world is not fair, and to making more money than his peers. In this way, the narrative of this voice encompasses specific events and figures. The connection with the opposing social–relational voice is only mentioned more or less in passing: "Fortunately, Mark's deceitful voice has been tempered by a strong opposing voice, which Mark calls social–relational." He adds how this voice is constituted as strong, reliable, honest, direct and loving, and how it is attached to certain figures, objects and places.

What is interesting in Raggatt's methodology is that he identifies specific categories that enable different voices to compose life narratives. These voices constitute the dialogical self. Raggatt's methodology provides a contextual understanding of voice. Yet, what to us seems problematic is the 'coincidental' and separate empirical mapping and presentation of each voice, particularly those that are oppositional and as such deeply related dialogically. This argumentation both holds for the article that we have been reviewing but also the chapter in this book regarding Raggatt's interaction of gender with body representations. Saying that the deceitful voice and the social–relational voice are oppositional implies that they have come into being as part of a dialogical relationship in which they act as counter-voices throughout their life narratives. Contextual understanding thereby means understanding each voice within the context of their *continuous dialogues* with other voices, which together constitute the dialogical self. Raggatt clearly perceives each voice as being co-constituted by particular social, cultural and historical attachments (outside the self), but neglects to look at how each attachment, each valuation of a particular voice, comes into being *in relation to* the attachments and valuations of other voices (inside the self). Thus, dialogicality refers not only to 'outward' contextualisation but also to 'inward' contextualisation.

When one aspect of a life narrative is presented under a certain name such as 'the deceitful voice', it is implied that there has always been a deceitful voice as an autonomous separate being. In contrast with this approach, we would like to return to the dialogical ontology stating that there can only be meaning-as-motion or, to put it differently, that voices are continuously emergent processes of becoming. In addition, from a dialogical point of view, there can be no autonomy without interdependency. The preceding example of a study based on a dialogical perspective draws attention to the following paradox. Although signifying a phenomenon (the separate voices in the study of Raggatt) is primarily an analytic step and does not automatically turn the phenomenon into a closed concept, it does call for considering the phenomenon an independent unit. In other words, whereas Raggatt's empirical work provides us with concrete methodological tools to elicit the developmental and contextual nature of voices, it also presents each of these voices as a closed unit. The result is not very different from the common social scientific approach (illustrated in Figure 1) against which we initially argued and in which units are characterised and defined as separate, as if they have a permanent existence independent of one another. This approach loses sight of all the intermediate qualitative transformations of the infinite moment-to-moment dynamics. We do not imply that this is Raggatt's intention. However, we think that somewhere along the line of (empirical) analysis 'meaning as being in motion' became transformed into 'meaning as being fixed'.

In later work Raggatt (2010) draws on the work of Peirce to develop a model that is not dyadic but triadic in nature, with the third component fulfilling the function of a mediating object between I-positions: "...a pattern of signification connecting and at the same time differentiating the opposed positions" (p. 409). This idea loosens up the dualist and closed nature of I-positions and leaves more space for ambiguity and interpretation. Although offering a more nuanced perspective, it remains important to be aware of our tendencies to fixate I-positions and their mediations in empirical work.

IMPRISONMENT OF MEANING

We have identified two boundaries: a limit in research scope and a limit in conceptual scope. We have illustrated the bounded nature of research by discussing empirical research based on dialogical theories. Why are these issues worth contemplating? Would it not be logical to simply state that research, dialogical research included, has its limitations?

We do indeed believe that it is natural for any type of research (and life for that matter) to have a certain focus and defined concepts. Boundaries are always at the core of meaning. Meaning is transformed into static categories that come to be seen and treated as real objects in themselves. As Säljö (2002) pointed out, when using language as a mediating tool for categorisation and communication, social scientific researchers tend to treat epistemic issues (e.g., intelligence) as "things" having ontologies with fixed meanings. No allowance is made for grey areas at the boundaries of meaning, and over time a definite line becomes established separating what is denoted from what is not denoted. Our argument here is that this transformation of meaning-in-motion into concepts is a natural process that we, as researchers, cannot escape when using categories to presuppose and comprehend what we are investigating. In fact, this natural process exactly exemplifies the dialogicality of dialogical research. Researchers delimit their research in reaction to previous research and in anticipation of future readers. Early studies on perception have shown how we tend to perceive the details for which we have a category and ignore those for which we do not (e.g.,

Bruner & Postman, 1949). Similarly, in the field of sociology, Schuetz (1944) notes how people tend to 'think as usual'. Consequently, as Gurevitch (1988, p. 1180) describes: "The stress on familiarity, however, forces one's attention not only to what is already known and figured out but also to the act of deliberate 'assuming away' of the unfamiliar as a part of everyday life". One could say that categories work like magnets and interfere with our open-mindedness to nuances. As Olson (1994) formulates it, once understanding is reached it is extremely difficult to 'unthink' it. Every scientific scope or concept, every meaning, even when it originates from dialogical understandings can simultaneously clarify and obscure our understanding. Hence, we become imprisoned in our meanings.

What is problematic is that boundaries, the imprisonment of meaning, seem to run counter to the intent of dialogical theories, which is to adhere to multiplicity and complexity by assuming 'meaning-as-motion'. We have now pointed to both the intent of dialogical theories and the limitations encountered in pursuing those intentions. This leaves us with the question how to address this problem.

CONCLUSION

When we want to adhere to dialogical assumptions, we should keep in mind that topics discussed scientifically are only analytically laid out in that manner. As Luria (1976) puts it, it is easy to mistake social representations for the world as such. To redress this misconception he proposes the assumption of a 'not-perfect-fit' between our knowledge of the world and the world as it is. For researchers this calls for open-mindedness and accountability (Bruner, 1990):

"I take open-mindedness to be a willingness to construe knowledge and values from multiple perspectives without loss of commitment to one's own values [...] It demands that we be conscious of how we come to our knowledge and as conscious as we can be about the values that lead us to our perspectives. It asks that we be accountable for how and what we know." (p. 30)

A dialogical perspective is valuable because it provides an initial way of accounting for and dealing with the complexities of social life. Moreover, it is dialogical arguments that reveal the natural limitations of scientific accounts, because they represent certain ways of what is called "reading" phenomena. A certain way of reading, by definition, means that some ways of reading are enabled and others are disabled. Besides inviting modesty, this suggests that we should scrutinise our own approaches and concepts and question how powerful they really are. How can we go about this? How can we deal with the limitations of the scope of our research or the magnetic tendency of once established categories? This is another way of asking how we can overcome what Langer (1989, 1997) calls 'mindlessness', that is, being locked in a rigid world entrapped by existing categories, where we rely on automatic behaviour and act from single perspectives. In opposition to mindlessness, Langer advocates 'mindfulness'. This encompasses the continual creation of new categories and openness to new information and new and multiple perspectives, and is in line with Bakhtin's comment about contextual meaning:

"Contextual meaning is potentially infinite, but it can only be actualized when accompanied by another (other's) meaning, if only by a question in the inner speech of the one who understands. Each time it must be accompanied by another contextual meaning to reveal new aspects of its own infinite nature (just as the word reveals its meanings only in context)." (Bakhtin, 1986, p. 146)

If we interpret "the one who understands" as the dialogical researcher, this quote can also be interpreted as a call for such openness. As Langer shows in her psychological studies, mindfulness and the creativity deriving from it require some uncertainty. Earlier, Dewey (1910) argued that 'thinking' (parallel to the notion of mindfulness) encompasses a state of hesitation, doubt and perplexity, and an investigation directed at the solution of a perplexity.

According to this reasoning, dialogical scientists should pay tribute to hesitation and doubt in making sense of the world. Currently, in social sciences, hesitation and doubt are only found in dialogues *between* scientists and *between* articles, and often only in specific settings such as the local workplace and (certain) conferences. However, on the whole, we, as researchers, have little opportunity to present our inner dialogues, driven by wonder and filled with doubts and hesitations. We wonder how we can make room for doubt and hesitation in dialogical science and how this can be used productively to advance dialogical research in a manner that is faithful to its ontological assumptions. We might not have presented satisfactory answers but we do hope that we have started a dialogue that might facilitate this quest.

REFERENCES

Abbey, E. (2007). Perpetual uncertainty of cultural life: becoming reality. In J. Valsiner & A. Rosa (Eds.), *The Cambridge handbook of sociocultural psychology*, (pp. 362-372). New York: Cambridge University Press.

Akkerman, S., Overdijk, M., Admiraal, W., & Simons, R. J. (2008). Beyond imprisonment of meaning: technology facilitating redefining. *Computers in Human Behaviour, 23*, 2998–3011.

Bakhtin, M. M. (1981). *The dialogic imagination: Four essays*. Austin: University of Texas Press.

Bakhtin, M. M. (1986). *Speech genres and other late essays*. Austin: University of Texas Press.

Bowker, G. C., & Star, S. L. (1999). *Sorting things out: Classifications and its consequences*. Cambridge, MA: MIT Press.

Bruner, J. (1990). *Acts of meaning*. London, England: Harvard University Press.

Bruner, J., & Postman, L. (1949). On the perception of incongruity: a paradigm. *Journal of Personality, 18*, 206–223.

Dewey, J. (1910). *How we think*. Mineola, NY: Dover.

Gergen, K. J. (1991). *The saturated self*. Basil Blackwell: Oxford.

Gergen, K. J. (1992). Towards a postmodern psychology. In S. Kvale (Ed.), *Psychology and postmodernism* (pp. 17–30). Sage: London.

Gergen, K. (1994). Exploring the postmodern: perils of potentials? *American Psychologist, 49*, 412–416.

Gregg, G. S. (1991). *Self-representation: Life narrative studies in identity and ideology.* Greenwood Press: New York.

Gurevitch, Z. D. (1988). The other side of dialogue: On making the other strange and the experience of otherness. *American Journal of Sociology, 93,* 1179–1199.

Hermans, H. J. M. (1994). Buber on mysticism, May on creativity, and the dialogical nature of the self. *Studies in Spirituality, 4,* 279–305.

Hermans, H. J. M. (1995). The limitations of logic in defining the self. *Theory & Psychology, 5,* 375–382.

Hermans, H. J. M. (1996a). Opposites in a dialogical self: Constructs as characters. *Journal of Constructivist Psychology, 9,* 1–26.

Hermans, H. J. M. (1996b). Voicing the self: From information processing to dialogical exchange. *Psychological Bulletin, 119,* 31–50.

Hermans, H. J. M., & Kempen, H. J. G. (1993). *The dialogical self: Meaning as movement.* San Diego, CA: Academic Press.

Hermans, H. J. M., Kempen, H. J., & Van Loon, R. J. P. (1992). The dialogical self: Beyond individualism and rationalism. *American Psychologist, 47,* 23–33.

Hermans, H. J. M., Rijks, T. I., & Kempen, H. J. (1993). Imaginal dialogues in the self: Theory and method. *Journal of Personality, 61,* 207–236.

Josephs, I. E. (1998). Constructing one's self in the city of the silent: Dialogue, symbols, and the role of "as-if" in self development. *Human Development, 41,* 180–195.

Langer, E. J. (1989). *Mindfulness.* Cambridge, MA: Perseus Books.

Langer, E. J. (1997). *The power of mindful learning.* Cambridge, MA: Perseus Books.

Luria, A. R. (1976). *Cognitive development: Its cultural and social.* Cambridge, MA: Harvard University Press.

Marková, I. (1990). A three-step process as a unit of analysis in dialogue. In I. Marková & K. Foppa (Eds.), *The dynamics of dialogue* (pp. 129–146). Hemel Hempstead: Harvester.

Marková, I. (1994). Mutual construction of asymmetries. In P. V. Geert & L. Mos (Eds.), *Annals of theoretical psychology. Vol. 10* (pp. 325–342). New York: Plenum.

Marková, I. (2003). *Dialogicality and social representations: The dynamics of mind.* Cambridge: Cambridge University Press.

Marková, I. (2006). On the 'inner alter' in dialogue. *International Journal for Dialogical Science, 1,* 125–147.

Miller, G. A. (1956). The magical number seven, plus or minus two: Some limits on our capacity for processing information. *Psychological Review, 63,* 81–97.

Morris, P. (1994). *The Bakhtin reader.* London: Edward Arnold.

Olson, D. R. (1994). *The world on paper: The conceptual and cognitive implications of writing and reading.* Cambridge: Cambridge University Press.

Raggatt, P. T. F. (2000). Mapping the dialogical self: Towards a rationale and method of assessment. *European Journal of Personality, 14,* 65–90.

Raggatt, P. T. F. (2010). The dialogical self and thirdness. A semiotic approach to positioning using dialogical triads. *Theory & Psychology, 20*(3), 400–419.

Raggatt, P. T. F. (2011). Gender, embodiment, and positioning in the dialogical self: Do males and females see eye to eye? In M. Märtsin, B. Wagoner, E. L. Aveling, I. Kadianaki, & L. Whittaker (Eds.), *Dialogicality in focus: Challenges to theory, method and application* (pp. 205-220). New York: Nova Science Publishers.

Sawada, D. & Caley, M. (2003). Structural coupling, wu-forms, and the discourses of education. *Proceedings of the 2003 Complexity Science and Educational Research Conference*, October 16–18, Edmonton, Canada, 45–66.

Säljö, R. (2002). My brain's running slow today. The preference for 'things ontologies' in research and everyday discourse on human thinking. *Studies in Philosophy and Education, 21*, 389–405.

Schuetz, A. (1944). The stranger: An essay in social psychology, *American Journal of Sociology, 49*, 499–507.

Valsiner, J., & Van der Veer, R. (2000). *The social mind. Construction of the idea.* Cambridge: Cambridge University Press.

Vygotsky, L. S. (1934/1986). *Thought and language.* Cambridge, MA: MIT Press.

Wertsch, J. V. (1991). *Voices of the mind. A sociocultural approach to mediated action.* London: Harvester Wheatsheaf.

Wertsch, J. V. (1997). Narrative tools of history and identity. *Culture & Psychology, 3*, 5–20.

In: Dialogicality in Focus
Editors: M. Märtsin, B. Wagoner, E.-L. Aveling et al.

ISBN: 978-1-61122-817-5
© 2011 Nova Science Publishers, Inc.

COMMENTARY 1 TO PART I:
CHALLENGES TO DIALOGICAL SCIENCE

Ivana Marková

Dialogical science is a future goal rather than a fully established field of scientific inquiry, states the Editorial of the *International Journal of Dialogical Science*. The Editorial explains that the objectives of dialogical science involve the construction and a further development of dialogical self theory and other theories which deal directly with the relationship between self and dialogue; the theory studies processes of communication and exchanges on a global scale involving persons, groups and cultures. The ambition of dialogical science is to position itself within the broad band of sciences ranging from neurobiology to humanities. Since 2000, international conferences on the Dialogical Self have attracted more and more participants, who enthusiastically take part in this new enterprise that promises to replace individualistic and mechanistic studies of the self and dialogue by social and dynamic perspectives.

In view of this optimism and the future orientation of dialogical science, let us pose the question as to why the authors of Part I of this book are concerned with 'challenges'? True, much remains to be explained. For example, what is it that could connect the study of brain neurons on the one hand and, say, a mundane conversation on the other hand? Or is dialogical science excluding from its frame of reference 'non-scientific' forms of dialogue like rhetoric? If it does exclude some forms, what kinds of dialogue are to be included? Nevertheless, all authors of Part I are thoroughly sympathetic to dialogical science, and they draw attention to certain dilemmas from the inside rather than from the outside of the field. If they sound alarmed from within, could it mean that some current concepts and practices in this developing field do not fully correspond to the authors' images of the future dialogical science? Or do their concerns reflect epistemological or topical uncertainties of this emerging field?

With these questions in mind, one could hardly comment on 'challenges' without considering the possible scope of this aspiring young science. I shall therefore, in the first part of my comment, outline the latitude of dialogical science and its movement during its short history. I shall then reflect on the 'challenges' as I understand them from the authors' points of view.

THE LONG PAST AND SHORT HISTORY OF DIALOGICAL SCIENCE

As it is well known, interest in dialogue as a literary, religious and philosophical genre has been well established in and through scholarly writings during several centuries BC in the Middle East, India and Europe. Wisdom, accumulated in the genre of dialogue during eons of time, has influenced human and social scientific thinking until today.

Nevertheless, we can say that it is the twentieth century and its aftermath that we can call the era of dialogue. Throughout the whole twentieth century and continuing to the twenty first century, several distinct literary, philosophical and religious approaches have been developing and profoundly changing the scholarly perspectives of dialogue. Although conceptual presuppositions of these approaches come from diverse sources, they all focus on conversation and dialogue as the fundamental prerequisites of humanity. In their diverse, yet complementary manners, they bring language and communication into the centre of scholarly interest.

Existential Dialogism

It has become more or less accepted that the sources of dialogism are sought, on the one hand, in Bakhtin's Circle and Vygotsky, and on the other hand, in American pragmatism as represented by William James, Charles S. Peirce, John Dewey, George H. Mead, among others (e.g., Gillespie, 2006; Hermans & Kempen, 1993; Hermans & Hermans-Konopka, 2010; Linell, 2009). Such connections seem to make good sense because all these scholars were concerned, though in their specific ways, with interaction between I and other(s) leading to the concept of dialogical self, constructivism, discourse and conversation analysis. However, other researchers warn of making a quick jump from the former to the latter because, after all, despite considerable similarities, there are also substantial differences between Bakhtin's dialogism and pragmatists' concepts of the self and dialogue (e.g., Taylor, 1991; Barresi, 2002). Many accounts of dialogism, despite their apparent breadth, are narrow because they neglect the perspective according to which dialogue is above all an ethical (though see, e.g., Taylor, 1991; Eskin, 2000; Ellis & Stam, 2010) and an ontological prerequisite of humanity. Considering ethics and ontology of dialogue, without any attempt to present a comprehensive review, I consider Mikhail Bakhtin (1895-1975), Hans-Georg Gadamer (1900-2002) and Emmanuel Levinas (1906-1995) to be the most representative scholars of dialogical approaches of the twentieth century. Depending on one's point of view, one could of course include some others, e.g. Paul Ricoeur (see Ellis & Stam, 2010). What is distinct about these scholars is that they, in their specific ways, substituted the traditional individualistic ontologies and epistemologies in language by dialogical ones. 'Dialogical' in this context does not mean that these scholars were primarily concerned with the self and dialogue as a face-to-face interaction, but that they posed fundamental questions about human and communicative resources of the self and others.

For Bakhtin, Gadamer and Levinas, dialogue is a form of being; it is existential. The term 'existential dialogism' was coined in the early nineteen twenties by the religious Neo-Kantian philosophers of the Marburg School. The self cannot be conceived in any other way but as interdependent with other selves in and through language and communication. There could be no humanity without the relation between I and thou, claimed Martin Buber (1923/1962). From this existential or ontological interdependence between I and thou, philosophers like Cohen, Rosenstock, Rosenzweig, among others, derived dialogism as epistemology, presupposing that knowledge is jointly generated by the self and 'others' throughout history as well as through symbolic and local dialogical encounters (Marková, 2003).

Mikhail Bakhtin

Building on the work of Neo-Kantians, Bakhtin formulated dialogism in the long life span of more than fifty years. Each dialogical encounter is formed in a unique relation between one human consciousness and another one (Bakhtin, 1981, 1929/1984, 1979/1986). This unique relation is a fundamental dialogical feature of the self; it takes place in the rich variety of environments differing from one person to another. Even within a single dialogical encounter the self takes on different positions (or speaks through different voices) depending on communicative genre, code-switching, emotions, and otherwise. Rejecting the notion of a unified language as an orderly system of signs, as well as the notion of communicative neutrality of the transmission of information, Bakhtin viewed daily speech as always judgemental, evaluative and orientated towards creating new meanings through a collaborative work of one's own and others' thoughts. Since words in a communicative encounter are always doubly orientated, i.e. towards the self and towards the other, they are always open to different interpretations. Dialogue does not necessarily lead to a resolution of discord. The fundamental feature of dialogue is a clash of ideas, their tension and transformation through their confrontation.

Hans-Georg Gadamer

Hans-Georg Gadamer is associated above all with hermeneutics and interpretation of texts, while his position with respect to the ontology of dialogue and conversation is largely overlooked. He explicitly draws attention to the primacy of dialogue in a variety of his writings (Dostal, 2002) and above all in *Truth and Method* (1975/2004). Many of his views on dialogue and conversation are very similar to those of Bakhtin and of later Wittgenstein. He sought "to approach the mystery of language from the conversation that we ourselves are" (2004, p. 370). By language he means above all a living dialogue or conversation, that is, language-in-use, and only secondarily a system of grammatical rules, syntax and vocabulary. He emphasises the dialogicality of language: we live language rather than use it as an instrument. And it is the living dialogue that always stands behind our dialogical understanding of texts, works of art, and traditions – in other words, it is living language that underlies hermeneutics. This means that the living dialogue is primary to the interpretation of text. Just like for Bakhtin, so for Gadamer, dialogue, whether internal or external dialogue with the self and others, is infinite; it is never complete and it never leads to something definitive. Our inner conversation simultaneously anticipates dialogue with others and so it introduces others into the conversation with ourselves (2004, p. 547).

Emmanuel Levinas

Finally, Levinas explores dialogue at an even more basic level than Bakhtin and Gadamer: for him, the first philosophy is the philosophy of dialogue and the dialogue cannot be anything but an ethical dialogue (Levinas, 1995, p. 108). All thinking, he continues, is subordinated to ethics. For Levinas, ethics underlies responsibility towards the other and this is what ultimately positions the self in the world. Levinas maintains that modern philosophy overemphasizes 'being' as activity, as an engagement in the world rather than as an engagement with others. Engagement with others is moral, obligatory and asymmetrical. The primacy of ethics over ontology means precedence of my responsibility to the other over my own existence (Levinas, 1978, p. 75-76). This also means that the ethics of dialogue precedes and pre-conditions dialogue in the everyday sense of the word, that is, exchange of mutual dialogical contributions. The self has no right to question what the other requires from him: his obligations and generosity to others is unlimited. This fundamental and a priori relation to the other, however, Levinas argues, is not ontology but religion. To approach the other person is to put my own freedom into question (1969, p. 303). These views of Levinas characterise a substantial difference from the dialogism of Bakhtin and Gadamer. In the ethics of Levinas's dialogue the other is guiding the self's position.

Towards a Dialogical Science

Although psychology, including the psychology of language, has always tended to associate itself with natural rather than social sciences, it could not remain untouched by the dialogical approaches of Bakhtin, Gadamer and Levinas, because the ideas of these scholars have been integrated into the European culture of the twentieth century. Even if they did not influence scientific psychologists directly, it would be hard for any intellectuals not to be affected by thoughts percolating through literature, education or daily talk. Nevertheless, despite the changing conceptions in the study of dialogue that these dialogical approaches have offered, postulating a scholarly inquiry as a science requires more than original ideas infiltrating culture. Science involves a systematic accumulating of knowledge and in this case, a systematic knowledge about dialogue and related phenomena. Moreover, science is built within an institutionalized recognition of the field in question: it requires specialist journals, international conferences, the establishment of University chairs, courses for the study of higher degrees and handbooks on 'the state of art'. In this sense the institutional beginnings of dialogical science are very recent and they take us to the year 2000 when the first conference on the Dialogical Self took place and to 2005 when the *International Journal for Dialogical Science* was launched. Nevertheless, it is unlikely that these institutional beginnings could have taken place without the already established foundations.

Building Blocks of Dialogical Science

Since the nineteen sixties and seventies we find a mounting criticism of the individualistically orientated studies of language that were above all reified in the claim that linguistics is a branch of cognitive psychology (Chomsky, 1968, p. 1). Numerous books focusing on the social context of language challenged the Chomskyan perspectives of individualistic and static inquiries into language and thought that were defined in terms of formal logical operations. Alternatives were sought focusing on explorations of language in social interactions, discourse, rhetoric, dramaturgical approaches and social change.

Second, due to technological advances in the nineteen sixties and seventies, it became possible to routinely audio- and video-record detailed features of dialogical speech like conversations, professional consultations, parent-child communications, and so on. These advancements largely contributed to new ways of looking at dialogue, speech, semantics and syntax. They led to new kinds of analysis, like conversation analysis, different forms of discourse analysis, observations of intersubjective relations in dialogue, and language acquisition in children. The advantage of these technological advancements was that video- and audio- observations could be repeatedly re-analysed, argued and negotiated in minute detail. The more the analysts observe, the more they see and hear. Video-analyses show micro-interactions defining pre-verbal dialogical synchrony between carers and babies, as well as asynchrony arising from the lack of dialogical sensitivity of partners; the implications of these findings for the development of language and communication became questioned and further studied.

The third, and perhaps most significant resource for the development of dialogical science, was the discovery of Bakhtin's work and publications of his papers and books in the West. The development and critiques of Bakhtin's work have led not only to creative elaboration of his ideas but also to terminological diversification. 'Dialogism', 'dialogicality', 'dialogistics', 'the dialogical self', 'the dialogical brain' and many other words and phrases with something 'dialogical' have become alternatives to the traditional 'monologism' and individualistic views of language and communication. The adjective 'dialogical' now refers to discourse, dialogue, verbal interaction, symbolic interaction, cultural exchanges, among other things. One consequence of this broad use of 'dialogical' is that this adjective almost loses its meaning and becomes no more than a word that signifies the allegiance of the user to the camp of 'dialogists'.

Diversities within Dialogical Approaches

The originality and richness of Bakhtin's newly discovered work surprised social scientists who, depending on their own inclinations, found in his texts diverse kinds of inspiration. With the benefit of hindsight, scholars writing on dialogue and social aspects of language commented that had they known Bakhtin's work earlier, they would have incorporated his ideas into their own thought when developing their theories. For example, Billig (1996), in an introduction to the second edition of *Arguing and Thinking,* published originally in 1987, states that omission of Bakhtin in his book "creates the greatest problem" (p. 17). The topics that he discussed in *Arguing and Thinking*, Billig points out, were all brilliantly and even more extensively covered by Bakhtin who stressed the dialogical and rhetorical nature of language. For Billig, it is above all Bakhtin's rhetorical force of utterances that he appreciates; Bialostosky, referring to similarity between Billig's and Bakhtin's ideas, comments on Billig's "reinvention of Bakhtin from Protagorean rhetoric" (Billig, 1996, p. 17). Rommetveit (1974), who, in *On Message Structure*, was concerned with intersubjectivity, communicative contracts and meta-contracts between speakers, and with ethical questions of dialogue, pointed out to me in a personal communication that had he known Bakhtin's work when writing his book, he would have used the Bakhtinian term 'co-authorship' rather than intersubjectivity, when referring to the mutual construction of messages between speakers. Moscovici (Moscovici & Marková, 2000, p. 274), too, reflected on the discovery of Bakhtinian ideas: "Thus in *Psychoanalysis* I differentiated between three systems of communication – diffusion, propagation and propaganda – according to the source, the goal and the logic of messages [...] it was before I discovered Bakhtin. Today I speak about communication genres". I myself, too, while referring to the Hegelian framework for the study of language and thought in *Paradigms, Thought and Language* (1982), have subsequently turned to a Bakhtinian dialogical approach. My own interest in Bakhtin was related in the first instance to his dialogical ontology and epistemology. Surely, one could find more examples of similar remarks in the literature on language and communication.

The Dialogical Self

Due to Bakhtin's influence, the term 'dialogical self' has become central in several scholarly approaches. Amongst the first ones, Charles Taylor (1991) in his paper *The Dialogical Self* discusses the self in the space of ethical questions, reflexive awareness and identity. For him, the kind of identity that is fundamental to a coherent sense of self relates humans to ethics, values and dialogical action. He explains that dialogical action is substantially different from the classic notion of co-ordination of movements, such as, for example, when one person throws the ball and the other person catches it. Such a notion of co-ordination, Taylor argues, does not capture the integration of the self and the other, their rhythm and cadence. However, such flow of movement is present, say, in dancing, sawing wood or conversation and this is the essence of a dialogical action. Of course, in a social theory, a dialogical action is often reduced to a mere co-ordination in the exchange of gestures. Referring to George Herbert Mead, Taylor argues that "taking the attitude of the other" is no more than another monological act within behavioural ontology. Here the self is socially constituted through taking attitudes of the other rather than through a mutually generated integrative action. Therefore, "we need not Mead and his like, but rather Bakhtin", Taylor (1991, p. 314) concludes. Moreover, he points out: "Human beings are constituted in conversation; and hence what gets internalized in the mature subject is not the reaction of the other but the whole conversation, with the interanimation of its voices. Only a theory of this kind can do justice to the dialogical nature of the self" (Taylor, 1991, p. 314).

Taylor's expression "Mead and his like" in the above quotation could also refer to William James who, as Barresi (2002) argues, provided a rich account of the self. Referring to Hermans, Barresi points out that we need to be careful with attempts to translate too quickly James into Bakhtin because these two authors are dealing with different theories of the self. To my mind, Barresi makes a similar point with respect to William James that Taylor makes with respect to Mead. In James's theory of the self, each thought, while connecting to past thoughts, is nevertheless, metaphysically independent. In contrast, Bakhtin's epistemological perspective is interrelated with the perspective of another person: it never displaces or overcomes the other (Barresi, 2002, p. 245). In Bakhtin's approach, the dialogical self is never enclosed either in self-positions, nor does it fuse with the other (Marková, 2003, p. 103; Bakhtin 1979/1986, p. 78; also Bakhtin, 1986/1993). Bakhtin's self and other are dependent on one another: they jointly generate language, thinking and knowledge. Nevertheless, they remain individual and responsible speakers, thinkers and knowers.

The concept of dialogical self developed by Hermans and his colleagues (e.g. Hermans & Kempen, 1993; Hermans & Hermans-Konopka, 2010) is theoretically derived from William James, George Herbert Mead as well as from Bakhtin. Numerous writings in this area have become fruitful and influential in promoting and institutionalising the field of the dialogical self. As Stam (2010) maintains, the list of articles and books now extends into hundreds and inevitably, with this expansion, both new elaborations emerge and critical voices re-evaluate the previous concepts. Challenges, critiques and new articulations reflect the authors' concerns and ideas of this fast growing field.

CHALLENGES TO DIALOGICAL SCIENCE
OR TO THE DIALOGICAL SELF?

The authors of Part I of this book raise several overlapping concerns that, in general, seem to express the view that this fast growing field is moving ahead too quickly without paying sufficient attention to conceptual, analytic and methodological issues. Since, understandably, different researchers are using the terms 'dialogical self' and 'dialogue' in diverse ways depending on the tradition of thought from which they come, and on theoretical perspectives to which they subscribe, the misunderstandings that arise, contribute to 'challenges'.

Metaphors and Nominalization

Both Billig (2011), and Akkerman and Niessen (2011), raise a substantial, old and well known problem in sciences: academics postulate metaphors or give objects and phenomena names, and then treat metaphors and names as the real things. It is not that there would be something wrong with metaphors. Referring to Vaihinger's (1935) *as if* philosophy, Billig maintains that metaphors can be vital for the creative insight. If the scientist acknowledges that metaphors are fictions, there could be no problems, Billig argues. Since the ancient Greeks metaphors have been used to communicate complex thoughts or simply to associate ideas with poetic images, nature, gods, evil, mechanisms or otherwise. Many great scholars and scientists, like Hegel or Darwin used metaphors to explain their theories. Metaphors link up one idea with another one and they also structure the listeners' or readers' meanings. The problems arise when the researcher forgets that metaphor is a fiction and treats it as a real object.

Akkerman and Niessen as well as Billig challenge the concept of dialogical self. Billig (2011) says: "The dialogical self is, of course, a metaphorical object – it cannot be seen, touched, or felt, but its existence is to be taken for granted, as well as its capacity for doing things" (p. 14). Billig's quote can be illustrated by the following example. Since the brain and brain metaphors now penetrate social sciences and humanities, it is not surprising to read: "we can speculate on how a dialogical self might actually be housed in a dialogical brain" (Lewis, 2002, p. 178). Here we have two metaphors, 'a dialogical self' and 'a dialogical brain' combined into one 'speculation'. Lewis attempts to model an internal monologue, hypothesising that internal monologue forms the basis of the dialogical self. The model assumes the link between an attentional system in the orbitofrontal cortex and associated affective and premotor systems in the brain. Lewis concludes that "the vitality and creativity of internal dialogues can be squared with the constraints of biological realism" (ibid., p. 187).

Yet the 'biological realism' is not so easily accepted by everyone, for example, by the anthropologist Ingold. As Ingold points out, cells in the brain interact with other cells both in the brain, and in the organism to which they belong. While the brain is embodied in the organism, it is the organism that interacts with its external environment, not the brain as such. The brain needs its embodiment to live; it needs oxygen, the flow of blood and chemicals; multilayered physiological processes all contribute to the emergence of the capacities of living beings (Ingold, 2004, p. 217). From this it is questionable whether we can assume that 'biological realism' justifies the metaphor of a 'dialogical brain' and 'dialogical self'.

The problem of metaphors is closely related to that of nominalization. Here again, Billig argues that nominalisation and the emphasis in sciences on the use of technical nominals encourages the substitution of names by 'real' things (see also Billig, 2008a, 2008b). Neologisms like 'nominalisation', 'dialogisation', 'globalisation' and others, all reify concepts and create fictional things. Akkerman and Niessen in their chapter raise the same issue. They point out that in order to capture reality, the researchers invent names. Names enable categorization of phenomena and they reify and solidify the world around us, providing the sense of identity and permanence. Thus dialogical researchers run into a paradox: while they emphasise dynamics and change, they use nouns that reify movement. We may ask: does reification bring the theory of dialogical self closer to science?

The Gap between Theory and Empirical Research

Akkerman and Niessen argue that dialogical theories are often unable to conduct empirical studies of social phenomena that would correspond to dialogical theories that, presumably, underlie empirical research. They see the main reason for this gap between theory and empirical research in the lack of concrete methods that are at researchers' disposal to explore the dialogical self. As an example of this problem they discuss an empirical study by Raggatt (2000), whose intention was to find a 'method of assessment' or a 'mapping' of the 'dialogical self'. The authors point out that while theoretically Raggatt builds on Hermans's and his colleagues' concept of the dialogical self, empirically, he is using traditional methods to explore the dialogical self, like semi-structured interviews. These are quantitatively analysed by, e. g. multidimensional scaling, to map the individual's webs of attachment. The authors point out that in the end the results of this work are not much different from the common social scientific approaches 'in which units are characterised and defined as separate, as if they have a permanent existence independent of one another'.

However, I wonder whether the real problem should not be sought in the ontological issues to which Akkerman and Niessen refer at the beginning of their chapter. I would argue that it is not the lack of dialogical methods which creates a gap between theory and empirical work but the fact that the researcher has not interiorised the dialogical theory and treats the data in the traditional monological manner. In other words, it is not the method that is insufficient but the way the method is conceptualised and used. One can use a 'dialogical method', e. g., a focus group, in a traditional mechanistic manner; equally, one can use semi-structured interviews in a dialogical manner by focusing, e. g., not only on the subjects' responses taken on their own but on the interdependence between subjects' responses and the social field within which the research is conducted (see also below). While Akkerman and Niessen are correct to challenge the gap between dialogical theory and empirical research, one can, nevertheless, raise another issue. It is clear from Akkerman and Niessen's chapter that they argue their point from the Bakhtinian perspective of the ontological interdependence between the self and other. However, is Raggatt's perspective Bakhtinian or is it a perspective of self-positioning? If Raggatt is concerned with the dialogical self in terms of listing different self-positions, perhaps one can argue that his empirical approach corresponds to his self-positioning theory.

Individualism and De-contextualised Dialogical Self

Both Haye and Larrain's (2011) and Joerchel's (2011) chapters raise in different ways, the importance of theoretical and empirical focusing on the interdependence between the self and other, and between their voices. Both chapters also emphasise the role of context or field and of culture as the forces interderpendent with the interacting participants. In other words, the interdependence between the self and other and their contexts constitutes a field, that is, an irreducible ultimate entity. This perspective has significant methodological consequences because the context, as part of the field, must be conceptualised just as clearly and profoundly as the psychological and social psychological characteristics of participants. This may seem obvious: one does not administer scales or questionnaires without good knowledge (historical, political, ethical, etc.) of the context in which the research is conducted. These points are implied in both chapters.

Haye and Larrain focus on Bakhtin's concept of utterance, which is a fundamental concept in his theory of speech or communicative genres. Nevertheless, despite Bakhtin's innovative conceptual contribution to the study of utterance as a unit of discourse, the authors propose to reconceptualise an utterance in terms of the dynamics of position-taking within interlocution fields. In asking 'what is an utterance?' they pose the question as to how is an utterance related to positioning. Is positioning the same as the utterance or is it different? In their emphasis on the openness of an utterance they argue that there is the risk involved in explaining the utterance simply as a positioning because this perspective would ignore that every utterance is engaged with numerous positions. Utterances respond not only to a previous utterance but to also to possible future positions and to immediate as well to imagined positions of others. All these other positions or voices take part in the discursive environment, orienting their movements and relations towards both neighbouring and distant utterances. In their analysis they show position-taking movements are never isolated processes but that they take place in a field of interdependent position-taking movements. This is why, they argue, the concept of positioning must be developed jointly with the field of interlocution.

By the field of interlocution they do not mean an external context but an inner component of the utterance. In contrast to other conceptions of self-positioning, according to Haye and Larrain positioning is a process taking place in the field. The authors refer to the way this concept is used in the theory of relativity, as a force binding phenomena together. In this case, the dialogical self and the field are constituted by tensions and conflicts of interests which provide space for multiple I-positions and their perspectives.

Joerchel's idea of the dialogical self as resonating with the other expresses a similar idea to that of Haye and Larrain. In Joerchel's chapter, too, culture emerges from interaction between individuals and can be located within the space between individuals. This too is an internal relation between the self and culture that embraces the concept of the field. This highlights the conception of culture as structural process which simultaneously organises the space in which positions move as well as the dialogical interactions between positions and thus also the dialogical self. For the theory of the dialogical self this means that it always develops within a cultural atmosphere which constantly, and usually unnoticeably, simultaneously resonates within each individual, structuring and formatting his or her dialogical interactions. Taking this resonating process seriously, the dialogical self can be viewed from a slightly different angle: the self constructs itself not only through the act of dialogue (as dialogue itself is already inspired by the general cultural atmosphere), but rather, resonating processes govern the dialogical processes and cultural atmospheric forces that inspire them. It is thus never *only* the individual position or voice, as suggested by Hermans and Kempen (1993, p. 118) which culturally influences the rest of the dialogical self system.

CONCLUSION

If we take a close look at the fast growing literature in the field of dialogism, we find that it is concerned above all with the dialogical self, while the concept of dialogical science is hardly ever mentioned. Even Hermans and Hermans-Konopka's (2010) book on the state of art of the dialogical self theory does not index 'dialogical science' as a term. One may even ask: what is the relation between dialogical science and the dialogical self? Has the dialogical self replaced dialogical science? If so, what are the implications of this shift?

If we reflect again on 'challenges' that the authors raise in Part I of this volume, we may conclude that these are directed at theoretical and methodological problems of the dialogical self and I-positioning rather than at challenges directed at the dialogical science. A science is usually built on specific theoretical presuppositions. For example, Newtonian science was built on the presuppositions of a mechanism; Einsteinian science is built on relations between forces; Chomskyan linguistics is built on Cartesian presuppositions of the individual cognition; and so on. The point of departure of dialogical science, I assume, is the ontological interdependence between the self and other(s) and its social (cultural, historical) vicissitudes. I suggest that the authors of Part I sound alarmed because they consider that 'dialogical' might (or does?) lose its ontological interactional basis by placing emphasis on the self and I-positioning rather than on the interdependence between the self and others. Indeed, their emphasis on problems of nominalisation, decontextualisation and lack of clarity in empirical research seems to confirm this suggestion.

In the meantime, researchers will expand dialogical theories as well as well as their critiques. Moreover, professionals in various spheres of life, like education, therapy or disability, search for new ways of improving communication with their clients. For instance, the presupposition of interdependence between the self and others and its multifaceted forms is fundamental for carers and clients in communication with the disabled, e.g. people with cerebral palsy (Marková, 2003), aphasia (Murphy, 2000), deafblindedness (Nafstad & Rødbroe, 1999) or learning disability (Cameron & Murphy, 2002). Indeed, many professionals in these areas find it necessary to focus on the basic presupposition of dialogical science, that is, on different forms of the self-other(s) interaction in their specific social contexts, rather than only on forms of the dialogical self and its positions.

REFERENCES

Akkerman, S. & Niessen, T. (2011). Dialogical theories at the boundary. In M. Märtsin, B. Wagoner, E. L. Aveling, I. Kadianaki, & L. Whittaker (Eds.), *Dialogicality in focus: Challenges to theory, method and application* (pp. 53-64). New York: Nova Science Publishers.

Bakhtin, M. M. (1981). *The dialogic imagination. Four essays by M. M. Bakhtin.* (M. Holquist, Ed., C. Emerson and M. Holquist, Trans.). Austin: University of Texas Press.

Bakhtin, M. M. (1979/1986). *Estetika slovesnovo tvorchestva.* Moskva: Bocharov. Trans. by V.W. McGee as *Speech genres and other late essays* (C. Emerson & M. Holquist, Ed.). Austin: University of Texas Press.

Bakhtin, M. M. (1929/1984). *Problems of Dostoyevsky's poetics.* (C. Emerson, Ed. and Trans.). Manchester: Manchester University Press.

Bakhtin, M. M. (1986/1993). *Towards a philosophy of the act.* (V. Liapunov, Trans. and notes). Austin: University of Texas Press.

Barresi, J. (2002). From 'the thought is the thinker' to 'the voice is the speaker': William James and the dialogical self. *Theory & Psychology, 12*, 237-250.

Billig, M. (1996). *Arguing and thinking: A rhetorical approach to social psychology. 2nd edition.* Cambridge: Cambridge University Press. Paris: Editions de la Maison des Sciences de l'Homme.

Billig, M. (2008a). The language of critical discourse analysis: The case of nominalization. *Discourse & Society, 19*, 783-800.

Billig, M. (2008b). Nominalizing and de-nominalizing: A reply. *Discourse & Society, 19*, 829-841.

Billig, M. (2011). Dialogical writing and dialogical theory: Reflections on Locke, Shaftesbury and fictional things. In M. Märtsin, B. Wagoner, E. L. Aveling, I. Kadianaki, & L. Whittaker (Eds.), *Dialogicality in focus: Challenges to theory, method and application* (pp. 3-18). New York: Nova Science Publishers.

Buber, M. (1923/1962). *I and thou.* Edinburgh: T.&T. Clark.

Chomsky, N. (1968). *Language and mind.* New York: Harcourt Brace Jovanovich.

Cameron, L., & Murphy, J. (2002). Enabling young people with a learning disability to make choices at a time of transition. *British Journal of Learning Disabilities, 30*, 105-112.

Editorial. *International Journal of Dialogical Science.*

Ellis, B. D., & Stam, H. J. (2010). Addressing the other in dialogue: Ricoeur and the ethical dimensions of the dialogical self. *Theory & Psychology,* 20, 420-435.

Eskin, M. (2000). *Ethics and dialogue in the works of Levinas, Bakhtin, Mendelshtam and Celan.* Oxford: Oxford University Press.

Dostal, R. J. (Ed.). (2002). *The Cambridge companion to Gadamer.* Cambridge: Cambridge University Press.

Gadamer, G.-H. (1975/2004). *Truth and method.* London and New York: Continuum.

Gillespie, A. (2006). Descartes' demon: A dialogical analysis of 'Meditations on First Philosophy'. *Theory & Psychology, 16*, 761-781.

Haye, A. & Larrain, A. (2011). What is an utterance? In M. Märtsin, B. Wagoner, E. Aveling, I. Kadianaki & L. Whittaker (Eds.), *Dialogicality in focus: Challenges to theory, method and application.* (pp. 33-52). New York: Nova Science Publishers.

Hermans, H. J. M., & Kempen, H. J. G. (1993). *The dialogical self: Meaning as movement.* London: Academic Press.

Hermans, H. J. M., & Hermans-Konopka, A. (2010). *Dialogical self theory: Positioning and counter-positioning in a globalizing society.* Cambridge: Cambridge University Press.

Ingold, T. (2004). Beyond biology and culture. The meaning of evolution in a relational world. *Social Anthropology, 12*, 209-221.

Joerchel, A. C. (2011). Locating the dialogical self within a cultural sphere. In M. Märtsin, B. Wagoner, E. L. Aveling, I. Kadianaki, & L. Whittaker (Eds.), *Dialogicality in focus: Challenges to theory, method and application* (pp. 19-32). New York: Nova Science Publishers.

Levinas, E. (1978). *Autrement que l'être ou au-delà de l'essence. [Otherwise than being or beyond essence]*. Leiden: Martinus Nijhoff.

Levinas, E. (1969). *Totality and infinity.* (A. Lingis, Trans.). Pittsburgh: Duquesne University Press.

Levinas, E. (1995). *Altérite et transcendance. [Alterity and transcendence]*. Montpellier: Fata Morgana.

Lewis, M. D. (2002). The dialogical brain. Contributions of emotional neurobiology to understanding the dialogical self. *Theory & Psychology, 12*, 175-190.

Linell, P. (2009). *Rethinking language, mind and world dialogically.* Charlotte: Information Age Publishing.

Marková, I. (1982). *Paradigms, thought and language.* Chichester & New York: Wiley.

Marková, I. (2003). *Dialogicality and social representations.* Cambridge: Cambridge University Press.

Moscovici, S., & Marková, I. (2000). Ideas and their development: A dialogue between Serge Moscovici and Ivana Marková. In S. Moscovici, *Social representations* (G. Duveen, Ed.). Cambridge: Polity Press.

Murphy, J. (2000). Enabling people with aphasia to discuss quality of life. *British Journal of Therapy and Rehabilitation, 7*, 454-457.

Nafstad, A., & Rødbroe, I. (1999). *Co-creating communication. Perspectives on diagnostic education for individuals who are congenitally deafblind and individuals whose impairments may have similar effects.* Dronninglund: Forlaget Nord-Press.

Raggatt, P. T. F. (2000). Mapping the dialogical self: towards a rationale and method of assessment. *European Journal of Personality, 14*, 65–90.

Rommetveit, R. (1974). *On message structure.* Chichester and London: Wiley.

Stam, H. J. (2010). Self and dialogue. Introduction. *Theory & Psychology, 20*, 299-304.

Taylor, C. (1991). The dialogical self. In D. R. Hiley, J. F. Bohman and R. Shusterman (Eds.), *The interpretive turn: Philosophy, science, culture* (pp. 304-317). Ithaca: Cornell University Press.

Vaihinger, H. (1935). *The philosophy of 'as if'.* London: Routledge and Kegan Paul.

In: Dialogicality in Focus   ISBN: 978-1-61122-817-5
Editors: M. Märtsin, B. Wagoner, E.-L. Aveling et al.   © 2011 Nova Science Publishers, Inc.

COMMENTARY 2 TO PART I: FROM 'ALREADY MADE THINGS' TO 'THINGS IN THEIR MAKING': INQUIRING 'FROM WITHIN' THE DIALOGIC

John Shotter

"What really *exists* is not things made but things in the making. Once made, they are dead, and an infinite number of alternative conceptual decompositions can be used in defining them." (James, 1909/1996, p. 263)

The authors of all the chapters in this section see the realm of the *dialogical* as offering not only new possibilities but also new challenges. And in their own different ways, they raise the whole question of what it is to conduct an inquiry into human social phenomena: how might one prepare oneself for the task; how can it actually be conducted; and how might its results be expressed or be presented in ways that are useful, not only to ourselves as inquirers, but also to others as the recipients of *the results* of our inquiries? In exploring how the authors of these chapters tackle these questions, instead of seeking *concepts* to *explain* how they go about conducting the different tasks involved, I want to explore the *practicalities* of what they propose, how their proposals might seem to play out in practice, both in their own further activities, but also out in the world at large. But before I do, I want to set out a number of preliminaries, to do with establishing a larger context within which to place the whole idea of being *dialogical*, along with the question as to whether a *dialogical science*, as such, is a real possibility – and if it is, what might it look like? For as I see it (given my task as a commentator to say what I think), none of these accounts, of what might be involved in bringing a *dialogical science* as such into existence, seem to me to be anywhere near radical enough.

AUTHORS' ORIENTATIONS: WHAT THEY *WANT* TO SEE

Many years ago, long before he opted for a more *dialogical* approach, Charles Taylor (1971) wrote about the need for a more *hermeneutical* turn in the human sciences, i.e., away from a concern with causes toward a concern more with meanings and understandings, and he noted: "These sciences cannot be '*wertfrei*'; they are moral sciences in a more radical sense than the eighteenth century understood. Finally, their successful prosecution requires a high degree of self-knowledge, a freedom from illusion, in the sense of error which is rooted and expressed in ones way of life; for our incapacity to understand is rooted in our own self-definitions, hence in what we are" (p. 51). And as Wittgenstein (1980) remarked in relation to our difficulties of understanding: "What makes a subject difficult to understand [...] is not that before you can understand it you need to be specially trained in abstruse matters, but the contrast between understanding the subject and what most people *want* to see. Because of this the very things which are most obvious may become the hardest of all to understand. What has to be overcome is a difficulty having to do with the will, rather than with the intellect" (p. 17). Thus overcoming these kinds of difficulty does not primarily involve *solving problems*, they involve more "a working on oneself [...] On one's way of seeing things. (And what one expects of them)" (p. 16), on one's way or ways of *relating* or of *orienting* oneself to events occurring one's surroundings (Shotter, 2010a).

This, then, is why I think that the authors of these four chapters are all being insufficiently radical: although they all bring important new issues into the arena of concern with dialogical phenomena, to a very large extent, they leave out their own self-definitions, their own ways of seeing things and what they expect of them, from the *dialogical* processes they are trying to elucidate. They leave out their own *embodied participation* in the processes of their concern – as well as the embodied participation of those they are studying. Whereas, as I see it, to the extent that "we are simultaneously actors as well as spectators on the great stage of life" (Bohr, quoted in Honner, 1989, p. 1), we need to bring to light, not just our own implicit 'assumptions' as the individuals we are, but also the implicit 'assumptions', or 'discursive background', constituting the overall "determining surroundings" (Shotter, 2009, p. 35) that determine the 'shape', so to speak, of the investigations we undertake. For we are not, and can never be, *outside* observers of the world as such; nor can we be simply located at particular places *in* it; rather, we are part *of* it, *participant parts* within the ceaseless, dynamic unfolding of the dialogically-structured surroundings within which we live and have our being.

This, I think, is the point that Bakhtin (1993) is trying to get at when he insists that an act of ours is only "truly real" when it "participates in once-occurrent Being-as-event [...] *in its entirety*" (p. 2). Otherwise, when it is characterized in a way that 'divorces' it from its immediate, responsive, and dynamic contact with its larger surroundings, it is (mis)characterized as owing its 'shape' only to other influences of a more pre-existing kind. As Bakhtin (1993) puts it: "My participative and demanding consciousness can see that the world of modern philosophy, the theoretical and theoreticized world of culture, is in a certain sense actual, that it possesses validity. But what it can see also is that this world is not the once-occurrent world in which I live and in which I answerably perform my deeds" (p. 20).

Thus, the changes required by the turn to the *dialogical* in our inquiries into human affairs, are not primarily epistemological changes, but ontological ones (Shotter, 2010), to do with changes in the ways in which *we relate ourselves* to the others and othernesses around us. For how we go out towards them, with certain already embodied reactions to their activities 'at the ready', so to speak, will determine what returning aspects of their expressive behaviour will count for us, will matter to us as a topic for further study. So, I agree whole heartedly with Akkerman and Niessen (2011) that "dialogical theories do justice to the complex nature of reality, but at the same time seem incapable of fully realising the potential of this ability because of propositional and linguistic characterization in research practice" (p. 53), and that "in the ontological sense presented in [their] chapter, all phenomena are considered dialogical" (p. 54). However, I still have to say that, as I see it, they also *to a crucial extent* still leave themselves out of the 'all' they see as ontological, in that they do not explore what is involved in working on themselves, on the embodied, taken-for-granted expectations determining how they get themselves ready to 'go out' to look for phenomena relevant to their inquiries into aspects of the *dialogical* of interest to them.

In other words, as I read all four of the contributions in this section, I see them all to a greater or lesser extent as still being oriented towards the construction of a *Dialogical Science* aimed at satisfying pre-existing academic and disciplinary criteria, i.e., as wanting primarily to see 'things' of relevance in *this* context – either in the terms of currently ongoing debates or in terms of acceptable conceptual frameworks – rather than as being oriented towards meeting the more unique and particular demands we face out in the concrete contexts we occupy in our everyday lives, a task that requires the critical examination, and the un-doing, of many of these narrow and restrictive criteria.

Past Concerns about the Conduct of Social Inquiry: 'Losing the Phenomena'

Fragmentation

Very briefly, I would like to look first at some of the ways challenges to a *science* of our social behaviour have been responded to in academe in the past, for some of the challenges we are still facing have been faced in the past. If we first turn to difficulties arising in relation to empirical studies – difficulties referred to by all the authors in this section in one way or another – we can find a number of them raised by Allen Newell, back in 1973, in a paper entitled: "You can't play 20 questions with Nature and win," in which he examined the then state of experimental psychology. He observed that: "every time we find a new phenomenon [...] we produce a flurry of experiments to investigate it" (Newell, 1973, p. 284), and on looking into his field of cognitive psychology at the time of writing, he produced a list of 59 such phenomena within, he says, "a few minutes." Although conceptualizing such phenomena made them amenable to experimentation, "it seems to me," he says, "that clarity is never achieved. Matters simply become muddier and muddier as we go down through time [...] this form of conceptual structure leads rather to an ever increasing pile of issues, which we weary of or become diverted from, but never really settle" (p. 288-289). And later in the article he added another important overall dimension to his concerns: "We never seem in the experimental literature to put the results of all the experiments together" (p. 296).

Will this be the fate of the results accumulating from our more empirical investigations in a dialogical science – their dispersion out into an ever increasing collection of separate, incommensurable fragments?

This danger is not easy to avoid, and I will return to it below. But for the moment, I would just like to introduce some comments from someone even earlier than Allen Newell. William James (1909/1906) in his *Manchester College Lectures* raised concerns about the very idea of starting our inquiries *intellectually*, by undertaking the task of *conceptualizing* the phenomena we want to study. For "when we conceptualise," he said, "we cut out and fix, and exclude everything but what we have fixed. A concept means a *that-and-no-other*. Conceptually, time excludes space; motion and rest exclude each other; approach excludes contact; presence excludes absence; unity excludes plurality; independence excludes relativity; 'mine' excludes 'yours'; this connexion excludes that connexion – and so on indefinitely; whereas in the real concrete sensible flux of life experiences compenetrate[1] each other so that it is not easy to know just what is excluded and what not" (p. 253-254). An amalgam of fragments is thus the inevitable consequence of this kind of approach that works in terms, not just of concepts defined in binary terms, but in terms of what I will call "representational" or "explanatory concepts," that is,, in conceptual terms that make no reference to human interests, traditions, institutions, etc., that is, to the surroundings within which they occur – concepts like *dialogical self* or *interlocation fields* that can be defined wholly in terms of context-free elements, and which need to be related to each other by rules, laws, or principles in such a way as to constitute a conceptual *framework*.

Finding a Living 'Cell' and the Importance of a Murky Tangle of Tiny Details: The Danger of Losing the Phenomena

Concerned to avoid trying to build a human science by patching together a collection of intrinsically separate and self-contained fragments, Vygotsky (1978) approached "the study of the mind having learned the whole of Marx's method [...] The whole of *Capital* is written," he thought, "according to the following method: Marx analyzes a single living 'cell' of capitalist society – for example, the nature of value. Within this cell he discovers the structure of the entire system and all of its economic institutions. He says that to a layman this analysis may seem *a murky tangle of tiny details*. Indeed, there may be tiny details, but they are exactly those which are essential to 'microanatomy'. Anyone who could discover what a 'psychological' cell is – the mechanism producing even a single response – would thereby find the key to psychology as a whole [from unpublished notebooks]" (p. 8, my emphasis). In other words, methodologically, Vygotsky does not proceed by trying to *represent* the arena of his study conceptually at all. Instead, he makes use of what we might call a "descriptive concept," a concept that requires a *murky tangle of tiny details* in giving an account of it, a concept that doesn't, so to speak, 'stand in' for a real life circumstance, but which in its description draws our attention to its *relations* to a whole array of other things in its surroundings.

By the term "descriptive concept," I do not mean to designate a way of thinking *about* something, but just as Wittgenstein (1953) uses the term "language-game [...] to bring into prominence the fact that the speaking of language is part of an activity, or of a form of life" (no. 23). I mean to suggest, as Vygotsky puts it, a murky tangle of tiny interconnected details to which we might possibly attend to in trying to make sense of a particular occurrence as witnesses to it.

Vygotsky (1986) thought that he had found that living 'cell' in "the conception of word meaning as a unit of both generalizing thought and social interchange," (p. 9), for, as he saw it, "unit analysis [...] demonstrates the existence of a dynamic system of meaning in which the

---

[1] From the participle stem of Latin *compenetro*, transitive verb meaning: to penetrate every part of.

affective and the intellectual unite [...] It further permits us to trace the path from a person's needs and impulses to the specific direction taken by his thoughts, and the reverse path from his thoughts to his behavior and activity" (p. 10-11). In describing the kind of analysis he meant here, he drew a distinction between it – *unit* analysis – and the attempt to analyze something complex into a structure of *elementary*, i.e., self-contained, namable parts. In making this most important distinction he noted: "The essential feature of this form of analysis [into elements] is that its products are of a different nature than the whole from which they are derived [...] Since it results in products that have *lost the characteristics of the whole*, this process is not a form of analysis in the true sense of the word. At any rate, it is not 'analysis' *vis-á-vis* the problem to which it was meant to be applied" (Vygotsky, 1987, p. 45, my emphasis)[2]. And he continues: "Because it causes the researcher to ignore the unified and integral nature of the process being studied, this form of analysis leads to a profound delusion. The *internal relationships* of the unified whole are replaced with *external mechanical relationships* between two heterogeneous processes" (p. 46, my emphases).

Garfinkel (2002) also discusses "losing the phenomena" (p. 264-267) in relation to "work-site specific contingencies" (p. 266), the murky tangle of tiny details to which practitioners must be responsive in bringing off a specific achievement in a specific context. To be attentive to these details, they must have come to embody specific anticipatory responses appropriate to making relevant local judgements in orienting themselves to such work-site contingencies. As an example, he discusses trying to replicate Galieo's experiments in which he rolled balls of different sizes and weights down a long wooden plank with a groove cut in it, inclined at an angler, starting at different heights. What became apparent in this replication – that 'went without saying' in Galileo's own account of his experimental arrangements – tas the importance of "initially hearing, listening to, becoming familiar with sounds of invariance" (p. 276). The experimenters' sensitivity to these sounds revealed to them "the board's own idiosyncratic properties" (p. 275), for, after a night of heavy rain, as they later learned, the board had absorbed moisture, so *"we lost our phenomena,"* he comments, "with no idea of why, or how, or what we had done to lose it, or where to look to find it again" (p. 276). In other words, although Galileo described the *results* of his experiments in detail, he 'took for granted' that recipients of them would find it boring and irrelevant if he described *all* the detailed work necessary to arrive at their reliable invariance.

Living 'Cells', Mechanical Assemblages and Non-localizable Influences

In seeking a living 'cell' as a focal unit in his "*unit* analysis", Vygotsky was seeking a form of analysis and ways of speaking that did not lead researchers to ignore the unified and integral nature of the processes being studied. He wanted expressions that, rather than (mis)leading us into *losing the phenomena* – i.e., failing to attend to their relation to the living whole from out of which they emerge – worked instead to draw our attention to the way(s) in which they are interwoven into it. This is why conceptual generalizations, explanatory or representational concepts, are of no use to us in our dialogically-structured inquiries: they are

---

[2] Here, I will quote from Minick's 1987 translation, as this issue is spelt out there in much more detail than in Kozulin's 1986 translation, although for all other purposes I will quote from Kozulin's version as it is, perhaps, the one most accessible to everyone.

the *outcomes* of a living, developmental process, and are therefore misleading when used in efforts to *represent* the ongoing, constitutive details of that process. They will inevitably divert our attention away from the *relational events* of interest to us, and (mis)lead us into seeking *separate elements* that could equally well be parts of a mechanical assemblage.

Thus what Vygotsky was concerned to do by focusing on the descriptive concept of "word meaning", was to distinguish between the growth and development of a *living being* from a 'seed' or 'embryo' embedded in a 'nutrient' environment, and the 'putting together' of a mechanical assemblage from a set of separate and nameable parts. For living beings develop from simple individuals into richly structured ones in such a way that their 'parts'[3] at any one moment in time owe, not just their character, but their very existence *both* to their *relations* to each other *and* to their *relations* with the 'parts' of the system at some earlier point in time. Thus their history is just as important as their momentary structure in their growth. This means that there is a *developmental continuity* in the unfolding of all living activities such that their earlier phases are indicative of at least the *style* of what is to come later. As a result, we can not only respond to their activities in an *anticipatory* fashion, but also, all the changes they undergo are *identity preserving* changes, which means that they retain their identity even while remaining 'open' to further changes – indeed, their 'incompleteness' is essential to their very nature as still growing and developing living beings.

By contrast, mechanisms whether simple or complex are constructed piece by piece from *objective* parts, that is, from parts which retain their character unchanged irrespective of whether they are parts of the system or not. And as such, a mechanism cannot be identified by name as such until the last part is put into its proper place and it 'switched on' or 'started up'. Mechanical systems will not 'go' until completed.

But there is more to it than this: Due to its spontaneous responsiveness to its surroundings a living 'cell's' embedding in its surroundings is, of course, of crucial importance too. Within the realm of the dialogical, Voloshinov (1986) brings out its importance thus: "the immediate social *situation and the broader social milieu wholly determine – and determine from within, so to speak – the structure of an utterance*" (p. 86, his italics). Hence the influences organizing our utterances and giving them their shape are neither wholly within the individual psyche, nor within the linguistic system:

> "*Any utterance,* no matter how weighty and complete in and of itself, *is only a moment in the continuous process of verbal communication*. But that continuous verbal communication is, in turn, itself only a moment in the continuous, all-inclusive, generative process of a given social collective [...] In its concrete connection with a situation, verbal communication is always accompanied by social acts of a nonverbal character [...] and is often only an accessory to these acts, merely carrying out an auxiliary role. *Language acquires life and historically evolves precisely here, in concrete verbal communication, and not in the abstract linguistic system of language forms, nor in the individual psyche of speakers.*" (p. 95)

---

[3] I put 'parts' in scare quotes as, strictly, they cannot exist at all as separate, self-contained 'things'; it is the part they *play* within a larger, still developing, larger organic whole which gives them their meaning or significance. Strictly, they exist only as *aspects* of it and as such, cannot be thought of as having their living function in separation from it; in separation from it they are at best *dead* shapes or forms.

In other words, some of the major influences at work in giving our utterances their expressive shape are *non-localizable* in the sense that the overall whole within which they make their appearance is crucially influential in the kind of appearance they make.

Bakhtin (1981) introduces the descriptive concept of the "*chronotope* (literally, 'time-space')" to give a name "to the intrinsic connectedness of temporal and spatial relationships that are artistically expressed *in literature*" (p. 84, my emphasis), to the diffuse, non-localizable influences at work in 'shaping' our forms of expression in a particular historical epoch. But, he goes on to say, "we must never confuse – as has been done up to now and is often done – the *represented* world with the world outside the text [...] However forcefully the real and the represented world resist fusion, [...] they are nevertheless indissolubly tied up with each other and find themselves in continual mutual interaction [...] As long as the organism lives, it resists a fusion with the environment, but if it torn out of its environment, it dies" (p. 253-254). Indeed, and I will expand on this much more later, as Dewey (1938/2008) notes, there is a pervasive, indivisible quality to the *situations* from within which we conduct our inquiries which not only "binds all constituents into a whole but it is also unique" (p. 74), and thus, as such, also constitutes or determines for us the 'objects' of our studies as the unique kind of objects they are.

Above, then, what I talked of in terms of the "determining surroundings" of our expressions is, thus, an aspect of the developing whole within which they occur and have their significance. When divorced from their surroundings, when characterized as entities simply in themselves – when observed and transcribed in recordings of one kind or another – our expressions become *products* which have lost the characteristics of the whole *process* from which they have been severed[4]. All this suggests the importance of distinguishing between what we might call "relational events," which occur and have their transitory existence only within the *intra*-play[5] between our outgoing bodily activities towards our surroundings and the incoming sensings occasioned within us as a result, and events *tout court*, i.e., supposedly objective and namable events occurring independently of our relationship to them which we collect by our use of various recording instruments (e.g., audio and video tape recorders).

For what is crucial about relational events, as we have seen above, is that they not only owe their character and their very existence to their relations to earlier events, but they also arouse anticipations within us as to what might come next. Indeed, as Billig (2011) points out, "according to Bakhtin, any utterance typically responds to a previous one and, in its turn, provokes others: 'The utterance is related not only to preceding, but also to subsequent links in the chain of communion' (Bakhtin, 1986, p. 94)" – an idea that has become central, as he points out, within almost all forms of conversational analysis. In other words, the 'glue', so to speak, holding together the different moments and meanings of our relationships to each other as they unfold over time are not general rules of any kind, but the particular *internal relationships* constituting a still unfinalized, living whole as it develops within a particular

---

[4] In much of our empirical work we work from tape recordings and transcripts. But such 'data' are only *representations* of the original events and as such, as 'things', they have *lost* much of what rendered them intelligible as significant social facts in the first place. This means that we have to try to replace what has been lost – people's bodily *orientations* towards events occurring around them, which are crucial to them experiencing them as social facts *of a particular kind* – by finding a place for such recorded events within an explicit conceptual framework of some kind.

[5] I say *intra*- rather than *inter*-play, as the activity involved is not between two or more already separate individuals, but occurs as a differentiation or inner articulation within an already existing holistic being.

situation – in other words, although it is already specified as a certain kind of unity, it is still open to further specifications within its *internal relations*, although only of "an already specified kind" (Shotter, 1984, p. 187).

The "Psychologist's Fallacy"

Above, then, we have seen the emergence of a familiar sequence of moves: the analysis of a living, holistic phenomenon into (an essentially mechanistic) a structure of separate parts, and then the proposal of a conceptual framework aimed at explaining their causal connections with each other. There have been some even earlier challenges to this approach than those I have already mentioned. William James (1890/1950) describes what he called *the psychologist's fallacy*. As he saw it, it occurs because:

> "The psychologist [...] stands outside of the mental state he speaks of. Both itself and its object are objects for him. Now when it is a cognitive state (percept, thought, concept, etc.), he ordinarily has no other way of naming it than as the thought, percept, etc., *of that object*. He himself, meanwhile, knowing the self-same object in *his* way, gets easily led to suppose that the thought, which is *of* it, knows it in the same way in which he knows it, although this is often very far from being the case. The most fictitious puzzles have been introduced into our science by this means." (p. 196)

In other words, we are very easily tempted into describing a *process*, an organized sequence of component tasks, in terms of the *product(s)*, the achievement(s), it was aimed at 'bringing off', whether it or they were in fact brought off or not. And again, what is lost in such a description is the 'relational glue', so to speak, that holds the sequence together as an organized whole.

About the nature of this 'glue', James (1890/1950) was very clear. In discussing its role in *the stream of thought* he remarked:

> "The truth is that large tracts of human speech are nothing but *signs of direction* in thought, of which direction we nevertheless have an acutely discriminative sense, though no definite sensorial image plays any part in it whatsoever [...] Their function is to lead from one set of images to another [...] If we try to hold fast the feeling of direction, the full presence comes and the feeling of direction is lost [...] Now what I contend for [...] is that 'tendencies' are not only descriptions from without, but that they are among the *objects* of the stream, which is thus aware of them from within, and must be described as in very large measure constituted of *feelings of tendency*, often so vague that we are unable to name them at all." (p. 252-254)

It is our *acutely discriminative sense* of the *unique directive* affect of the *feelings of tendency* present to us at each unfolding moment of our living activity – which guides us in anticipating what is next to come – but which are lost if we try to hold on to them sufficiently to name them in some general way. It is our urge to name these transitory, but no less real events, gives rise to the fallacy. Indeed, as I have already intimated above, what we lose – what scientific psychologists and linguists lose – when we and they try to *explain* in theoretical terms the meaning of an isolated utterance, divorced from the surroundings in which it had, or can have its life, is not what the words mean (in some conventional or dictionary sense of word-meaning), but what a particular person, *in a particular situation*, meant in saying them. In short, it is their *uniqueness* that is lost. Voloshinov (1984) puts it as follows: "the task of understanding does not basically amount to recognizing the form used, but rather to understanding it in a particular, concrete context, to understanding its meaning in a particular utterance, i.e., it amounts to understanding its novelty and not to recognizing its identity" (p. 68)[6].

The 'Dialogical' as a Descriptive Concept

Finally, in this section, I would like to focus on the notion of "descriptive concepts" that I introduced in my discussion of Vygotsky's efforts to find a living 'cell', a unit that would in "unit analysis" *orient* us towards *relating ourselves* to "the existence of a dynamic system of meaning in which the affective and the intellectual unite" (Vygotsky, 1986, p. 10). I introduced it as we need, of course, to know *what it is* in any sphere of inquiry that we are inquiring into. But there are two ways, not just one, in which we can approach the task of conceptualizing that *whatness*. We can seek to *formulate* an appropriate concept, or we can, in a Wittgensteinian (1953) sense, take it that a crucial word or phrase – a phrase like "the dialogical" – picks out in its *use* an array of crucially inter-connected features in our everyday activities that have not been appropriately attended to before. In formulating a concept, as individual researchers, we have to argue for the crucial importance of a theoretical object that possesses, we claim, a certain collection of features, so that rules can be specified for bringing some, but not other, events under its aegis – so that, for instance, some exchanges can be deemed to be properly *dialogical* events, whereas others will be excluded. Such concepts then can give rise, we hope, to representational theories that we, again as individuals, try to use to *explain* events *after* they have happened, to determine their antecedent causes and to make *predictions* (on the assumption that the future will be like the past).

Our use of descriptive concepts is quite different. Talk of "utterances", "writing", "the dialogical", "rhetorical", "identity", "personhood", or whatever, etc., is not talk of well-defined objects; the use of such words is pre-theoretical. As Wittgenstein (1953) puts it, when we use such words as those above, "and try to grasp the essence of the thing [they seem to represent], one must always ask oneself: is the word ever actually used in this way in the language-game which is its original home? – What we do is to bring words back from their metaphysical to their everyday use" (p, 116). If we wanted to be really technical about it, we could say that their use is *ontological* rather than *epistemological*, that is, their use is to do with drawing our attention to the fact that, at this moment, we are being confronted by a qualitatively special kind of event, an occurrence of a distinctive kind with its own unique way or mode of *being* in the world. Hence we must approach it or orient towards in a way different from our usual ways, either with different anticipations and expectations, at the ready, or with the expectation that we must undertake an 'exploratory' approach to it. Thus a descriptive concept is global and prospective and open to yet further *internal* articulation, to being internally enriched, so to speak, as a result of our further experiences with the

---

[6] What constitutes a linguistic form as such, Voloshinov (1986) says, "is not at all its self-identity as signal but its *specific variability*" (p. 69) – see my comments above on unities which, although already specified as unities of a certain kind, are still open to further specifications of an already specified kind.

phenomenon in question, while a theoretical concept is retrospectively and definitively defined. "One cannot guess how a word functions," says Wittgenstein (1953). "One has to *look at* its use and learn from that" (p. 340).

What, then, is the special nature of the *dialogical* phenomena we are setting out to study in studying the dialogical? What are their special qualities? Can they be captured in concepts constructed from features defined in terms already well-known to us? Or do they demand the development within ourselves of a new kind of awareness, and thus the noticing of kinds of phenomena not previously noticed?

Clearly, if it really is the case that there is something uniquely special about the dialogical that we feel we haven't yet understood, the first option will not do: Attempting to discover the nature of this special quality by following intellectually devised plans, methods, or procedures will simply result in the continual rediscovery of sameness. For the coordinated execution of planned actions depends upon all concerned sharing, *prior to the execution of the research*, a set of already existing concepts relevant to the formulation of the plan, thus all the new plans will depend on old concepts. As I see it, genuinely innovative changes in a research area need to be 'deep' changes in the sense of changes in our 'ways' of thinking, 'ways' of seeing, of hearing, 'ways' of 'making connections' between events, 'ways' of talking, and so on (Hanson, 1958; Kuhn, 1970)[7]. In short, they are changes in what 'we think with', changes in how we relate to, or orient ourselves towards the situations we find ourselves to be 'in'.

THE CHAPTERS: COMMENTARY

Clearly, the overall task facing the authors in this section is that of exploring challenges to a *dialogical science*, or a *science of the dialogical*. They each have their own specific theme or topic they wish to explore and their own distinctive approach to it. I will therefore comment on each one separately. However, as the first chapter by Michael Billig is distinctive in that, while the other three see their task as being to do with *conceptualizing* dialogical phenomena and thus with creating conceptual frameworks for *scientific* purposes, Billig sees his as setting his concerns within the larger context of our everyday practical concerns. For this reason I will spend more time on Billig's chapter. For, as he sees it, the task is not so much as, say, Haye and Larrain put it, of arriving at "insights for the development of proper discourse analytic tools" (p. 34) for use by a group of professional experts within the boundaries of an academic discipline, but of placing these issues within the much larger context of public discussion and debate. As Rorty (1979) put it now some time ago, rather than seeing knowledge as something arrived at by it being *properly* formulated in theoretical frameworks and arrived at by *proper* scientific methods, we should see "*conversation* as the ultimate context within which knowledge is to be understood" (p. 389).

---

[7] Hanson (1958) notes that "in a growing research discipline, inquiry is directed not by rearranging old facts into more elegant formal patterns, but rather by the discovery of new patterns of explanation... Let us examine not how observation, facts and data are built up into general systems of physical explanation, but how these systems are built into our observations, and our appreciation of facts and data" (p. 2-3). And Hanson goes on to examine the already implicitly *theory-laden* nature of what we take to be the basic facts and data we collect in our inquiries – are we assuming a world of separate particles or a holistic world of an indivisible nature?

Billig: Styles of Writing and the Status of Fictional Things

Michael Billig (2011) is concerned in general with whether a dialogical approach requires a different style of writing than a monological approach, and in particular with the tendency towards 'nominalization', i.e., writing in terms of 'named things' in one's investigations. Straightaway, it is clear that Billig feels no need to conceptualize or theorize the dialogical, as such, in making it clear what he is discussing. He either assumes that a sufficiently clear use of the word, *dialogical*, already exists amongst the community he is addressing, or that it will become clear in the course of his discussion. Similarly for many of the other descriptive terms he uses, such as 'cognitive psychologists', 'critical psychologists', 'dialogical psychologists', 'monological' versus 'dialogical use of language', and so on, we have to look at his use of these and learn from them as his text unfolds. For we already know what he means – don't we? Well in one sense we do but in another we don't.

If we were to insist on unambiguously definitive definitions from the start, then he (and we) would be in trouble, but if we allow that he is offering us global, prospective, *descriptive concepts*, then there is the chance of him articulating them as he goes on with a sufficient degree of precision to complete the task he has in hand. Indeed, as he makes clear towards the end of his chapter, while he has made a special effort to avoid technical terms and passive sentence structures (without eliminating them altogether), his style of writing has been conventional; he has not felt driven to fashion a new, so-called *dialogical* style of writing.

He begins his explorations of whether a different style of writing is required in taking a dialogical approach, rather than a monological one, by noting, most importantly, that "an academic discipline is always more than theory and methodology: it must be written down" (Billig, 2011, p. 3) – a topic not often treated as a topic of crucial importance (but see Bazeman, 1988; Geertz, 1975; Myers, 1990; Shotter, 2008). He then goes on to distinguish between cognitive and dialogical psychologists by claiming, that while cognitive psychologists take an individualistic, information processing approach, "by contrast, critical psychologists, especially discursive psychologists, tend to view human thinking as being rooted in the practical and dialogical use of language" (p. 4), and he himself writes as a discursive psychologist. This means that we must look not at linguistic forms he uses *in themselves*, but at his use of language in its natural 'habitat', so to speak, in relation to its surroundings.

So what is it to *use* language in a practical and a dialogical way? Billig introduces us to it via a discussion of John Locke's and the Earl of Shaftesbury's (virtually Locke's 'foster-son') different writing styles. As he points out, Locke treated the mind as a self-contained entity and assumed that it worked by, passively, receiving impressions through our senses which "agree to the reality of things" (Locke, quoted in Billg, p. 4). The function of language was thus, for Locke, "the means by which we can transfer ideas from one person to another" (p. 5). Locke used the word "idea" for the most basic unit of thought, including in this category every kind of mental *content*, i.e, mental *object*, from concrete sense impressions to abstract intellectual concepts; the crucial feature of an idea for Locke was its ability *represent* something beyond itself – and it was merely the task of language, a secondary task, to represent ideas in a plain and simple, unadorned fashion.

By contrast, claims Billig, Shaftesbury saw language as having the primary task of assessing the validity of our ideas, not merely transmitting them. Our claims to knowledge cannot be accounted as true because they are well founded, but because finally they have been subjected to the courts of public criticism. This, notes Billig (2011), led him to "a dialogical account of mind" (p. 6), an account of how to conduct their own thinking. "Before offering views in public, aspiring authors should conduct internal dialogues. They should divide themselves into separate parties. "Divide yourself" was his advice" (p. 6).

Billig makes three important points about Shaftesbury's style of writing and thinking: (1) that it belongs in an argumentative context and that he sought "to write in a way that expressed the importance of continuing dialogue" (p. 8); (2) that he "wrote rolling sentences, with fine phrases and extensive metaphors [and] much of his writing gains from being read aloud, in order to capture its cadence" (p. 7); and (3) that in it he "was arguing for the priority of practice over theory" (p. 9). These are all extremely important points, but before I comment on them further, I want to turn to what Billig has to say about academic writing and the "nominal style" – a style in which academics "name a whole process by a single nominal [...] [thus to] linguistically turn processes into things" (p. 11) – and also about the use of passive verb forms and metaphorical fictions.

Those who use nominals justify their use by suggesting that they "act as a form of short-hand, enabling academic writers to avoid constantly spelling out in detail exactly what they are referring to" (p. 11), and that such technical terms "are more precise than those of ordinary language" (p. 11). Billig, however, counters both these claims.

He points out that nominalization turns processes that happen over time into already existing things (see James above on "the psychologist's fallacy"). They hide the agent of actions, and in so doing "reify the contingent world, presenting it as being filled with necessary things rather than being created by human actions" (p. 11) – we thus come to (mis)treat ourselves as victims of processes we ourselves have instituted. Further, he points out, once in existence, writers use technical terms in "a variety of different, and often mutually inconsistent, ways" (p. 11) – the very use of the term 'nominalization' being itself a case in point (Billig, 2008b, 2008c). One could also add to Billig's list that fact that they must, of theoretical necessity, refer to context-free elements unrelated to the surroundings within which they occur, and as a consequence, they exclude *the murky tangle of tiny details* of relevance to our understanding the unique meaning of people's utterances in the unique context of their uttering of them. Further, in discussing our use of metaphors in our writing, Billig not only points to their usefulness – I would say, their *inevitable use* (Lakoff & Johnson, 1980; Rorty, 1979; Wittgenstein, 1953) – but also to their dangers if nominalized. For then we end up depicting "a world filled with metaphorical fictions, accomplishing all manner of actions" (Billig, 2011, p. 13), all of which, seemingly, happening, as Karl Marx put it, 'behind our backs'.

As I see it, then, Billig's achievements in this chapter are important ones, but they need to be situated in a very different overall context to that of the other three chapters in this section. Like Locke and Shaftesbury, Billig does not see himself as working to produce *dialogical theories*, nor does he see himself as writing for specialist academic readers, but for more general readers (hence his choice of words and style of writing). Consequently, he has no need of de-contextualized, theoretical terms, his terms are contextualized. He sees himself as writing into the context of an ongoing *debate*, and in *that context*, he sees no difficulty with our uses of technical terms and fictional objects, as such. It is "the closing down of debate" (p. 15) by a group's insistence that only *they* know their *proper use* of a term that he is objecting to.

On this front, there are a couple more comments I would like to make on issues Billig raises. One is that at the very end of his chapter, Billig makes a case for still including Locke's seemingly *monological* insights into the way we, as individuals, look upon and think about our world, into our current discussions about what matters to us in our daily lives. To some, this might seem inimical to everything we are trying to achieve, but in fact, the opposite is the case. Indeed, as Bakhtin (1984) himself makes clear, to place an utterance within an ongoing, multi-voiced conversation – especially into a conversation intertwined in with our everyday practical living with the others around us – is to give that utterance a significant role in our lives, whatever the style of its expression. This is not to say that its style is not important, but it does mean that no utterance can simply be dismissed from our considerations.

Another is, as I noted above, Billig claims that Shaftesbury's writing gains from being read aloud, in order to capture its cadence, but he doesn't say *what* it is that is gained by voicing it aloud. Here I would like to return to my remarks above about living movements – that they have a developmental continuity which allows us to anticipate *possible* next movements. This, I think, can be connected with Bakhtin's (1986) remark, that "from the very beginning, the utterance is constructed while taking into account possible responsive reactions [of others], for whose sake, in essence, it is actually s created [...] The entire utterance is constructed, as it were, *in anticipation of encountering this response*" (p. 94, my emphasis), and, suggests Bakhtin, one can experience (hear) in a speaker's *accenting* or *intoning* of their utterances these anticipations of how another will respond – with agreement, disagreement, reluctant agreement, sympathetic agreement, grudging disagreement, and so on. These anticipations are the 'glue' holding the 'fragments' of an utterance together as a unitary whole; there is no need to suppose that underlying rules, laws, or principles are needed for this task.

Do I, then, in light of the resources I set out at the beginning of this chapter, have any objections to what Billig claims? Yes, I do. As I see it, he still puts far too much emphasis on our use of language in itself, and not enough on its use when intertwined in with other of our much more practical activities within particular practical contexts. He places far too much emphasis on intellectual debate and leaves our everyday collaborative activities out of account. Billig is an academic, and it seems to me, his identity as such affects his ways of seeing things and what he expects of them. As I see it, the issue is not simply the opening up of academic debates – many of which will still remain enclosed within academic seminar rooms – but to provoke many more practical explorations, out in the world of our everyday lives together, of the *relations* between our actual verbal utterances and our practical actions. For the development of our *practical, embodied* understandings in this realm – the capacities we have to understand which are rooted in who we are as practitioners, as nurses, as bankers, as teachers, as doctors, etc., etc. – is an undertaking still in its very beginnings. Billig leaves us still within the ivory (and concrete) towers of academe.

Joerchel: Beginning with Two – Instead of One

Amrei Joerchel (2011) begins her chapter with a quotation from Sloterdijk[8], about the different spaces within which we live – which he calls *spheres* – as always having been taken for granted without ever being made conscious and explicit, and that this has led to our misunderstanding ourselves. This, I think, is a very apposite claim to make in the current context. It is one that I have broached myself in my talk above of what I called our "determining surroundings" (Shotter, 2009). In a sense, we might say that taking a dialogical approach to human behaviour is also to take an ecological approach too, in that, as I suggested in my preliminary remarks above, we need to see all our activities as emerging within the dynamics of an unfolding flow of *intra*-related activities. This is a view that Joerchel herself wants to take, "a view of culture which manifests itself within the interrelatedness of individuals and their environment (Boesch, 1991; Valsiner, 2003)"; a perspective she wants to discuss and elaborate "with the concept of a cultural sphere as inspired by Boesch (1991) and Sloterdijk (1998, 1999, 2004)" (p. 19).

But also, as a kind of way-station in her discussion, she wants to criticize the attempts by Hermans and his colleagues (Hermans & Kempen, 1998; Hermans, 2001a; 2001b; Hermans & Dimaggio, 2007) to conceptualize the relations between dialogical selves and their surrounding culture in terms of "culture positions," for, as she sees it, "revealing and analyzing cultural positions and voices (and not the processes between them) implies the same reification of culture that Hermans and colleagues aim to transcend [...] The habitual processes and intersubjective matrices which constitute the self are lost"[9] (p. 21). She quotes from Hermans and Kempen's (1998) – who seem to suggest that the experience of an artist, say, of Arabic origin working in Germany, can be "conceptualized in terms of two separate *cultural positions* (Arabic and German) that are available and between which the person shifts from time to time" (p. 1118, my emphasis) – and she points out that it is the very conceptualisation of such position as *separate entities* that cuts them off from the larger context in relation to which they have their being.

To overcome the seemingly sharp separation of selves and cultures, she turns to the idea of a *cultural action field* as outlined in psychology by Boesch (1991), who suggests that different actions fields provide different *action opportunities* – an idea clearly consonant with Gibson's (1979) the notion of *affordances* he outlined in his ecological approach to perception. And like Gibson, but following Sloterdijk (1998, 1999, 2004), Joerchel also suggest that individuals come to *resonate* or to be *attuned* to the action opportunities available to them within their current *sphere* of activity.

At this point, it might be relevant to quote Bakhtin's (1986) ideas along the same lines: "Each separate utterance is individual, of course, but each sphere in which language is used," he notes, "develops its own *relatively stable types* of these utterances. These we may call speech genres. The wealth and diversity of speech genres are boundless because the various possibilities of human activity are inexhaustible, and because each sphere of activity contains an entire repertoire of speech genres that differentiate and grow as the particular sphere develops and becomes more complex" (p. 60).

---

[8] http://www.petersloterdijk.net/, March, 2010
[9] See my comments above on "losing the phenomena."

The importance of this, as Joechel notes, is that both the kind of person we can be, a person's *self*, as well as the aspects of culture influencing who we can be, are inseparable and thus mutually constitutive. She sets out to highlight this through the provision of two central exemplifications: the resonance of occurring between two lovers, and the intersubjective intimacy occurring at the beginning of life.

What is special about these kinds of intimate relations – in which, as Bakhtin (1986) puts it, we meet each other "'without rank', as it were" (p. 97) – is that we experience ourselves as 'being in' something larger than ourselves, and thus, not so much exerting our own wills as conforming to the 'calls' coming to us from whatever it is that we are 'in'. "It is this atmosphere of profound trust, the speaker reveals his internal depths," says Bakhtin (1986, p. 97). But what is also very special about an expression of ours in such a sphere, is that "it always creates something that never existed before, something absolutely new and unrepeatable and, moreover, it always has some relation to value (the true, the good, the beautiful, and so forth). But something created is always created out of something given (language, an observed phenomenon of reality, an experienced feeling, the speaking subject himself, something finalized in his world view, and so forth). What is given is completely transformed in what is created" (Bakhtin, 1986, pp. 119-120). Indeed, as well as what Joechel quotes from John Donne's (1896) *The Ecstasy*, she could also have quoted:

He – though he knew not which soul spake,
Because both meant, both spake the same –
Might thence a new concoction take,
And part far purer than he came.

For, as Joechel herself observes, "a very distinct novel space emerges for mother and child or for two lovers due to the resonating processes of one human being with the *vis-à-vis*, this space in turn emerges within a cultural sphere which simultaneously has a history and permanently undergoes restructuring as novel spaces emerge (Sloterdijk, 1999, 2004)" (p. 27). And it is the very novelty – or better, *relevant uniqueness* – of these spaces, and the 'calls' they exert on us to be 'more than we already are', so to speak, 'calls' that are also 'shaped' to an extent by historical and cultural influences, that are of crucial importance in our development.

Joerchel thus introduces us, like Billig, to crucial features of a dialogical approach to our understanding of our own human activities – features which in my estimation are of crucial concern to us. But unlike Billig, there is a continual refrain running through her chapter: it is her concern with how certain theoretical entities *should be conceptualized*. As I see it, this urge to conceptualize continually gives rise to a fundamental *aporia* at the heart of her work in this chapter. While Billig is content to go out into the as yet unfinalized openness of current debate, and to situate his remarks there, Joerchel seems to see herself as in contest with Hermans' and his colleagues' conceptualisations, and to claim that her conceptualisations are better than theirs. The *aporia* in her work, as I see it, is this: if we take her conceptualisations as clear and well-defined they will "cut out and fix, and exclude everything but what we have fixed," in William James's words, and then they will inevitably lead to the very "static and localized notion of culture" (p. 29) of which she accuses Hermans and Kempen, or else they will lead still to an indeterminacy of meaning for which no resolution is possible. In other words, Joerchel does not seem to have felt the need to examine the sources of her own urge *to seek definitive conceptualisations*, she simply seems to take it for granted that this just *is*, or *should be*, the first step in one's inquiries[10].

As I intimated at the outset, I don't think Joerchel is being sufficiently radical in that she is not questioning whether this *is* a necessary starting point for one's inquiries. If we turn to our more practical involvements in everyday life, as Akkerman and Niessen (2011) point out, Dewey (1910) suggested that our need for thought arouse out of a state of perplexity, hesitation, and that our sense of the qualitatively unique nature *that* state should be our proper starting point for our further inquiries – I will examine this further below.

Haye and Larrain: Bakhtin's Notion of 'the Utterance' – A 'Psychological' Cell

Like Joerchel, Haye and Larrain (2011) are also fundamentally concerned with *conceptualizing* central topics within the dialogical approach to human phenomena in ways that "contribute to a theoretical understanding of the dialogical nature of discourse in order to provide insights for the development of proper discourse analytical tools" (p. 34). Like Vygotsky's search for a "single living 'cell'" (1978, p. 8), Haye and Larrain seek "the minimal whole of discursive communication, such that the extra-verbal situation and the affective tones, as essential ingredients of language, are articulated as a unit" (p. 35). Not surprisingly, they find it in Bakhtin's (1986) concept of the utterance.

They then proceed in a very comprehensive fashion to list the provisos that Bakhtin (1986) himself issued against trying to capture the nature of dialogically-structured activities with a formal system. As their list is so complete I will not repeat it here. However, after having outlined his provisos, they go on to comment that his account "is not free from conceptual difficulties and important ambiguities [...] As a matter of fact, Bakhtin's work does not give us a clear and consistent system of well-defined concepts, each with a single and fixed meaning" (Haye & Larrain, 2011, p. 36).

At this point, I'm very tempted to say: Of course not. Providing us with a fixed and unambiguous meaning for all the terms he uses is not Bakhtin's aim at all. His aim is to stimulate us into noticing a whole indefinite range of *possible* features of utterances that might in the circumstances of our concern be of importance to us, and to do this, he uses the concepts he introduces like a 'living' metaphor might be used rather than a 'dead' one. For instance, in suggesting that language is like a city (without mentioning any particular city), Wittgenstein (1953) gives us pause for thought, and we find that we can make use of it in a whole range of different ways to bring to light many otherwise unnoticed properties of possible relevance to us in our inquires. Once a metaphor has become *literalised*, i.e., become a dead metaphor, it ceases to be suggestive in this way; we do not pause for further thought when we, literally, think of the supports of a table as its *legs*. Thus rather than being concerned with the vagueness or ambiguity of Bakhtin's account of the utterance, just as a

---

[10] What Joechel also seems to have been forgotten, or not noticed, as important in Hermans and Kempen's (1993) original work, is the comparison they made between Descartes and Vico, and the importance they attached to Vico's (1744/1968) notion of a "wholly corporeal imagination" (p. 117). "Whereas Descartes was convinced," they say, "of the power of lucid and clear (disembodied) thinking, Vico believed in the power of (embodied) imagination" (p. 7). Indeed, this initial focus on the primacy of bodily activity seems to have been forgotten by all concerned, including Hermans and Kempen.

metaphor can *conceal* something from us as a result of its selective *revealing*, we perhaps need to ask ourselves whether it conceals anything from us in a similar manner, or whether it is adequate to the tasks we face.

As Haye and Larrain see it, their first task is to differentiate, not so much dialogical *uses* of the term 'utterance' from non-dialogical uses, as dialogical *conceptions* from other, not particularly dialogical conceptions of it. And it is this switch in orientation, from Bakhtin's focus on our words in their speaking, as they issue from the living body speaking them, to a focus on a pattern of already spoken words now separated from the body that spoke them, that I find troublesome. For, as Bakhtin himself notes, what makes an utterance *dialogical* is not something that can be categorized objectively, as a separate entity in itself. It is something *in the attitude of the speaker* that gives an utterance its dialogicality, and that as such makes its appearance as a transitory, relational event within an ongoing dialogue that *can be heard* as such by recipients and analysts alike, if they are attuned to it.

Now it is not that Haye and Larrain are unaware of the distinction between words in their speaking, and the patterns discernable in already spoken words. Indeed, they themselves note – in criticizing the attempt "to conceive of the utterance as the event of responding to another *in context*" (p. 38) – that language needs to be "thought of as movement rather than a thing, as a transit rather than a state, as activity rather as potentiality" (p. 38). But although they say this, they continually forget the living body that expresses the language in question, and in consequence, they still slip back, it seems to me, into *thingifying* talk. For instance, they claim that Bakhtin's (1986) emphasis on "the *responsive* quality of discourse does not illuminate how each utterance becomes a link of an 'organised chain of other utterances' (p. 69)" (p. 38). And this leads them to suggest that "for many purposes, this explanation of utterances as active responses does not yet disclose the distinctly dialogical nature of discourse. For it would again be possible to think that single phrases or verbal expressions [...] are [...] basic acts of discourse" (p. 38). What they seem to forget in their search for a consistent system of clear and well-defined concepts, is that, as Bakhtin (1986) points out, "from the very beginning, the utterance is constructed while taking into account possible responsive reactions, for whose sake, in essence, it is actually created [...] From the very beginning, the speaker expects a response from them, an active responsive understanding. *The entire utterance is constructed, as it were, in anticipation of encountering this response*" (p. 94, my emphasis).

Finally, I need to comment on Haye and Larrain's important introduction – like Joerchel's emphasis on Boesch's and Sloterdijk's talk of action spheres – of "fields of interlocution" (p. 78). As I myself pointed out above, they point to both Bakhtin's and Voloshinov's emphasis on the role played by the surrounding extra-verbal situation in shaping our utterances. It does not exert its influence *from the outside* as a separate set of identifiable influences, but *from within* something very like, they say, the space of a game – except, as they quite correctly comment, "the metaphor [of a game] is limited in the sense that, in the case of utterances, the interlocution field is not fixed, as the rules of a game are" (p. 45). But if there are no fixed rules, how is it possible, we might ask, for us ever to arrive at precise sense of the emotional atmosphere pervading a person's utterance or to determine accurately its meaning? The question becomes even more complex if it is the case, as Haye and Larrain say (echoing Voloshinov's comment quoted above, on recognizing an utterance's *novelty*), that "in analysing utterances it is important to focus not on identifying repeatable forms or contents but in discovering their singularity" (p. 48). Haye and Larrain leave these questions dangling, tantalizingly, in the air.

I will return to them below, however, in discussing the importance of Dewey's (1938/2008) account of *qualities*, and the fact that a situation in all its unfolding details is held together as a complex whole by being constituted and characterized throughout by a single, unique quality, a quality that "is sensed or *felt*" (p. 73). And this prompts me to end this section with a comment on whether Bakhtin's account of the utterance works to *conceal* anything from us, whether it is adequate to the tasks we face? Following Bakhtin (1984, 1986), Haye and Larrain speak only of *voices, consciousnesses, speaking personalities* (all of which are, in Billig's terms, *nominalized* entities), but not of that aspect of our experiences that occur on the bodily side, so to speak, of the relational events occurring within the intra-plays within which we are involved as living, responsive, and feelingful bodies – in the literature drawn on by Haye and Larrain, Bakhtin makes little mention of bodily experiences.

Akkerman and Niessen: Beyond Dichotomies to 'Double Descriptions'

Interestingly, precisely some of the concerns I have had with some of the other chapters in this section are explicitly voiced by Akkerman and Niessen in their chapter. While dialogical theories seem capable, on the one hand, of doing justice to the complex nature of reality, they wonder, on the other hand, whether this potential can be realized because of limitations in the "propositional and linguistic characterization of research practice" (p. 55) – its primary limitation being its conduct in terms of a set of dichotomies commonly implied in almost all social science research, such as individual versus social, mind versus matter, and such like, where one in the pair precludes the existence of the other. Whereas, within a dialogical approach, as they see it, "these dichotomies are defined as coexisting only *in relation to* or *in dialogue with* each other" (p. 55, original emphasis).

In Bateson's (1979) terms, when two (or more) sources of 'information' (his term) become entwined in this way, they "give information of a sort different from what was in either source separately" (p. 31) – a phenomenon that he calls of "double description" occurs, and when it does, it gives rise to 'information' of a quite different "logical type"[11] from that in the two (or more) sources producing it. For example, the entwining of the two flows of neural activity issuing from our two eyes in the optic chiasm gives rise to binocular vision; the slight but related *differences* between our two eyes work, not only to improve contrasts and resolution at edges, but much more importantly, to create a sense of *depth*. While depth itself is invisible, what we see when we see 'in depth', is how far or near to us things are *in relation to our bodies*, i.e., how things are arrayed in an inter-related way before in terms of the ease or difficulty of our being able to reach them by our bodily movements. In other words, what Bateson calls information of a different *logical type*, is not information available to us objectively 'out in the world'. It is 'in' the dynamically unfolding relations between ourselves

---

[11] Ryle (1949) gives the following example of what he calls a "category mistake" that can arise out of expecting to encounter facts as if they belonged to one logical type or category (or range of types of categories), when they actually belong to another: "A foreigner visiting Oxford or Cambridge for the first time is shown a number of colleges, libraries playing fields, museums, scientific departments and administrative offices. He then asks 'But where is the University?... It has then to be explained to him that the University... is just the way in which all that he has already seen is organized" (p. 17-18).

and our surroundings; and in the intra-play between our outgoing activities and the incoming responses they occasion we create "relational dimensions" between them, *depth* being just such a relation – and indeed, we talk metaphorically of our dialogues as sometimes having 'depth', as taking us into an extensive 'landscape' of intra-related thoughts and images.

Besides pointing out the need to move from exclusionary dichotomies to dialogical relations between aspects of the phenomena we deal with, Akkerman and Niessen also discuss – in a way that connects with Billig's account of the perils of *nominalization* above – our seeming need "to name aspects of the world as we encounter them to enable us to act in the world in a meaningful manner" (p. 56). About this, as they note, naming is (often) accompanied by 'disambiguation' and that this reduces interpretative alternatives and consequently complexity. Further, while they have found it possible to advance contextual understandings on some occasions within a particular situation at hand, they have found it impossible to adhere consistently and fully to this approach in conducting empirical studies of social phenomena based on dialogical theories – as, presumably, a phenomenon precisely named in one context does not turn up under exactly the same name in another.

Rather than illustrating these difficulties with a piece of their own attempted empirical research, they select an investigation by Raggatt (2000), in which he set out to study the supposedly different narrative identities or voices of a single individual, with his own corresponding attachments and stories to tell. But the trouble is, as they see it, Raggatt's study presented each of the individual's different voices "as a closed unit" (p. 60). Thus, as a result, they say, his work is similar to "the common social scientific approach against which we initially argued and in which units are characterised and defined as separate, as if they have a permanent existence independent of one another. This approach loses sight of all the intermediate *qualitative transformations of the infinite moment-to-moment dynamics*. We do not imply that this is Raggatt's intention. However, we think that somewhere along the line of (empirical) analysis 'meaning as being in motion' became transformed into 'meaning as being fixed'" (p. 60, my emphasis).

I can only comment that this, by now, is a common refrain: the methods commonly employed in social scientific research seem to "lose the very phenomena" that they are meant to clarify.

How might we counter this tendency? Akkerman and Niessen make two suggestions: Referring to a comment of Luria's (1976), that it is easy to mistake social representations for the world as such, they suggest that to redress this misconception, we need to become more open-minded as well as being accountable. In saying this, they follow Bruner (1990), who sees open-mindedness as a willingness to be multi-perspectival in one's understandings, without a loss of commitment to one's own values, and as also making the effort to become conscious of *how we came to* our own knowledge and of the values that have led us to our ways of seeing things – and the expectations we hold regarding them. Their second suggestion takes up Ellen Langer's (1989. 1997) work on mindfulness and creativity, and her claim that both start with uncertainty, with a sense of there being 'something' genuinely novel that is not yet known. And they link this to John Dewey's (1910) similar claim that thinking begins with hesitation, doubt, and perplexity, and they end by suggesting that we "should pay tribute to hesitation and doubt in making sense of the world" (p. 62), and how this can be used productively to advance dialogical research in a manner that is faithful to its ontological assumptions.

I agree with this wholeheartedly, and I will take up this theme – of beginning our inquiries with our disquiets rather than with efforts to construct a conceptual framework that captures what is already well-known to us – in my conclusions section below. But here I need to point out that, yet again, although they mention the need to be *accountable* Akkerman and Niessen do not follow up in any sustained way what paying tribute to doubt and hesitation in one's inquires would actually look like, sound like, and feel like. They do not describe how their suggestions would, in fact, radically change the actual practical conduct of our inquiries, how starting from felt disquiets would give rise to a very different kind of investigation from starting with a conceptual system or framework.

CONCLUSION: FROM CONCEPTUAL FRAMEWORKS TO FELT DISQUIETS WITHIN ARENAS OF LIVING ACTIVITY

"In my beginning is my end,"
(T.S. Eliot, *East Coker*)

Above, then, we have seen both the dangers of fragmentation and of losing the very phenomena we think of ourselves as inquiring into. What is evident in reading all these chapters, is that for all the authors what is there in the background – the reality within which we live our lives which they all draw on in formulating their claims – is something which, oxymoronically, we must describe as both vague but very specific. Its specificity provides them with standards against which they can continually measure the adequacy of their formulations, the comprehensiveness of their claims, the accuracy of their conceptualisations, and so on; but it is its vagueness – its multi-dimensional complexity – which allows it to be verbally formulated in a multiplicity of different ways in different situations. However, there seems to be a tension between this multi-dimensional complexity and our urge to seek clear and unambiguous formulations from within which to conduct our inquiries. Do we always need to begin our inquiries in *this* manner?

In wanting to "begin our study of the mind from within" (James, 1890/1950, p. 224), William James was well aware that, in introducing his metaphor of *the stream of thought*, he was introducing something very vague. Indeed, it is "the re-instatement of the vague to its proper place in our mental life which I am so anxious to press on the attention," he said (p. 254). But he thought the claim "that we can have no images but of perfectly definite things" (p. 254) in traditional psychology was ridiculous. "The traditional psychology," he said, "talks like one who should say a river consists of nothing but pailsful, spoonsful, quartpotsful, barrelsful, and other moulded forms of water. Even were the pails and the pots all actually standing in the stream, still between them the free water would continue to flow. It is just this free water of consciousness that psychologists resolutely overlook. Every definite image in the mind is steeped and dyed in the free water that surrounds it. With it goes the sense of its relations, near and remote, the dying echo of whence it came, the dawning sense of whither it is to lead. The significance, the value, of the image is all in this halo or penumbra that surrounds and escorts it" (p. 255).

It is the very vagueness of the metaphor of the stream provides a cornucopia of possibilities, each of which suggesting something of importance to consider in our attempt to study our minds from within. Akkerman and Niessen quote Valsiner and Van der Veer's (2000) comment that "appropriating [Bakhtin's] ideas has enriched contemporary social sciences theoretically, while leaving them baffled as to the kind of empirical work that needs to follow (p. 390)" (p. 58). No doubt similar comments were made years ago about the irrelevance of William James' work – particularly what he had to say about *the stream of thought* – to empirical studies in social science. But the bafflement arises, as I see it, from the fact that traditional psychologists are still unprepared to adopt the study of mental phenomena *from within*, and stay resolutely resolved to study it *from the outside*.

It is at this point that I would like to return to Akkerman and Niessen's reference to Dewey, and to their suggestion that we should make room for doubt and hesitation in our investigations.

In his *Logic: The Theory of Inquiry*, Dewey (1938/2008) points out that, while psychological theories take "a *singular* object or event for the subject matter of its analysis. In actual experience, there is never any such isolated singular object or event; *an* object or event is always a special part, phase, or aspect, of an environing experienced world – a situation" (p. 72). In other words, as I mentioned above, each unique situation we occupy is held together as a complex unity by the fact that it pervaded throughout by a single quality, a global bodily sense of the situation we are in. It is the uniqueness or singularity of this pervasive quality that is of crucial importance to us in our inquiries. Thus, as Dewey (1938/2008) sees it, "discourse that is not controlled by reference to a situation is not discourse, just as a mass of pied type is not a font much less a sentence. A universe of experience is a precondition of a universe of discourse. Without its controlling presence, there is no way to determine the relevancy, weight, or coherence of any designated distinction or elation" (p. 74). Further, it is only as a result of our "sensitivity to the quality of a situation as a whole" that a problem as such can be grasped as the problem it is; "in ordinary language, a problem must be felt before it can be stated" (p. 76).

Thus strangely, instead of beginning our investigations by trying to form systematic theories or conceptual frameworks – which as Dewey sees it are so "fixed in advance that the very things which are genuinely decisive in the problem in hand and its solution, are completely overlooked" (p. 76) – we should begin our inquiries by being prepared to go 'into' our perplexities and uncertainties, 'into' our feelings of disquiet at what we already know, 'into' our confusions and bewilderments. And this is where our *descriptive concepts* have a crucial role to play, for in guiding what we look for and pay attention to, they can *direct* and *organise* our explorations in such a way that we can begin to 'find our way about' within them, and thus the guidance we need in overcoming our disquiets. As Dewey (1938/2008) puts it, "the peculiar quality of what pervades the given materials, constituting them a situation, is not just uncertainty at large; it is a unique doubtfulness which makes that situation to be just and only the situation it is. It is this unique quality that not only evokes the particular inquiry engaged in but that exercises control over its special procedures" (p. 109).

Briefly, we can see that what Dewey is proposing here is very different from what we might call *theory-driven* research currently popular in scientific psychology. As we have seen, this kind of research works in terms of explicitly identifiable entities, stated in unambiguous, context-free terms, related to each other in terms of specific rules or laws within a systematic, causal framework, that holds true in all places at all times – in short, it works in terms of *generalisations* and *idealisations*. And it is popular because it is aimed at informing us of the specific interventions we need to make to cause the specific changes we desire. Clearly, what

I have called *relational events* – events that only have their existence in the unfolding, dynamic relations between our outgoing bodily activities and their incoming results – seemingly, play no part in such a form of research. But equally clearly, a major disadvantage in this kind of research practice is that what is excluded, the situational details that are lost in its generalisations and theoretical idealisations still remain to influence events in practice – but now in an unaccountable and unaccounted for manner.

We can call the kind of inquiry Dewey (1938/2008) outlines (which I have supported in this chapter), practice-situated or situation-specific research. As he terms it, this kind of "inquiry is the controlled or directed transformation of an indeterminate situation into one that is so determinate in its constituent distinctions and relations as to convert the elements of the original situation into a unified whole" (p. 108). Or, in more everyday terms, it aims at turning a bewildering situation into one in which we can feel 'at home' and no longer feel 'lost'. So, although Dewey talks of overcoming *problems*, as I mentioned at the outset, overcoming a difficulty of this kind does not primarily involve *problem-solving*, it involves more "a working on oneself [...] On one's way of seeing things. (And what one expects of them)" (Wittgenstein, 1980, p. 16), on one's way or ways of *relating* or of *orienting* oneself to one's surroundings (Shotter, 2010a). As Wittgenstein (1953) puts it, the difficulty one faces initially "has the form: 'I don't know my way about'" (no. 123), and when one does become oriented, then one can exclaim: "Now I can go on" (no. 154).

This, then, is a kind of research conducted within specific arenas or spheres of practical activity with the aim of resolving specific confusions, disquiets, bewilderments, perplexities, etc., within them – it is not aimed at results of a general kind. I have explored this kind of practice-based action research extensively elsewhere (Shotter, 2005, 2006, 2007, 2008, 2009, 2010a and 2010b), so I will not go into its nature further here. Suffice it to say that in most of our everyday practical exchanges with those around us, the difficulties we face are not theoretical difficulties, difficulties to do with explaining the causes of their behaviour. The difficulties we face in understanding a person's utterances are not a matter of our solving problems, of 'working out' what the words they address to us 'add up' to; they are orientational issues: we need to move from being 'all at sea' to knowing 'how to go on' with them. We need to develop within ourselves – in the course of our talk with them – the appropriate embodied anticipations that will allow us to exhibit to them the responsive understandings they expect. Science is aimed at manipulating things, not at understanding them 'from within'. It makes its own idealised abstractions of 'things' and operates upon these static, dead, and completed 'objects', trying to effect whatever changes are permitted by their definition. But, as William James (1909/1996) commented long ago, "logic being the lesser thing, the static incomplete abstraction, must succumb to reality, not reality to logic. Our intelligence cannot wall itself up alive, like a pupa in its chrysalis. It must at any cost keep on speaking terms with the universe that engendered it" (p. 207). And we can do this if we can discover how reorient ourselves from wanting to work from within conceptual frameworks to solve problems, to working within arenas of living activity to resolve disquiets.

REFERENCES

Akkerman, S. & Niessen, T. (2011). Dialogical theories at the boundary. In M. Märtsin, B. Wagoner, E. L. Aveling, I. Kadianaki, & L. Whittaker (Eds.), *Dialogicality in focus: Challenges to theory, method and application* (pp. 53-64). New York: Nova Science Publishers.

Bakhtin, M. M. (1981). *The dialogical imagination.* (M. Holquist, Ed., C. Emerson and M. Holquist, Trans.). Austin, TX: University of Texas Press.

Bakhtin, M. M. (1984). *Problems of Dostoevsky's poetics.* (C. Emerson, Ed. and Trans.). Minneapolis: University of Minnesota Press.

Bakhtin, M. M. (1986). *Speech genres and other late essays.* (V. W. McGee, Trans.). Austin, TX: University of Texas Press.

Bakhtin, M. M. (1993). *Toward a philosophy of the act.* (V. Lianpov, Trans. and notes, M. Holquist, Ed.). Austin, TX: University of Texas Press.

Bateson, G. (1979). *Mind and nature: A necessary unity.* London: Fontana/Collins.

Bazerman, C. (1988). *Shaping written knowledge: The genre and activity of the experimental article in science.* Madison: University of Wisconsin Press.

Billig, M. (2008b). The language of critical discourse analysis: The case of nominalization. *Discourse & Society, 19,* 783-800.

Billig, M. (2008c). Nominalizing and de-nominalizing: A reply. *Discourse & Society, 19,* 829-841.

Billig, M. (2011). Dialogical writing and dialogical theory: Reflections on Locke, Shaftesbury and fictional things. In M. Märtsin, B. Wagoner, E. L. Aveling, I. Kadianaki, & L. Whittaker (Eds.), *Dialogicality in focus: Challenges to theory, method and application* (pp. 3-18). New York: Nova Science Publishers.

Boesch, E. E. (1991). *Symbolic action theory and cultural psychology.* Berlin: Springer-Verlag.

Bruner, J. (1990). *Acts of meaning.* London: Harvard University Press.

Dewey, J. (1910). *How we think.* Mineola, NY: Dover.

Dewey, J. (1938/2008). *Logic: The theory of inquiry.* In *Vol.12 of The later works, 1925-1953.* (J. A. Boyston, Ed.). Carbondale, IL: Southern Illinois Press.

Garfinkel, H. (2002). *Ethnomethodology's program: Working out Durkheim's aphorism.* (A. Warefield Rawls, Ed. And Intro.). New York & Oxford: Rowman & Littlefield Publishers.

Geertz, C. (1973). *The interpretation of cultures.* New York: Basic Books.

Hanson, N. R. (1958). *Patterns of discovery.* Cambridge: Cambridge University Press.

Haye, A. & Larrain, A. (2011). What is an utterance? In M. Märtsin, B. Wagoner, E. L. Aveling, I. Kadianaki, & L. Whittaker (Eds.), *Dialogicality in focus: Challenges to theory, method and application* (pp. 33-52). New York: Nova Science Publishers.

Hermans, H. J. M. (2001a). The dialogical self: Toward a theory of personal and cultural positioning. *Culture & Psychology, 7*(3), 243-281.

Hermans, H. J. M. (2001b). Mixing and moving cultures require a dialogical self. *Human Development, 44,* 24-28.

Hermans, H. J. M., & Kempen, H. J. G. (1993). *The dialogical self: Meaning as movement.* San Diego, CA: Academic Press.

Hermans, H. J. M. & Kempen, H. J. G. (1998). Moving cultures: The perilous problems of cultural dichotomies in a globalizing society. *American Psychologist, 53*(10), 1111-1120.

Hermans, H. J. M. & Dimaggio, G. (2007). Self, identity, and globalisation in times of uncertainty: A dialogical analysis. *Review of General Psychology, 11*(1), 31-61.

Honner, J. (1987). *The description of nature: Niels Bohr and the philsophy of physics.* Oxford: Clardendon Press.

James, W. (1890/1950). *Principles of psychology,* Vols. *1 & 2.* London: Macmillan.

James, W. (1909/1996). *A pluralistic universe: Hibbert lectures at Manchester College on the present situation in philosophy.* Lincoln and London: University of Nabraska Press. (original work first published 1909).

Joerchel, A. C. (2011). Locating the dialogical self within a cultural sphere. In M. Märtsin, B. Wagoner, E. L. Aveling, I. Kadianaki, & L. Whittaker (Eds.), *Dialogicality in focus: Challenges to theory, method and application* (pp. 19-32). New York: Nova Science Publishers.

Kuhn, T. S. (1970). *The structure of scientific revolutions, 2nd edition, enlarged.* Chicago, IL: University of Chicago Press.

Lakoff, G., & Johnson, M. (1980) *Metaphors we live by.* Chicago: University of Chicago Press.

Langer, E. J. (1989). *Mindfulness.* Cambridge, MA: Perseus Books.

Langer, E. J. (1997). *The power of mindful learning.* Cambridge, MA: Perseus Books.

Luria, A. R. (1976). *Cognitive development: Its cultural and social.* Cambridge, MA: Harvard University Press.

Myers, G. (1990). *Writing biology: Texts in the social construction of scientific knowledge.* Madison, WI: University of Wisconsin Press.

Newell, A. (1973). You can't play twenty questions with nature and win. In W. G. Chase (Ed.), *Visual information processing* (pp. 283-306). New York: Academic Press,

Raggatt, P. T. F. (2000). Mapping the dialogical self: Towards a rationale and method of assessment. *European Journal of Personality, 14,* 65–90.

Rorty, R. (1979). *Philosophy and the mirror of nature.* Oxford: Blackwell.

Ryle, G. (1949). *The concept of mind.* London: Methuen.

Sloterdijk, P. (1998). *Sphären I: Blasen.* [Spheres I: Bubbles.] Frankfurt: Suhrkamp.

Sloterdijk, P. (1999). *Sphären II: Globen.* [Spheres II: Globes.] Frankfurt: Suhrkamp.

Sloterdijk, P. (2004). *Sphären III: Schäume.* [Spheres III: Foams.] Frankfurt: Suhrkamp.

Shotter, J. (2005). Inside processes: Transitory understandings, action guiding anticipations, and withness thinking. *International Journal of Action Research, 1*(1), 157-189.

Shotter, J. (2006). Understanding process from within: An argument for 'withness'-thinking. *Organization Studies, 27*(4), 585-604.

Shotter, J. (2007). Inside the moment of thinking and speaking: "The quiet weighing of linguistic facts." *Review of Contemporary Philosophy, 6,* 194-223.

Shotter, J. (2008). Embodiment, abduction, and difficulties of orientation: On coming to feel 'at home' in the world. *History and Philosophy of Psychology, 10*(2), 27-39.

Shotter, J. (2009). Perplexity: *Preparing* for the happening of change. In S. Lowe (Ed.), *A guide to the perplexed manager* (pp.135-176). London: Sage.

Shotter, J. (2010a). Movements of feeling and moments of judgement: Towards an ontological social constructionism. *International Journal of Action Research, 6*(1), 1-27.

Shotter, J. (2010b). Dialogical dynamics: Inside the moment of speaking. In J. Streek (Ed.) *New adventures in language and interaction* (pp.256-269). Amsterdam & Philadelphia: John Benjamins Publishing Co.

Taylor, C. (1971). Interpretation and the sciences of man. *Review of Metaphysics, 34,* 1-51.

Valsiner, J. (2003). Culture and its transfer: Ways of creating general knowledge through the study of cultural particulars. In W. J. Lonner, D.L. Dinnel, S. A. Hayes, & D. N. Sattler (Eds.), *Online readings in psychology and culture* (Unit 2, Chapter 12), (http://www.wwu.edu/~culture), Center for Cross-Cultural Research, Western Washington University, Bellingham, Washington USA.

Valsiner, J., & Van der Veer, R. (2000). *The social mind. Construction of the idea.* Cambridge: Cambridge University Press.

Voloshinov, V. N. (1986). *Marxism and the philosophy of language.* (L. Matejka and I.R. Titunik, Trans.). Cambridge, MA: Harvard University Press. (Original work first published 1929).

Vygotsky, L. S. (1978). *Mind in society: The development of higher psychological processes.* (M. Cole, V. John-Steiner, S. Scribner, and E. Souberman, Eds.) Cambridge, MA: Harvard University Press.

Vygotsky, L. S. (1986). *Thought and language.* (A. Kozulin, Trans.). Cambridge, MA: MIT Press.

Vygotsky, L. S. (1987). *Thinking and speech.* In *The collected works of L. S. Vygotsky: Vol. 1.* (R. W. Rieber and A. S. Carton, Eds, N. Minick, Trans.). New York: Plenum Press.

Wittgenstein, L. (1953). *Philosophical investigations.* (G.E.M. Anscombe, Trans.). Oxford: Blackwell.

Wittgenstein, L. (1980). *Culture and value.* (G. Von Wright, Intro., P. Winch, Trans.). Oxford: Blackwell.

Wittgenstein, L. (1981). *Zettel, 2nd Edition.* (G.E.M. Anscombe and G.H.V. Wright, Eds.). Oxford: Blackwell.

PART II: REFLECTIONS ON DIALOGICAL METHODOLOGIES

In: Dialogicality in Focus   ISBN: 978-1-61122-817-5
Editors: M. Märtsin, B. Wagoner, E.-L. Aveling et al.   © 2011 Nova Science Publishers, Inc.

Chapter 5

REPAIRING RUPTURES:
MULTIVOCALITY OF ANALYSES

Brady Wagoner, Alex Gillespie, Jaan Valsiner, Tania Zittoun,
João Salgado, Livia Simão

INTRODUCTION

Dialogical thinkers have long known that consciousness is a kind of irreversible flow that passes through similar (but not identical) positions; yet, the methodological tools to analyse these complexities have not been wholly adequate. Analytic strategies need to be developed that demonstrate both how to identify positions and analyze their spatial/temporal relationships. To this end, the present chapter aims to concretely explore researchers' reasoning in conducting a dialogical analysis of intra-psychological discourse. Six researchers were given the task of independently carrying out a dialogical analysis of Angel's (1985) stream-of-consciousness short story *The Guerrillero* (see Appendix A).

The main object of the text is the narrator – a woman named Felicidad Mosquera. Felicidad is both the thinker and that which is thought about, she is knower and known, subject and object—in short, what James (1890) called the 'I' and the 'Me'. But we also find in Felicidad's stream of thought a number of significant others, such as her lover, her tormenters, and their previous victims (i.e. "Him" and "Them") which Felicidad can use to reflect on herself. Thus, Felicidad's stream of thought is replete with I-positions and dialogical tensions between them.

The plot of the story is very simple: in the context of a civil war, a woman is expecting some soldiers who might abuse her for having hosted a rebel fighter, the Guerrillero. The text narrates her experience of inner change, from a state of strong panic when thinking of being searched by soldiers, through a recollection of her amorous experiences with the Guerrillero, to a heroic state of great calm and readiness in the face of whatever is awaiting her.

How can we analyze these profound intra-psychological movements from a dialogical perspective? In what follows five approaches are advanced. These approaches were first developed for a symposium at the *Fifth International Conference for the Dialogical Self*.

They have since been revised, shortened and brought together for the present chapter. They are followed by a discussion and a conclusion, which bring the approaches into dialogue and reflect on the exercise of conducting multiple independent analyses of the same text.

THE I, THE ME AND THE OTHER
IN THE STREAM OF THOUGHT
ALEX GILLESPIE

This analysis has two stages. First, the text was analysed to identify active I-positions. Second, the dialogical relations between these I-positions were analysed in order to understand Felicidad's transition from fear to defiance.

Identifying I-positions

1. The Narrating 'I'

Although the text is very dialogical, it is narrated by one person throughout—that is, Felicidad. Her stream of thought moves from a state of panic and fear about torture, toward a calmer, more confident position, in which she prepares to open her door and look her assailants in the eyes.

2. Me in the Past

There are two versions of Felicidad's past self. First, there is the self that fell in love with the Guerrillero, and thus got her into her predicament. This past self is described as naïve: too helpful, too concerned, and too sympathetic to the Guerrillero and his plight. But, the love experienced by this former self is described in authentic terms. Second there is the past self that is described as "cool-headed" and having a "watchful heart". This more cautious past self would "never let" herself become "trapped" in such a predicament. Arguably this "cool-headed" self prevails within the text and becomes the narrating 'I' at the end of the text.

3. Me in the Present

The self in the present refers not to the narrating 'I', but to the self in the situation described by the narrating 'I'. This self is described as crying, fearful, moaning, cursing, and moving furniture to block the door.

4. Me in the Future

The future self is a space of imaginative possibility that remains unfixed. It shifts from initially being tortured and raped and thus confessing the whereabouts of her lover, to a more defiant stance, in which despite being tortured, she does not confess. The final emergent future self is cool-headed, confident and unflustered.

5. *Counterfactual Me*

The counterfactual 'Me' is Felicidad's imagination of her situation had she not fallen in love with the Guerrillero. This is an unrealised self, which is a wishful escape from the predicament.

6. *"Him"*

The representation of "Him," the Guerrillero, is quite constant. He was in a predicament when she found him in her house. She helped him and found him to be handsome. He helped her with the firewood and the water pump. They fell in love. Their relationship is passionate and authentic. He is not only in the past, he is also in the future, and in the future he moves from originally being betrayed by her, to not being betrayed and thus being able to fight on.

7. *"They"*

"They" will "arrive with their machetes". "They" will potentially burn her hands, slice her open and/or rape her. The belief that "they're coming" provides the rupture, which motivates the stream of thought. Although their violence is constant, their knowledge about her relationship to the Guerrillero changes.

Initially, Felicidad assumes that they know what has happened: that is why they will be "asking you where in hell he has hidden himself". It is assumed that they know that she knows, and because of their violent means, "they'll force you to betray him". Then she realises that they cannot know. The reason they will be saying that they know is to try and scare her into telling.

8. *Previous Victims*

Felicidad refers to three specific victims: Celta lost her parents; Calixta had her hands put in a fire, and Prospero's wife who was found dead in a well sliced open. She also refers to the others in general who have been raped and who have had their houses burnt down. Although these victims are in the past, they are relevant for Felicidad's own future because she fears becoming like them.

Analysing the Transition

The stream of thought can be analysed in terms of two basic movements (depicted in Figures 1 and 2, respectively). Initially Felicidad is engrossed in her future 'Me'—images of what has happened to other victims blends with the future 'Me'. The belief is that "They" (the torturers) are coming, that "They" know what has happened, and that "They" will torture her into confessing. This leads her to lament her past, and her actions with "Him," the Guerrillero. Her counterfactual self, which does not have to contend with machetes, arises at several choice points: (a) She could have gone with the Guerrillero when he left, (b) she could have made him say good bye on the night they met, (c) she could have said good bye to him once he had healed, (d) she could have noticed that she was falling in love, (e) she could have chosen not to go with him on the fateful walk that ignited her desire for him.

The second movement of thought grows out of the memories of being with her lover associated with the lament. Felicidad realises that nobody could actually know what happened in the fields, and that their relationship is a secret and will only become public if she confesses. Her resolve strengthens due to her desire to protect him, her belief that her assailants might be calling her bluff, and the belief that so long as she does not confess "He" will fight on. "They can search your very innards, cut you in two with their machetes, drill into your senses, pierce your heart, they will find nothing."

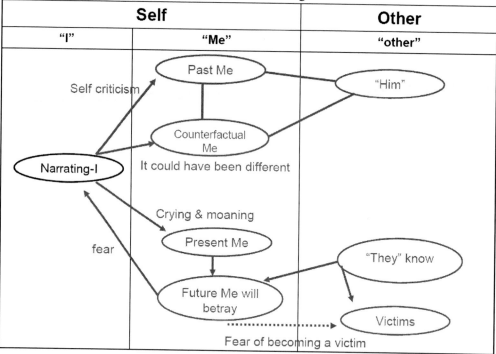

Figure 1. The rupture and lament.

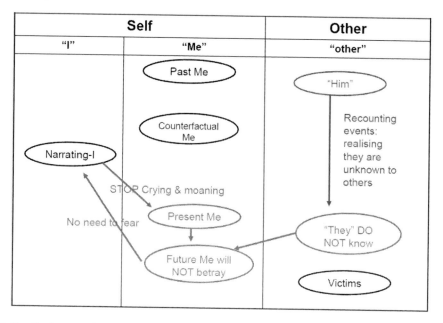

Figure 2. Realisation, resolve and self-regulation.

The realisation leads to a reconstruction of the situation. Initially "They" were thought to know what happened; now "They" are re-represented as not knowing. Initially her betrayal of the Guerrillero is seen as inevitable, then it becomes within her control. As these thoughts are integrated, they lead to a plan of action, and a new resolve. The narrative 'I' takes control, and directs Felicidad in the present, encouraging her not to cry and moan, and not to block the door. Instead, the self-regulatory process encourages her to open the door and look her assailants in the eyes. "Don't cry and moan any more. Open the door yourself. Stand upright in the doorway. Hold their eyes."

From this analysis we see that not only are there I/Me dynamics, which are essential to this dialogical stream, but that "others" (or more specifically others-within-self) are essential to that stream as well. The stream of thought begins with the thoughts attributed to others and reaches its major turning point through the reconstruction of those attributions (namely that "They" don't know what happened).

DOUBLE DIALOGICALITY –
THE SELF SURROUNDING ITSELF
JAAN VALSINER

The dialogical self is dynamic—yet structured. The introspective short story allows us to glimpse into the ways in which the dialogical process moves, which entails rapid movement through loops, between I-positions, that are constructed as the flow of experience moves ahead.

The 'bare story' of an ordinary encounter between Her and Him is very simple:

He looks at her
He asks her for salt
She puts salt in his hand
His hand barely touches hers

This is just the mundane everyday act of passing the salt. Yet the short story writer narrates it differently—with extensions (from *The Guerrillero*, p. 119):

I can't understand. *Felicidad Mosquera*,
I don't recognize *you* any longer.
I never thought *you*'d change this fast,
Go from black to white, as you did,
from one day to the other.
Because the trembling you felt
when he looked at you with his dark eyes
or the stammering, like a little girl
when he asked for the salt
and barely touched you with his fingers
as you put it in his hand,
everything in you turned upside-down

the current changed, your cables crossed
so how in *God*'s name *didn't you* notice it?
So the internal domain of the story is constructed here:

He looks at her	She trembles
He asks her for salt	She stammers
She puts salt in his hand	She feels everything turned upside down
His hand barely touches hers	

This is merely the subjective meaning-making counterpart of what happened—not yet indicative of any aspect of the dialogical self. To get to the dialogical self, we need to see how the external (events) and the internal (feelings) become related through reflexivity. Reflexivity rises above the event<>experience relationship, constituting a meta-level (Figure 3). This reflexivity requires semiotic mediation—that is, signs of various kinds.

Note that reflexivity is constructed by the Self, not by the Other(s). Of course, it is through the myriad of social suggestions by the Other(s) that particular forms of reflexivity are made available. Types of attributions (e.g. *"he made me* tremble" versus *"I started to tremble* because of him" etc.) are directed by such suggestions.

The reflexivity entails a scenario where the *internal becomes external* so as to make it possible to examine the internal—by taking MYSELF-OUTSIDE-MYSELF (ME→ YOU-as-ME→ ME) as position, or emphasizing what the OTHER did to MYSELF. This is done by constructing voices ("I say...", "you say"... "X says") that create temporarily fixed I-positions.

Again from *The Guerrillero* (p. 119):

I-position *move*	*Voiced* dialogicality
ME→ OUT→ ME	*I* can't understand. *Felicidad Mosquera,*
ME→ OUT→ ME	*I* don't recognize *you* any longer.
ME→ OUT→ ME	*I* never thought *you*'d change this fast,
ME→ ME	Go from black to white, as you did, from one day to the other.
ME→ ME	Because the trembling you felt
ME→ OTHER→ ME	when he looked at you with his dark eyes or the stammering, like a little girl
ME→ OTHER→ME	when he asked for the salt and barely touched you with his fingers
ME→ OTHER	as you put it in his hand,
ME→ ME	everything in you turned upside-down the current changed, your cables crossed
ME→OUT→ME	so how in *God*'s name *didn't you* notice it?

The important focus is that of projecting the ME into the same role outside of the "inside self" as the Other. Thus, in *"I don't recognize you* any longer" the "I" and "you" are the same, yet they become distinguished as Subject (I) and Object (you). The voice of "I" emerges to relate to "you."

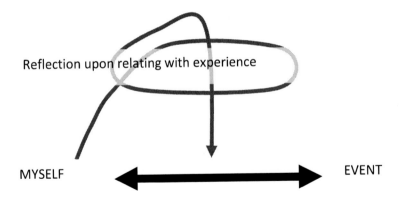

Figure 3. Reflexivity in event<>experience relation.

Transitory Nature of I-positions

So we have a Self-system in which an I-position can be momentarily transferred from inside to outside to make it possible for the self to reflect upon itself ('self mirror'). This reflection entails use of *hypergeneralized affective sign fields* (Valsiner, 2007). These fields emerge in the hierarchy of meaning-making as a result of the process of generalization where the generalized signs 'take over' the whole of the personal culture and give it affective framing. The person feels meaningfully towards some object—and that feeling is total. Through such signs the fluidity of the ongoing relation of the self to the event is both clarified and maintained. The best existing example in psychology is the phenomenon of values.

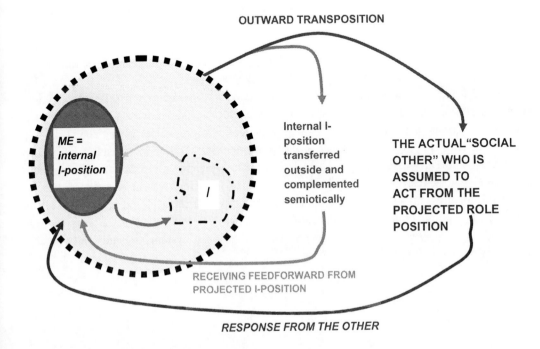

Figure 4. The trialogical self (after G. H. Mead).

Specifically, what is the function of "don't recognize" and "any longer". It is a backward-oriented account which has the function of forward-oriented regulation – "I used to, but no more". In the RECOGNIZE◇non-recognize duality of meaning the priority relation reverses (recognize◇NON-RECOGNIZE), as it is mapped on the distinction within irreversible time. These distinctions are made dynamically within coordination of three dialogical loops (Figure 4)—compare also with Figure 3 and 'I-position moves' chart above.

In Conclusion: Double Redundancy

The flexibility of the dialogical self system is guaranteed by double redundancy. The first redundancy is the *rapid movement* of I-positions between locations (inner/outer self domains—in Hermans' 2002 terms). That rapid movement, like a human gaze in observing visual images, guarantees that there is necessarily *dialogicality in time*. No previous I-position location is ever re-visited (even if it is similar, it is not the same). Integration of I-positions—Present and Future—is immediately unfolding (*A →moving into →B*, rather than discretely oppositional—*A in contrast to B*) in the process of experiencing. This is a contrast between methods of looking at I-positions that pre-construct these as discrete positions ("you now" vs. "you 5 years from now"). The functioning of the Dialogical Self is in a flow—perhaps best captured by Marková's (1990) three-step process—not in contradictions between static given positions.

The second redundancy is in at least _two_ 'social others'—the externally transposed inner position, and actual other person (Figure 4). The internal I-position (itself a double—of ME◇I loop) faces in parallel two 'mirrors'—which may enter into dialogical relation between themselves, as well as with the internal position. In that 'triangle' the lack of one component, out of three, does not eliminate dialogicality (the other person may be absent if the externalized inner I-position creates contrast with the ME◇I system). The ME◇I system is never absent. It feeds the constant movement of the externalized I-position. The 'inner self' becomes surrounded by two kinds of 'social others'—externalized and generalized internal I-positions, and actual other people who reflect upon the person.

So, the I-positions move and move rapidly if need be, thanks to self-reflexivity which becomes possible through such moves, as well as enables further moves. Voices create the flow of I-positions, a relationship that in time generates more voices. The 'core self'—a maintained status quo of the system—is *in that movement* (rather than in any static entity 'in' the person), and can be seen in Felicidad falling in love against all odds for no externally specifiable "causal reasons". So we become fascinated with fugitives or with the riches of boring millionaires, or with symbolic expressions of power, property, and propriety—all in the same way—to feed into our dynamic self-system. *The very social and very Dialogical Self is thus deeply egocentric*—and that egocentricity (as an open system) depends fully on the social world.

RUPTURES AND RESOURCES IN MOVEMENT
TANIA ZITTOUN

The text, as flow of consciousness, can be read as a transformative process after an experience of rupture. It can be treated as a semiotic process of sense making – involving linking, distancing from, and transforming embodied and/or cultural experiences. I work with the idea that such processes can be analyzed along four dimensions: their time-space orientation; their identity positioning; the degree of belief in the 'reality' of an event; and finally, the distance one takes towards that experience. The narrator's position can thus be studied as it follows a trajectory in a space organized by these dimensions. This allows me to identify the role of semiotic resources in such trajectory changes.

A Psychological Rupture

The reader realises that, throughout the text, Felicidad changes position and state of mind. This change is crystallised in the first and last three lines of the text. Comparing them suggests a change in the *subjective relational position* of Felicidad facing the immediate future – that is, the arrival of armed forces looking for the Guerrillero hidden by her. Felicidad moved from fear, shame and passivity in beginning of the text, to pride and self-assurance at the end. This change is here considered a semiotic elaboration, provoked by a rupture in Felicidad's life (i.e. her relationship to the Guerrillero). This is an intra-psychological rupture expressed in the conflict between two I-positions (narrator and 'you'— or 'I' and 'Me'). The events of the rupture also change Felicidad's relationship to others and social reality.

If the relationship to the Guerrillero is the rupture, then the position of 'fear' expressed at the beginning of the text, is an immediate result of contemplating this rupture—its social meaning, and its possible consequences. In this respect, the position of 'pride', at the end of the text, is the result of a semiotic elaboration of the *personal sense* of this rupture (Zittoun, 2006). The text is hence the means and the externalisation of the transition process (from this to that position) and the language is the semiotic operator of this transformation.

Four Dimensions

The text is constructed as a narrator addressing a 'you', both being part of the same person—Felicidad. These two 'voices' are themselves not static. As the text progresses, they evolve through different positions. I propose to organise these movements along four dimensions:

1. *The (social) position of the narrator*: Positions of the narrator can be seen as representing various I-positions (Hermans, 2002), that is, internalised voices of relevant social others, as well as forms of radical otherness ("They" of the soldiers; "He" of the Guerrillero);
2. The *time-space* of the scene in which "you" is located (in the past, present or future);

3. The *degree of reality* of the scene depicted: *what did happen* is real; *what would have happened if* is counterfactual, that is, imaginary; *what will happen* is undetermined;

4. The *degree of distancing* ranging from just above the subconscious (below semiotic elaboration), to the embodied, here-and-now experience, to more descriptive or factual, images, to more diffused, values or emotional tones ('hyperconscious' in Valsiner, 2007). These are marked by the use of different semantic fields, some being at the level of organic event – trembling, blood, membranes, muscles – others at the level visual descriptions, while still others are at the level of good/bad values, suggested by mentions of signs of God and Devil.

Movements of the Text

The goal of my analysis is to understand how this rupture is elaborated. To do this, I identified the main movements of the text, and characterised the *semiotic operators* of change.

The text can be decomposed in seven parts on the basis of substantial changes in time-space locations. Each of these parts has then been closely analysed by means of the two last dimensions identified above (distancing and degree of reality). I used the two other dimensions only when the analysis required it. Here I simply present the synthesis of this analysis, which identifies key semiotic resources and operators of Felicidad's psychological transformation.

1. *They'll arrive:* Fear and passivity characterise the text from the beginning, until the twice repeated "That's how it is" (p. 119, l. 9). The starting point is, under the threat and the eyes of the other, in a present situation of fear and miscomprehension, a situation of alienation. The first scene is in that sense pre-symbolic.

2. *If-only* (p. 119, l. 10-13): The narrator engages in a counterfactual reasoning: if she had gone with him–the Guerrillero–(which she did not do) she would not have been exposed to that fate. The first semiotic operator enabling a change of perspective is a subjunctive, "you should", which in contrast to "that's how it is", enables distantiation and opens *an imaginary space* of possibility.

3. *Hosting the Guerrillero* (p. 119, l. 13-p. 120, l. 20): This is the narrative heart of the text, where we get a full narration of what happened. The text is alternating between the descriptions of the Guerrillero through the perceptions of Felicidad, the actual shared events (staying longer, eating, going for a walk), and her shocked comments, expressing distance between her past and present self. In that space, the whole experience of the relationship with the Guerrillero is given a first meaning. The *first field-like symbolic resource* that enables her to hold together the diverse characteristics of that experience (i.e. initial feeling of fear, alienation, and presence of others, etc.), is the imaginary concept of the *devil* – from the Greek *diabolos*, what separates. In other words, the narrative is given a sense and a direction by a set of a highly distanced or hyperconscious values. It is however diffusing in the whole narration, as it brings the author to specific actions and experiences.

4. *They're coming* (p. 120, l.20-26): Following this 'separation' the narrator seems to be located outside herself, in the position of the others – that of "They" coming for her.

This brings her to a catastrophic imagination of the immediate future, in which "They" will use a classical means of torture – saying that they know, to make you go for it. Yet this opens *a second imaginary space*, in which the narrator can see herself from the perspective of the others. In so doing, she realises that she has nothing to hide. In that sense, the classical torture trick becomes *a semiotic resource to operate a reflective short-circuit.*

5. *But only God and you are witnesses* (p. 120, l. 27-p. 121, l. 4): The short-circuit, marked by the *"but"* – a semiotic marker of interruption in a flow of thinking/speaking – enables in turn a vivid re-presenting of the past in the present, in a new thinking space. This time, the semiotic means to express the scene are at the level of organic experience, or just above the sub-conscious (Valsiner, 2007) that is, below the presence of fact, values, judgements, presence of the others. It is paradoxically through this inner experience of union, that a new semiotic field emerges – that of the divine or the sacred, in an Augustinian manner. Hence, "God" invoked here is the new triangulation point, the semiotic operator, which enables the solution of the conflict between the I-positions. "God" thus plays here the role of the *symbolon* – etymologically, that which unifies what is separated.

6. *And who's to judge you... Not a whisper* (p. 121, l. 4-l.9): This passage is pulling together the two strings of the previous one: the inner ineffable nature of the experience of the encounter between the Guerrillero and Felicidad; and the connection to God as "you" is under "His" protection. Hence, paradoxically, by this juxtaposition, the encounter, which is impossible to see, and belongs only to her, becomes of divine nature. In other words, after the experience of fear of total annihilation (4), the narrator could open a space and find the distance given by the idea of God to live again the actual experience around which the whole text is constructed. From this perspective, a new field-like semiotic resource is available; that of the 'holy', which cannot be found even if the "heart is pierced", and that only God can see. Note that the 'inner space' as the place where God can be found is a classical religious theme (see Marková, 2007, on Saint-Augustine). In this paragraph, as in the previous one, the narrator is no longer refusing her connection to the "you". One might say that the experience of this inner-transcendent place enables the resolution of the conflict between the two I-positions. This deploys a *second hyperconscious field-like symbolic resource* of the holy or the righteous (or the martyr?), which dictates images (pierce the heart), and has various consequences, at the level of action (not moaning, not swearing) as well at the level of embodiment (stand upright).

7. *Don't look like that... Hold their eyes* (p. 121 l. 9-15): It is through this new semiotic field that the initial situation is re-signified; in the present, it is now a situation of the righteous having nothing to fear from what is to come. Indeed: the fight has already taken place.

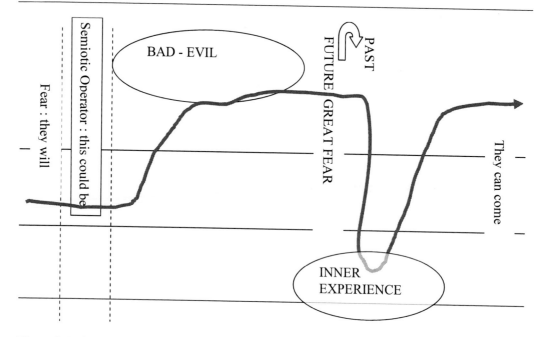

Figure 5. Trajectory of the Felicidad's position.

These movements can schematically be represented in the figure below (Figure 5). The horizontal line, from left to right, represents the flow of the text. The vertical lines represent the level of semiotic distancing: the line below represents embodied experience, the top line represents *hypergeneralised affective sign fields* (such as BAD) (Valsiner, 2007; also see Valsiner's analysis above). The line moving up and down represents the location of the narrator's position; the brusque alteration of that line can be linked to the narrator's use of specific semiotic mediators.

This analysis reveals the role of semiotic operators like "you should", and "but" which can bring a confrontation of perspectives and therefore distancing. However they are a surface manifestation of deeper imaginary experiences – it is after imagining radical alienation that the narrator can take distance manifested by a "but". The analysis also shows the narrator's use of symbolic resources taken from a religious system – God, the Devil, which, when triggered, bring along rich semantic fields, which in turn are diffracted at various levels of semiotic mediation. The main function of these semiotic resources here is to open imaginary spaces, in which the person can explore alternative positions or views. Hence, it can be said that the trajectory of the narrator is shaped by a series of experiences in imaginary spaces, enabled or expressed by semiotic resources which reroute the flow of consciousness.

POSITIONING MICROANALYSIS
JOÃO SALGADO

This analysis is based on a new procedure called *positioning microanalysis* (Salgado & Cunha, 2010), which represents an attempt to build a research strategy coherent with the general principles of a dialogical perspective. It is far beyond the scope of this section to present our theoretical options and guidelines (see Marková, 2003; Leiman, 2002; Linell, 2009; Salgado & Gonçalves, 2007; Valsiner, 2007). Here I will simply say that meaning-making is seen as a matter of responsivity to others within a surrounding and co-constructed semiosphere. Thus, human beings are conceived as communicational agents that are constantly responding to situations with semiotic tools and, therefore, assuming and reassuming semiotic positions.

The following positioning microanalysis of the text *The Guerrillero* aimed to: (1) illustrate how to depict different positions, and (2) identify patterns of relation between these positions. The purpose was to show the potentialities of an analysis focused on inquiring into the dynamics of stability and change of positioning and repositioning.

Step 1: Division into response units

The Positioning Microanalysis procedure usually starts with a division into 'response units' (Auld & White, 1956; Hill, 1982) that correspond broadly to the minimal independent grammatical units of meaning. This procedure was performed by two judges who were able to reach a high level of consensus (above 90%) and to distinguish 79 units. Then, the author of this section analysed the entire text.

Step 2: Detecting the 'field of positioning'

This field represents the overall context of meaning-making and is composed of a generally stable organization of Ego-Other-Object: the person is dealing with some task around an object or theme invoking, implicitly or explicitly, relevant social others to the occasion. In this case, the field was considered generally uniform along the entire text, since the narrator is constantly dealing with the same theme: the relationship (and the consequences of that relationship) between Felicidad Mosquera (who is also the narrator) and the Guerrillero.

Step 3: Constructing a hierarchy of positions of sub-positions

The next step consisted of the analysis of each unit with the following instruction: to categorize each response unit in terms of the self-position assumed in that segment towards others and the world. Each categorization was systematically compared with the previous ones, enabling the construction of the hierarchy of positions and sub-positions presented in Table 1.

Most of the text develops as a monologue, in which the narrator addresses Felicidad Mosquera about her love affair with a Guerrillero – a monologue with an explicit dialogical structure. As we can see, there are five main positions, with several sub-positions: it starts with the narrator assuming (1) a warning position towards Felicidad Mosquera that quickly turns into (2) a reproaching/blaming position. Then, (3) the narrator recalls episodes of the encounter of Felicidad Mosquera and the Guerrillero (recalling position). The initial part of text dwells in an interplay between these three different positions, apparently feeding each other. Initially, the warning position feeds a great despair and rage towards those past steps – giving rise to the reproaching position. This is the position that dominates the first part of the monologue. By its turn, reproaching leads to the evocation of past events. However, suddenly, we see a dialogical shift towards a totally different position – (4) near the end the narrator assumes an accepting tone towards her love affair and (5) finally encourages Felicidad

Mosquera to deal bravely and without remorse about her fate. The development throughout time of the main positions is described in Figure 6—the vertical axis is of the five positions of the narrator, while the horizontal axis represents the 79 units of the text (both identified above).

This sudden transition between the initial cycle (positions 1-2-3) and the emergence of a novel position is a rather interesting point of analysis, since it may be parallel to sudden and drastic changes within oneself. In order to better understand what happened in that transition, it is necessary to return to the data in order to check what happened before this shift. This strategy fits the overall aim of the microgenetic approach of developmental science (Valsiner, 2007).

Table 1. Positions and sub-positions of the narrator

Positions	Sub-positions
1. Warning position: The narrator (N) warns Felicidad Mosquera (FM) of the danger	1.1. The narrator (N) describing "them" as an unavoidable and terribly threatening
	1.2. N describing what they'll do to her (FM)
	1.3. N describing FM's fate as a fatality
2. Reproaching/blaming position: N reproaching or blaming FM	2.1 N telling FM what she might have done
	2.1.2. Running away with him
	2.1.2. Refusing to help him
	2.2. N describing what would not be happening if she had acted differently
	2.3. N showing FM what would be happening if she had acted differently
	2.4. N regretting and reproaching FM about what she did in the past
	2.4.1. Regretting
	2.4.2. Recriminating and cursing
	2.5. N alienating FM
	2.5.1. N describing FM as blind
	2.52. N affirming FM "possessed" by a different identity ("you were not you")
3. Recalling position: N recalling FM her story with him	3.1. N recalling her of how she helped him when he was injured
	3.2. N affirming FM as enamored of him
	3.3. N recalling his courtship
	3.4. N recalling their meeting on the river bank
4. Accepting position: N accepting FM's love story 5. Encouraging position: N encouraging FM to surpass her fear and to accept her fate	

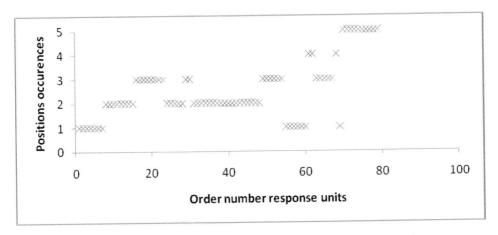

Figure 6. Occurrences of the positions throughout time.

The reproaching attitude, intermingled with the recall of her love affair, gives episodic vividness to the past events. The narrator explores how she was "transformed by his touch". The narrator alienates Felicidad Mosquera, depicting her as "possessed" or mad. However, operating as counter-voice to this position, the narrator is getting in touch with Felicidad Mosquera's deep love for that man. Thus, the voice of Felicidad Mosquera was actually the addressed one and the recall of those romantic and sensual episodes brings that experience to the foreground. At that moment, fear overcomes her again, because she returns to the warning position. However, the vividness and concreteness of that powerful voice of passion breaks through, and the narrator shifts to a new position, declaring the complete acceptance of the passion and addressing God as the only possible judge of what happened. The narrator finally accepts the passionate love, while describing the meeting on the river banks. Here, the storyteller is no longer a simple narrator, since she starts to describe what only God and Felicidad Mosquera were able to know: how she felt while making love to him. Here, the identity of the narrator is revealed: it must be either God or Felicidad Mosquera, herself. Then returning to the problem at hand – position 1 – she becomes able to find a new future – and an encouraging position (position 5) is assumed, voicing the acceptance of her own fate and eventual death and sacrifice.

Concluding Comments on Positioning Microanalysis

In sum, the shift to a new voice that breaks the initial stability and in-feeding of different positions seems to take place through the contact with a counter-voice that was initially maintained at the foreground – as the voice of a counter-position, which those initial positions were fighting against. The contact, in itself, was facilitated by the recapturing of the passionate past experience, whose concrete qualities and felt dimension opened a gate to giving a new meaning to the same situation.

FELICIDAD'S CHALLENGE, A CHALLENGE TO US
LIVIA SIMÃO

The aim of the present analysis was to take the story as an opportunity for illustrating some aspects of I-Other (world) relationships, understood as culture and time bounded processes in personal development. The first step of the analysis was impelled by the question 'Who is Felicidad Mosquera?' The only way of knowing Felicidad is listening to her, in the sense of *letting her touch us* (Gadamer, 1959), taking advantage of the situation in which Angel launches us, as hidden listeners in Felicidad's self-talks.

In Spanish Felicidad means *happiness*, and this installs, at the onset of the tale, an expectation that disquiets us throughout the story. By listening to Felicidad we grasp the ambiguities of her life: her impotence facing the sin of her destiny which causes her anguish and *unhappiness*, and also her internal rebellion against that sin, actualized through a perseverant remembering and a pervasive revival of her intensely *happy* past moments with her lover. In this flux of emotions the more she feels near a dead-end situation, the more she dives into her best memories. At the last moment, she takes some control over the situation by making a deal with herself. In reality it is a deal settled in the celebration of the past victories, maybe as a revengeful consolation, bringing the *happiness of past times back to her and in so doing giving her some dignity in the present.* In this sense, it is a deal that makes it possible for her to transcend the circumstantial and 'objective' attributes of the here and now lived situation.

The second step was to try to understand the other character that had the power to bring about *Felicidad's stream of thoughts and emotions* (James, 1890). The Guerrillero is like a strong figure in pastel, who surreptitiously arrives, bringing intense inner transformations in Felicidad, allowing her *happiness*—perhaps the only sublime and evanescent moment of coincidence between herself and the meaning of her name.

Then he disappears, carrying Felicidad's *happiness* with him, as if paying for a double transgression: having actively experienced the pleasure of love with a forbidden and dangerous lover. However, the *Guerrillero* allowed her to feel *other feelings*, think *other thoughts*, and act *other acts*—in short, to be *other*. Astonished, a little bit angry, a little bit scared, but maybe also proud, she realizes that there is another unexpected and unknown *Felicidad Mosquera* dwelling in herself.

Above all, she is not alone any more, as she now has the companion of *other voices* in herself, the "Is" and "Yous" to whom she can now talk. Her former *quiet dialogue, in which the I and the Self were in unison,* has shifted into a more complex dialogue. From her 'monological inner monologue', Felicidad passed through a 'polyphonic inner monologue' (Rommetveit, 2003). This change allowed her to question her *past* attitudes and inquire about the *future*.

Felicidad's Experience of Negativity

By sheltering the Guerrillero in his *dual otherness—as foreigner and fascinating—* Felicidad could have what is called 'an experience of negativity' (Gadamer, 1959). This kind of experience happens in the *present*, is addressed to the *past* and is essential for preparing the person for the *future*. This enables a constructive change in the relation between one's internal and external world. In this process of reconfiguring I-world relationships one prepares oneself for the future (Boesch, 1991; Valsiner, 1998).

For Felicidad, this happened through a polyphonic internal dialogue with her new fellows, the "Yous" who are, *simultaneously, "Is" and "Yous" in herself*, sometimes approving and encouraging her, sometimes criticizing, scaring and warning her. Such a polyphony enabled a shift in the symbolic relations within her self-experience of temporality: instead of *a comprehensible past and a good or regular expectation for the future, viewed from her present,* she is now in a situation of *striving for self-understanding and self-planning in the present, facing a challenging and scary future, in the light of an unexpected intensely happy past.* This means that she could cope with the affective-cognitive challenge posed by the whole unexpected situation, and reach a reorganization of her self-experience in a new coherent whole (Diriwächter, 2008).

The relevance of past experiences that came as remembrances and reviviscences is not in replicating experiences, which would be strictly impossible and psychologically not desirable for preparing for the future. Their value is exactly in being another (new) present experience, addressed to the past, in view of the future. The psychological value of the internal dialogue lies exactly in being a reinterpretation of remembrances, reviviscences and anticipated meanings about a situation. As far as it is never a replication, it prevents her from confirming her expectations, and thus she enlarges her horizons (Gadamer, 1959), allowing new constructions in her I – Other (world) relationships (Simão, 2010). From the *present* situation, Felicidad rectifies her expectation about herself, in face of the requirements for understanding herself in the *past* situation. Her thought and expectation about the future flows, then, in a new direction.

This new subjective configuration, by its turn, brings new decisions, honouring a compromise born in the interplay of the *I's* and *You's* inner dialogue. This is a compromise implying autonomy, but not in isolation, as it carries with it the *onus on the I-Other relationship*. However, all these are possible only if the person could attend to the call of the otherness.

Felicidad's Illusion

One of the ways by which one can be touched by that call is to let oneself be *illusioned* by the other. Being *illusioned* embraces not only the illusory character of an event (as if it were false or a misunderstanding, which sooner or later will cause the person who believes in it *disillusion*), but also keeps its former Romantic meaning: *the imaginary anticipation of pleasure, future, joy and delight.* Its address to the future occurs in the form of anticipation and projection of some event (Marías, 1984).

To be *illusioned* creates a duality between reality and unreality, past and present, possible and impossible, as the *illusioned* person relies on the image of something that comes back from the past, but in a new way. Illusion also refers to one's life projects, to who one wants to be and what one feels one needs to be, even with heavy doubts about its accomplishment. In sum, it touches on the issue of authenticity of one's life projects. Being illusioned is a process of making discoveries about ourselves and others by living through the labyrinths of mistakes, misunderstandings and transformations we make (Marías, 1984).

The process of discovery, in which the Guerrillero was Felicidad's object of illusion, also concerns Felicidad herself. Self-discovery involves opening one's self to not-yet-explored aspects of one's interiority. This is, indeed, a tri-fold process of personal discovery: the discovery of *the Guerrillero by Felicidad*; the discovery of *Felicidad by herself* in her relationship with him; and, finally, the discovery of *the Guerrillero in his own eyes*, illuminated by the light of the illusion he has awakened in Felicidad.

DIALOGUING THE ANALYSES
BRADY WAGONER

The above five analyses illustrate the complexity of psychological processes that can be found in a seemingly simple short story. Gillespie outlines the I-positions inhabiting Felicidad's stream of thought, and shows how they are systemically related and re-organized through the narrative. Valsiner illustrates how external events and internal feelings become related through self-reflexivity, in which the I moves outside of the Self into external positions to reflect on itself as Me. Zittoun focuses on personal sense making after a rupture, whereby Felicidad uses a variety of semiotic mediators to regain stability in her self-system. Salgado tests his method of *positioning microanalysis* on the text, which uncovers existing I-positions and their patterned occurrences through the temporally evolving narrative. Simão attends to the changing I-world relationships in the text and their existential significance for Felicidad and ourselves. More detailed versions of all of these analyses can be found online at http://www.dialogicalscience.com/Program.htm.

Gillespie, Zittoun, and Salgado all focused on identifying the different *steps*, *phases* or *movements* in the text with their different networks of positioning. We find a clear convergence (with minor variations) in their analyses, which occurs in spite of the fact that their analytic methods and theoretical focus differed from each other. Table 2 below outlines how each characterised the text's general phases. It should be noted that the different phases identified here do not correspond precisely in all the analyses but rather involve a high degree of overlap. For example, Zittoun distinguishes between phase 5 and 6, while the other analyses merge them into one, and Gillespie does not mention phase 4. Furthermore, Salgado's analysis is much more fine-grained in its characterisation of text phases (similar to the level Valsiner worked at), but at the same time he covers the text as a whole. As such his analysis has the advantage of capturing some of the brief returns to earlier positions which are generally left out of the other analyses. As such his analysis has the advantage of capturing some of the brief returns to earlier positions which are generally left out of the other analyses. This can be helpful in understanding the transition between the different phases (which is our primary interest); yet, to do this, positioning microanalysis must be supplemented with an interpretation of holistic meanings and relationships in the text itself, as the other analyses do and Salgado does in interpreting the final movements of the text.

One surprisingly underdeveloped feature of all the analyses was the importance of Felicidad's social context in occasioning her stream of thought—as such there is a risk of making the stream overly subjective. Felicidad's self-dialogue is driven to overcome (or at least temporarily stabilise) inner tensions emerging from being in the middle of a civil war and taking a side in it by helping the Guerrillero: she worries about being tortured for information and betraying her lover, as well as strives to resolve contradictory meanings in her memories—did she act foolishly or courageously? It is only in the context of war that decisions like whether to help a wounded person take on such existential weight. Of course, context is partly addressed by attending to the different role positions mentioned (e.g. the Guerrillero, the torturers, past victims, etc.) but this seems to miss the larger social *meaning* or *value* (see Valsiner) of the struggle for those involved. Simão does mention, at the end of her analysis, Felicidad's "discovery of the Guerrillero in his own eyes". I take this to mean that the larger struggle he is engaged in becomes Felicidad's own personal struggle, part of her 'life-project'. Simão also mentions that 'Felicidad' means *happiness* in Spanish—also often used in contexts of congratulations—yet, no one mentions her last name "Mosquera", which is likely a reference to Tomas Cipriano de Mosquera, a courageous general who led the successful liberal rebel army during the 1860-1862 Colombian civil war. Thus, Felicidad Mosquera's name also hints at the local values surrounding the struggle.

Table 2. Comparison of text phases identified in three analyses

	Phase 1	Phase 2	Phase 3	Phase 4	Phase 5	Phase 6	Phase 7
Gillespie	Rupture	Lament	Realization		Resolve		Self-regulation
Zittoun	They'll arrive	If-only	Hosting the Guerrillero	They're coming	But only you and God are witnesses	Who's to judge you... not a whisper	Don't look like that... Hold their eyes
Salgado	Warning	Blaming	Recalling	Warning	Accepting		Encouraging

In attending to social context we also find important symbols used by Felicidad, in her stream of thought, to resolve her inner tensions—Zittoun aptly notes the etymology of 'symbol' is that which unifies. The most important among these come from Catholicism. It is significant that all the analyses that focused on the different phases of the text identified the key line, "But only God and you are witnesses"—after which she proceeds to describe the details of her highly sexual memories with the Guerrillero. It might appear strange to have God attached to these memories, but Obeyesekere (1981, 2010) has found that eros and agape, sexual and divine love, are often found together in spiritual ecstasy, in religions around the world. Thus, God needs to be added to Gillespie's catalogue of I-positions and brought into play as both 'witnessing' (past Me) and 'protecting' (future Me's) (in Figure 2). In evoking "God" Felicidad creates a *hyper-generalized affective field* (see Valsiner and Zittoun) of spirituality, in which having someone "pierce your heart" takes on the meaning of martyrdom (like Christ on the cross). Her struggle is deeply personal (no one knows of her relationship to the Guerrillero) yet utilizes the social meanings of her community (religious symbols) to express and resolve inner tensions, and thus she also has the potential to communicate something to the community at large (she could become a Martyr for the rebel cause).

Conclusion: Methodological Reflections on the Multivocality of Analyses

What can we learn from this exercise in the multivocality of analyses about conducting a dialogical analysis? In his chapter, Billig encourages dialogical thinkers to write dialogically by voicing contrary ways of thinking about an issue. This is *not* to be done to pre-emptively silence potential objections from others, as many contemporary writers in fact do; but rather, it serves the purpose of opening up further dialogue, ensuring that this is not the last word on the subject. Yet, given the rigid style constraints of most academic publishing and difficulty of getting one's ideas heard at all, it is natural for us to be wary writing dialogically. In the present chapter we have, to a certain extent, circumvented this problem by offering different analyses of the same material without attempting to integrate them into a single finalized perspective. In setting these analyses side-by-side, contrarieties become visible between them (rather than within a single author). It is crucial that the same material be analysed by all to have a common ground against which differences emerge.

The discussion explored the differences and developed (vis-à-vis the other analyses) another distinct analytic perspective —where Felicidad's self-dialogue emerges from tensions inside her social situation and is resolved through cultural tools found there. Even though this last analysis (in the discussion) synthesizes ideas from the previous analyses, it does not cancel out the other analyses into a higher form (as in Hegelian dialectic); rather it provides another position from which to dialogue and develop the other analyses. This was done by bringing together analytic tools from each of the analyses, as well as exploring what was left out (e.g., social context). The other analysis might in turn find inspiration for developing their analytic approaches through the reconfiguration of ideas in the discussion.

Although there were limitations, our exercise in the multivocality of analyses made an important step forward. We set out with the aim of opening up dialogue on analytic strategies in dialogical science, which the exercise has certainly achieved. In setting up this exercise we created a social situation, in which there is a problem, tension or rupture for ourselves. Like Felicidad, we overcome it through self-reflection, drawing on symbolic resources and voicing the perspectives of others. In the externalization of rich analyses we see a diversity of emerging research techniques and theoretical ideas, which provide tools for others to creatively adapt in their own research contexts. It is from the dynamic tension between different perspectives (such as these) and appropriations to new contexts that further innovations will emerge within the field dialogical science.

APPENDIX A: THE GUERRILLERO
ALBALUCÍA ANGEL

Now they'll see, Felicidad Mosquera, when they all arrive with their machetes, threatening, asking you where in hell has he hidden himself, then you'll confess. They'll ask. They'll force you to betray him because if you won't talk they'll take the old folks, like they did two days ago with your friend Cleta, remember, or they'll put your hands into the fire, like Calixta Peñalosa, or they'll slice open your belly, after all—all of them—have used your body. That's how it is, Felicidad. That's how it is. You should have gone with him, then you wouldn't have suffered. You wouldn't be dragging yourself around, crying and moaning, looking for anything that might do as a weapon, pushing the few bits of furniture against the door. That night, when Sebastian Martinez's dogs began to howl as if they'd smelled the devil, and you saw him there, suddenly, standing ever so still, his trousers in shreds and his white shirt all bloody, then you should have spoken, said anything, any excuse to make him whisper good-night and creep back where he'd come from, but no, too bad it didn't happen that way. Bad luck, Felicidad. You made him come in without a word, you pulled up a chair for him, he let himself fall heavy as lead, and then you saw the other wound on his skull: *I'm tired*, was all he mumbled; and then collapsed like a horse on the floor. Whatever got into your head, Felicidad Mosquera? What evil star dazzled you then, what evil wind blew through your heart to stir up the fire, to blind you? Because you were blind, blind. The shivers you felt when you looked upon his face and realized he was so handsome. That you liked his black moustache. The nervous urgency with which you went to boil water and prepare the herb plasters, somehow wasn't yours. Because you've always been cool-headed. A watchful-heart. Careful. You never let yourself be trapped into these things. Whatever happened to you, tell me. Whatever came over you when instead of saying good-bye, once he felt better, and began to go out at night to take a walk, to get firewood, offering to pump water, instead of saying yes, well thank you, see you sometime, you said no, it was no trouble, why didn't he stay a few more days. What happened, damn you. I can't understand. Felicidad Mosquera, I don't recognize you any longer. I never thought you'd change this fast, go from black to white, as you did, from one day to the other. Because the trembling you felt when he looked at you with his dark eyes, or the stammering, like a little girl, when he asked for the salt and barely touched you with his fingers as you put it in his hand, everything in you turned upside-down, the current changed, your cables crossed, so how in God's name didn't you notice it. Putting salt into another person's hand is stupid, brings bad luck. Bad tidings. And what about that day when instead of letting him go off on his own to get some air, you flushed, all red in the face, when he offered to walk together for a while, and crossing the bridge he held your waist, because it shakes so much was his excuse, but you felt how the heat boiling on his skin began to seep into you, burning, hurting, a cry inside you. A deep, deep moan. They're coming, Felicidad Mosquera. They'll come shouting that they know. Kicking everything in the house, as they did with Prospero Montoya's wife, when they left her stuck inside the well, her belly sliced open and the baby inside. They won't let you make the slightest move. When they arrive like that they're all ready to kill you. To leave no trace. They'll say they know so that you go for it. But only God and you are witnesses. The only witnesses of the meeting in the fields, on the river bank, between the scented sheets; who else will swear if only you felt the delight, the sex entering your body, searching your smoothness, changing you into streams, twilight, sea; who else will know the movement of your thighs, burning, your hands searching; touching the groin forcing sweetly your way into life. Who else heard his groans. His loving search. His long, drawn-out orgasm as you sank into a silence of moist membranes, a quick throb of blood, a hurried quiver of muscles, which then relaxed rippling through the entire body, an inside scream bursting upwards, like a torrent. And who's to judge you, Felicidad Mosquera, if only God and you can swear that this is true. No one will dare. They can search your very innards, cut you in two with their machetes, drill into your senses, pierce your heart, they will find nothing. Not a whisper. Don't look like that. Throw your fear overboard. Don't curse any more: he's far away and all that counts is that he lives and carries on fighting. You won't say a word. Not even if they set fire to your shack, ram themselves into you, or bottles, or do what they did to others to drive you crazy; take courage, Felicidad

Mosquera, don't cry or moan any more. Open the door yourself. Stand upright in the doorway. Hold their eyes.

ACKNOWLEDGMENT

We would like to thank the book's editors for their invaluable comments on earlier drafts of this chapter.

REFERENCES

Angel, A. (1985). The Guerillero. In A. Manguel (Ed.), *Other fires: Short fiction by Latin American women* (pp. 119-121). New York: Three Rivers Press.

Auld, F., & White, A. M. (1956). Rules for dividing interviews into sentences. *The Journal of Psychology, 42*, 273-281.

Boesch, E. E. (1991). Symbolic action theory and cultural psychology. Berlin: Springer.

Diriwächter, R. (2008). Genetic Ganzheitspsychologie. In R. Diriwächter & J. Valsiner (Eds.) *Striving for the whole: Creating theoretical syntheses* (pp. 21-45). Somerset, NJ: Transaction Publishers.

Gadamer, H. G. (1959/1985) *Truth and method*. New York: Lexington.

Gillespie, A. (2006). *Becoming other: From social interaction to self-reflection*. Charlotte, NC: Information Age Publishing.

Hermans, H. (2002). The dialogical self as a society of mind. *Theory & Psychology, 12*(2), 147-160.

Hill, C. E. (1982). Counseling process research: Philosophical and methodological dilemmas. *The Counseling Psychologist, 10*, 7-19.

James, W. (1890). *Principles of psychology*. Cambridge, MA: Harvard University Press.

Marías, J. (1984/2006). *Breve tratado de la illusion [Short Treatise about Illusion]*. Madrid: Alianza Editorial.

Marková, I. (1990). A three-step process as a unit of analysis of dialogue. In I. Marková & K. Foppa (Eds.), *The dynamics of dialogue* (pp. 129-146). Hemel Hempstead: Harvester Wheatsheaf.

Mead, G. H. (1934). Mind, self & society from the standpoint of a social behaviorist. Chicago: University of Chicago Press.

Obeyesekere, G. (1981). Medusa's hair: An essay on personal symbols and religious experience. Princeton: Princeton University Press.

Obeyesekere, G. (2010). Deep motivation and the work of culture in Christian penitential ecstasy. In B. Wagoner (Ed.) *Symbolic transformation: The mind in movement through culture and society* (pp. 120-141). London: Routledge.

Perret-Clermont, A. (2004). The thinking spaces of the young. In A. Perret-Clermont, C. Pontecorvo, L. Resnick, T. Zittoun, & B. Burge (Eds.), *Joining society: Social interactions and learning in adolescence and youth* (pp. 3-10). Cambridge: Cambridge University Press.

Rommetveit, R. (2003). On the role of "a psychology of the second person" in studies of meaning, language and mind. *Mind, Culture and Activity*, *10*(3), 205-218.

Simão, L. M. (2010). *Ensaios dialógicos: Compartilhamento e diferença nas relações eu-outro. [Dialogical essays: Sharing and difference in I-Other relationships]*. São Paulo: HUCITEC.

Valsiner, J. (1998). *The guided mind: A sociogenetic approach to personality*. Cambridge, MA: Harvard University Press.

Valsiner, J. (2007). *Culture in minds and societies: Foundations of cultural psychology*. New Delhi: Sage.

Zittoun, T. (2006). *Transitions: Development through symbolic resources*. Greenwich, Connecticut: Information Age Publishing.

In: Dialogicality in Focus   ISBN: 978-1-61122-817-5
Editors: M. Märtsin, B. Wagoner, E.-L. Aveling et al.   © 2011 Nova Science Publishers, Inc.

Chapter 6

VOICES OF GRAPHIC ART IMAGES

Marcela Lonchuk and Alberto Rosa

INTRODUCTION

We live surrounded by pictures of many different kinds. Paintings, photographs and engravings cover the walls of our homes, illustrate the pages of the books we read, and cover large surfaces of urban space for the purposes of decoration, advertising or propaganda. Everyday objects, such as coins, bank-notes, tickets and stamps are also covered with figures of graphic art. Video-clips, video-games, and movies are omnipresent in private as well as public spaces.

Ours is a world of signs. Coloured lines on the floor signal where we can cross hazardous traffic, while coloured lights tell us when to move or stop. Pictures of our relatives populate wallets in our pockets reminding us to what family we belong. Religious, historical and mythical images populate urban landscapes and decorate buildings, appealing to our feelings and urging us to act in a particular way. Arrangements of colours (flags), as well as photographs or engraved profiles of individuals (queen, king, or president) on coins, tell us where we are, hint at the power of the State and make us feel foreign or at home. Pictures of suffering children make us feel sympathy and urge us to support the advertised organisation.

Signs and images do not only populate our environment, they also are the means through which a considerable amount of our experience gets shaped. How much of what we know or believe to be real has actually been directly perceived? Is it not true that an enormous amount of what we take to be our experience and knowledge of the world reaches us through signs and images? It may be true that we dwell in a reported world as much, if not more, than the world we experience directly.

Beyond their apparent immediacy, these images have all the force of the 'semiotic making' (Greimas, 1979). They have a cognitive and pragmatic power capable of constructing objects and making them communicative devices capable of conveying cultural values and calling for a particular kind of action. Images and graphic art are not only naïve representations of absent objects; they are communicative artefacts capable of making one see something, to believe it to be real or fantastic, to feel moved or indifferent, inclined to act in a particular way or another, or even to belong to a particular group.

This chapter addresses how pictorial images are understood, how meaning is attributed to them and how one feels while interpreting what the image is about. The thesis we are going to examine here is that understanding and interpreting images is done through argumentative dialogues involving different I-positions.

WHAT IS AN IMAGE? WHAT IS IT CAPABLE OF DOING?

Images in graphic art are a means of presenting something absent, for representing something else – either real or fictional, concrete or abstract. They are made for the sake of communication, for calling attention to something, or for producing some effect on others. They are shaped in such a way as to optimize their communicative intention. Last but not least, images are not only drawn, pictured or sculpted, but they can also be explained and interpreted through language. This makes us believe that it is possible to communicate what one understands when interpreting a graphic image, something very useful when devising a methodology to study the process of its interpretation.

Pictorial images are capable of presenting things with some kind of felt immediacy. If when looking at Figure 1a one was asked, "*what is this?*", one may immediately answer "a pipe", as if this were a real pipe from which one may smoke, even if one is very much aware that this is not the case. The effect of the picture, however, changes dramatically when some words are added to the image (see Figure 1b). What does it refer to now? Obviously there is neither a single, nor simple, answer to this question. It opens an interpretative process which was precisely the intention of René Magritte (the author of a painting inspiring Figure 1) - to make apparent the separation between the image and its referent. Magritte, Michel Foucault (1983) and others developed a well known discussion about the risks of taking representation and real life experience for granted. One may say that there is no simple reading of an image. Images are always interpreted, even if the interpretation appears quite straightforward.

a

This is not a pipe

b

What is this? Such a question, when asked before these two pictures, will take to rather different answers.

Figure 1. Figure 1a represents a pipe, but, what does figure 1b represents? It seems to be more an argument than a representation.

Figure 2. What does this represent?

Graphic art images appear instantiated on material objects (paper, cloth, metal or whatever). They are objects which stand for other objects, either real or fictitious. When looking at Figure 2, one feels compelled to say, *"this is Justice!"* It is as if one were before a picture of a well known real life character. However, there is no iconic similarity between the image and its referent. Justice is an abstraction. It has no physical shape and its representation as a woman is a result of *convention*.

This image is far from simple. It conveys many messages together. The way the woman stands suggests strength and determination, but it also shows caring as the delicacy of the position of her hands reveals. Feeling a balance without seeing what is being weighed, suggests making decisions without prejudice. The column and stairs remind one of classical buildings, which often house institutions. All this, together with the absence of another conventional sign of justice (the sword on the other hand of the balance – meaning an armed force supporting and enforcing the law) substituted by the globe under one hand, suggests the decision to refrain from even suggesting the possibility of using coercive force. In sum, taking all this into account, one may end up thinking that we are being presented with a representation of International Justice.

This picture, then, denotes a particular symbolic object, but it does so by presenting an argument that is distributed among the different figures which together make up the whole display (a young woman, a balance, a globe, etc). Each of its conventional elements is, in their turn, made up of different individual features, each one of them signalling towards a particular meaning (wavy lines = hair; a circle with patches of light and colours inside = the Globe; some vertical and horizontal lines = steps + columns = the façade of a building, etc.). In other words, this image, behind its deceiving simplicity, hides a complex architecture.

In order to understand what the picture is about, the observer must group together lines and colours so that different signs are formed. It is only then, that these signs become capable of denoting some objects and connoting others. Eventually all these elements get combined forming a complex symbolic object – Justice in this case. In semiotic parlance we may say that this process is one of recursive semiosis, creating new signs again and again, which end-up producing an argument. We only become aware of this process when the picture breaks conventionality; when it puzzles us, and we have to start making conscious inferences towards working out a feasible argumentative interpretation.

Images, then, are capable of acting as signs (giving meaning to elements in the space). They can present and represent real material objects (such as a pipe). They can even give figurative shape to abstract entities such as Justice, or create virtual or fictitious characters, capable of giving substance to stereotypes and social representations such as John Bull or Don Quixote (see Figure 3). These latter objects are not abstractions coming from arguments, but rather characters in narratives. This gives the images the ability to act as signs in the narrative, and the images also convey a moral that the narrative conveys. When this happens, the image is not just suggesting, presenting or representing something. It is also *saying something to me* (the observer). It becomes a communicative device. It addresses an audience, and the observer feels affected by what he or she understands the message to be about.

a   b

Figure 3. *a. John Bull* is a personification of England first created by John Arbuthnot (1667-1735), a Scotsman. The John Bull character was that of a drinking man, hard-headed, down-to-earth, averse to intellectualism, fond of dogs, horses, ale, and country sports. He appeared first as a character in satiric stories, and then in cartoons. During the Napoleonic Wars, John Bull became the national symbol of freedom and of loyalty to king and country. John Bull is the personification of the character of the English: honest, generous, straightforward, with a zest for life and ready to stand up and fight for what he believes in. *b. Don Quixote* is the protagonist of a novel by Miguel de Cervantes (1547-1616). He is presented as a noble but crazy character, which sees himself as carrying out the heroic duty of fighting against imaginary enemies, searching for a delirious good, always getting defeated and making a fool of himself. In the early 20th century, after Spanish defeat in the Spanish-North-American War (1898), some intellectuals made him to appear as some sort of personification of one side of the Spanish character, the other side would be represented by Sancho Panza - his plebeian, mercenary and much down to earth servant.

Figure 4. Three versions of the same composition produced at the time of 1st World War for recruiting purposes. The first two (1914) depict Lord Kitchener, British Secretary of State for War. The third represents Uncle Sam (a personification of the US coming from as early as the 1812 war, but without a popular pictorial representation until this poster came about). It was designed by James Flagg in 1917.

This latter feature makes graphic art a privileged means for reaching wide audiences. Posters and advertisements are very often used as vehicles not only to let the public know about a happening or to seduce them into buying something, but also to move them to act according to some moral values. In some cases, the observer is addressed directly (see Figure 4). In this case images are directly and unavoidably addressing the audience itself, so that there is no way one could avoid feeling that the message concerned them. The pictures (or rather, the characters appearing in the picture) are *talking to me*. They are capable of exercising quite a strong illocutionary[1] force upon some public (Searle, 1969).

---

[1] Illocutionary force refers to the speaker's intention of producing an utterance (Searle, 1969). It is an instance of a type of culturally defined speech act capable of making the audience feel or act in a particular way (e.g., commanding, promising, warning, begging, etc.).

In sum, images are capable of making absent objects present, of giving shape to abstract entities, of creating fictional characters that embody generalizations; they can provide the figurative nuclei[2] of social representations (Moscovici, 1984). What is more, they can suggest and convey arguments; they are capable of making one feel that what the image presents or *says* concerns them. In other words, they have the capability of making me aware of myself by making me feel that what the image (re)presents concerns me.

How Can Images Be Understood?

From what has been said so far, it follows that for images to be understood, one should first start constructing them as objects, and taking them as signs referring to other objects. Going back to one of our earlier examples (Figure 1), to have the possibility of getting involved in the consideration of the argument suggested in Figure 1b, one first needs to have fallen into the trap of the immediacy suggested by Figure 1a. One has to feel that one is seeing a pipe, so that one may then feel puzzled by the caption stating "this is not a pipe".

Thus viewed, the picture is a rhetorical device prompting one to carry on along the line of the argument there presented. I have to feel affected by the image. It has to produce in me an aesthetic effect – to make me *feel strange* as I observe it. Otherwise I would not be bothered to keep paying attention to it in order to figure out what the picture means. I have to feel aroused enough to produce utterances and so continue to initiate dialogue.

Understanding a picture, then, is not just about identifying the referents of the images there presented. It is also to enter into a dialogue with the meanings suggested by the signs presented in the display. This requires one to go into the effort of constructing an argument that does not only gather together the signs coming from the picture itself, but also those the observer summons when interpreting that picture in a particular spatial and temporal context.

Feelings, Appraisal and Awareness

Feelings are one of the effects the presentation of signs has on the agent. If we were to speak in Peirce's parlance, feelings are *interpretants* coming together with the sign and the object in the process of semiosis, so that meaning could be produced. Peirce's semiotic logic takes meaning to be the result of semiosis (a triadic relationship including sign, object and interpretant - (in contrast to Saussure's dyadic link between the sign and its referent). An *interpretant* is a sign in the mind appearing together with the *representamen* (a previous sign) and the object it signifies. Interpretants are susceptible to becoming signs for new recursive semiosis, so that with new aspects of the object, new meanings may be produced. So viewed, feelings do not only result from semiosis, but they also can act as signs of an object.

Feelings play the function of a central representation for the organization of responses (Scherer, 2004). When so doing, they also act as a sign of one's own agency. Feelings are a

---

[2] 'Figurative nucleus' is a key concept within Serge Moscovici's theory of social representations. It refers to an image structure that reproduces a conceptual structure in a visible manner. This results from the process of objectification, in which abstract representations become concretized in a conventional manner and get projected into the world, so that concrete instances could be taken as embodying that representation.

semiotic outcome of earlier actuations, but they are also signs for the direction of future ones. They result from appraisal processes which trigger motivational processes, giving emotional value (meaning) to objects, events, agents and performances; and they do so, because they affect one's sense of the self (Frijda, 2004).

Feelings not only refer to what the stimulus makes me feel (pleasure, pain – so that I find the object pleasant or painful), but also to how I feel vis-à-vis the experienced object or event (awkward, at ease, disgusted, pleased). It even refers to how I feel towards myself (or somebody else) as a result of acting as an agent (satisfied, restless), when judging how I carried out a task (proud, useless, ashamed), or when appraising my own performances vis-à-vis other agents (arrogant, humble, sympathetic, envious, jealous, despicable). These feelings can exist because emotions are recursive, they are applied again and again upon every outcome of each recursive semiosis; they appraise the object, the actuation, the agent (either somebody else, or myself as another –if such a thing has first been constructed as an object). Appraisals, in a way, are affective judgments deriving from the use of norms (social rules). They produce feelings of an aesthetic and moral nature, as well as acting as signals for the re-adjustment of actuations, for the governance of one's own self.

Therefore, the utterances I produce before the presented picture are not just a reply to 'what the image says' (as if the image were capable of *saying* anything), but it is *my* replay. My utterances are arguments which respond to the arguments I attributed the image to be saying. But they are also a consequence of how I felt, of the position (Davis & Harré, 1990) I take.

We believe that feelings do not act only as interpretants of the signs that images are. They can also change their function and set the *grounds* from which new semiosis can be produced, so that new aspects of the image could be taken as signs, and so new meanings could be attributed to the image. In Peirce's semiotics the *ground* is what makes the sign capable of signifying an object, it is something they have in common; it is an abstract category that can only come from earlier experience (his better known example is that of black acting as a sign of a stove, because both share *blackness* -the ground; Peirce, C.P.1931-58, I1.495).

Argumentation

Interpretation is a dialogical and argumentative process. Interpreting complex images is an argumentative process of object construction, in which objects get constituted and become signs for new, different objects, which then become signs for something else, and so on, in a process which C.S. Peirce called recursive semiosis. These arguments are not only cognitive devices, they are also affective, they give value to what the objects mean, to whom the observer is, and also to the arguments produced, and so trigger new counter-arguments.

The way we have been using the word *argument* here, deserves some explanation to avoid misunderstandings. An argument in Peirce's semiotics is a type of sign gathering together several previous semiosis involving symbols (*dicent-signs*). A dicent-sign, in turn, is an interpretant coming from a semiosis in which the symbol is a conventional sign pointing to a regularity (a legisign). For example, the concept of a ball would be an argument gathering together dicent-signs stating that it is spherical, it bounces, etc; i.e., that it gathers a set of properties which together make it such an object. This way of conceiving an argument makes it very close to the concept of schema, even if these symbols are not words, but instead, images, gestures or ritualized movements (Rosa, 2007). Holding a tennis racket by the handle and hitting the ball with the strings sending it above the net of the court is an enactive dicent-sign showing one is familiar with the argument of what the racket is, what it is for, etc. Enactive arguments (motor schemas) come from experience and provide embodied knowledge of how to move around in a familiar world, to know what things are, and what to do with them. The understanding of Figure 1a is one of these arguments – one *feels* that "this is a pipe" and does not need to utter it to anybody.

There is another more familiar use of the term argument, related to verbal communication and rhetoric. van Eemeren (2002; 2003), van Eemeren, Grootendorst, Jackson & Jacobs (1993; 1997), within the framework of pragma-dialectics, conceive arguments as complex speech acts (Austin, 1962; Searle, 1969) aiming to solve a dispute by a methodical exchange of utterances.

Most of the time, the first kind of argument does not require any kind of conscious awareness, while the second does, since the instrumental operations carried out for problem solving involve the use of conventional signs in social communication, either with others in conversational exchanges, or with oneself as another in egocentric (Vygotsky, 1934) or private speech (Winsler, Fernyhough & Montero, 2009).

Neither kind of argument comes out of the blue, nor are they ever completely produced anew. Arguments come together organised in pre-packaged schemas connected to cultural contexts, personal experiences and concerns. In the case of spoken arguments we can trace these cultural products in the very linguistic structure of the produced utterances.

Interpreting complex or contradictory artistic displays, as the case of Figure 1b shows, requires going into spoken argumentation, even if it happens in private speech. If the interpretation happens in a social situation, such as an interview, the interviewee may quite easily share with the interviewer the on-going process of making sense of the figurative display.

Topoi

The concept of *topos*, first used in Aristotle's *Art of Rhetoric* (1991), offers a useful tool to connect individual arguments with cultural productions. It is a way of making an issue present in a conversation by making use of the applicable discourses available within the cultural tool-kit. Topoi are discursive packages conveying beliefs held in a community, suggesting routes to reach specific conclusions from particular utterances (Anscombre & Ducrot, 1983). A lexicon contains a package of *topoi*. How these *topoi* appear in utterances carry within them the way in which these issues are appraised – they include social, aesthetic and moral values.

From a pragmatic outlook, *topoi* have also been considered in political sociology. Hedetoft (1995) identified territory, language, sports, immigration and war as the five *topoi* of national identity appearing in a research project carried out in several Western European countries. It was around these five issues that the nationalist discourses studied elaborated their arguments.

Topoi are the key issues appearing in the argumentative dialogue about a particular issue. If somebody goes through the trouble of arguing about something, it is because she or he feels that it concerns them. When a *topos* makes itself present when interpreting an image, it is because there is something in the image that acts as a sign of that meaning, or because something happened in the argumentative process that made it come about. One must have some particular interest, some particular bias so that one is sensitive towards that particular issue, so that from many different elements one chooses something in particular, and so makes it a sign of something else – a *topos*.

It should be remembered that it is the *ground* that makes it possible for a sign to refer to an object. As said before, the ground is an abstract idea coming from earlier experience, but that abstract idea comes about because of the way the agent approaches the display. The ground is not arbitrary (it has to have some foundation in what is presented), but it also results from the intention, the attitude one takes when approaching the display. One tries to understand what one sees, but what one sees is not too far removed from what one feels concerned about. When interpreting a picture, one is also projecting one's own worries.

In sum, the consideration of the *topoi* appearing when interpreting a graphic display is of interest, since they are methodological devices capable of acting as a sort of pivot linking ground and feelings together, as well as social discourses and inner concerns.

Social Voices and Dialogical Understanding

Bakhtin's (1981) ideas about heteroglossia were introduced into psychology some time ago (Wertsch, 1991). According to him, our speech is a constant recycling of others utterances, ventriloquating other voices. The very process of understanding a text when reading it in silence is also a dialogue in which different voices produce arguments and counter-arguments. These voices speak social languages carrying ideologies, and so express meanings from different positions, as if at times different characters took possession of one's own voice (Voloshinov, 1997). The I of the speaker can then be conceived as a set of *I-positions* in a continuous dialogue – a *dialogical self* (Hermans, 1996).

Such a view conceives the speaker as a multitude of voices in dialogue, and thinking as a dialogical argumentation in which different voices present themes and counter-themes in a polyphonic manner (Bakhtin, 1981). When acting, when speaking, when solving problems and thinking, one resorts to signs, to utterances, to formulae and arguments and to social positions, and voices them in an inner dialogue in order to try to make sense of what one is facing, to figure out what that is, and what to do.

The public space houses many discursive forms addressing issues of interest from many different outlooks. Elements of this public cultural toolkit get instantiated when a voice uses a particular discursive form and so appropriates a particular way of picturing an issue. When an individual ventriloquates a voice, he also borrows an I-position, holds a particular view on an issue, carries along an ideological outlook and presents a *topos* in a particular way.

UNDERSTANDING AN AMBIGUOUS POLITICAL POSTER

The complex process of understanding can be seen quite clearly when one faces the task of understanding a complex and ambiguous graphic display that makes one feel intrigued and implicated. For this to happen, it has to refer to something quite related to the interpreter's sense of self, as well as having some contextual relevance, beyond the interpreting situation.

We are now going to present the results of our interpretation of how a task devised along these lines was carried out by an individual. This will show how the processes we have been referring to, appear when actually interpreting an image, as well as providing the opportunity to go into the examination of other elements worthy of consideration, which have not been mentioned so far.

The participant was María (fictitious name), a 43 year old university graduate and business woman, working as an executive for a U.S. multinational company. She is an Argentinean, living in Buenos Aires, and as part of her job she has to travel a lot around the Americas and Africa. She was individually interviewed in 2008 and asked to think aloud when figuring out what the graphic display meant to her. Her answers were recorded, transcribed[3] and later analyzed.

The poster used in this study (see Figure 5)[4] belongs to a series showed in an exhibition presented at the Argentinean consulate in Barcelona in 2004 under the highly ironic title "God is Argentinean", which plays with the arrogance taken to be one of the features of Argentinean national character. The exhibition was meant to be a reflection on the current state of Argentina, following its 2001 economic debacle, which had ended the brief period of prosperity after the bloody military dictatorship of the 1970's and 1980's and Argentina's defeat in the Falkland Islands War.

When looking at her argumentation, three rather well defined steps can be distinguished in her process of interpretation. First, choosing signs for constituting objects. Second, setting one of these objects as the issue around which the bulk of the argument will develop. And, third, constructing and appropriating the object *national identity*.

---

[3] The transcription of Maria's original spoken interpretation in Spanish is as follows:

"Las barricadas cierran calles | pero abren caminos || yo | cuando la ví así la imagen con el barbijo | lo primero que pienso es en la contaminación ambiental | nos toca qué se yo de cerca | yo estaba pensando | vinculado pensás en lo de las papeleras | la otra vez el humo que hubo que quemaron los campos y es como || sabés qué me da la sensación con este barbijo | porque ¿es un barbijo no? | ¿o no? || no sé | todo depende | si lo ves como un barbijo | ahora si lo ves como un pañuelo que se está tapando la cara | te suena a qué | a un ladrón | entonces UN LADRÓN ARGENTINO Y LUCHADOR | mmmmm | o sea es jodido el mensaje | porque te están diciendo | a mí esto me da la sensación como de que | cara de santo | y encima es Cristo | cara de santo | te ponés un coso | decís un luchador y en el fondo sos un chorro de lo peor | ehhh | y acá hablan de las barricadas | esto es por los cortes | cuando cortan rutas y eso | no sé | yo lo relaciono con eso | porque así así las barricadas cierran calles pero abren caminos || es con el tema de | sí | ¿CAMINOS PARA QUÉ? Es mi pregunta | caminos para no cosas buenas | no sé como otros lo han interpretado pero || para mí lo que más fuerte es | es la imagen no | porque te hace pensar dos cosas | a mí primero me hizo pensar en | sin mirar más | ahora bueno con todo este tema que hay de contaminación | pero ahora que lo miro bien | es justamente | con cara de santo | tapado así como los chorros | argentino y luchador | jodido para mí el mensaje en ese punto | y para mí eso es la ley | eso que la gente te corta calles y te dice | estamos luchando por algo justo | que por ahí | en el fondo no es nada justo | sino que están mirando de beneficiarse ellos | porque en realidad | el que está trabajando y tiene que llevar pan a su casa está laburando no está cortando calles | eso estamos todos de acuerdo | porque cuando yo voy a veces a ver clientes y las calles estaban cortadas | los tipos comiendo mandarinas en la mitad de la | 187 | no estaban mirando | bueno | de buscar el bien común || estaba cortando porque alguno le dijo |bueno | tenés que ir a cortar allá | bueno me hace acordar un poco a la imagen de que nos hacemos los santos pero que en realidad somos unos ladronzuelos | eso."

[4] The author of the image is Oscar Luis Alonso. The exhibition, entitled "Dios es Argentino" was organised by Eric Olivares (Istuto Europeo di Design. Barcelona, España. www.iedbarcelona.es), Julio, 2004, Curators Elenio Pico y Luciana Leveratto. http://www.moluanda.net/diosesargentino/

ARGENTINEAN
AND FIGHTER

BARRICADES
BLOCK ROADS BUT
OPEN PATHS

Figure 5. The content of the poster is rather ambiguous. It plays with a well known element of Catholic iconography (Christ as *Sacre-Coeur*), but the human figure could also be a woman. S/he is wearing a piece of cloth covering part of his/her face. The two legends appearing in the poster are translated at the right hand-side of the figure. The second one became quite popular after May 1968.

The following paragraphs will present a translation of significant excerpts of Maria's argumentation, followed by our analysis and comments[5].

First Step: Constituting the Objects

"…when *I saw* the image like this, with a <u>mask</u>, the first thing *I think* of is environmental **pollution** [… if *you* see this <u>as a mask</u>".

"If *you* see this <u>as a scarf</u> hiding the face, *<u>it sounds like it is saying</u>* [CHARACTER- THE IMAGE]- **a thief, an Argentinean and fighter thief**. <u>**This is a bloody message**</u>. Because *<u>they</u>* [CHARACTER- THE IMAGE?] are telling *you, I feel*, that face of a saint and on top of everything else is Christ. Saint's face, *you* put something on, *you* say *you* are a fighter and at the bottom *you* are the worst thief."

"Here *<u>they</u>* [CHARACTER- THE IMAGE?] speak of barricades. This is because of **blocking roads** [recent national event] … Opening paths to where? This is *my* question."

Paths to nothing good.

María starts fixing her attention on the piece of cloth covering the mouth, which she first takes to be a mask. She takes this object to be a sign of pollution, which she relates to recent national events - a dispute between Argentina and Uruguay about a recently opened cellulose

---

[5] The text of these excerpts is marked in such a way as to highlight significant features for analysis according to the following key: Three dots (...) refer to a pause; underlined word (such as '<u>**Sign**</u>') refers to 'something acting as a sign'); bold (such as '**object**') means 'objects created by signs'). Bold and underlined refers to <u>**Ethical appraisals**</u>. Markers of dialogicality are always in italics, as follows: *I* and *you* (plain italics), *<u>Characters</u>* (italics and underlined) and ***Protagonists*** (bold italics).

plant, or to some incidents of burning fields resulting from a political dispute about agricultural taxation which produced clouds of smoke covering parts of Buenos Aires City and made many people wear masks in the streets. So pollution seems to be the first object she takes to be the meaning of the mask she viewed, which itself is taken as the main sign in the display.

From the beginning she speaks in first person singular, but suddenly she starts addressing herself as *you*. Following this, the cloth covering the mouth becomes a sign of something different, a scarf. After this, another positioning and another voice appear, attributed to the image which is now seen acting as a speaker. This voice tells her a rather shocking message: the scarf means a *thief*, which she immediately interprets as an *Argentinean and fighter thief*, an interpretation that shocks her.

After this, she again uses a *you*. But this time it does not refer to herself – it is a sort of substitute for anybody, although this is not just anybody; it is an equal, it is a *you*, which could also be myself – as will be shown later on.

Then she moves to another part of the image, the legend at the bottom. This brings her to constitute a third object: setting up road blocks[6], a common nightmare of travelling Argentineans, something which she also disapproves of.

So far, her dialogical argumentation involves the use of two voices (I and You), and a third (the author of the image). She constitutes three objects: "pollution", "an Argentinean fighter and thief", and "setting up road blocks".

Second Step: Appropriating Objects

It is interesting to see how María seems to be so shocked by her own understanding, that she repeats her words again, as shown below, in a sort of recapitulation, before going ahead with her argumentation.

> "This [image] makes *me* think of two **things**: (…) first **pollution**, but now when *I look* better more carefully, it is just with a saint's face, **so covered as thieves, Argentinean and fighter**. <u>**A bloody point the message makes**</u>".
> "This is **the law** for *me*".

But this repetition is for the purpose of discarding the first object, and leaving aside the third (as a sort of property of the second), to focus on thieves "with a saint's face", and pretending to be Argentinean and fighters. This takes her to a new object: the law. An object she mentions in an ambiguous way. Is it a rule she sets for herself, or is it her view of the law?

---

[6] Demonstrators setting up road blocks is a rather common event in Buenos Aires. Participants in these demonstrations ('piqueteros') usually wear a scarf covering their faces, so they cannot be identified.

Third Step: Setting and Appropriating a New Object – We, and the Way we Are

So far María has made herself present in her arguments only as an interpreter, but then she shows that she herself feels addressed by the message she thinks the image conveys. Her reaction to this call is quite unexpected. She sets a completely new scene to make sense of her new interpretation.

> "*People* cut off your streets and say *they* are doing something for justice. That really **is not just at all**, *they* are **looking after their own benefit**. [*PROTAGONIST 1-*DEMOSTRATORS]
>
> In truth, *those who are really working* and have to take bread home are not blocking cutting streets. (...) [*PROTAGONIST* 2 WORKER]
>
> When I am sometimes visiting clients, and see people blocking cutting streets. *Fellows* [*PROTAGONIST* 1 DEMOSTRATORS] eating mandarin oranges in the middle of the road, they were **not looking after the common good**. They were blocking cutting because *someone* [*PROTAGONIST* 3 UNIONIST] told them - 'you have to block there'. Cut there'.
>
> This reminds *me* of the image that *WE* pretend to be saints but *WE* really are little thieves".

The object she had seemed to forget (setting up road blocks) appears here again, but now within a narrative she introduces in her argument in which new third parties appear: first, demonstrators (with an explicit negative evaluation); then, dishonest unionists; and finally workers trying to earn their living. But this is but an explanation of the earlier main object, the thief, as it clearly appears in the closing statement.

Here María does not argue with herself anymore. María's *I* and *you* are absent in this paragraph. Rather, three different protagonists occupy the scene she sets in her argumentation, which creates a sort of dramaturgical performance that exemplifies a social conflict.

Her earlier enigmatic reference to the law receives some clarification here. In a rather indirect and euphemistic way she seems to be saying what she believes: do not trust political activists when they claim to be doing something for justice, they are obeying people who are acting in their own interests.

This negative view of her own country does not cause her to refrain from showing her feelings of belonging. Her own voice reappears again, but now included in a *we*. This makes clear the second referent of the *you* in the first step of our analysis. The others are thieves, but they are my equals, I could be like them. Even if reluctantly, she recognises herself within the image she despises. It is a sad conclusion not too far from a confession of collective sin, but also a declaration of solidarity with sinners, before an image whose religious appearance was evident from the beginning but whose catholic connotations did not so far appear very explicitly in her interpretation.

The Dialogical Structure of María's Interpretation

The excerpts we have just examined show a dialogical structure to María's interpretative argumentation, worthy of some comments.

It is interesting to note the use she makes of pronouns referring to herself. She seems to take a rather passive outlook, refraining from appearing as active in her interpretation. Her use of *I* is mainly passive in a sort of empiricist way – *I saw, I feel*; she only says *I think* as a consequence of seeing *"(when I see an image like this, with a mask, the first thing I think of"*; *"This makes me think of"*; *"This reminds me of"*). Her only positive action appears in an explanatory sentence for setting a scene we will soon examine in some detail (*"When I am sometimes visiting clients, and see people"*). She only once refers to herself in an active sense but even then she does so in a rather oblique way (*"Opening paths to where? This is my question"*).

Her use of *you* is also very interesting. She chooses it for presenting the sign that will drive her interpretation into the *topos* "thieves" which appears as the *leit-motif* of the bulk of her interpretation (*"if you see this as a scarf"*). It is only within this argument that the *you* appears, and it does so several more times, but playing different functions. First, as an addressee of the message the image tells her (*"they are telling you, I feel"*); but immediately after, the *you* that appears could be herself or somebody else, since it appears in the form of reported speech (*"you put something on, you say you are a fighter and at the bottom you are the worst thief"*). This is interesting. It is the poster which is saying that to her, as one of the *you*s to whom the image is talking. The image appears as a *character* (Voloshinov, 1997) in the argument, talking to María, taking her as an interlocutor. Curiously enough, that *character* is also presented as a third person plural (*"they are telling you"*).

The dialogical argumentation does not only involve *I*, *me* or *you*, but also a third party – the image, *they*, who talks to me (*"they are telling you"*, *"they speak of barricades"*, see excerpt 1). But there are also other third parties who come into the dialogue. They are *protagonists* (Voloshinov, 1997) of scenes narrated within the argument, they do not talk to María, they go on with their own business, as she says – *"they are blocking streets, eating mandarin oranges [...] not looking after the common good"*; or it is *someone* telling *them"*. Three different protagonists appear: lazy demonstrators following orders, one dishonest chieftain, but also the honest worker *"who [...] has to take bread home"*.

As this analysis shows, María has constructed her argument in such a way as to avoid showing her moving from one *I-position* to another. She has chosen another strategy. She did not only move between the *I*, the *me* and the *you*, but also summoned other voices to present views from which to elaborate her final interpretation of what the meaning of the message is. It is at this point that she reunites all the voices together in a *we* – *"we pretend to be saints, but really we are little thieves"*.

CONCLUSION: THE CONTENT OF THE INTERPRETATION AND THE PROCESS OF ITS SHAPING

When looking at Maria's interpretation of the poster there are several issues worthy of commentary. Some refer to the content of the message she believes the poster conveys, while others have to do with the argumentation from which Maria's final interpretation and positioning arise.

Concerning the content, we will first pay attention to her choosing of one element of the image from which to construct the whole argument: the scarf. Once its interpretation as a mask is discarded, the scarf signals thieves, represented by mercenary demonstrators following the command of corrupt unionists. What is more, the latter are presented as the image of the dishonest population of a country to which she cannot avoid feeling committed to.

This way of interpreting the piece of cloth covering the mouth of the human figure in the poster drives her to overrun any other possible interpretation of the poster as a whole. For her the poster carries a sarcastic meaning - thieves pretending to be saints fighting for justice, while really they are crooks.

On the one hand this has an easy contextual explanation. Setting up road blocks by demonstrators, who actually are unemployed (or unemployable) inhabitants of the shanty towns of the outskirts of the city, who act as political shock force rioters in the pay of union chieftains, is an all too frequent event, to the despair of the bulk of the population.

But on the other hand, the image has other components that María seems to have overlooked completely. To start with, the heavy presence of religious signs (it appears in the conventional posture of the *Sacre Coeur*), but also the rather ambiguous gender of the human figure, who could be a man or a woman. If it were the latter, it could also remind one of the title of one contemporary Argentinean novel "Santa Evita", by Tomás Eloy Martínez (1995). But there is something else. White scarves worn by women in Argentina is a sign of the *Plaza de Mayo Mothers* and later also *Grandmothers*. Originally they were a group of courageous women who silently demonstrated in Buenos Aires at the Plaza de Mayo, opposite the building of the presidency of the Republic, demanding news of their children and grandchildren who had disappeared during the bloody military dictatorship of the 1970s. They were seen as a sign of civic courage at the time, and later as one of the key actors fighting for justice once the military regime was toppled. Although it is true that currently Argentina wants to leave behind that nightmare, and that what is left of this group of women has turned into a sort of phantom organisation attempting to play a rather pathetic political role in current national politics, and has lost a lot of the respect they enjoyed before, it is also the case that they remain a strong symbol of civic courage. As a matter of fact, the legend explaining this poster in the exhibition (see http://www.moluanda.net/diosesargentino/) explicitly refers to the *Plaza de Mayo Mothers*, although it also plays with other meanings – a mask to protect from pollution, demonstrators behind barricades with white handkerchiefs above the guns of surrendering Argentinean soldiers in the Falklands.

It is paradoxical that a poster that seemed to be designed for conveying a message of courage (but also peace) before adversity, ends up being interpreted as a sign of hypocrisy and corruption. One cannot avoid pondering whether this is a consequence of María's worries about the current state of her country.

As it hardly could be otherwise, the interpretation of what the image means is also shaped by the setting in which the interpretation is produced. María is not speaking her thoughts into the air; she is talking to an interviewer who asked her to think aloud her thoughts while figuring out what the poster meant to her. So, when María talks, most of the time she has two addressees: the interviewer and herself, although not always on an equal basis. One may say that sometimes she neglects one for the sake of the other. This clearly happens when she becomes surprised by some of her own utterances. Then she begins developing arguments that most probably would have not appeared if she were on her own. The interview not only highlights but also encourages the dialogical process of interpretation. Thinking aloud in an interview is a sort of mixture of reporting one's retrospection to somebody else, engaging in new dialogues and, when so doing, going further into developing arguments.

This shows clearly in some elements of her interpretation. At the beginning some verbs appear in past tense as she is reporting her interpretation (*"when I saw the image like this, with the mask"*, *"I was thinking"*). But soon only the present tense appears, while the past tense only shows when referring to events within narrative arguments.

María's dialogical argumentation is a lively discussion among different voices which ends up producing an "image" of 'how we are' ("we *pretend to be saints but we really are little thieves"*). The ongoing argument involves the self of the interpreter appearing in different positions, as a perceiver, as a believer, as an addressee, but also as an actor walking in on an imagined scenery to carry out an action (*"if you wear something, and you say"*), an actor who could be anyone, but also yourself/herself.

The flow of interpretation suddenly changes when she gets an insight into what the image tells her (*"an Argentinean and fighter thief"*). This is a message she utters, but it is as if she were told by somebody else (*"bloody message* [...] *they are telling you"*; *"here they talk about barricades"*). It is told by they, in plural.

Why is it a "they*"* who speaks? Why not the poster, the human figure there portrayed, the graphic artist or whoever or whatever else? Perhaps this "they" is announcing the "we" of the final utterance. Maybe they are the 'others' María despises. The protagonists telling her the shocking "bloody message" are as foreign to her as the characters she despises. But these very same characters are also her peers. In her own words: "*if you wear* [...] *if you say"*. These *they*, are also a *you*, are equal to *me*; *they* and *I* belong to the same *we*.

Images have an illocutionary force when they are capable of making one feel concerned and moved. For this to happen, some elements of the figure have to be taken as signs of something affecting the self. If the objects signalled by the signs are felt as unpleasant, but cannot be rejected as foreign to oneself, because they are predicated to be a part of one's identity, the only way to come to terms with this object created by the semiotic process is to make it appear as uttered by somebody else's voice (a protagonist addressing me), or even to set a sort of dramatic performance in which different characters act and speak.

This is a case in which figuring out what a display means involves not only a dialogue among voices coming from different I-positions, but also voices of several third parties which one is reluctant to recognise as part of one's self, but are not foreign to one's identity. This shows how one's own social identity may go beyond the limits of the I-positions of the self. Or, even more, the boundaries of the self are fuzzy, somehow blurring who are the *they* I feel foreign to me, and who are the *we* to whom I feel to belong.

There is little doubt that self and identity are different concepts. We believe though that it would be worth exploring further the intricacies of how they relate to each other in different circumstances.

REFERENCES

Anscombre, J.C., & Ducrot, O. (1983). *L'Argumentation dans la langue. [Argumentation in language title]*. Bruxelles: Mardaga.

Aristotle (1991). *The art of rhetoric.* (H. C. Lawson-Tancred, Trans.). London: Penguin Classics.

Austin, J. (1962). *How to do things with words.* Cambridge, MA: Harvard University Press.

Bakhtin, M. (1981). *The dialogical imagination.* (C. Emerson & M. Holquist, Trans.). Texas: University of Texas Press.

Bakhtin, M. (1993). *Toward a philosophy of the act.* (V. Liapunov, Trans.) Austin: University of Texas Press.

Davies, B., & Harré, R. (1990) Positioning: The discursive production of selves. *Journal for the Theory of Social Behaviour, 20*, 43–63.

Foucault, M. (1983). *This is not a pipe.* California: University of California Press.

Frijda, N. (2004). *Emotion and action.* New York: Cambridge University Press.

Greimas, A. J. (1979). *Dictionnaire raisonné de la théorie du langage. [Reasoned dictionary of theory of language]*. Paris: Hachette.

Hedetoft, U. (1995). *Signs of nations.* Aldershot: Dartmouth.

Hermans, H. (1996). Voicing the self: From information processing to dialogical interchange. *Psychological Bulletin, 119,* 31-50.

Martínez, T. E. (1995). *Santa Evita.* Buenos Aires: Planeta.

Moscovici, S. (1984). The phenomenon of social representations. In E. M. Farr & S. Moscovici (Eds.), *Social representations* (pp. 3-70). Cambridge, MA and Paris: Cambridge University Press and Maison des Sciences de l' Homme.

Peirce, C. S. (1933-1948). *Collected papers.* Cambridge: Harvard University Press.

Rosa, A. (2007). Acts of psyche. Actuations as synthesis of semiosis and action. In J. Valsiner & A. Rosa (Eds.), *Cambridge handbook of sociocultural psychology* (pp. 205-237). New York: Cambridge University Press.

Scherer, K.R. (2004). Feelings integrate the central representation of appraisal-driven response organization in emotion. In A. S. R. Manstead, N. Frijda & A. Fischer (Eds.), *Feelings and emotion* (pp. 136-157). Cambridge: Cambridge University Press.

Searle, J. (1969). *Speech acts. An essay in the philosophy of language.* Cambridge: Cambridge University Press.

van Eemeren, F. (2002). *Argumentation: An overview of theoretical approaches and research themes.* Amsterdam: University of Amsterdam.

van Eemeren, F. (2003). The development of the pragma-dialectical approach to argumentation. *Argumentation, 17,* 387-403.

van Eemeren, F., Grootendorst, R., Jackson, S., y & Jacobs, S. (1993). *Reconstructing argumentative discourse.* Tuscaloosa, AL-London: University of Alabama Press.

van Eemeren, F., Grootendorst, R., Jackson, S., y & Jacobs, S. (1997). Argumentation. In T. A. van Dijk (Ed.), *Discourse as structure and process. Discourse studies: a multidisciplinary introduction* (pp. 208-229). London: Sage.

Voloshinov, V. (1997). La palabra en la vida y la palabra en la poesía. Hacia una poética sociológica. [Word in life and poetry. Towards a sociology of poetics] In M. Bakhtín. *Hacia una filosofía del acto ético. De los borradores y otros escritos,[Toward a philosophy of the act. Drafts and other manuscripts.]* (pp. 106-137). Barcelona: Anthropos.

Vygotsky, L.S. (1934). Thinking and speech. In R.W. Rieber & A.S. Carton (Eds.), *The collected works of L.S. Vygotsky. Problems of general psychology* (pp. 39-285). New York: Plenum.

Wertsch, J. (1991). *Voices of the mind.* Cambridge, MA: Harvard University Press.

Winsler, A., Fernyhough, Ch., & Montero, I. (2009). *Private speech, executive functioning, and the development of verbal self-regulation.* Cambridge: Cambridge University Press.

In: Dialogicality in Focus ISBN: 978-1-61122-817-5
Editors: M. Märtsin, B. Wagoner, E.-L. Aveling et al. © 2011 Nova Science Publishers, Inc.

Chapter 7

DIALOGUES ABOUT RESEARCH

Pernille Hviid and Zachary Beckstead

INTRODUCTION

From a dialogical research perspective, the self is rooted in the community in which the person engages and participates. In interaction with the community people develop I-positions from which they voice themselves, and thereby construct a dialogical self as a landscape of different I-positions. In principle it is assumed, that every new relationship gives rise to new I-positions. As James (1890) famously said: "a man has as many social selves as there are individuals who recognize him and carry an image of him in their mind" (p. 294). The specific relation we here address is the one established by researcher and research-participant in the field of research. We will explore dialogues within this field and reflect on the possible implications of such dialogues for research as well as for researchers and research-participants.

DIALOGICALITY AND THE DIALOGICAL SELF

Analysis of the research encounter in its multiple dialogicality is key to understanding how psychological knowledge is constructed from the data generated between researcher and researcher-participant (Hermans, 1991). Yet, what is dialogicality in the context of research? Josephs (2003) demonstrates how dialogicality has been a rather fuzzy term, often closer to being used as a metaphor than a well fleshed out conceptual framework. The term has often pointed to concrete talk between two (present and non-present) interlocutors, a model of man (Buber, 2002), and a model of meaning-making (Josephs, Valsiner & Surgan, 1999). For Marková (2003), dialogicality refers ontologically to social phenomena as having an oppositional nature (i.e., something is defined by what it is not), with these dialogical components being in tension and creating conflict and thus change instead of being grounded in static universals. Therefore, social phenomena are constantly in change and "situated in and interdependent with their external contexts, rather than being in self contained systems"

(p. 16). Additionally, Marková explicates the epistemological characteristics in the following way:

"(1) The human knower understands, creates, and constructs his social reality by way of signs and representations rather than to adopt them as ready-made codes. (2) Semiotic relationship is a triadic relationship involving the two (at least) interlocutors and a sign or a representation of an object. Therefore, epistemologically the basic unit of the construction of knowledge is a triad or a three step semiotic process of communication. (3) The construction of knowledge proceeds through interdependence between culturally and collectively transmitted signs which are reconstructed, given new meanings, and are changed in the experience of individuals." (Marková, 2003, p. 16)

This conception of dialogicality of course has significant implications for research encounters. First, since the research-participants are actively constructing their reality through signs, the implication is that any research question (i.e., from the very ordinary to the complicated) must be interpreted and made sense of by the research-participants. What may seem to be a clear question or request from the perspective of the researcher (e.g., "tell me about your home") may be understood in various ways by the research-participant. Communication is inherently fuzzy and vague (Rommetveit, 1985), and therefore, leaves room for misunderstandings (intentional and unintentional) and divergence of meanings. Whether it is a request to "tell me about your life" or a standard item on a questionnaire (Wagoner & Valsiner, 2005), the responses of participants can move into unanticipated directions as the process of meaning-construction unfolds (see Josephs, Valsiner & Surgan, 1999 for a discussion of *mean-acting*). Of course only methods sensitive to this possibility are capable of recognising and exploiting this aspect of dialogicality.

Josephs (2003) also notes that dialogicality often implicitly has the value-laden meaning of 'togetherness' or intersubjectivity and mutual understanding; yet this is not (always) the case, as we just noted above. As we demonstrate below, this dis-harmony can serve as the basis for novelty and surprises as the researcher is confronted by the emergence of reconstructed meanings in the research encounter. Furthermore, it is more than a reconstruction of meaning that occurs as researcher and research-participant meet. Research-participants (and researchers) *as* persons can act otherwise – ignore instructions or questions, mock the researcher (or research-participant), form alliances with other participants to obstruct data collection, transgress social boundaries, violate social norms or the emergent norms in the research setting, pursue their own projects or not participate in the research altogether.

Furthermore, dialogicality has been used to elucidate and elaborate notions of the self. According to the theory of the dialogical self, the self is conceived as "*social,* with the other, not outside, but in the self-structure, resulting in a multiplicity of dialogically interacting selves" (Hermans, Kempen, & van Loon, 1992, p. 23, original emphasis). The dialogical self is modelled as a multi-voiced system with separate I-positions, or alternative perspectives, that are derived and construed by the person from encounters with real and imagined others (Hermans, 1995, 2001). The self is inherently social even when alone or in isolation, since others occupy positions within the self. The self from the dialogical perspective has at its disposal simultaneously existing I-positions that come into contact with each other in agreement, opposition, ridicule, conflict and contradiction and thereby allow one I-position to modify, dominate, and possibly silence other I-positions.

The self-system changes and is changed by intra-psychological dialogues as well as by dialogues between concrete others or discourses that the person comes into contact. It is through these encounters that new I-positions emerge. Theory and research on the dialogical self have investigated the dialogical processes that occur as people move towards their uncertain futures (e.g., immigration or students moving towards professorship, Bhatia & Ram, 2001; Bhatia, 2002; Tappan, 2005).

A key aspect of the dialogical self for the thesis of this chapter is that I-positions can be endowed with voices that have 'stories to tell' about the world and the self. One implication of this is that research-participants *and* researchers enter the research setting with a range of perspectives and 'stories to tell' about the self and their worldviews. Hermans, Kempen and van Loon (1992) note that these voices can be constrained by various conditions. The researcher speaks from the I-position of socially guided and internalised understandings of what it means to be a researcher, whereas the research-participant often speaks from a position less constrained by knowledge of what a research-participant 'is' or should be. This means that the trajectory of the research encounter is not fixed and, therefore, there is a potential for the emergence of novel I-positions for the participant's self.

ENTERING THE FIELD

Researchers and research-participants 'enter' the research-setting and meet each other with a multitude of I-positions derived from encounters with concrete and imagined others in differing and overlapping social institutions and conditions.

The emergence of the activity 'doing research' begins with ideas and interests (perhaps fuzzy at first) of the researcher based on personal goal-orientations (e.g., to get published, to improve the world, to understand X better, to gain fame). These general goals are made more concrete as researchers engage in dialogues with advisors, colleagues, the laboratory group, the research literature, societal messages, and their own previous experiences. These others make the research questions more concrete and also provide guidance on what are the proper methods and techniques for collecting data. Thus, as researchers, before we enter any research setting and encounter research-participants, we engage and communicate with 'real' and imagined others; and these others play a crucial role in orienting researchers on how to conduct research. From the perspective of the dialogical self, these dialogues also take place 'within' the researcher as different voices, derived from the researcher's experience, encounters with others and social roles, communicate, agree or contradict each other. However, for much of psychological research this heterogeneity of voices moves towards a single voice in the methodological and technical sense (e.g., questionnaires, surveys) as well as in rhetorical sense as used in the final reconstruction of the research encounter presented in journal articles or conference presentations.

Furthermore, the many I-positions or voices that are in play (or could be in play) guiding what researchers do, how they *should* act before, after, and during research, and how they (should) relate to the research-participants, are channelled and move towards a unified position (e.g., a researcher is objective and completely competent, in charge and in control).

Thus the voice of the researcher can expropriate (at least temporarily) the other voices within the self-system; it can silence or swallow other competing voices of the researcher as *person*. For example, the researcher in Milgram's (1974) studies did not react when 'teachers' increased the electric shock on 'learners' but maintained his position as 'experimenter' in spite of the anxiety of participants.

Similarly, outside the research setting, the research-participant as *person* moves back and forth between numerous social roles—son, father, co-worker, worshipper—that are textured by encounters with real and imagined others. Our point here is that the research-participant does not enter the research with *one* story or perspective on the world (including themselves), but with a multiplicity or polyphony of positions that can be in agreement or in contradiction, and with a vague understanding of what psychological research is about, stemming from, for instance, media sources. Ordinarily the research setting (e.g., a laboratory or a classroom where questionnaires are filled out) is removed from the participants' everyday settings and encounters, and they come to the 'pristine' environment of research with untidy, unsystematic and often incoherent attitudes, beliefs, and feelings.

Thus, while the researchers might have convinced themselves that the research situation is neutral, it can range from the unusual to the bizarre from the perspective of the research-participant because research in a laboratory is not functionally related to their life-worlds (Tajfel, 1972). This requires the participant to construct a new I-position (i.e., 'I am a research-participant') and accept it – rather than continue using old ones (e.g., 'I am your friend'). The research setting thus provides a unique context for the emergence of a new voice or perspective for the research-participant that can enter into dialogue with other I-positions.

CONSTRAINING THE SOCIAL ROLES

It is usually the researcher who has structured the field and defined the range of possible choices for the research-participant in psychological research. The researchers themselves typically maintain a safe distance from the research-participants in order to avoid problems of reactivity, stemming from the fear that revealing too much information would compromise the study, possibly in ways desired by the researcher. However, as we argued above, this commonly employed monological perspective in research (Aronsson & Hundeide, 2002), also makes the research setting inherently ambiguous: research-participants are told that they are discussing a mutually engaging phenomenon with the researcher, whilst the researcher is investigating, for instance, the 'theory of mind' of the research-participant. Ambiguity in the research situation is thus created by researchers' attempts to 'shield' their hypotheses and intentions in order to attain authentic beliefs and responses, and by research-participants' simultaneous efforts in trying to 'read the mind' of the researcher and through that escape from the fuzziness of the situation. In other words, while the researcher has made an effort to eliminate traces and obscure their intentions, the research-participants are oriented towards anticipating the subtle cues and gestures of the researcher and research materials and are searching for the latent meanings.

Consider for example the process of filling out a questionnaire. Seeing an item in a questionnaire stimulates an inner dialogue for the research-participants in which they attempt to decode the meaning of the question (and intent of the researcher) and to provide a suitable answer. The process of filling out a questionnaire is thus a dialogical process, as research-participants struggle to create a 'typical' response— that somehow reflects the whole range of the person's experiences (Wagoner & Valsiner, 2005). Yet, research-participants' inner dialogues, in spite of the dialogical process through which answers are arrived at, are almost never explicitly recognized by the researcher during data collection or in later reports of the findings. The outcome response – the 'near-to-truth' answer given by research-participant – becomes interpreted by the researcher as if it was a unitary representation. While the research-participant can refuse to answer items on a questionnaire or write comments on the margins, these responses do not usually enter the later stages of data analysis. In other words, 'mainstream' psychological research is oriented towards preventing anomalies, boundary crossings, and other transgressions in the research setting.

In spite of these best efforts of researchers, research does not always proceed smoothly along unambiguous trajectories. Psychological research operates between the boundaries of control/non-control. In spite of the efforts of the researcher to impose order upon the research and the research setting (control), uncontrollable events and reactions in both the research and research-participant can emerge. These 'failures' are rarely reported in the final products (publication or presentation) of research, and therefore a 'cleaner' and more coherent picture of the research process emerges than in fact is warranted.

CRITICAL DIALOUGES ABOUT RESEARCH

In the preceding we have presented problems of dialogicity in empirical research. We have argued that both researcher and research participant enter the empirical zone of research with different kinds of prior experiences and tacit expectations to what is going to happen. We have also assumed that an unbalanced positioning of power between researcher and research-participant, which partly stems from meta-constraints of what is considered to be valid science, create dialogical problems. This makes the research-participants submissive to the more or less implicit ideas of the researcher, or creates a situation where both parties try to define the common agenda of the meeting and seek to maintain the frustrating and energy consuming mutual blindness. In what follows we will present empirical work aimed at exploring these problems, and the new challenges arising therein. The study aimed at investigating children's experience of their own development. Five 12-year-old children participated in three 1.5 hour interviews at their youth club.

Children's Experiences of Communication in and outside Research

As researchers of child development we are aware how often children are put in dialogical difficulties not only within but also outside research context. Referring to Grice's principles of communication Aaronsson and Hundeide (2002) characterise the majority of research conversations with children as being monological. That is, while children believe that they are communicating with the researcher about a subject of shared relevance, the researcher is in reality 'measuring', for example child's cognitive abilities. This type of conversation is not completely different from children's everyday experiences in, for instance, schools and preschools. As Mehan (1979) has pointed out, children are obliged to learn the communicative rules of 'known-answer-questions' during their institutional trajectory: they learn that a question from an adult most probably does not mean that the adult does not know the answer, but rather that the adult is examining whether the child knows the right answer or not.

To break that everyday communication pattern we chose to be as explicit as possible about our research agenda and made an effort to 'translate' our rather complex theoretical position into ideas that we thought 12-year-old children could grasp and work with.

Theoretically, our approach to developmental studies is cultural-historical (Vygotsky, 1998; Rogoff, 2003), with a strong emphasis on children's actions (Valsiner, 1997, 2000), their experiences (Vygotsky, 1998; Gottlieb, 2003), their meaning-making and reflections upon the world and themselves (Gillespie, 2006), their engagements (Hviid, 2008) aspirations and developing interests (Vygotsky, 1998), but also acknowledging the institutional traditions (Mehan 1986; McDermott, 1993) that are canalizing their developmental pathways (Hedegaard & Chaiklin, 2005) as well as the numerous social and symbolic resources or blockings they are offered (Zittoun, 2006) and choose or reject along the way. We consider temporal concepts like 'the new', 'the changed' and 'the remaining the same' to be important to track (Sato, 2007) in children's developmental trajectories.

As an attempt to offer an unambiguous and theory-consistent position to the participating children, they were told that books on children's development were written by adults largely without asking children. The children were critical of this information and accepted to join the work and help the researcher[1]. As a agreement of communication the researcher urged the children to resist being misunderstood by the researcher, since it would be unpleasant to them and create 'bad research' for the researcher. Children often referred to this when they corrected the interpretations of the researcher: "I know it is difficult to understand, since you haven't been there", "OK, lets try once more" or "Yes, that is most often what people think, but...". Moreover children were told that the researcher was equally interested in good and bad experiences, and that both were needed in order to get an authentic picture of the children's developmental experiences. Rather than selecting between 'good' and 'bad' the researcher urged the children to deal with issues of importance to them.

The Life-map Method

The concept of development is a rather abstract one for 12-year-old children to deal with. To support their participation they were asked to draw maps of their lives. They were asked to describe the places they had been over time, the particular meanings they ascribed to them, the choices they made, the changing interests they developed and the conflicts that appeared. So children drew tracks, roads, bumps and highways between different places, such as nursery, kindergarten, home and the football club. They drew symbols and wrote comments to their maps, marking their specific engagements, such as horses, Harry Potter's Golden Lightning, new friends, whereby the researcher was given sense of engaged pasts, present and possible futures situated in time and space. Other children chose to depict their life not as a

---

[1] The interviews with children were conducted by the first author of the chapter.

map, but as a 'mood-line' that went up and down (or straight) according to their remembrance of their mood in a particular period.

These drawings worked as 'papers in progress' between researcher and research-participants and both parties referred to the drawing during the interview to understand and explain, but the children always had the final word on whether or not to represent the specific themes on the map. For instance, one of the children decided not to draw his nursery, since it was to him, only "a small bump on the road". At other times a child's detailed comments, which to the researcher appeared to be things of lesser importance, were put on the paper, such as the release of the first translated Harry Potter book.

From the researcher's point of view, through the specific constraints of the empirical setting we tried to create an authentic zone of cooperation by relating to the children's lives and life circumstances, by promoting their choices and specific interests, and by supporting their resistance to misunderstandings or misinterpretations. Good and bad experiences were considered equally important, and the researcher positioned herself as someone who needed help and knowledge from the children.

In this chapter we will focus on some of the data from the last interviews with two of the five children. These cases are selected since they raised critical issues about the research practice, and thus are the ones we learn the most from.

In the last interview, the researcher drew on the map a small 'zone of research–bubble'. The children were asked to 'enter' it and reflect on three questions: 1) how the research had made an impact on their life experience, 2) how they would judge the data they had created as participants, and 3) did they have suggestions as to how to improve the research setting and procedure.

Jonathan: If you Come Closer you will Get More from me

Like other children, Jonathan thought that he got something out of his participation. He came to remember more things and he became "self-wise", as he explained. Yet he raised some clear critical points regarding the research, as the following dialogue indicates[2].

> Interviewer: I wonder whether you have any good advice regarding how to interview?
> Jonathan: You should have spent 20 minutes telling me about yourself. Where you live, whether you have a boyfriend, and what your hobbies are. Because that way it is actually easier to answer more questions, and you can go into depth when you know a little about the person.
> Interviewer: Yes, but why? I can well understand what you say, but why?
> Jonathan: Because, I believe you can trust the person better the more you know the person, you know who the person is. Then, I know how you are. Then I can decide whether I should put a limit on the different kinds of things or whether one can just chat away. Now I'm just chatting away because I know that this is an education for you, so I help you with a thing, and so I just tell you.

---

[2] All the interviews were conducted in Danish and translated to English. An effort has been made to retain the general 'feel' of children's talk.

Jonathan appealed to a more multi-faceted presentation of the researcher/person, since it could clarify what he would share with her, which would in turn make his contribution more precise. He called for other I-positions of the researcher. The researcher explained her positioning.

> Interviewer: ... for instance in therapy, I don't know if you know anything about that, but there there's a rule that you don't do it, so we haven't really learnt it, we are not told that we should do it. So it is really exciting that you say that you think that one should.
> Jonathan: Now we are in a rather different situation. In fact, it is not you helping me, but actually me helping you.
> Interviewer: Yes. (Laughs) That's an important difference.
> Jonathan: It is your decision, but I advise you to do it. Then there would be another style of psychologists. That would only be good.

Jonathan seemed to know that therapists are *helping* their clients, but again he pointed out that the roles were reversed here, since it was Jonathan who was helping the researcher, which demands "another style of psychologists". From here on the researcher started investigating the influence of the researcher-position from Jonathan's point of view. Could it be that Jonathan would have responded differently, if he had been interviewed differently by the researcher? Or would he have answered differently if he was interviewed by someone else? Jonathan was certain that his perception of the interviewer had a huge impact on his participation and thus on the elaboration of data.

> Interviewer: Yes, but why do you believe that?
> Jonathan: Yes OK, let's take it again (giggles)
> Interviewer: No, no, but why would it be different if the person was someone other than me?
> Jonathan: Because the person has different attitudes towards different things, they have different questions and different points of views. They would ask questions in other ways and I would answer them in other ways. If you ask questions as you do now, I answer as I do now, if you asked other questions in other ways, I would reply in ways that suited that way.
> Interviewer: But if I wrote my questions down [and gave them] to another person, those that I had planned from the start, do you believe it would be more or less the same interview?
> Jonathan: Sort of... But no ... not at all.
> Interviewer: So it's also something about how I am when I ask you?
> Jonathan: Yes. That's it. I mean, I don't know how you are personally, but believing that you are who you are, I have said those things I have said. If it was another person, I would approach her, like she is, in that way ...

Jonathan also claimed that he would have answered differently had the interview sequence been repeated by the same researcher, because he had already "changed" through the first 'round' of questions. Either way, the social situation at hand would have been different, and so would the data. Despite this, when he evaluated the content of what he actually said, he recognised himself in it.

> Interviewer: If you were to evaluate the story given to me and the drawing you have made then: is it a picture of your life? Could there be another picture? Could it have looked totally different?

Jonathan: Hmmm, if I had been another person, of course.

Interviewer: No, no. It is you.

Jonathan: Or if you had told more about yourself?

Interviewer: No, I just really mean ... (thinks)

Jonathan: You are thinking

Interviewer: Yes. It is difficult. Now it's really more how you think the story reflects you. Is that how you think your life has been, within the limits you think I should know about?

Jonathan: Yes. I think I have done a good job. It [the map] reflects much of myself but there are still a lot of things that you don't know about me. I could have gone into depth here a hundred times as much. A hundred times as much. In broad outline ... in broad outline... Like a map without cities. That is how it is, yes.

In Jonathan's search for the 'best practice' – from his perspective – he called for positions other than a classical researcher I-position. His argument was that the topic of the research – his personal development – could only be explored in depth through such a close personal encounter. He seemed to say: Come closer, and you will get more from me. In principle, the proposal to enhance collaboration is logical and convincing, and thus rubs against the researcher's attempts to create a satisfying cooperative framework for the empirical investigations.

But were there other reasons, beyond the achieved quality of research, why Jonathan would have wanted a closer relationship with the researcher? Or, put another way: why didn't all the kids ask us to come closer? Which other experiences and I-positions in Jonathan's life might support that need?

Jonathan's life-map and his narratives about his life gave us some hints for interpretation. Jonathan was generally very much on his own with regard to adults. It had been like that for most of his life. Both of his parents were very ambitious in their careers. We judge them to be highly interested and competent employees, but rather absent parents. His brothers and his sister had left home years ago. He was, in his own words, "always the last to be picked up at kindergarten", "always the last to be picked up at the leisure centre", a boy who spent a lot of time with "stupid nannies, who were mostly watching Lotto on television." His cats gave him some comfort, and the older boy upstairs, who was beaten up by his drunken father, was a close friend of his.

As a 12-year-old boy, Jonathan washed his own clothes, did the shopping, and made dinner for himself and for his parents. When asked, "Do you always make the dinner for your parents?" he replied: "No, sometimes they have already eaten, before coming home." Jonathan had difficulties in school too, since he was diagnosed as dyslectic at the time of interviewing, and therefore preparing for a school change. Jonathan explained that his life was a bit tough, but as he saw it he had two options: he could stand and wait for the bus that never came, or he could simply start walking. So he walked. Besides, there were also advantages connected to his parent's occupations; next week he was going to New York with his father, who had received an award for his work. He was looking forward to flying in Business Class. But all in all, there were good reasons why Jonathan would want a person, who was interested in him and his life, to come closer, and stay longer.

Jonathan's personal situation was demanding, but he managed. He is an absolutely unique and fascinating person. But so are many other children that the researcher comes in contact with. Obviously researchers cannot build close and continuous relationships with all of them. Or could they? Besides this issue, the consequences of such close encounters are unforeseeable; it is way beyond the contract with children's parents, not to mention the ethical dilemmas involved. It would be very difficult. But could it be made to work?

Lucy: Too Many Hearts to Bear

Lucy had great difficulties making her life map. She could not figure out how to do it. She asked the researcher how the other children had approached the task and was told that some made spatial representations over time whereas others made lines, depicting their mood through different periods. Lucy wanted to try the mood-line. While she did that, narratives of her life at home, amongst friends and boy-friends, in school and in leisure time activities came to life. But Lucy was never satisfied with her drawing. "It's ugly!" she stated in the second interview. In the third interview, the researcher opened the possibility that she could draw a new one. She felt like making a less coherent map, with different non-linked episodes, but rejected the opportunity to make a new drawing, because she found it "difficult to draw situations". Prompted by the researcher's remark that the drawing was already filled with situations, Lucy stated: "*I don't know ... I guess this is how it has been, right?*"

It seemed that the drawing Lucy had made both fitted and did not fit Lucy's life. At first the researcher considered this to be a) a technical problem related to drawing, perhaps Lucy was generally discontented with her drawing abilities; b) a representational problem, perhaps the map did not catch the important aspects of her life; or c) a theoretical one, perhaps Lucy did not see her life as continuous sequence but rather as bits and pieces. These considerations might all be true. But could she have other reasons to consider the drawing ugly, yet at the same time see it as "how it has been"? We believe she had, and this raises a new problem for the contemporary child-centred research. Lucy made some discoveries while drawing her mood-line. She was surprised to see how often she had fallen in and out of love during the 12 years of her life. Since kindergarten, boyfriends replaced each other in a continuous sequence, and "the boy I was in love with at that particular time" seemed to make a real episode of Lucy's life. She was very critical about this new discovery; she called her love "un-serious".

> Interviewer: What do you come to think of, when you look at the drawing?
> Lucy: There are too many hearts, considering that I am only a seventh grader.
> Interviewer: Why are there too many hearts?
> Lucy: It looks like a lot. It has taken up too much of my everyday life ... I think it is strange, that I suddenly stop [being in love] and then there is a new one, maybe I have liked none of them at all, maybe I only believe I am in love all the time ... its always: Now I don't like him anymore, now I like a new one.

As Lucy was looking at the map, the map looked back at her and voiced her continuous falling in and out of love. Comparing herself with her female friends she commented that they had not fallen in love that often, and they did not talk about boys all the time as she did. From other narratives we came to know that it was precisely her falling in love with boys that was the core of many conflicts with other girls and harassing behaviour from other girls. She quarrelled, for instance, with her best friend because of a boy they both "wanted", and she ended losing both the friend and boyfriend. In other conflicts, she was teased by female friends because of her fast-changing rather dramatic love. She was falsely told by other girls that the "love of her life" at that time was seeing another girl. She was hurt by this untrue information, withdrew from her peers and even the boy she loved seemed annoyed with her. There were also many broken hearts in Lucy's narratives. Still, "the boy she was in love with" made her heart beat, made her attend school and made her endure teasing female friends.

Her "girl-behaviour" was criticised also in other corners of her life. Her father considered her style of dress to be much too vulgar for her young age. Looking back on it, she agreed with his judgment that it was "too much", but at that time she was blind to the vulgarity.

Lucy was not content with her life. The researcher tried at one point to share her own childhood loves with Lucy, and talked about love as something fine and precious. But Lucy's point of view was firm: it was not fine. It was "ugly and unserious"; ugly together with many other ugly things in her life. Lucy's narratives were about people who were not very attentive to her needs (her family members), people who were not very kind to her (bullies in school), boys who did not respond to her feelings towards them, difficulties in school subjects, worries that she therefore might not become a doctor as she wanted, and analysis of her life wherein she was rather critical about her own behaviour. Lucy had many sad and difficult stories to tell; they coloured almost all her different I-positions.

During the research interviews then Lucy started an auto-dialogue about who she was, and had been, with the help of other voices looking at her and reacting to her: friends, boyfriends, parents and teachers. She came to view her life very critically. Although the researcher did not voice criticism, the research activity set in motion Lucy's reflection about who she was. The map was a research device and it 'screamed' back at her. The map was precisely as ugly as she considered her life to be; an ugliness not due to a technical problem or a representational problem, but due to an existential problem.

> Interviewer: Do you feel, that you have told me too much?
> Lucy: In fact I think of it as some kind of relief, to tell one person everything. Other people might ask about one particular thing, and I tell that, and other people ask about something else, but there is never anybody … even my mother doesn't know my full [story]

Although telling was some kind of a relief to Lucy, she had until now preferred the 'chopped up' version of her life. Why did Lucy agree to look at her life, in the first place, through the research, when she did not want to see? Why did Lucy choose to participate in research? It was explained in a clear and child-friendly way that the research was about the children's experience of their life and development. Why would she proceed to deepen the knowledge of her hurtful life? The truth of the matter is that she read the invitation differently.

> Lucy: I thought it was like the other time, to a women's magazine, but it was not … I had not anticipated that I would tell my life story.
> Interviewer: So, you have been interviewed before?
> Lucy: Yes, in "Alt for Damerne" ("All for the ladies")
> Interviewer: And that was different?
> Lucy: Yes

How could a 12-year-old girl know the difference between an interview for a women's magazine and a research interview? She could not, and so she agreed to participate in something other than the research intended. Besides this point, like other children who participated, Lucy saw new aspects of her life while participating, like all the hearts she was to draw. She could not foresee that.

Our interpretation is that it was tough for Lucy to look at her life, but perhaps even tougher to keep it inside herself or 'chop it up', so no one – not even herself or her mother – would notice her difficulties. The contemporary child-centred strategy offered Lucy a chance to look with the researchers, but at something she did not like looking at – her life. Our interpretation is perhaps flavoured by our research agenda, since we, as researchers are equally interested in coming to understand 'good' and 'bad' life trajectories. Children like Lucy might have another point of view.

DISCUSSION: SURPRISES, EMERGING I-POSITIONS AND ETHICAL DILEMMAS

As these research examples illustrate, 'entering the field' and encountering others (potential research-participants) is not without challenges, tensions and surprises. The categories of 'researcher' and 'research-participant' and what these mean (to both researcher and to research-participant) are not simply given but are also ambiguous, negotiated and challenged. Both children discussed here did at different times question the researcher and the research activity and thereby produced conditions for the researcher to see herself and her practice in a new light. Likewise, the researcher and research activities invited the research participants to recall memories of different important places and activities in their lives, to describe their engagements and social positions and, on another level, to move between different I-positions by looking at the drawing, thereby promoting opportunities for self-reflection. Both children saw themselves in new light, as "self-wise" or as someone who had occupied herself too much with falling in love. These meetings thus created a multitude of opportunities for both parties to 'become other' (Gillespie, 2006) and thereby develop new understandings of themselves and the activity.

Researchers' Surprises

Two examples of surprises are particularly worth mentioning at this point. First, the case of Jonathan illustrates the reversal of positions between 'researcher' and 'research-participant'. As Jonathan points out to the interviewer, he is helping her instead of the other way around. A point acknowledged and recognised by the interviewer's laughter. And this laughter is significant since it indicates that the interviewer is 'caught' in deviating from her own principles in the research setting, while the child stays within the contract.

It is surprising how difficult the reversal of positions between children and adults and between psychologists and research-participants is. This exchange alters the trajectory of the dialogue between researcher and research-participant and Jonathan immediately "advises" the interviewer to adopt a style or approach more conducive to openness between both parties. Later in the interview, Jonathan is the one questioning the interviewer and the interviewer suddenly is the one struggling to answer questions. Indeed, this exchange leads to and is guided by the emergence of new I-positions for both Jonathan ("I-as-knower", "I-as-researcher") and the interviewer ("I-as-research-participant").

The second example of dialogicality in the research encounter is illustrated with the case of Lucy. Recall that Lucy ended up sharing more of her life story than she anticipated. This stemmed in large part from her misreading and misinterpreting the research invitation. From the perspective of the researchers, the instructions and details of the invitation were clear and spoken and written in a 'child-friendly' manner. However, as we mentioned earlier, the instructions (conceived as signs) are not necessarily the same for the researcher and research-participant. Lucy, like all participants, had to make-sense of the 'collectively transmitted signs' (Marková, 2003) and drew on her past experience (obviously unknown to the researchers) to do so. What was clear to the researchers (i.e., a multifaceted interview exploring the life of children) was not grasped by Lucy.

Moving and Melting I-positions

In analysing the data it becomes clear, how children's self-positioning in the research was informed by and 'fertilised' by their positioning elsewhere, in their everyday life. Jonathan's participation is the clearest example of that. His argument, that the personal information given had to be mutual to work in an interview on personal development, is in line with a scientific rationality, but it was also in line with his personal needs in his everyday life.

Lucy's wish do draw disconnected social situations could point to a theoretical problem of how to conceive the person – as fragmented or as unified – but it was, at the same time a strategy she had relied upon outside the research setting, in order not to be confronted with her unhappiness. Thus the research-participants drew upon what they more or less consciously knew to be a strategy of life to them or a need to them.

The I-positions of the 'research-participant' were thus informed by other positions developed in their everyday life and social encounters, as well as in relation to the specific proposals to and criticism of the research that reached far into their lives outside of the research setting. This does not discard their critiques on a theoretical level, rather the opposite. When facing a rather loosely constrained new context, as the 'zone of research', they seemed to invest their whole lives into that space and with all that, they made helpful comments on the research and its conceptions. We can therefore not point to any distinct research-participant I-position; what we see instead is different positions melting into each other. To make it even more complex, Jonathan stated that he would answer differently, if he was to be asked again, since he had already changed, during the first interview. He incorporated his experiences of his participation in the research so fast that the interview, as a locus of the negotiation of I-positions, also became a process of reflection on the part of Jonathan that transformed his visions of his own life process that is the very object that the researcher's interviews aimed to understand.

Moving towards Democratic Research

It is tempting to seek shelter in the old-fashioned monological type of research when looking at these complexities for both parties. The monological conversation is something children already know very well, appropriate easily and even contribute to. It comes easy to an adult in an ordinary adulto-centric society too. Besides, the academic society approves it, and questions of research validity to be thus answered are simple, straightforward and clear. By applying that conversational logic, Lucy would not be involved and invited to look at her difficult life together with the researcher and Jonathan would not feel the need to invite the researcher, to come closer thereby putting her in a very difficult ethical situation. But the monological research is just as difficult to believe in today, as it is to believe in the observational method where observer is merely a 'fly on the wall'. There is no escape.

The research presented here did manage to create some degree of mutual relevance; we observed children describing their participation in the process as making them "self-wise". But we also met Lucy to whom the process of self-reflection and reflections on her general life situation was painful, a situation that called for much more support to her life outside the interview setting, than the research offered. Jonathan invited the researcher to 'come closer and stay longer', which probably would have been beneficial for both parties. Lucy did not make that strong invitation, probably due to her very late understanding of what the activity was about. We suspect that she would have been much more proactive, had the research better matched with the timings of her movements. Without wanting to belittle the children's motivation to 'help the researcher', we assume that the full vitality of the research activity comes alive when both parties envision 'a better life' trough the participation. The 'zone of research' also managed to create some degree of collaboration between the participants. It seems to be beneficial to the quality of research and the participation of the child that research is translated as far as possible and framed by an explicit contract, making it possible for participants to resist misinterpretations and to comment on the research procedure.

The radical consequence of these dialogical challenges, as we see it, is not to simplify the research activity, but to complicate it even further. In walking the line to its end we anticipate a solution based on the establishment of communities of researchers and research-participants, where the objectives and the direction of the research as well as the intervention in practice outside the empirical 'zone of research' is constituted and created as a shared agenda with importance to both parties. This also implies that both parties agree on the interpretation of the research, the necessary intervention of the research as well as the decision of when to begin and when to terminate the activity. It is for the research to sort out issues of ethics, economy and to make that possible in research-time.

ACKNOWLEDGMENTS

We would like to acknowledge the work of Ditte Winther-Lindqvist, who carried out some of the interviews as part of her educational training, as well as Brady Wagoner for his constructive reading and commenting on the text.

REFERENCES

Aronsson, K., & Hundeide, K. (2002). Relational rationality and children's interview responses. *Human Development*, *45*, 174-186.

Bhatia, S., & Ram, A. (2001). Locating the dialogical self in the age of transnational migrations, border crossings and diasporas. *Culture & Psychology, 7*, 297-309.

Bhatia, S. (2002). Acculturation, dialogical voices and the construction of the diasporic self. *Theory & Psychology*, *12*, 55-77.

Buber, M. (2002). *The Martin Buber reader: Essential writings*. A. D. Biemann (Ed.). New York: Palgrave Macmillan.

Gillespie, A. (2006). *Becoming other: From social interaction to self-reflection*. Charlotte, NC: Information Age Publishing.

Gottlieb, G. (2003). Probabilistic eigenesis of development. In J. Valsiner & K. J. Connolly (Eds.), *Handbook of developmental psychology* (pp. 3-18). London: Sage.

Hedegaard, M., & Chaiklin, S. (2005). *Radical-local teaching and learning. A cultural-historical approach*. Aarhus: Aarhus University Press.

Hermans, H. J. M. (1991). The person as co-investigator in self-research: valuation theory. *European Journal of Personality, 5*, 217-234.

Hermans, H. J. M. (1995). The limitations of logic in defining the self. *Theory & Psychology, 5*(3), 375-382.

Hermans, H. J. M. (2001). The dialogical self: Toward a theory of personal and cultural positioning. *Culture & Psychology*, *7*(3), 243-281.

Hermans, H. J. M., Kempen, H., & van Loon, R. J. P. (1992). The dialogical self: Beyond individualism and rationalism. *American Psychologist, 47*(1), 23-33.

Hviid, P. (2008). Next year we are small, right? Different times in children's development. *European Journal of Psychology of Education*, *23*(2), 183-198

James, W. (1890). *The principles of psychology. Vol. I.* New York: Dover Publications.

Josephs, I., Valsiner, J., & Surgan, S (1999). The process of meaning construction: Dissecting the flow of semiotic activity. In J. Brandstadter & R. Lerner (Eds.), *Action & development: Theory and research through the life span* (pp. 257-282). Thousand Oaks, CA: Sage.

Josephs, I. (2003). Varieties of dialogue: Instead of an introduction. In I. Josephs (Ed.), *Dialogicality in development* (vii – xvii). Westport, CT: Praeger Press.

Marková, I. (2003). Dialogicality in the Prague school of linguistics: A theoretical retrospect. In I. Josephs (Ed.), *Dialogicality in development* (pp. 3-33). Westport, CT: Praeger Press.

McDermott, R. P. (1993). The acquisition of a child by a learning disability. In S. Chaiklin & J. Lave (Eds.), *Understanding practice. Perspectives on activity and context* (pp. 269-305). New York: Cambridge University Press.

Mehan, H. (1979). "What time is it Denise?" Asking known information questions in classroom discourse. *Theory into Practice*, *18*(4), 285-294.

Mehan, H. (1986). *Handicapping the handicapped. Decision making in students educational careers*. California: Stanford University Press.

Milgram, S. (1974). *Obedience to authority*. New York: Harper.

Rogoff, B. (2003). *The cultural nature of human development*. New York: Oxford University Press.

Rommetveit, R. (1985). Language acquisition as increasing linguistic structuring of experience and symbolic behaviour control. In J. Wertsch (Ed.), *Culture communication and cognition: Vygotskian perspectives* (pp. 183-204). Cambridge: Cambridge University Press.

Sato, T., Yasuda, Y., Kido, A., Arakawa, A., Mizoguchi, H., & Valsiner, J. (2007). Sampling reconsidered: Idiographic science and the analysis of personal life trajectories. In J. Valsiner & A. Rosa (Eds.), *Cambridge handbook of sociocultural psychology* (pp. 82-106). Cambridge: Cambridge University Press.

Tajfel, H. (1972). Experiments in a vacuum. In J. Israel & H. Tajfel (Eds.), *The context of social psychology: A critical assessment* (pp. 69-121). London: Academic Press.

Tappan, M. (2005). Domination, subordination and the dialogical self: Identity development and the politics of "idealogical becoming". *Culture & Psychology, 11*, 47-75.

Valsiner, J. (1997). *Culture and the development of children's actions. A theory of human development.* New York: Wiley.

Valsiner, J. (2000). *Culture and human development.* New Dehli: Sage.

Vygotsky, L. S. (1998). *Child Psychology. The collected works of L. S. Vygotsky, Vol. 5.* New York: Plenum Press.

Wagoner, B., & Valsiner, J. (2005). Rating tasks in psychology: From static ontology to dialogical synthesis of meaning. In A. Gűlerce, A. Hofmeister, I. Staeuble, G. Saunders & J. Kay (Eds.), *Contemporary theorizing in psychology: Global perspectives* (pp. 197–213). Concord, ON: Captus University Publications.

Zittoun, T. (2006) *Transitions: Development through symbolic ressources.* Charlotte, NC: Information Age Publishing.

In: Dialogicality in Focus
Editors: M. Märtsin, B. Wagoner, E.-L. Aveling et al.   © 2011 Nova Science Publishers, Inc.
ISBN: 978-1-61122-817-5

COMMENTARY TO PART II:
DIALOGICAL METHODOLOGIES IN PRACTICE

Kyoko Murakami

INTRODUCTION

I shall discuss methodological issues of social science research practice – analysis and research process in response to reading the three chapters showcasing analyses of materials (story, image and talk-in-interaction). My intention is not to argue a specific position to dialogical self theory and its research practice, but to simply have a dialogue. I shall address methodological challenges and concerns in the critical community of social scientists including intertextuality, visual analysis and the importance of research contexts and reflexivity of research practice.

INTERTEXTUALITY IN ANALYESES

The multi-authored contribution by Wagoner et al. (2011) uncovers I-positions in relation to others as a unit of analysis. In particular, beyond the obvious analytical conclusion of multivocality, the work brilliantly reveals the inevitable variability of the analyses, as well as showing voices as a unit of analysis that is variable. Rather unsurprisingly we are faced with a variety of unique analytical texts, as a result of applying the dialogical self theory to the same material *The Guerrillero* by the Columbian writer Albanlucía Angel. The variety of the researchers' styles of writing within the chapter shows their distinctive analytical logics, principles and preferred strategies of treating the research object (the story) as a static text. These analytical texts constitute a discursive community of argumentation for the dialogical self theory, showing intertextuality of the analyses conducted on the same material. According to Rose (2007), "[i]ntertextuality refers to the way that the meanings of any one discursive image or text depend not only on that one text or image, but also on the meanings carried by other images and texts" (p. 142). The chapter authored by Wagoner et al. reflects the way in which each analyst relates to the text (a short story in this case) with other texts including the analyst's personal beliefs and values, theoretical preferences and methodology, and epistemic stance (how the researcher comes to understand and claim his/her knowledge). When it comes to working with the politically charged, sensitive topics featured in Angel's story, we see the process of analysis being imbued with the challenge of grappling with the analyst's own moral dilemmas as well as with the storied dilemmas.

The concept of intertextuality opens up a way of thinking about the research process, namely triangulation and the reliability of data analysis by multiple researchers. A singular research object (a story), by virtue of the collaboration produces an intertext of analyses. The intertext in its multiple forms yields infinite possibilities for interpretation, like many other discursive practices. The chapter as an intertext can provide a fruitful way of entering into dialogue with others in the dialogical self research community – an opportunity to explore further possibilities for alternative interpretations and the amalgamation and hybridization of analyses.

Dialogical self theory's analytic strategy of focusing on I positions provides a window into individual subjectivity and meaning making in dialogue with social others. Yet, in the analytic practice, it is important to recognise that the linguistic I's and reflexive pronouns are manifested differently within world languages. For instance, in the case of the Japanese language, which I am familiar with, linguistic pronouns are marked very differently from the English language and quite often not marked at all. In demystifying the view of English (Anglo)-specific 'I', Harré (1998) extends the grammar of self and unveils the intricacies of I's as context-bound. Needless to say, the dialogical self theorist works with data in other languages. This is not to say that the dialogical self researcher should produce analysis on the data in other languages. Rather it raises the challenge, commonly shared by qualitative researchers, of operationalising concepts (such as self, identity, personhood and subjectivity), a process that is not straightforward and depends on the individual researcher.

Following its assumption that 'I' is multivocal, dynamic and relational as an agent of action, the dialogical self analysis captures self in terms of time. I-positions are thought of as being time-bound, including varieties of I-positions 'me in the past', 'me in the present', 'me in the future' and various points of time in the process of self in the making. But what is meant by 'me in the past' for instance? Why is it important to highlight? Surely, the systematic hunt for 'I''s in the text yields a helpful starting point in the analytical process, achieving data reduction. In this stage of the research process, the analyst reduces the text into a matrix of I's and generates categories that reflect each researcher's aims and theoretical agenda. Here, in the analyses of Felicidad's recollection of harrowing past experiences, time is seen as being linear and chronological (*chronos*). We tend to conceive time unproblematically in terms of *chronos*, but Greek concepts of time also include *kairos,* opportune time in English translation, referring to a moment in time when something special happens (Martin-Vallas, 2009). The latter concept of time – *kairos* – might help us to understand Felicidad's lived experience.

In the following, building on the time-bound analysis of I-positions, I temporarily traverse to the literary field, especially to the notion of stream of consciousness, to which Wagoner et al make an ephemeral mention. At present, my thinking on this issue is admittedly premature. The attempt would hopefully stimulate an interest in producing an analysis that captures the dynamics, relationality and fluidity of self beyond the commonplace notion of time and place.

Stream of Consciousness

Stream of consciousness, coined by William James (1842-1910), is an influential concept in modern psychology (see also Shotter, 2011, p. 84). It also contributed to the development of a literary genre and the way human experience is expressed, read and analysed in a literary form at the turn of the 20th century. According to Humphrey (1954), stream of consciousness as a literary label is an genre for presenting the psychological experience of a character in fiction. He argues that "[S]tream-of-consciousness fiction differs from all other psychological fiction precisely in that it is concerned with those levels that are more inchoate than rational verbalization – those levels on the margin of attention" (Humphrey, 1954, p. 2). Thus, the conventional distinctions – I as author, narrator, and animator – can be challenged and blurred. Simply put, the story written in the style of stream-of-consciousness is characteristically devoid of chronological time, leaping in syntax and ignoring other writing rules. "The combination of omniscient description with internal monologue will recall to the reader the method used in 'Mrs Dalloway' and 'To the Lighthouse'" (Humphrey, 1954, p. 117) by Virginia Woolf, one of the pioneers of stream-of-consciousness novels. As an example of the influence of stream-of-consciousness fiction, the short story *The Guerrillero* is illuminating. Of particular interest here is the use of elaborate symbolism to express the dream qualities of consciousness within a lucid story, reflecting Humphrey's characterisation. The reader is introduced to a dream-like world, with an effective yet incoherent and disjointed montage of symbols, used in the representation of Felicidad's inner dialogues. The story, written in the style of the stream of consciousness, removes the reader from anything specific – even though there are a number of specific, local details that can be envisioned and imagined. *The Guerrillero* is one such story that defies the reader's traditional expectations of plots and story lines according to the chronological time (*chronos* or *kronos*). By doing so, the story weaves together the voices of the author, narrator and animator. *The Guerrillero* depicts *kairos* time as experienced by the author-narrator-animator (as Felicidad sees, feels, remembers, asks questions and thinks of things).

In my first reading of *The Guerrillero*, I simply could not 'follow' the story. Only after repeated reading and consulting an introductory commentary, did I come to speculate and appreciate the invocation of a specific political history of oppression and other contexts in which the story is situated. The text is filled with implicit, subtle and intricate meanings, which make it difficult to understand the plot. We can note the absence of a plot, which disrupts a sense of sequential time (*chronos*) in the events featured in the story. This is characteristic of the stream of consciousness novel. In the story, various pronouns were marked with the past-present-future time frame. Certainly the analyses trace and document transitions triggered by ruptures (Zittoun, 2006) in the protagonist's encounters and interactions with others. Focusing on I-position as a non-static multivocal subject, the story signifies Felicidad's 'becoming'.

A strong sense of becoming can be better understood when considered in light of Henri Bergson's (1859-1941) process philosophy (Middleton & Brown, 2005, p. 59). Bergson's work is developed against traditional Western philosophy, which is concerned with 'substance' – explaining the matter of things, and their essential qualities, rather than exploring the relationship between things or the transformation within things (Middleton & Brown, 2005). This has had a profound effect on the methodology of social sciences, as Middleton and Brown argue in line with Bergson's view that the things we experience in the world around us become secondary. Against the narrative tradition, in an unadulterated way, *The Guerrillero* depicts the very Bergsonian notion of Felicidad's experience in the way she experiences the world around her. Her world can be seen in continuous motion with the 'I's' and Me's in dialogues occurring in different times and spaces. Bergson elaborates this idea of becoming in terms of duration – the time of living (*durée*). Duration is the experience of time passing. It involves a succession of conscious states, enabling conscious beings to break their absorption in the present moment. For Bergson, consciousness is constituted as an 'organic whole', where states blend into one another (Middleton & Brown, 2005, p. 63). Bergson's concept of becoming and duration, in my view, might help us understand Felicidad, in the way her various senses of self are anchored in the stream-of-consciousness and in the concept of duration (*durée*) that is unbreakable and indivisible. Analysing I-positions according to conventional time and place may thus reduce Felicidad's experience into substance. The analysis then is simply to 'explain' the substance. This does not mean, however, that we are able to understand Felicidad's experience in the way that Bergson and James may have approached it – as *durée* and stream of consciousness.

VOICES IN IMAGES

In the dialogical self theory, multivocality is a prominent concept. Voices are not confined to speaking subjects; they can be projected onto images and pictorial media. Lonchuck and Rosa's (2011) analysis illustrates that images and pictures are polysemic and as signs, are carriers of ideological messages. The images and pictures pose dialogical self researchers an added methodological challenge as they are seen to be deceptively static and fixed to a specific space in time. In this section, I shall reflect on the ideas provoked by Lonchuk and Rosa's analysis, underlying the view that the act of analysis of the visual experience can be considered as forming a relationship between the authors/analysts and the images in a given moment.

Graphic art images are complex representations of the dynamic interaction between society and individuals. Increasingly, with the advent of digital media, we as researchers benefit from capturing the world as both living and lived in the way experiences come to matter. Especially, coupled with latest popularity of visual methodologies (e.g., Banks, 2001; Prosser, 1998; Rose, 2007), social science researchers work with the images, paying great attention to the context and surroundings where the images are placed—the environment and people. The dialogical self researcher seeks to understand the situated meanings of the image as signs by focusing on the dialogical relation which the image forms with the person (including the researcher). The visual methods researcher focuses on the 'use' of images in the analysis, incorporating ethnographic descriptions of the context in which the images are put to use and their function.

Visual methods used to be more the confined interest of the scholars of cultural studies. However, the analysis by Lonchuck and Rosa demonstrates that it is possible to study self in dialogue with others in a work of art. Their analysis confirms the importance of examining aspects of the material and physical world, which has been explored by Valsiner (2008). He recognises the abundance of signs in the living environment and its impact on the human psyche and psychological functions.

Whilst illustrating how images can be made sense of and interpreted, the analysis begs a question about an obscure stance of the analyst – whether the analyst ontologically remains outside the phenomenon of the pictorial images being viewed in a location, context and point in time. Out of a concern with methodological issues of ontology and epistemology, I ask where the dialogical self researchers position themselves when acknowledging and synthesising the perspective of the analyst and their relationship with the research object and the context within the analysis. With Lonchuck and Rosa's analysis, who is the 'one' who sees, feels and make sense of the images? Who is the 'I' – an imagined, generic viewer or the analysts themselves? How would the analytic act differ from that of the 'ordinary' viewer? Whose interpretations is the analysis representing? These questions might help clarify the epistemic stance that the researcher-analyst makes in analysing the images. How does one come to know the voice(s) in art and pictorial images? In what circumstances is the research relationship with the images formed? These questions and issues defy the positivistic notion of validity aimed at ensuring the scientific value of meanings and interpretations that the analysts draw. The questions prompt dialogical self researchers to ascertain their stance and approach to the knowledge they produce. In the following I shall elaborate on this point by considering the notion of reflexivity using the chapter by Hviid and Beckstead.

REFLEXIVITY

The chapter by Hviid and Beckstead (2011) addresses the issues regarding what is commonly known as criteria for good research, such as validity, reliability and ethical issues. Clearly, judging from its theoretical assumptions and focus, dialogical self research values reflexivity – the self-awareness – of the researcher. Although of ethnomethodological origin, reflexivity is a term that has been influential across social science disciplines. Reflexivity is a significant feature of social research and occupies a central methodological concern for ethnographic researchers (Hammersley & Atkinson, 2007). It recognizes an ontological stance that "researchers are inescapably part of the social world that they are researching" (Cohen, Manion, & Morrison, 2007, p. 171). Here, in line with Hammersley and Atkinson's definition, I would like to consider how reflexive understanding of research practice shapes and reshapes the relationship between the researcher and the researched. The researcher's awareness of what is being studied in terms of reflexivity certainly echoes Hviid and Beckstead's concerns. They grapple with a troubling complexity of *topos* (context/place, mentioned by Lonchuk and Rosa), the research field, problematising the influence the researcher as part of the field has on the data (Hviid and Beckstead). Rather than trying to eliminate researcher effects, Hviid and Beckstead acknowledge and disclose their own selves in the research, seeking to understand their part in, or influence on the research. The concept of reflexivity seems to resonate with the spirit of the dialogical self theory, supporting the view that the orientations of research will be shaped by their socio-historical locations, including the values and interests that these locations confer upon them. It also rejects the idea that social research is, or can be, carried out in some autonomous realm that is insulated from the wider society and from the biography of the researcher, in such a way that its findings are unaffected by social processes and personal characteristics.

Furthermore, the methodological issues in dialogical self research, as discussed in the three chapters, seem to suggest an exploration of self as a critical project, according to Gillian Rose:

> "Reflexivity is an attempt to resist the universalizing claims of academic knowledge and to insist that academic knowledge, like other knowledges, is situated and partial. Reflexivity is thus about the position of the critical, about the effects that position has on the knowledge that the critic produces, about the relation between the critic and the people or materials they deal with, and about the social effects of the critic's work." (Rose, 2007, p. 137)

What Hviid and Beckstead document in their chapter is what Hammersley and Atkinson typically call "the researcher's ethnographic text of the field as part of the general process of reflexivity in that it helps to construct the social phenomena it accounts for" (2007, p. 202). Their discussion implies recognition of the extent to which researchers shape the phenomena that they study. "The careful ethnographer will be aware that all classes of data have their problems, and all are produced socially; none can be treated as *transparent* representations of *reality*" (Hammersley & Atkinson, 2007, p. 130, original emphases). According to the dialogical self theory, the researchers undertake various positions, in and out of the research field with their attention to the details of the research setting and participants, with an emerging sense of negotiated research ethics and power relations that their research interaction is manifested through.

PROCESS OF SELF AS OPEN AND AMBIGUOUS

Along with two other contributions, and perhaps more strongly than them, Hviid and Beckstead stress the openness and inherent ambiguity of the social relations initiated and developed by research. "Any research question [...] must be interpreted and made sense of by the researcher-participants" (Hviid & Beckstead, 2011, p. 148). The question posed by the researcher provides multiple/infinite possibilities for the respondents/participants' answers, as "research participants and researchers enter the research setting with a range of perspectives and 'stories to tell' about the self and their worldviews [...] [and] the trajectory of the research encounter is not fixed" (Hviid & Beckstead, 2011, p. 149). "There is [thus also] a potential for the emergence of novel I-positions for the participant's self" (ibid.). These reflections of the dialogical self researcher accord with the contemporary methodological critique of orthodox psychology and other social sciences.

Unique to their contribution, Hviid and Beckstead put forward a strong awareness of research as being in the institutional structure and the process of research intersecting with the social life of the research participants. They also explicate how institutional traditions "are canalizing their developmental pathways" together with the "numerous social and symbolic resources or blockings" that are offered to/taken away from them and taken up/rejected by them (p. 152). Therefore, although the research setting is an open and ambiguous social process, it is not free from the rules or ideological messages of the research setting which provides an institutional framework. In social science research, judgement as to what is ethically right or appropriate is a grey area, subject to negotiation. In order to better understand the acts of research participation, the researcher takes great pains to observe and make sense of what is going on, documenting social conventions and regulations of how the researcher and the researched interact and, jointly construct meaning. Within dialogues between the researcher and the researched (however asymmetrical they may be), research participation is reciprocal. The research participant, likewise, observes the researcher in an on-going interaction, working out the goals of the research and producing the 'right' answers. The research-mediated interaction is no different from any other form of social interaction. The interpretative task at the stage of analysis might go beyond a focus on I-positions of the researcher and the research participant. The nuanced accounts of restrictions to access, taboos and socially managed positions are produced in research interviews. In such institutional research, it is difficult to separate the self and the institution. Having said this, it is not possible to ensure that social science research, including the dialogical self research, can claim the real, true and factual status of the researched knowledge. These thoughts leave Hviid and Beckstead, and the dialogical self researchers more generally, with a myriad of dilemmas and contradictions.

IN CLOSING

In this commentary, I have addressed some common threads in dialogical self research based on the three chapters which analyse fiction (a short story), pictorial images, and a reflexive account of research interviews. Variability in the unit of analysis as well as the outcome of the dialogical self analyses in analysing speech sheds light onto the process, especially the living and lived experience of a person. Wagoner et al's chapter underlies the importance of time and the process of becoming in understanding the dynamic and relational sense of self. The dialogical self analysis goes beyond describing the substance of the phenomena in question, following Bergson's philosophy. Furthermore, the context of self-making is an important focus, as demonstrated by Lonchuk and Rosa. Reflexivity of the dialogical self researchers, particularly evident in Hviid and Beckstead's chapter is well explored. The authors of the three contributions provide a helpful opening to a methodological dialogue. Their work helps develop further methodologies and creatively applies the dialogical self theory to advance in rigor, appealing to a wider range of social science researchers.

REFERENCES

Banks, M. (2001). *Visual methods in social research*. London, Thousand Oaks, New Delhi: Sage Publications.

Cohen, L., Manion, L., & Morrison, K. (2007). *Research methods in education. Sixth Edition*. London: Routledge

Hammersley, M., & Atkinson, P. (2007). *Ethnography: Principles in practice. Second Edition*. London: Taylor & Frances.

Harré, R. (1998). *The singular self: An introduction to the psychology of personhood*. London: Sage.

Humphrey, R. (1954). *Stream of consciousness in the modern novel.* Berkeley, CA: University of California Press.

Hviid, P. & Beckstead, Z. (2011). Dialogues about research. In M. Märtsin, B. Wagoner, E. Aveling, I. Kadianaki & L. Whittaker (Eds.), *Dialogicality in focus: Challenges to theory, method and application* (pp. 147-162). New York: Nova Science Publishers.

Lonchuk, M. & Rosa, A. (2011). Voices of graphic art images. In M. Märtsin, B. Wagoner, E. Aveling, I. Kadianaki & L. Whittaker (Eds.), *Dialogicality in focus: Challenges to theory, method and application* (pp. 129-146). New York: Nova Science Publishers.

Martin-Vallas, F. (2009). From end time to the time of the end: some reflections about the emergence of subjectivity. (L. de Galbert, Trans.). *Journal of Analytical Psychology, 54,* 441–460.

Middleton, D., & Brown, S. D. (2005). *The social pscyhology of experience: Studies in remembering and forgetting.* London: Sage.

Prosser, J. (Ed.). (1998). *Image-based research: A sourcebook for qualitative researchers.* London: Falmer Press.

Rose, G. (2007). *Visual methodologies: An introduction to the interpretation of visual materials.* London: Sage.

Shotter. J. (2011). From 'already made things' to 'things in their making': Inquiring 'from within' the dialogic. In M. Märtsin, B. Wagoner, E. Aveling, I. Kadianaki & L. Whittaker (Eds.), *Dialogicality in focus: Challenges to theory, method and application* (pp. 77-102). New York: Nova Science Publishers.

Valsiner, J. (2008). Ornamented worlds and textures of feeling: The power of abundance. *Critical Social Studies, 1,* 67-78.

Wagoner, B., Gillespie, A., Valsiner, J., Zittoun, T., & Salgado, J. (2011). Repairing ruptures: Multivocality of analyses. In M. Märtsin, B. Wagoner, E. Aveling, I. Kadianaki & L. Whittaker (Eds.), *Dialogicality in focus: Challenges to theory, method and application* (pp. 105-128). New York: Nova Science Publishers.

Zittoun, T. (2006). *Transitions: Development through symbolic resources.* Charlotte, NC: Information Age Publishing.

PART III: DIALOGICALITY IN SOCIAL PRACTICES

In: Dialogicality in Focus   ISBN: 978-1-61122-817-5
Editors: M. Märtsin, B. Wagoner, E.-L. Aveling et al.   © 2011 Nova Science Publishers, Inc.

Chapter 8

Innovative Moments in Psychotherapy: Dialogical Processes in Developing Narratives

*Miguel M. Gonçalves, Carla Cunha, António P. Ribeiro,
Inês Mendes, Anita Santos, Marlene Matos and João Salgado*

Introduction

This chapter presents an overview of the research programme that is being developed in our research centre addressing narrative change processes in psychotherapy. Our departing point was the narrative metaphor of psychotherapy (Angus & McLeod, 2004; Bruner, 2004; Hermans & Hermans-Jansen, 1995; White & Epston, 1990) and the emphasis on the narrative construction and re-construction of the self (Bruner, 1986, McAdams, 1993, Sarbin, 1986), which assumes that clients transform themselves through the stories they tell – to themselves and to others. We also proceed from the idea that self-narratives entail particular dialogical processes that can become visible or be enhanced in the psychotherapeutic setting. Furthermore, by adopting this dialogical and narrative standpoint, therapists and clients can use this inner multiplicity as an opportunity for identity changes.

While this general metaphor of 'clients as storytellers' has framed our work in psychotherapy research, the re-authoring model of White and Epston's (1990; see also White, 2007) and the dialogical perspective of Hermans and collaborators (Hermans, 1996; Hermans & Hermans-Jansen, 1995; Hermans & Kempen, 1993; Hermans & Dimaggio, 2004) have been shaping our conceptual lenses in the study of change in therapy.

In this chapter we elaborate upon a central concept of our research: the concept of *innovative moments* (*IMs*, also named as *i-moments* in previous publications), drawn from White and Epston's (1990) notion of 'unique outcome' and discuss the dialogical dynamics that are involved in IMs emergence and development in therapy.

CHANGE AS NARRATIVE RE-CONSTRUCTION OF THE SELF

Over the last decades, several authors within the narrative and dialogical fields have been acknowledging the centrality of 'telling stories' in human lives (e.g., Bruner, 1986; McAdams, 1993). Self-narratives are the result of the human effort to create meaning from our experience in the world and to have our perspectives validated by others, to whom we are dialogically intertwined (Gonçalves, Matos & Santos, 2009). The construction of meaning through self-narratives involves a process of interpretation, selection and synthesis of life experiences (McAdams, 1993). Complex elements of episodic memory, personal and social expectations, emotional and interpersonal experiences are selected and integrated into a personal account in the form of a story. The story is performed to others in the specific act of telling it, simultaneously projecting a certain present view into the future. The segments of the experience that are integrated in our self-narrative frames are shaped by our prior salient and more familiar experiences, both with social others and with ourselves. Additionally, the stories we tell are also constrained by the interlocutor and the context (for example, our self-narratives vary according to the social role we are assigned in a given context).

Therefore, given the multivocal nature of these sources of narrative production (see Hermans, 1996), self-narratives involve processes of dialogical negotiation, disagreement and conciliation between self and other (this 'other' can be specific social others, broader cultural messages and prescriptions, or even other parts of oneself).

Hence, the process of narrating a story pictures the self, as narrator, in dimensions that go beyond the narrated content. Self-narratives present the possibility of simultaneously revealing our authorship – by the way we view ourselves – and disclosing our position in the world – by the way we present ourselves to others (Wortham, 2001). As Hermans (1996) claims, this means that the self is simultaneously embedded in the content of the story and the act of telling it to another person. According to some authors (Hermans, 1996; see also Sarbin, 1986), this dual feature of agency and positioning of the self – both as an author/narrator and a social actor – is critically embedded in the unfolding narrative process, and it is through this process that self can be transformed.

According to the re-authoring model of White and Epston (1990), clients frequently seek therapeutic help when the self has lost its ability to flexibly interpret the world, becoming trapped within redundant forms of meaning-making that are no longer capable of incorporating the diversity and multiplicity of lived experience. Clients become entrapped in 'problem-saturated stories' (White, 2007; White & Epston, 1990) – that is, narratives that dominate and minimize the possibilities of creative and flexible meaning, and thus become problematic.

These all-encompassing stories usually favour one perspective over multiple others (being more monological than dialogical; Hermans & Hermans-Jansen, 1995), and tend to be fixed around a single dominant problematic theme (see Neimeyer, Herrero & Botella, 2006; Santos & Gonçalves, 2009). As a consequence they constrict personal adaptability and undermine other possibilities for thinking and acting (Gonçalves et al., 2009). For example, a client seeking therapy in order to deal with daily anxiety and panic attacks, may narrate several stories in the session that illustrate how he or she is too afraid to engage independently in everyday life activities, always needing to be taken care of by other members of the family.

In this case, fear is the theme of the problematic self-narrative and avoidance behaviours appear as compliance with the problem's rule.

Congruently, therapy can be an opportunity for gaining awareness of the constraining power of these problematic self-narratives and developing alternative, more flexible ones. Following White and Epston (1990):

> "when persons experience problems for which they seek therapy, (a) the narratives in which they are storying their experience and/or in which they are having their experience storied by others do not sufficiently represent their lived experience, and (b), in these circumstances, there will be significant and vital aspects of their lived experience that contradict these dominant narratives." (p. 40)

Thus, with the acknowledgement that there are always details of lived experience not assimilated by the problematic self-narrative, the therapist's action in re-authoring therapy should lead to the search for these opposing aspects or 'unique outcomes' in the client's life. According to White and Epston (1990), the concept of unique outcome refers to all details outside the problematic self-narrative that appear as exceptions to the problem's prescriptions and an attentive therapist would be listening to them within the stories brought by their clients. In the above example, our client that is currently consumed with panic attacks can remember a situation in the past when he or she was able to leave home alone and did not experience any panic attack as predicted (i.e., a unique outcome towards fear). White and Epston (1990) have argued that:

> "As unique outcomes are identified, persons can be encouraged to engage in performances of new meaning in relation to these. Success with this requires that the unique outcome be plotted into an alternative story about the person's life." (p. 41)

Along these lines, by bringing the client's awareness to these exceptional moments opposing the power of the problem, therapy can introduce novelty in meaning-making and, thus, create opportunities for the emergence of new self-narratives (White, 2007). Social validation (by the self, the therapist, meaningful social others) is essential in the development of the new self-narratives since narratives are always performative acts and, as such, produce relational results and new lived realities to which, in turn, we must reinterpret and adapt to.

When we began our research project, we directly took the notion of 'unique outcome' to analyse data but our terminology evolved along with our findings (Gonçalves et al., 2009). We now prefer the notion of IMs for two main reasons: first of all, 'unique' might convey the misleading idea – for readers unfamiliar with the re-authoring model – of rare experiences appearing outside the problematic rule; however, these exceptions occur quite frequently in therapy, even in unsuccessful cases. Secondly, the term 'outcomes' stresses results or outputs and, as we shall argue, these innovations reflect a developmental process building up towards a given outcome at the termination of therapy (that traditionally is classified into good or poor outcome). It is because we are more interested in the developing nature of narrative transformations in therapy that we favour the notion of IMs over unique outcomes.

INNOVATIVE MOMENTS AS OPPORTUNITIES FOR THERAPEUTIC CHANGE

In our initial studies of re-authoring therapy with a sample of women who were victims of domestic violence (Matos, Santos, Gonçalves & Martins, 2009), we inductively identified five categories of IMs: 'action', 'reflection', 'protest', 're-conceptualisation' and 'performing change' IMs (Gonçalves et al., 2009). We will now present these categories, illustrating them with clinical vignettes. In each example, an IM is identified according to the problematic self-narrative specific to the case[1].

Action IMs are events when the person acted in a way that is contrary to the problematic self-narrative.

> Clinical vignette 1 (problematic narrative: agoraphobia)
> Therapist: Was it difficult for you to take this step (not accepting the rules of "fear" and going out)?
> Client: Yes, it was a huge step. For the last several months I barely went out. Even coming to therapy was a major challenge. I felt really powerless going out. I have to prepare myself really well to be able to do this.

Reflection IMs refer to new understandings or thoughts that undermine the dominance of the problematic self-narrative, sometimes involving a cognitive challenge to the problem or cultural norms and practices that sustain it. In this sense, reflection IMs frequently assume the form of new perspectives or insights of the self, somehow contradicting the problematic self-narrative.

> Clinical vignette 2 (problematic self-narrative: depression)
> Client: I'm starting to wonder about what my life will be like if I keep feeding my depression.
> Therapist: It's becoming clear that depression has a hidden agenda for your life?
> Client: Yes, sure.
> Therapist: What is it that depression wants from you?
> Client: It wants to rule my whole life and in the end it wants to steal my life from me.

Protest IMs involve moments of critique, confrontation or antagonism towards the problem (directed at others or at oneself), its specifications and implications or people that support it. Opposition of this sort can either take the form of actions (achieved or planned), thoughts or emotions, but it necessarily implies an active form of resistance, repositioning the client in a more proactive confrontation to the problem (which does not happen in the previous action and reflection IMs). Thus, in this type of IMs we can always distinguish two positions in the self (implicit or explicit): one that supports the problematic self-narrative and other that challenges it; in these moments the second position acquires more power than the first.

> Clinical vignette 3 (Problematic self-narrative: feeling rejected and judged by her parents)
> Client: I talked about it just to demonstrate what I've been doing until now, fighting for it.

---

[1] These clinical vignettes were based on Gonçalves et al. (2009).

Therapist: Fighting against the idea that you should do what your parents thought was good for you?

Client: I was trying to change myself all the time, to please them. But now I'm getting tired, I am realising that it doesn't make any sense to make this effort.

Therapist: That effort keeps you in a position of changing yourself all the time, the way you feel and think.

Client: Yes, sure. And I'm really tired of that, I can't stand it anymore. After all, parents are supposed to love their children and not judge them all the time.

Re-conceptualisation IMs are closer to stories due to their time sequencing nature. In these types of narratives there is a personal recognition of a contrast between the past and the present in terms of change, and also the personal ability to describe the processes that lead to that transformation. It is because the person is capable of describing the processes underneath the achieved changes – through a meta-reflective level – that these IMs go further than action, reflection and protest. Not only is the client capable of noticing something new, but he or she is also capable of recognizing him or herself as different when compared with a past condition, due to a transformation process that happened in between. Thus, they always involve two dimensions: a) a description of the shift between two positions (past and present) and b) the transformation process that underlies this shift.

Clinical vignette 4 (Problematic self-narrative: domestic violence and its effects)

Client: I think I started enjoying myself again. I had a time...[2] I think I've stopped in time. I've always been a person that liked myself. There was a time... maybe because of my attitude, because of all that was happening, I think there was a time that I was not respecting myself... despite the effort to show that I wasn't feeling... so well with myself... I couldn't feel that joy of living that I recovered now... and now I keep thinking "you have to move on and get your life back".

Therapist: This position of "you have to move on" has been decisive?

Client: That was important. I felt so weak in the beginning! I hated feeling like that.... Today I think "I'm not weak". In fact, maybe I am very strong, because of all that happened to me, I can still see the good side of people and I don't think I'm being naïve... Now, when I look at myself, I think "no, you can really make a difference, and you have value as a person". For a while I couldn't have this dialogue with myself, I couldn't say "you can do it" nor even think "I am good at this or that".

The final category is *performing change IMs*. They refer to new aims, projects, activities or experiences – anticipated or acted – that become possible because of the acquired changes. Clients may apply new abilities and resources to daily life or retrieve old plans or intentions postponed due to the dominance of the problem.

Clinical vignette 5 (Problematic self-narrative: domestic violence and its effects)

Therapist: You seem to have so many projects for the future now!

Client: Yes, you're right. I want to do all the things that were impossible for me to do while I was dominated by fear. I want to work again and to have the time to enjoy my life with my children. I want to have friends again. The loss of all the friendships of the past is something that still hurts me really deeply. I want to have friends again, to have people to talk to, to share experiences and to feel the complicity of others in my life again.

---

[2] "..." - stands for a pause in the conversation.

According to Bruner (1986), narratives always imply two landscapes: on the one hand, there is the 'landscape of action' that refers to who the actors are, what actions are taking place, and what setting or scenario is framing the development of the plot. On the other hand, there is the 'landscape of consciousness' that refers to what the actors know, feel, think, value or plan. If we take Bruner's two dimensions, we could clearly say that action IMs belong to the 'landscape of action' while reflection IMs belong to the 'landscape of consciousness', each being "pure" representatives of that particular dimension. Protest IMs, in turn, can occur in one landscape or the other, or even have elements from both; likewise, performing change can be situated at both landscapes, since they can refer to new feelings or thoughts ('consciousness') and also actions and plans ('action') triggered by change. Re-conceptualisation IMs, as they involve a meta-reflective level, usually combine elements from both landscapes, integrating them.

Levels of Development in Narrative Innovation

In recent works (Ribeiro, Bento, Salgado, Stiles, & Gonçalves, in press; Ribeiro, Bento, Gonçalves, & Salgado, 2010), we have been trying to understand the possible role of IMs in therapeutic development with the notion of change as a multilevel process. This is inspired in the work of Fogel, Garvey, Hsu and West-Stroming (2006) that use this idea in the study of early dyadic mother and child interaction. These authors depart from the notion of 'frame' as their observation unit. Frames are "segments of co-action that have a coherent theme, that take place within a particular location (in space or in time), and that involve particular forms of mutual co-orientation between participants" (Fogel, Garvey, Hsu & West-Stroming, 2006, p. 3). These authors distinguished two typical frames: the 'guided object frame' (when the mother is guiding the play with the child through the use of objects) and 'the non-guided object frame' (when the child picks the toy and starts playing with it autonomously, without the adult's help). When studying the mother and child interaction, they noticed changes at three levels, each with different implications. A 'level 1 change' relates to a "natural" variability in the way mother and child play (on one day mother and baby can be playing with a ball and on the next day with a doll, but the 'guided object frame' is similar, since they maintain identical gestures and games towards the object). A 'level 2 change' happens when an innovation appears within the segment (within the 'guided object frame', the child, for the first time, throws the object to the ground and the mother picks it up). Finally, a *level 3 change* implies a clear developmental change (this can occur if, following our example, the child starts playing a new game of throwing and reaching a toy, this time without the help of the adult, repeating it over time and stabilizing a 'non-guided object frame').

Applying these three levels to psychotherapeutic change, we could say that, clients enter therapy with problematic self-narratives (White & Epston, 1990), in which a redundant theme is repeated over and over again, despite the possibility of telling and storying different events or situations (a "natural" variability equated to level 1 changes). For example, in depression, there is an enduring theme of hopelessness and helplessness in the client's problematic self-narratives, while in anxiety disorders, danger and avoidance constitutes the rule or the plot connecting the stories together. Once in a while, something different emerges in the stories told during therapy as an exception to the problematic rule; that is, an IM (paralleled to level 2 changes). For example, the client has a different emotional experience that was not congruent with her or his expectations concerning the problem or plans, something divergent from the boundaries and power limitations set by her or his difficulties. If these innovations are noticed, elaborated and valued as something "interesting" and "worthwhile" by therapist and, more importantly, by client, they can lead to enduring developmental transformations (level 3 changes). We parallel level 3 changes in psychotherapy to the development of a new self-narrative, through the elaboration of IMs that emerge. We will later also discuss the processes that allow the elaboration of changes from level 2 to level 3 and also how this process can be undermined, leading to the maintenance of the problematic narrative.

DESCRIBING THE INNOVATIVE MOMENT CODING SYSTEM

The five types of IMs presented above were systematised in the *Innovative Moments Coding System* (IMCS; Gonçalves, Ribeiro, Matos, Santos & Mendes, in press), a qualitative method applicable to various research projects, from single cases to samples from different therapeutic models and even interviews about problems outside psychotherapy. The application of the IMCS requires at least two trained coders. Their training requires the familiarisation with the relevant theoretical notions and coding procedures, through several training exercises. We have structured the training in order to develop the various skills required for the methodological application of IMCS.

Then, these two coders engage independently in an initial reading/listening/visualisation of the materials (sessions or interviews) in order to be familiarized with the problems under analysis and their development. Afterwards, the coders meet in order to discuss and agree in terms of what the problematic self-narrative is and the different dimensions that it involves (personal, interpersonal, professional, etc). A list of problems is, then, consensually elaborated in close approximation to the client's self-narrative (in terms of words, expressions, metaphors). The following independent identification of IMs departs from this first step. IMs are always identified in their relation to the previously/initially identified problematic self-narrative and it takes into consideration the specificity of the problem: for example, the act of "*walking away from the situation*" can be regarded as an IM in relation to a problem of domestic violence; alternatively, in a different case, it can be part of the avoidant behaviour that sustains a panic disorder.

Each session is analysed independently by each coder, according to three steps that result in three IM indexes (for further details, see Gonçalves, Ribeiro, Matos et al., in press):

1. Identifying IMs and defining their onset and offset in the session. The *temporal salience* of IMs is then, computed, as the percentage of time (in seconds) occupied by each IM. We consider that the duration is a preferred measure to the frequency of IMs since it reflects more closely their narrative elaboration. Several indexes of IM temporal salience can be computed: we can have an interest in computing the temporal salience of each type of IM in each session or the IM temporal salience for the entire case (as the mean score of IMs' temporal salience in all sessions).
2. Categorizing IMs in terms of the five types (Action, Reflection, Protest, Re-conceptualisation and Performing Change).

3. Identifying who elicited IMs, i.e., who was responsible for their *emergence*. There are mainly three possibilities: a) the IM was explicitly produced by the therapist (through a question or commentary about the client), being accepted and further elaborated by the client; b) the therapist implicitly triggers or facilitates a client' subsequent IM, through an indirect form (asking, for example: *What have you learned from this experience?*); or c) the IM emerges spontaneously from the client, without therapeutic guidance. The decision of which of these three possibilities applies to each IM is performed after the other two indexes are addressed.

MAJOR FINDINGS OF IMS' RESEARCH PROJECT

Since the coding of IMs involves the analysis of each session in a therapy case, second by second, we have been working with relatively small samples (contrasting successful and unsuccessful cases) or conducting intensive case-studies. Up until now, our major findings derive from one sample of narrative therapy with women who were victims of domestic violence (N=10 participants; Matos et al., 2009), emotion-focused therapy (EFT) with depressed clients (N=6 participants; Mendes, Ribeiro, Angus, Greenberg, & Gonçalves, 2010) and client centred-therapy also with depressed clients (Gonçalves, Mendes, Cruz, Ribeiro, Sousa, Angus & Greenberg, submitted). Additionally, several case-studies from different therapeutic orientations have also been studied at a more microanalytic level (Gonçalves, Mendes, Ribeiro, Angus, & Greenberg, 2010; Ribeiro, Gonçalves & Ribeiro, 2009; Ribeiro, Gonçalves & Santos, in press; Santos, Gonçalves, Matos, & Salvatore, 2009; Santos, Gonçalves, & Matos, 2010).

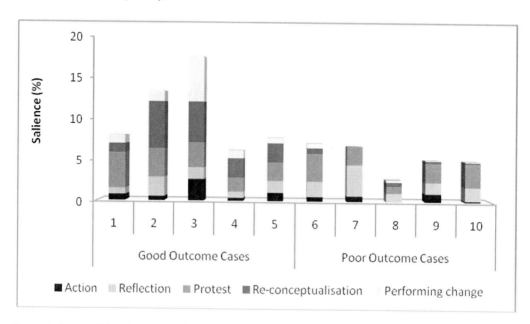

Figure 1. Successful and unsuccessful cases in narrative therapy.

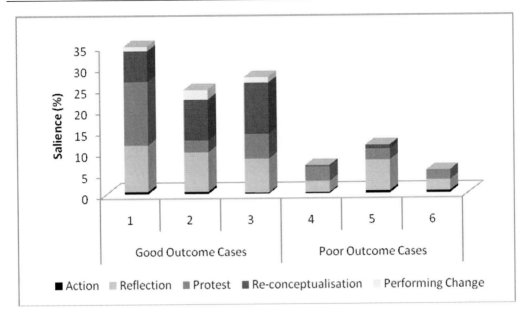

Figure 2. Successful and unsuccessful cases in EFT.

We will proceed now to an overview presentation of the EFT and domestic violence samples findings, which are also congruent with what we have found in several case-studies (Gonçalves et al., 2010; Ribeiro et al., 2009; Ribeiro, Bento et al., in press; Santos et al., 2010; Santos et al., 2009). These studies contrasted groups with differential therapeutic outcomes - successful or unsuccessful - distinguished through the assessment of symptoms carried out at the beginning and end of therapy. The following figures illustrate our main findings in the narrative sample (in Figure 1) and in the EFT sample (in Figure 2).

A first look at these figures shows that the overall temporal salience of IMs is higher in successful cases when compared to unsuccessful ones. Nevertheless, IMs also appear in unsuccessful cases. A closer look shows us that re-conceptualisation and performing change IMs, while present in the successful groups, are almost absent in the unsuccessful samples (in EFT performing change IMs are completely absent). These findings led us to enquire about the processes that generate these different outcomes and the role that re-conceptualisation and performing change seems to play in this development. We will later return to this issue.

We will now focus on a more process-oriented view through the analysis of two contrasting cases of narrative therapy, presented in Figures 3 and 4, which represent prototypical cases of successful and unsuccessful therapy. These figures display the evolution of the several types of IMs in therapy, on a session-by-session basis (plus the follow-up interview at 6 months after the end of treatment).

In Figure 3, which represents a depiction of IM development in a successful case, we can observe an increasing tendency of IMs temporal salience that appears from the beginning of therapy. If we look at session two, in particular, we already see 'action', 'reflection' and 'protest' IMs; furthermore, in session 4, all the five types emerge, continuing to increase their presence until the end (see Santos et al., 2009, for an elaborated account upon this specific case-study).

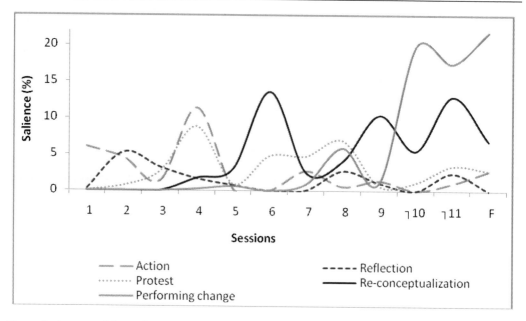

Figure 3. A successful case in narrative therapy (11 sessions plus follow-up).

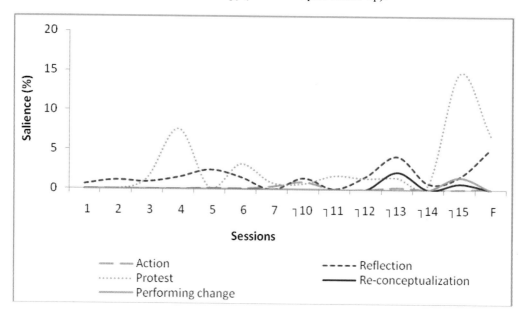

Figure 4. An unsuccessful case in narrative therapy (15 sessions plus follow-up).

Contrastingly, in an unsuccessful case, not only is the temporal salience of IMs lower, but its diversity is also much more restricted. As we can see in Figure 4, which represents the development of IMs in an unsuccessful case, reflection and protest IMs are present but they are not followed by re-conceptualisation and performing change IMs, as we see appearing and increasing in successful cases from the middle stage until the end of therapy. In other words, most of the time, action, reflection and protest IMs are present in unsuccessful cases from the beginning until the end of therapy (and can even slightly increase their temporal salience) but the differences in terms of overall temporal salience are clear as far as successful cases are concerned.

To summarize our global findings in terms of IMs' emergence and evolution in therapy, we can say that successful cases are typically characterized by a progressive tendency in the diversity and temporal salience of IMs from session to session. In the beginning of therapy, action, reflection and protest IMs start emerging and becoming more prominent as the treatment progresses. These IMs are then followed by re-conceptualisation that emerges in the middle of the process and continues increasing until the end. Performing change IMs tend to appear after re-conceptualisation. In turn, unsuccessful cases are typically characterized by a lower diversity and temporal salience of IMs, with action, reflection and protest being the main IMs, most of the time without a clear trend to increase from the beginning until the end of treatment. Re-conceptualisation and performing change IMs do not appear typically or have a very low temporal salience.

An interesting commonality between both groups is, to us, the presence of IMs from the first session until the end, regardless of the therapeutic outcome. This means that, if we took the terminology of Fogel and collaborators (2006), level 2 changes appear in therapy even when the final outcome is poor. In other words, even when the problematic narrative dominates in the beginning and keeps its power balance unchanged until the end, there are always novelties appearing and opportunities for new narratives to be developed, even if they are ignored, trivialized or dismissed after their emergence.

According to our studies, these results in the context of psychotherapy were also replicated in daily life changes (i.e., changes related to personal problems, transitions and processes of adaptation to life events that occur outside the therapeutic context). Cruz and Gonçalves (in press) conducted an exploratory study based on interviews with a non-clinical population that asked participants (N=27) to identify three types of difficulties in their lives: past (and solved) difficulties, current difficulties (in the moment of the interview) and persistent difficulties (present for more than 6 months). In this study the presence of re-conceptualisation IMs was the characteristic that distinguished solved from present difficulties (with statistically significant results). Furthermore, a similar study by Meira (2009; see also Meira, Gonçalves, Salgado & Cunha, 2009) on non-therapeutic change with a longitudinal design replicated the same findings about 're-conceptualisation (17 participants were interviewed about a personal problem every couple of weeks, for four months).

The consistency of these findings within and outside the therapeutic context suggests that re-conceptualisation is a key factor for sustaining narrative changes and the construction of new self-narratives. In the next section, we will elaborate upon a model of narrative change, supported by the several findings presented above and other case-studies that systematically pointed to the same results.

A MODEL OF NARRATIVE CHANGE IN PSYCHOTHERAPY

In our view, narrative change implies not only diversity of IMs but also specific interrelations between them. Due to the complexity of self-changes, it is unlikely that sustained changes could develop from a specific type of IM (Gonçalves et al., 2009). So, according to our findings, change starts with IM diversity, namely in the form of 'action' and 'reflection' IMs. These are more elementary forms of innovation that appear as early forms of opposing the problematic self-narrative (being level 2 changes). Nevertheless, these IMs are vital since, if recognized by the self and validated by others, they become the first signs that something new is taking place and that change is on its way. These novel actions, thoughts or intentions, either triggered by the therapist's questions or spontaneously recognised by the client, defy the dominant problematic themes that prescribe redundant behaviour. The way these innovations appear can be quite idiosyncratic to the person or situation: sometimes they appear through new actions that lead to new thoughts and intentions, other times through new insights about the problem's maintenance that feed new actions. We have also noticed protest IMs present from the first session on, in some cases. This can be due to the fact that not all clients enter therapy at the same stage of change (see Prochaska, DiClemente & Norcross, 1992). Some seek therapy already engaged in an active state, while others are still very contemplative and ambivalent and may take more time reflecting and exploring the problem before they gather enough motivation to enter in more active stages (Prochaska et al., 1992; see also Gonçalves, Ribeiro, et al., in press). We consider protest IMs an interesting type of innovation since they trigger a strong attitudinal movement against the problem and entail new positioning of the self in relation to the surrounding world.

Independent of the starting point, the idea is that these three forms of IMs keep feeding each other and amplifying their occurrence. For example, as the person starts recognising that the avoidance of certain activities only maintains the problem of fear, she might decide and plan to start doing small things that defy the problem (reflection IM) and actually starts re-experimenting in his or her daily life with previously abandoned activities (action IMs) while at the same time protesting frequently in therapy towards the problem's assumptions (protest IMs).

At a certain point of therapy (usually in the middle of the process) re-conceptualisation IMs start to appear. We contend that these IMs are very important to the consolidation of further narrative changes, given that unsuccessful therapeutic processes and non-resolved personal problems usually do not exhibit them.

Since re-conceptualisation IMs are grounded in two important features: a) the contrast between present and past and b) a meta-level narration of the processes that made this transformation possible, they seem to be a type of narrative which is more complex than the previous IMs. As we have argued before, not only is its structure closer to the structure of a story (given its sequencing of events and higher narrative coherence), but it also gives a meta-level view of the agent in a story about change. In this sense, it pictures the actor in a given path towards self-transformation and, at the same time, frames the story in a new narrative perspective from the author (the person positions him or herself as different). Furthermore, these IMs also foster other action, reflection and protest IMs, acting like a meaning-making gravitational field towards future production of meanings and experiences. Since the person – as a changed narrator – assumes a different authoring position towards the self and the world, his or her narratives give coherence to the several types of novelties, acting as a meaning bridge (Osatuke & Stiles, 2006) between the old and new versions of the self. Thus, re-conceptualisation has the power of integrating old patterns into new ones, through a synthesis process (Santos & Gonçalves, 2009).

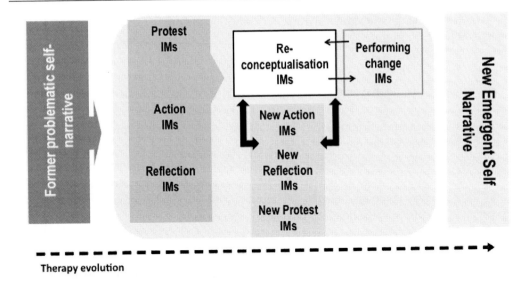

Figure 5. A heuristic model of successful psychotherapy.

Finally, performing change IMs emerge and represent the expansion of the change process into the future, as new experiences, projects and intentions emerge due to the transformations achieved. The future projection of a story is vital for an expansion of new self-narratives: as several authors suggest (Crites, 1986; Omer & Alon, 1997; Slusky, 1998), new stories need to have a future. Figure 5 illustrates the processes described above in successful psychotherapy.

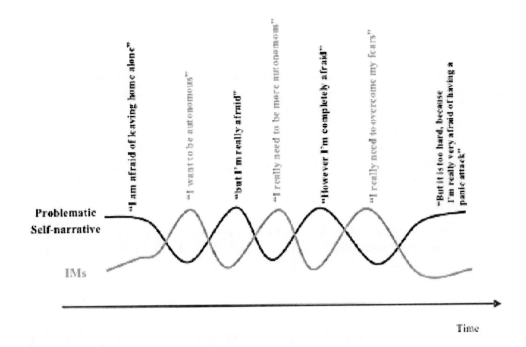

Figure 6. Mutual in-feeding producing a dynamic stability between opposing voices.

We consider that all the variability that occurs within the problematic self-narrative (dark rectangle at the left of figure 5) is related to level 1 change that obeys the usual "rules" of the problem (for example, when the client narrates being vulnerable to the fear over and over again, despite the differences in events and situations). The emergence of IMs, in the middle section between the double braces, represents level 2 changes: something novel that is emerging and being noticed by the participating agents. Nevertheless, we think that the emergence of re-conceptualisation IMs is the starting point of a flow of processes that lead to level 3 changes: the development of a new self-narrative (pictured at the right of the figure above). This is the distinguishing feature between successful cases and unsuccessful ones. So, the next logical question is to enquire about what processes occur in unsuccessful cases that do not trigger developmental changes. Or, more specifically: What processes interrupt the emergence of re-conceptualisation IMs in unsuccessful cases?

A MODEL OF NARRATIVE STABILITY IN PSYCHOTHERAPY

If we compare the initial stages of successful and unsuccessful cases, they seem quite identical: action, reflection and protest IMs are present (although in some unsuccessful cases the temporal salience of these IMs is lower from the beginning). Clearer differences reside in the middle of therapy when, in the absence of re-conceptualisation, the potential power to foster change of the three previous IMs, is not built upon and amplified. Thus, despite some innovations, the person returns to the same narrative, not being able to challenge its dominance.

Exploring the processes that prevent the emergence of re-conceptualisation and, thus, facilitate the dominance of the problematic self-narrative, involves taking into account IMs potential to challenge a client's usual way of understanding and experiencing, generating uncertainty. IMs can be easily understood as episodes of self-discontinuity and, thus, uncertainty (Gonçalves & Ribeiro, in press; Ribeiro & Gonçalves, 2010). We have argued that the development of IMs into a new self-narrative depends on the way people manage the emergence of uncertainty. Ignoring or avoiding uncertainty, by returning to the problematic self-narrative and, thus, attenuating IMs' meaning, in order to promote a sense of continuity or coherence, may sustain the maintenance of the problematic self-narrative. The following example shows how, although the client elaborates an IM, its meaning is soon attenuated by a return to the problematic self-narrative that restores self-continuity (i.e., reinstates the power of the problematic self-narrative):

Clinical vignette 6
Client: **Sometimes, I feel able to face my fears... I feel this strength inside me** [Reflection
IM], *but then it suddenly disappears, as if my fears return and takeover!* [Continuity
restoration by returning to the problematic self-narrative]

When uncertainty is not overcome during the therapeutic process, the problematic self-narrative and IMs may establish a cyclical relation that blocks the development of the self. This process is akin to what Valsiner (2002) described as 'mutual in-feeding': a dynamic balance between two contrasting voices in the dialogical self (e.g., voice A: "life is good", voice B: "life is bad") that feed each other in a perpetual movement back and forth. The voices seem to be moving and quite unstable, but the dynamics actually remain the same as time goes by. It is a case of stability through a very dynamic process in the dialogical self. In our clinical example of a person with panic disorder, in the first sessions he or she could express a voice A that says "I am afraid of leaving home alone" and voice B that says "I must overcome my fears in order to become more autonomous". According to the IMs coding system, voice A is an expression of the problematic self-narrative, while voice B expresses a reflection IM. Despite the novelty, they could be feeding each other infinitely, in a redundant back and forth movement that keeps the person within the same vicious cycle (see Figure 6).

Furthermore, this back and forth movement between voice A and voice B can even lead to a more striking polarization of meanings, in what Valsiner (2002) calls 'mutual escalating' of voices. The most interesting thing is that, despite the small variability gained through the oscillation between the voices as time passes, the relationship between them remains the same as it was in the beginning.

The process of mutual in-feeding has been addressed by other authors in different theoretical perspectives. In personal construct theory, it is sometimes referred to as 'slot rattling' (Kelly, 1955), a dance between two poles of the same construct. In strategic therapy, it is related to the 'ironic process' (Shoham & Rohrbaugh, 2002) of first order changes that only lead to an escalation of the problem (Watzlawick, Weakland & Fisch, 1974). And in the assimilation model of Stiles and collaborators (Brinegar, Salvi, Stiles & Greenberg, 2006) this is paralleled with a 'rapid crossfire' between two divergent voices.

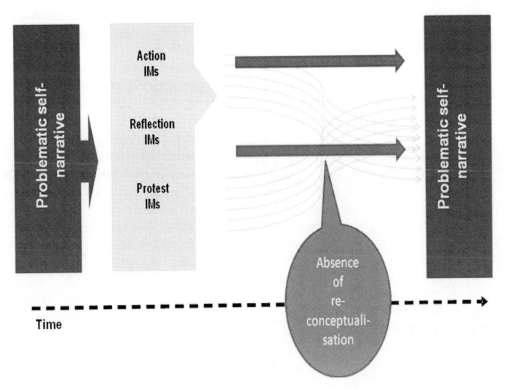

Figure 7. A heuristic model of unsuccessful cases.

We have been empirically observing the phenomenon of 'mutual in-feeding', by analysing whether IMs present 'Return-to-the-Problem Markers', as in the following example:

Clinical vignette 7

Client: **"This week I decided to face some of my fears as we agreed in the last session ... I decided to go to the mall [Reflection IM]**, *but when I was on my way to the mall, I was suddenly caught by an incredible agitation. I felt I couldn't breathe, as if I had a cramp, but I could do nothing. [RPM]*

A study recently conducted by our team with the sample of women who were victims of domestic violence contrasted the successful group with the unsuccessful group to explore whether there would be significant differences in terms of the percentage of IMs with RPMs. As we suspected from the argument presented before, our results in this sample indicate that the unsuccessful group had a significantly higher percentage of IMs followed by RPMs (namely action, reflection and protest).

Our results also suggest that the presence of mutual in-feeding is rare in re-conceptualisation. One possible reason for this is that these IMs already dialectically integrate both opposites (past and present or, in other words, problematic voice and innovative one), making it difficult for an oscillation between them. Performing change IMs also escape this process of mutual in-feeding because they tend to emerge only after re-conceptualisation, being more characteristic of later stages of therapy. Moreover, according to the definition of performing change IM, they are the anticipation or planning of new experiences and projects. Since these projects and new experiences appear as a generalisation of the change process into other life domains and into the future, it is likely that they are not involved in a return to the problem. Figure 7 summarizes the processes that occur in unsuccessful cases.

We initially tried to understand mutual in-feeding mainly through the analysis of unsuccessful cases, but we concluded, later on, that this vicious cycle, although typical of unsuccessful cases (Santos et al., 2010), is not exclusive to them (Ribeiro, Bento et al., in press). Thus, it is important to note that successful cases also presented signs of mutual in-feeding that are surpassed as therapy progresses. The dialogical processes that allow evolution from mutual in-feeding to another type of dialogical relation and the role of the therapist in it are important dimensions that still need to be studied.

In this sense, we are now directing our research efforts to the exploration of the role of the therapist in these two specific situations: a) in the promotion of IMs – particularly in the facilitation of re-conceptualisation, and b) in the surpassing of mutual in-feeding. Up until now, we only have analysed data from case-studies (Cunha, Mendes, Gonçalves, Angus & Greenberg, 2009; Ribeiro, Loura, Gonçalves, Ribeiro, & Stiles, 2010). These preliminary findings indicate that the promotion of IMs is usually associated with the previous use of more directive interventions from the therapist (namely, direct guidance in therapeutic in the midst of therapeutic tasks or open questions to facilitate self-awareness). Focusing now on the therapist's response to mutual in-feeding, preliminary findings indicate that mutual in-feeding tend to persist during therapy when the therapist respond to it by understanding predominantly the innovative voice (by amplifying it), instead of understanding the problematic voice (trying to explore what it is in the client's experience that prevents change). In such cases, clients might feel that the therapists do not understand them, invoking a "strong reactance on the part of the client, often hardening the client's stuck position" (Engle & Arkovitz, 2008, p.390). Instead, surpassing of mutual in-feeding, involves empathic understanding not only for innovative voice(s) but also for problematic one(s) (Stiles & Glick, 2002).

CONCLUSION

Although at this point we cannot infer a causal relationship between mutual in-feeding and re-conceptualisation, our data suggests that the emergence of re-conceptualisation is strongly associated with a decreasing in the mutual in-feeding.

This integrative power of re-conceptualisation tends to give coherence to the meaning of other IMs and gives directionality to the change process, thus beginning to dissipate the redundancy of the problem in clients' daily lives. The recognition of oneself as different and the awareness of exceptions to the problem can start a 'domino effect' (Watzlawick, Weakland & Fisch, 1974) that leads to a level 3 (developmental) change and to successful psychotherapy. Furthermore, since re-conceptualisation implies the contrast between past and present, and aggregates the old self with the transformed self, it achieves a new sense of unity in the dialogical self, surpassing the former dualities and ambivalence usually inherent to a mutual in-feeding process between opposing voices. The self's multiplicity of experiences and perspectives become integrated in a more flexible way, with new resources at its disposal to deal with difficulties and a future-oriented view that triggers and amplifies new performances of change.

One of the powerful processes entailed by re-conceptualisation that, in our view, is responsible for this, is the development of a meta-position, allowing for a self-observation process. Through self-observation, new insights are created and new connections are established (see Castonguay & Hill, 2006 for a comprehensive discussion of insight in psychotherapy). This facilitates the development of a new sense of personal agency and the commitment to a new way of life where, through repetition, the novelties become familiar.

ACKNOWLEDGMENT

This chapter was supported by the Portuguese Foundation for Science and Technology (FCT), by the Grant PTDC/PSI/72846/2006 (Narrative Processes in Psychotherapy) and also the PhD grants: SFRH/BD/30880/2006; SFRH/BD/29804/2006 and SFRH/BD/46189/2008. We are very grateful to Les Greenberg and Lynne Angus for allowing us to use of transcripts from the York Project I.

REFERENCES

Angus, L. E., & McLeod, J. (2004). Toward an integrative framework for understanding the role of narrative in psychotherapy process. In L. E Angus & J. McLeod (Eds.), *The handbook of narrative and psychotherapy: Practice, theory and practice* (pp. 367-374). Thousand Oaks: Sage.

Brinegar, M. G., Salvi, L. M., Stiles, W. B., & Greenberg, L. S. (2006). Building a meaning bridge: Therapeutic progress from problem formulation to understanding. *Journal of Counselling Psychology, 53*, 165-180.

Bruner, J. (1986). *Actual minds, possible worlds*. Cambridge, MA: Harvard University Press.

Bruner, J. (2004). The narrative creation of self. In L. E. Angus & J. McLeod (Eds.), *The handbook of narrative and psychotherapy: Practice, theory and research* (pp. 3 - 14). Thousand Oaks: Sage.

Castonguay, L. G., & Hill, C. (Eds.) (2006). *Insight in psychotherapy: Definitions, processes, consequences, and research directions*. Washington, DC: American Psychological Association.

Crites, F. (1986). Story time: Recollecting the past and projecting the future. In T. R. Sarbin (Ed.), *Narrative psychology: The storied nature of conduct* (pp. 152-173). New York: Praeger.

Cruz, G., & Gonçalves, M. M. (in press). Mudança inovativos e momentos de inovação: Um estudo exploratório [Spontaneous change and innovative moments: An exploratory study]. *Psychologica*.

Cunha, C., Mendes, I., Gonçalves, M. M., Angus, L., & Greenberg, L. S. (2009). *Therapist and client interventions and the promotion of narrative innovative moments in Emotion Focused Therapy: A preliminary study with the case of Lisa*. Poster presented in the 40th Meeting of the Society for Psychotherapy Research, Santiago, Chile.

Engle, D., & Arkowitz, H. (2008). Viewing resistance as ambivalence: integrative strategies for working with ambivalence. *Journal of Humanistic Psychology, 48*, 389-412.

Fernandez, I., & Faretta, E. (2007). Eye movement desensitization and reprocessing in the treatment of panic disorder with agoraphobia. *Clinical Case Studies, 6*, 44-63.

Fogel, A., Garvey, A., Hsu, H. C., & West-Stroming, D. (2006). *Change processes in relationships: A relational-historical approach*. New York: Cambridge University Press.

Gonçalves, M. M., Matos, M., & Santos, A. (2009). Narrative therapy and the nature of "innovative moments" in the construction of change. *Journal of Constructivist Psychology, 22*, 1–23.

Gonçalves, M. M., Mendes, I., Cruz, G., Ribeiro, A., Sousa, I., Angus, L., & Greenberg, L. (submitted). Innovative Moments and change in client-centered therapy. *Psychotherapy Research*.

Gonçalves, M. M., Mendes, I., Ribeiro, A., Angus, L., & Greenberg, L. (2010). Innovative moments and change in emotional focused therapy: The case of Lisa. *Journal of Constructivist Psychology, 23*, 267-294.

Gonçalves, M. M., & Ribeiro, A. (in press). Narrative processes of innovation and stability within the dialogical self. In H. J. M. Hermans & T. Gieser (Eds.), *Handbook of dialogical self theory*. Cambridge: Cambridge University Press.

Gonçalves, M.M., Ribeiro, A.P., Stiles, W.B., Conde, T., Santos, A., Matos, M., & Martins, C. (in press). The Role of Mutual In-Feeding in Maintaining Problematic Self-Narratives: Exploring one Path to Therapeutic Failure, *Psychotherapy Research.*

Gonçalves, M. M., Ribeiro, A. P., Matos, M., Santos, A., & Mendes, I. (in press). The Innovative Moments Coding System: A coding procedure for tracking changes in psychotherapy. In S. Salvatore, J. Valsiner, S. Strout, & J. Clegg (Eds.), *YIS: Yearbook of Idiographic Science - Volume 2.* Rome: Firera Publishing Group.

Hermans, H. J. M., & Dimaggio, G. (2004). *The dialogical self in psychotherapy.* New York: Brunner-Routledge.

Hermans, H. J. M. (1996). Voicing the self: From information processing to dialogical interchange. *Psychological Bulletin, 119*, 31-50.

Hermans, H. J. M., & Hermans-Jansen, E. (1995). *Self-narratives: The construction of meaning in psychotherapy.* New York: The Guilford Press.

Hermans, H., & Kempen, H. (1993). *The dialogical self: Meaning as movement.* San Diego, CA: Academic Press.

Kelly, G. (1955). *The psychology of personal constructs.* New York: Norton.

Matos, M., Santos, A., Gonçalves, M. M., & Martins, C. (2009). Innovative moments and change in narrative therapy. *Psychotherapy Research, 19,* 68-80.

McAdams, D. P. (1993). *The stories we live by: Personal myths and the making of the self.* New York: William Morrow.

Meira, L. M. A. (2009). *Mudança Narrativa: Estudo sobre processos de inovação pessoal na resolução de problemas de vida.* [Narrative change: A study upon processes of personal innovation in the resolution of life problems]. Unpublished PhD thesis. University of Minho.

Meira, L., Gonçalves, M. M., Salgado, J. & Cunha, C. (2009). Everyday life change: Contribution to the understanding of daily human change. In M. Todman (Ed.), *Self-regulation and social competence: Psychological studies in identity, achievement and work-family dynamics* (pp. 145-154). Athens: ATINER.

Mendes, I., Ribeiro, A.P., Angus, L., & Greenberg, L., & Gonçalves, M.M. (2010). Innovative moments and change in emotion-focused therapy. *Psychotherapy Research, 20,* 692-701.

Neimeyer, R. A., Herrero, O., & Botella, L. (2006). Chaos to coherence: Psychotherapeutic integration of traumatic loss. *Journal of Constructivist Psychology, 19*, 127-145.

Omer, H., & Alon, N. (1997). *Constructing therapeutic narratives.* Northvale, NJ: Jason Aronson.

Osatuke, K., & Stiles, W. B. (2006). Problematic internal voices in clients with borderline features: an elaboration of the assimilation model. *Journal of Constructivist Psychology, 19*, 287-319.

Prochaska, J. O., DiClemente, C. C., & Norcross, J. (1992). In search of how people change: Applications to addictive behaviours. *American Psychologist, 47,* 1102-1114.

Ribeiro, A. P., Gonçalves, M. M., & Ribeiro, E. (2009). Processos narrativos de mudança em psicoterapia: Estudo de um caso de sucesso de terapia construtivista [Narrative processes of change in psychotherapy: A case-study of successful constructivist therapy]. *Psychologica, 50*, 181-203.

Ribeiro, A. P., & Gonçalves, M. M. (2010). Innovation and stability within the dialogical self: The centrality of ambivalence. *Culture & Psychology, 16*, 116-126.

Ribeiro, A. P., Bento, T., Gonçalves, M.M., Salgado, J. (2010). Self-narrative reconstruction in psychotherapy: Looking at different levels of narrative development. *Culture & Psychology, 16*, 195-212.

Ribeiro, A. P., Bento, T., Salgado, J., Stiles, W. B., & Gonçalves, M. M. (in press). A dynamic look at narrative change in psychotherapy: A case-study tracking innovative moments and protonarratives using *State-Space Grids*. *Psychotherapy Research.*

Ribeiro, A. P., Gonçalves, M. M., & Santos, A. (in press). Innovative moments in psychotherapy: From the narrative outputs to the semiotic-dialogical processes. In S. Salvatore, J. Valsiner, S. Strout, & J. Clegg (Eds.), *YIS: Yearbook of Idiographic Science – Volume 3.* Rome: Firera Publishing Group.

Ribeiro, A. P., Loura, J., Gonçalves, M. M., Ribeiro, E., & Stiles, W. B. (in preparation). How the therapist responds to mutual in-feeding during therapy?

Santos, A., & Gonçalves, M. M. (2009). Innovative moments and change processes in psychotherapy: An exercise in new methodology. In J. Valsiner, P. C. M., Molenaar, M. C. D. P., Lyra, & N. Chaudhary (Eds.), *Dynamic process methodology in the social and developmental sciences* (pp. 493-526). New York: Springer.

Santos, A., Gonçalves, M. M., Matos, M., & Salvatore, S. (2009). Innovative moments and change pathways: A successful case of narrative therapy. *Psychology and Psychotherapy: Theory, Research and Practice, 82*, 449–466.

Santos, A., Gonçalves, M. M., & Matos, M. (2010). Innovative moments and unsuccessful in narrative therapy. *Counselling and Psychotherapy Research.* DOI: 10.1080/14733140903398153.

Sarbin, T. R. (1986). The narrative and the root metaphor for psychology. In T. R. Sarbin (Ed.), *Narrative psychology: The storied nature of human conduct* (pp. 3-21). New York: Praeger.

Shoham, V., & Rohrbaugh, M. J. (2002). Brief strategic couple therapy. In A. S. Gurman & N. S. Jacobson (Eds.), *Clinical handbook of couple therapy. 3rd Ed.* (pp. 5-25). New York: Guilford.

Slusky, C. E. (1998). Strange attractors and the transformation of narratives in family therapy. In M. F. Hoyt (Ed.), *The handbook of constructive therapies: Innovative approaches from leading practitioners* (pp. 159-179). San Francisco: Jossey-Bass.

Stiles, W. B., & Glick, M. J. (2002). Client-centered therapy with multivoiced clients: Empathy with whom? In J. C. Watson, R. Goldman, & M. S. Warner (Eds.), *Client-centered and experiential therapy in the 21st century: Advances in theory, research, and practice* (pp. 406–414). London: PCCS Books.

Valsiner, J. (2002). Forms of dialogical relations and semiotic autoregulation within the self. *Theory & Psychology, 12*, 251-265.

Watzlawick, P., Weakland, J., & Fisch, R. (1974). *Change: Principles of problem formation and problem resolution.* New York: Norton.

White, M. (2007). *Maps of narrative practice.* New York: Norton.

White, M., & Epston, D. (1990). *Narrative means to therapeutic ends.* New York: Norton.

Wortham, S. (2001). *Narratives in action: A strategy for research and analysis.* New York: Teachers College Press.

In: Dialogicality in Focus   ISBN: 978-1-61122-817-5
Editors: M. Märtsin, B. Wagoner, E.-L. Aveling et al.   © 2011 Nova Science Publishers, Inc.

Chapter 9

EMPATHY AND EMOTION FROM THE PERSPECTIVE OF DIALOGICAL SELF THEORY

Thorsten Gieser and Hubert Hermans

INTRODUCTION

Empathy has a long history in psychology and philosophy, and rightly so. It has been described as a phenomenon in its own right, as an ability, as a state of mind, as an emotional state. But it is more than that. It is what enables us to transcend our self, to acknowledge and understand other people as experiencing subjects like ourselves. Ultimately, it is even the attempt to putatively experience what someone else is experiencing. In this sense, empathy is a fundamental aspect of human relationships, of two selves in communication. We can see now why empathy is so important for understanding the dialogical self. Not only does it provide us insights into how a self can go 'beyond the skin' of the individual; it also tells us something about dialogical relationships, which rely on our ability to assume exterior positions, to experience them as I-positions, and to give them a 'voice'.

To illustrate these points we look at empathy in the psychotherapeutic context, where so much depends on conversations and a developing 'spiral of understanding' between client and therapist. To start with, we present a brief history of the concept of empathy followed by a first interpretation in terms of dialogical self theory. We then move on to introduce a case study drawn from Alfred Margulies' classic work *The Empathic Imagination* (1989). Our discussion of the material starts by showing how spoken words, as evocative sounds, can create perceptual and emotional imaginary landscapes that can be experienced by both client and therapist. What is more, the therapist might even feel into this landscape *as if* it were his own, thereby sharing the client's perceptions and emotions to a degree. We argue that a state of 'first-order phenomenology' (Lambie & Marcel, 2002), an experience of emotional immersion, is necessary for empathy to develop and that it is the 'secondary-order awareness' of emotion which transforms this process of 'feeling-into' into a process of distancing. Both processes, so we propose, are essential for the therapeutic success. To complicate the matter, we then demonstrate that a closer look at the emotions involved in our case study reveals that shared perceptions do not necessary result in the same shared emotion. Through a detailed description of the empathetic process in terms of dialogical self theory we explicate how different parts of the therapist's and client's selves, both interior and exterior, relate to each other and to different levels of emotion, especially 'primary' and 'secondary' emotions (Greenberg, 2002). Distancing ourselves from the confinement of the case study, we conclude this chapter with an elaboration on the importance of empathy for dialogicality and the dialogical self in general.

EMPATHY AS SHARED PERCEPTION

The term empathy is the translation of the German word *Einfühlung* ('feeling-into'). Titchener (1909) created the word from the Greek *en pathos* ('in suffering/passion') by analogy with the word 'sympathy' (see Wispé 1986 and 1991 for elaborations on the sympathy/empathy distinction). The concept of *Einfühlung* was first used by psychologists within the field of aesthetics and form perception in the last quarter of the 19th century. They understood that aesthetic appreciation demands a projection of the self into the object of beauty (Wispé, 1990, p. 18). At the beginning of the 20th century, the concept was transferred from the context of subject-object relationships to that of subject-subject relationships, i.e., to the question of how we know others (e.g., Lipps, 1903; 1905). According to Lipps, we can feel into the emotions of others by seeing shame in the blushing, anger in the clenched fist, or joy in the radiant smile (Stein, 1964, p. 70). It was in this sense that the concept of empathy was subsequently employed in various psychological sub-fields like personality theory, social psychology, developmental psychology, and – most importantly for this article – in psychotherapy (see Duan & Hill, 1996; Eisenberg & Strayer, 1990 for reviews).

The definitions employed to date describe empathy in various related ways that may be translated as sympathizing with someone, feeling with/for someone, responding to someone, understanding, participating, being sensitive to someone, or taking the role of the other. Carl Rogers, one of the advocates of empathy in inter-personal relationships, defines it in terms of:

> "*Entering the private perceptual world of the other* and becoming thoroughly at home in it. It involves being sensitive [...] to the changing felt meanings which flow in this other person... It means *temporarily living in his/her life* [...] It means frequently checking with him/her as to the accuracy of your sensings, and being *guided by the responses you receive* [...] To be with another in this way means that for the time being you lay aside the views and values you hold for yourself in order to enter another world without prejudice." (1975, p. 4, our emphases)

More recently, empathy has been understood as a complex multidimensional phenomenon that includes both cognitive and affective components and control systems, and that varies in degree with personality factors, relational factors and situational context (see e.g., Vreeke & van der Mark, 2003 or Preston & de Waal, 2002 for recent elaborations). It is not our intention here, however, to analyse empathy in all of its aspects in any detail. Following in Carl Rogers' footsteps, our concern is rather with an interpretation of empathy as a mode of shared perception and emotion.

EMPATHY FROM THE PERSPECTIVE OF DIALOGICAL SELF THEORY

We assume that empathy is both a dialogical and a self-related phenomenon. A dialogical perspective is needed in order to understand the relationship between people as involved in a process of cognitive and affective interchange. A self-perspective is required to understand how dialogical processes *between* people are intimately related with dialogical processes *within* the selves of the participants. Therefore, "dialogical self theories" in which the notion of self and dialogue are conceptually combined, are useful to analyze how people involved in empathetic communication establish meaningful relationships not only between each other but also between *different* aspects of their multifaceted selves. In their first inception of dialogical self theory, Hermans, Kempen, & Van Loon (1992) criticized the assumption that the self is organized around *one* centre or core. Rather than conceptualizing the self as organized from a centralized headquarter, they proposed a (partly) decentralized self that is extended to the world with the social other as not purely outside but also inside the self. Instead of considering the self as a centralized agent with a unifying view on the world, the authors conceived the self in terms of a dynamic multiplicity of relatively autonomous 'I-positions' that are organized in an imaginal landscape. In this conception, the I is always bound to particular positions in time and space but has the possibility to move from one position to the other in accordance with changes in situation and time. In this process of positioning and repositioning, the I fluctuates among different and even opposed positions, and has the capacity to imaginatively endow each position with a voice so that dialogical relations between positions can develop that renew and innovate positions involved. Such dialogical relationships are contrasted with monological relationship in which one or a few positions are dominant in the self, with the result that other positions are silenced or suppressed or otherwise not allowed to speak from their own specific point of view.

In order to understand empathy from the perspective of dialogical self theory, it is necessary to make a distinction between two kinds of I-positions (a) internal ones that refer to personal and social aspects of the self (e.g., I as a professional, I as a perfectionist, I as vulnerable) and (b) external positions that refer to people or aspects of the environment that are felt as belonging to the self (e.g., my father, my colleague, my friends, my house). In other words, I-positions are not only aspects of the self that are located "inside the skin" but also aspects that are, in the sense of James (1890), constituents of the self as *extended* to the world. An empathetic person has the capacity to understand the internal and external positions of the other and of oneself in their differences, addressivity, responsiveness, and power dynamics. A person who is empathetic is building up a new landscape in his own self in which both the internal and external positions of the other are constructed and reconstructed in their mutual dynamic relationships, *as if* he is the other. When empathy develops, the internal and external position repertoire of the other becomes increasingly familiar to the empathic person both in its content and organization. Empathy becomes really dialogical when the empathic person is able to *respond* to the other by developing a new space in his extended self in which the position repertoire of the other is interiorized and reconstructed, but also able to *address* the other in such a way that the position repertoire of the other receives a new developmental and integrative impulse. As part of this process the empathetic person develops a feeling for the *power dynamics* in the position repertoire and gains insight in the organization of the repertoire in which some positions are dominated or even suppressed by other ones. As a result of the addressivity, responsiveness, and insight in the power dynamics on the part of the empathetic person, the other feels not only understood but also liberated and renewed.

THE CASE EXAMPLE: A NIGHTMARE

The case example used here is drawn from Alfred Margulies' classic work *The Empathic Imagination* (1989). In this book, Margulies presents a phenomenological account of empathy in his everyday clinical practice. One of his examples deals with the nightmare of a client:

"My son and I were going to a park, just for a walk. We were separated – no, he ran ahead and I started to go up into town, [...], and I started to go up the road between two buildings. There was a feedmill [sic] and a bridge or a walkway connecting two buildings and there were men hanging from the walkway and grabbing people as they walked that way. And my son was ahead of me and I went another way and I got to the park. And there was this row of doors, and I kept opening the door to see if my son was there and he wasn't – and I was absolutely terrified and then I woke up. And I kept thinking something had happened to him and he wasn't there. And I thought I wasn't there and if he cried out I wouldn't be there.

The other part of the dream that stands out is the road that was around the feed mill – it was full of ruts and like covered with shit and very slippery and difficult to walk on. And I remember looking down at it and I was surprised and I just kept walking..." (Margulies, 1989, p. 55)

At this point, the client begins to associate and leaves the immediacy of her dream and Margulies brings her back, asking her to describe the scene further:

"It was surprising to me. It was sort of [...] the thing was, it was slippery and full of ruts. And I didn't want to fall down. It was like I thought I wouldn't get out – but I did. I remember there being a building and the road coming down out of the building and down the hill and when I was on the hill, that's when I realized what it was. It was full of ruts, and not soft, but hard and I was sinking into it and I was sliding over it, afraid I'd fall [...] There wasn't a smell. It was sort of like coming upon it and being surprised and when I realized what it was, but rather than being caught up, I had to get where I was going, I had to get to the park. Being more scared kept me from being bogged down." (Margulies, 1989, p. 55)

As the client describes this dream in more detail, Margulies has an unexpected empathic experience:

"Throughout this narrative I had been forming another impression that was like a deja vu to me. I had experienced it before, though it felt strange and uncanny to me, a compound sensory image that she had once described with vivid and distressing affect. The mental representation I had was strong with a slippery feeling, a tactile and kinesthetic sensation that was not part of her original description of the event or even how I recalled it as told by her, but that now seemed integral. I hesitated to comment, wondering if this image were my projection onto her dream [...] Awkwardly I decided to go with my hunch, 'I am not sure of its relevance, but it reminds me of the scene you once described of being a little girl and watching the pigs being slaughtered – I don't know if it's the slippery part of the image that seems a part of it, though you hadn't described it that way.'

'It's funny,' she reflected, 'That was sort of blood and guts, and slippery. There was a barn there – a *red* barn. Its [sic] like when you hang a pig up after you slaughter it; it's like those men hanging in the dream ... just suspended there...'

'Like slaughtered pigs?' I say.

'Yeah, the way they were suspended. The feed mill in the dream was old and painted red too. Last night I went outside in the garden to plant holly hocks... they were blossoming. My neighbour grew them.'

I think holly hocks, ham hocks. 'The neighbour who had the pig slaughter?'

'Yes!' she laughs, 'I also remember once sliding down her walkway during a light snow and I ran right into her husband and knocked him down.' He was the one who slaughtered the pigs." (Margulies, 1989, p. 56)

This session ended and Margulies took up some of its loose threads later on. Together with his client, he explored the role of violent men in her life and tried to reconnect compartmentalized episodes of violence that she had witnessed and dreamt of.

DISCUSSION

Now, to make explicit the empathetic processes involved in this case a model of the self is needed that is capable of showing the organisation of positions and the dynamics of positioning on which empathy relies. In dialogical self theory one of the best models is that of the PPR (see Hermans, 2001), a matrix of external and internal positions that makes up one's 'society of the self'. By describing and interpreting empathy in terms of a PPR we are able to access complex patterns of dialogical relationships and follow the dynamics of movement between positions; not only within one self (the client or the therapist) but also between selves. What we mean by that will become clear shortly.

At the start of the therapy we can assume that Margulies introduced his client as a new external position in his (PPR). This new position is still quite 'hollow': with a face, a name, perhaps a few snap judgements about her general appearance but without an awareness of her life history, her character traits, her significant others or the power dynamics that govern her relationships. During the course of the next therapeutic sessions, he gradually elaborated her one position into a full set of internal and external positions (a full external PPR). And here we go beyond the original formulation of the PPR as conceived nearly a decade ago. Other people are rarely present in the PPR as one solidified external position; they are usually present as complex patterns of their internal and external positions as we know them. Simplified, yes, we relate to others from an internal position to an external position. But more realistically, this external position is made up of many facets and constitutes a whole PPR within ours. In Margulies's case, he heard more and more about her life, more and more people were introduced to him, and the client became invested with personal, individual traits and stories. For example, the client told him about her career, the family finances, her marriage, her son, her father's obsession with hunting, her fascination for violent men, and so on. These narratives not only introduced 'significant others' as external positions to the therapist, but also gave insights into her internal positions (e.g., the mother, wife, the anxious, etc.), together with their relationships and power dynamics in her life.

At the same time, something else is going on. Within the PPR of the therapist, the newly formed positions of his client are simultaneously linked not only within the network of the client's other positions but also with the past experiences of the therapist himself. In Margulies' own words:

"As I become engaged with the inner life of another, I experience a growing sense of familiarity with a built-up internal landscape. Oftentimes this is not so conscious to me. I enter a private world constructed from associations and images stimulated by my patient and drawn from my own personal past experience." (1989, p. 53)

Thus we learn more about the process by which positions are created. As soon as they 'enter the stage' (to use a metaphor Hermans, 2001, used in describing the PPR), positions are exposed to the 'pulling power' of already established positions that resonate with them in some way. There must be 'recognition', in some sense, of the other in me, that draws the new position towards the old. It is as if the established positions gaze at a simulacrum appearing and tentatively probe into it, trying to discern whether this simulacrum is a mirror of themselves or a new external position in its own right. From the quote above we may conclude that the more 'associations' one finds the greater the pull and recognition.

But before we elaborate on the importance of this pull and recognition of positions for empathy let us briefly explore why and how positions can appear as simulacrums, especially in the therapeutic context. It is important to remember here that narratives, especially in the therapeutic context, are not simply descriptive reports but re-lived experiences (see Jackson, 1998). Put differently, "stories are lived before they are told" (MacIntyre, 1984, p. 212). The words of narratives bring to life once again the sensual experiences of a more or less distant past: the sight of the son running away from her, a slippery road full of ruts and covered in excrements, the feeling of her sinking into and sliding over the ruts, the marvellous absence of any smell in this situation. These words re-create, in both telling client and listening therapist, the world of the 'dreamscape', and with each new sentence, with each new piece of sensory information, this dreamscape becomes more real and experience-able. But it is not only the words of the story told that enrich the dreamscape. The remembered sensual experiences themselves open up a whole world of other emotions and memories, as so pointedly remarked by Marcel Proust who once lost himself in memories when he tasted a *madeleine*:

"But when from a long-distant past nothing subsists, after the people are dead, after the things are broken and scattered, ... the smell and taste of things remain poised a long time, like souls, ready to remind us, waiting and hoping for their moment, amid the ruins of all the rest; and bear unfaltering, in the tiny and almost impalpable drop of their essence, the vast structure of recollection." (2006, p. 210)

Likewise, the anthropologist Tim Ingold (2000, p. 409) argued that "*words gather their meaning from the relational properties of the world itself.* Every word is a compressed and compacted history". Margulies remembered a particular instance in his work that illustrates this point clearly:

"As I gain greater familiarity with the world of the other, I then have a Proustian echo of recollection. With one patient, for example, I recall a farm in my mind's eye, the fields, the roads, the old lady who fed the patient/me ginger snaps and bananas – all experiences I have lived empathically through her. I do not recall in my own life whether I have ever even had ginger snaps and bananas together, but I can almost taste them on my mind's tongue. Moreover, I sometimes recollect such empathic sensations more readily than does the patient from whom I have learned them!" (1989, p. 54)

These recollections are again more than re-lived sensual experiences; they are filled with emotional experiences as well. According to Antonio Damasio (1999), each perceived (social and natural) environmental stimuli becomes associated with particular body signals (the emotion) and are thereby 'marked' with positive (e.g., happiness or pride) or negative values (e.g., fear or disgust); values that make us either approach or retreat from the stimulus. Emotions are hence understood only in their relationship between individuals and the world they live in and perceive. To 'speak' about a past experience evokes the same relationships that became associated with the emotions in the first place.

Two consequences arise from the above: First, when the client's dialogical self within the PPR of the therapist crystallizes, it does so with certain emotional values attached. Her emotional reactions are either being verbally expressed; being expressed by changes in tone of spoken words; or being visible in facial expressions, gestures and body posture (see Ekman, 1999). Second, when we follow Damasio's hypothesis, listening to the client's emotional accounts (and watching her bodily emotional expressions) create an emotional response in the therapist as well. In this context, Ingold (2000, p. 21) argued: "To show something to somebody is to cause it to be seen or otherwise experienced". Analogously, to tell somebody something is to cause it to be heard or otherwise experienced. As almost every perception is accompanied by emotion, to draw attention to something is not only a statement of *what it is* but also of *how it is*. It is a statement not just of a word but also of a relationship between narrator, the words and the world that they denote. To follow someone's pointing finger, or words in this case, is therefore to become involved in a relationship, or, in other words, *to feel into* a relationship.

The therapist feels into the client's relationships by attending to her in a sympathetic mode in order to establish rapport. He is therefore likely to respond to her emotional expression with a similar one, perhaps accompanied by a compassionate feeling. When hearing about something the therapist is also familiar with (e.g., having a son, problems in a relationship), his past emotional reactions will become associated, too. Margulies remarks:

"It is not merely my reaching into resonant experience from my own life (for example, that I have, parallel to the patient, fond boyhood memories of eating cookies and feeling happy and secure). It is more: I now have memories empathically derived and elaborated into a relatively coherent form from someone else's experience... I reach deep down into my internalized inscape of the other." (1989, p. 54-55)

The emotions felt now establish a link to the client such that both focus their attention on the same aspects of her inner landscape, sensually as well as emotionally. Margulies was dwelling in his client's inner landscape, which he built up in his own PPR. But not merely as an observer. He perceived this landscape from the client's position, hence as a déjà vu. In terms of the dialogical self, this means that one of his inner positions (e.g., his feeling of strangeness) related to the external positions of the client (e.g., her son who disappeared). However, these external positions should normally be related to the client self positions, not to the therapist self positions. Two things must have happened. First, the boundaries between client self positions and therapist self positions must have loosened so that her positions can be experienced as belonging to the sphere of the therapist self positions. Second, the client self positions must have been silenced in order for the therapist to have a first-person experience of the dream and not simply an observation of what the client is doing in the dream story.

How is it possible that the therapist experiences the memories of his client as his own in these moments? We have already mentioned two aspects of the answer. First, the telling of the client's narratives has created an emotional link between the emotional values the client attached to the characters of her stories and the emotional response of the therapist that arose while he listened to her. Second, in the empathic moment the client's narratives evoked a detailed, meaningful, inner landscape both in herself and the therapist. We shall finally point to a last answer to this question by bringing in an analogy with the phenomenologist Merleau-Ponty's concept of *duplicité*, that is the phenomenon of 'touching and being touched'.

When we shake hands, for example, we can either feel our hand shaking another person's hand or our hand being shaken by somebody else. We can voluntarily switch our focus of attention to either feeling, knowing that the other feeling is never out of reach. Similarly, we can use our right hand to touch, for instance, a table, with our left hand being passive. Again, we always know that the passive hand can become active if we wished so. On the basis of these realisations, a 'transfer of sense' can take place which allows us to perceive the hand of another person in a similar way as we perceive our own passive hand. We are able to *feel into* the experience of another person's hand because of its similarity to our own hand. We have experienced our hands as both perceiving subject and perceived object (often with one hand being part of the background of the active hand that is in our focus of attention). As we experience the other's hand as object in the same background, we may experience the other's passive hand then like we experience our own passive hand." (Merleau-Ponty, 2003, p. 223 and 225)

We argue that a similar bodily logic is at work when we empathize through speaking and listening. Whenever we speak, we simultaneously hear our voice. We may be so involved in our speaking that we merely hear our voice while in other instances we may actively listen to what we are saying. Our voice can hence be understood either in our 'hearing background' or 'listening focus' (Ingold, 2000). Whenever we have a conversation, we hear our own voice and the voice of the other. Moreover, in a friendly conversation we also tend to adjust our use of words or phrases, pronunciation and intonation to our fellow conversant. This enables us to feel into the experience of another person's voice because of its similarity to our own voice. What further contributes to this empathy is that, in the course of a conversation, we experience a continual switching of attentional focus, between our voice either in the background or in focus and the other's voice either in the background (e.g., when both of us speak simultaneously) or in focus. In either case, our voices become linked in one experiential *Gestalt* and hence we may feel into another person's narratives *as if they were our own*.

However, the thus created sensory and emotional bond does not lead the client and the therapist to have identical emotions. If we recall, the client said she felt "afraid" and "scared" for her son. We can also infer from her statements about the slippery road surface - full of excrements, and the fact that she was trying to avoid falling into this mess – that she felt disgusted. Now Margulies, on the other hand, did not share her concern for the son but instead felt something "strange" and "uncanny" in connection with a "tactile" and "kinaesthetic" feeling of slippery-ness. It seems like Margulies was – sensorily – in the narrated dreamscape, together with her, but the world opened up to him through these sensations was different from hers. For her, the feeling of being disgusted by the slippery road surface was a compound sensory and emotional image linked up with being scared for her son. For him, the tactile and kinesthetic feeling of slippery-ness was linked with a feeling of slippery-ness from another episode of the client's life, namely her memory of a pig slaughter scene. It was the inconsistency or discrepancy between his and her experience of the relevance of this perception (of slippery-ness and what it meant) that led to his strange and uncanny feeling.

Margulies mentions that his client once told him about the "blood, squealing and slaughter" of this memory with "vivid and distressing affect". We could describe this original affect as the client's *primary emotion* (Greenberg, 2002), the initial response to a concrete stimulus situation. In her dream, the slippery surface and the red barn are drawn from this original experience and should have brought up the primary emotion once again. Yet it was obscured by a new situational *secondary emotion* of being scared (for her son). According to Greenberg (2002), secondary emotions often cover a deeper emotion which a person might be afraid to acknowledge. Consequently, the client focused her attention on the feeling for her son rather than the distressing memory of slaughter and violence.

In a way, Margulies expected unconsciously for the primary emotion to come up in the client and his empathetic bond to her loosened when he realised that his and her experience of the scene differed (he suddenly had a "strange" and "uncanny" feeling). Listening to her story, he re-lived the dream with her in a state of what Lambie and Marcel (2002) call *first-order phenomenology*. In this state, one *lives* the emotion without being aware of the fact that one *has* an emotion or what nature this emotion is. Margulies' sudden feeling triggered his attention which led to a *second-order awareness* (Lambie & Marcel, 2002) of the emotions that he and his client shared empathetically a moment ago. As we have previously argued, when Margulies empathetically relived the story of his client (in a state of first-order phenomenology) he experienced her external positions as his own while the boundaries between his and her PPR must have become highly permeable. Second-order awareness, then, re-establishes the boundaries between their PPRs, introduces some distance between the therapist's and the client's positions, and thereby leads to a renewed acknowledgement of the client's interior positions by the therapist. From Margulies' perspective, we could say that the distance between the reflective *I* and *my* emotion generates a perceived distance between *I* and *You*. Awareness of the shared emotion, then, breaks the empathetic link and re-introduces the distinction between me and the other which was meaningless a moment ago. It opens up a 'space for dialogue' that enables the recognition of multi-perspectivity, multi-positionality, as well as positional history and context (see Hermans & Hermans-Konopka, 2010).

Yet the question remains how the therapist could empathetically share his client's perceptions and emotions in a state of first-order phenomenology and then suddenly have a different perceptual and emotional experience in their shared narrated dreamscape. We suggest the answer to this question lies in the fact that the client's PPR in the therapist's PPR developed primarily through listening to her stories. But whereas the client's own PPR in her dialogical self is intimately linked with *her* positional histories and contexts, the therapist creates a client's PPR in his dialogical self that relates to other positions in the client's stories and *his* personal positional histories and contexts. In other words, his own perceptions, memories and conceived meanings influence his experience of her inner landscape. Yet because Margulies acquires only a condensed version of her positional histories through the stories, in some respects his experience of her PPR may be more condensed or focused than hers. Silencing his own histories, he focuses on her without being easily distracted by associations that would lead her away from the current experience. Hence he might have a strong 'tactile' and 'kinesthetic' experience of the slippery surface that she did not have. Her PPR was far too diversified to pay attention to such a small detail. Furthermore, her secondary emotion led her to focus her attention on the son rather than on the situation which might have led to recognize her primary emotion linked to the slaughter memory.

So it was a differing sensory perception (together with its emotional tone) that made Margulies feel something 'strange' and 'uncanny', which – in turn – let him recognize that there are actually two *I*-positions in the narrated dreamscape: he is only accompanying his client there; it is not his dreamscape. Nevertheless, he recognized something important that she did not. Once he realized this, his task was to make her perceive what he had perceived; in other words, to make her perceive her dreamscape from a different I-position: not her as in I-am-scared-for-my-son, but her as in I-am distressed- by-this-slaughter-imagery. In this way, she could acknowledge that she was present as two I-positions in her dream and then start a dialogical relationship between her two positions. Thereby she might access the message the primary emotion holds for her (about the role of violence and violent men in her life).

As we see at the end of the dialogue presented in the first part of this chapter, the reflective process triggered by the therapist (as a 'promoter-position' in the self of the client, so to say) led her to explore various aspects of her primary emotion which eventually result in her laughing. We may interpret that as the start of a 'counter emotion', a helpful response to an initial emotion (Hermans & Hermans-Konopka 2010), developing which might have a positive influence on her ongoing therapy and a repositioning of herself in her PPR.

CONCLUSION

We may ask, what purpose has empathy then for the therapeutic process as a whole? Margulies' answer to this question is that it starts a 'spiral of understanding' where client and therapist sensually explore the now shared inner landscape and thereby uncover more and more meaningful aspects in the client's life history.

"In an edge-of-consciousness way I entered my patient's separate experiences, which then remained *in my mind* with their own intense sensory traces, ready to come to life. Despite the ultimate unknowability of the other, there was a coherence of world view that I could approximate from within my own distinctive world view. Moreover, this coherence extended into the shadows of her inscape, into its dormant possibilities. That is to say, *the inscape of this other person had its heretofore unelaborated absence-in-presence that became articulated in my own mental representation of her experience.* It was through the **empathic dialectic** that I then brought into consciousness my experience of her inscape, which was then affirmed in her connecting to my connections, pushing the spiral of understanding further. We explored reflected inscapes together, me blind and imagining, her frightened and recoiling." (1989, p. 57, our emphasis in bold print)

The last sentence highlights that these moments of shared experience are not only empathic in nature. They are but moments, accompanied by other moments where the therapist only guides the client through her inscape, or has to distance himself even more from her in order to reflect on what he was told. The psychotherapeutic process described in this chapter is therefore a dynamic process of distancing and feeling into, of emotional reflection and emotional immersion. But we would also like to take it a step further and argue that empathy, broadly conceived, is more than a complex psychological phenomenon; it is the ontological basis of dialogue and dialogical relationships as such. Too often we tend to narrow down the notion of dialogue to an interplay of words (see Gieser, 2008 for an alternative embodied approach). Yet this case study has shown that what makes dialogue possible in the first place is an ability to feel into someone else's positions, perceptually and emotionally. The 'spiral of (cognitive) understanding', that is the dialectic aspect of dialogicality, does not only rely on the recognition of distance between positions, a fundamental distinction between I and Thou alone. Dialogue needs also the merging of positions, the overcoming of distance. Without empathy we would not know how to assume another position - internal or external – and thus would not be able to 'connect to connections', as Margulies put it.

That the latter point is essential to the dialogical self has most recently been pointed out by Hermans and Hermans-Konopka (2010) who described the dialogicality of emotion as follows:

> "We assume that an emotion is dialogical when it meets a real, remembered, imagined or anticipated position in the other or the self and is influenced, renewed, understood, consoled or, in the broadest sense, influenced by that position in a way that the emotion, and the self more in general, is developing to some higher level of integration.". (p. 29)

The key word here is "integration". To integrate means to open oneself, to allow oneself to be affected and touched (the Latin *tangere* in 'integration'), to affect and touch others, and to draw this experience together to form a whole that is an extension of the self, a dialogical self. If we thus speak of dialogicality we mean this continuous *movement* between positions, of feeling into and distancing, alongside the static turn-taking *points* of a dialogue. As we have seen, just to listen to someone draws us into their world and them into ours. A dialogue is not only a linguistic phenomenon; it is a perceptual and emotional basis for empathy.

REFERENCES

Damasio, A. (1999). *The feeling of what happens: Body and emotion in the making of consciousness*. New York: Harcourt.

Duan, C., & Hill, C. (1996). The current state of empathy research. *Journal of Counselling Psychology, 43*, 261-274.

Eisenberg, N., & Strayer, J. (1990). Critical issues in the study of empathy. In N. Eisenberg & J. Strayer (Eds.), *Empathy and its development* (pp. 3-13). Cambridge: Cambridge University Press.

Ekman, P. (1999). Facial expressions. In T. Dalgeish & M. Power (Eds.), *Handbook of cognition and emotion* (pp. 301-320). Sussex: Wiley & Sons Ltd.

Gieser, T. (2008). Me, my prey, and I: Embodiment and empathy in the dialogical self of a Siberian Hunter. *Studia Psychologica: Special Issue on the Dialogical Self, 6*, 41- 53.

Greenberg, L. (2002). *Emotion-focused therapy: Coaching clients to work through feelings.* Washington, DC: American Psychological Association.

Hermans, H. J. M. (2001). The construction of a Personal Position Repertoire: Method and practice. *Culture & Psychology, 7*, 323-365.

Hermans, H. J. M., & Hermans-Konopka, A. (2009). Dialogical self theory: Positioning and counter-positioning in a globalizing society. Cambridge: Cambridge University Press.

Hermans, H. J. M., Kempen, H. J. G., & Van Loon, R. J. P. (1992). The dialogical self: Beyond individualism and rationalism. *American Psychologist, 47*, 23-33.

Ingold, T. (2000). *The perception of the environment: Essays on livelihood, dwelling and skill.* London: Routledge.

Jackson, M. (1998). *Minima ethnographica: Intersubjectivity and the anthropological project.* Chicago: University of Chicago Press.

James, W. (1890). *The principles of psychology. Vol. I.* London: Macmillan.

Lambie, J., & Marcel, A. (2002). Consciousness and the varieties of emotional experience: A theoretical framework. *Psychological Review, 109*, 219-259.

Lipps, T. (1903). Einfühlung, innere Nachahmung, und Organempfindungen. [Empathy, inner imitation, and visceral feelings] *Archiv für die Gesamte Psychologie, 1*, 185-204.

Lipps, T. (1905). Das Wissen von fremden Ichen. [The knowledge of other Is] *Psychologische Untersuchungen, 4*, 694-722.

MacIntyre, A. (1984). *After virtue: A study in moral theory.* Notre Dame, Ind.: University of Notre Dame Press.

Margulies, A. (1989). *The empathic imagination.* New York: W.W. Norton & Co.

Merleau-Ponty, M. (2003). *Nature: Course notes from the College de France.* Evanston, IL: Northwestern University Press.

Preston, S., & de Waal, F. (2002). Empathy: Its ultimate and proximate bases. *Behavioural and Brain Sciences, 25*, 1-20.

Proust, M. (2006). Another memory. In J. Drobnick (Ed.), *The smell culture reader* (pp. 210-211). Oxford: Berg.

Rogers, C. (1975). Empathic: An unappreciated way of being. *Counselling Psychologist, 5*, 2-10.

Stein, E. (1964). *On the problem of empathy.* The Hague: Martinus Nijhoff.

Titchener, E. (1909). *Experimental psychology of the thought processes.* New York: Macmillan.

Vreeke, G., & van der Mark, I. (2003). Empathy, an integrative Model. *New Ideas in Psychology, 21*, 177-207.

Wispé, L. (1986). The distinction between sympathy and empathy: To call forth a concept, a word is needed. *Journal of Personality and Social Psychology, 50*, 314-321.

Wispé, L. (1990). History of the concept of empathy. In N. Eisenberg & J. Strayer (Eds.), *Empathy and its development* (pp. 17-37). Cambridge: Cambridge University Press.

Wispé, L. (1991). *The psychology of sympathy.* New York: Plenum Press.

In: Dialogicality in Focus   ISBN: 978-1-61122-817-5
Editors: M. Märtsin, B. Wagoner, E.-L. Aveling et al.   © 2011 Nova Science Publishers, Inc.

Chapter 10

Gender, Embodiment, and Positioning in the Dialogical Self: Do Men and Women See Eye to Eye?

Peter Raggatt

Introduction

"…the self experiences his external body (the one the Other sees) as a series of disparate fragments, dangling on the string of his inner sensation." (Ann Jefferson, 1989, p. 154)

"No matter how much you think you're making sense they're still looking at your boobs."

Melissa Madden Gray, 2008, p. 7

These quotes point in different ways to the phenomenology of our embodied social relations. In sharing experience there is always a spatial and experiential 'gap' to be negotiated, suggesting that dialogue will always be constrained by our different positions. Our bodies are an important part of this dialogical (dis)engagement. The quote from Jefferson evokes the quandaries of the mirroring experience – the image we see of ourselves in the mirror is always incomplete and can never match the view that others see. We can only make a guess about the other's view. The second quote, from a popular Australian feminist comic, is also rich in signification. It parodies the gender wars; implies a predatory sexuality in men; and references the 'objectification' of women's bodies. But the joke can also be read as giving a social (gendered) context to the same disengagement between self and other proposed in Jefferson's more dispassionate phenomenological description.

Notwithstanding these observations the topic of 'embodiment' has received only limited attention in discussions of the dialogical self, perhaps because notions of dialogue and 'dialogism' invoke the spoken word as primary medium. In this chapter I will address aspects of embodiment as a form of positioning within a dialogical self theory (DST) framework. I will also report some findings from a survey of positioning and embodiment amongst midlife adults. Taking the lead from Gray's observation, I will focus specifically on the interaction of gender with body image representations, and consider how these relate to positioning in a DST framework. The findings point to problems of cross-gender communication and conflict that can be illuminated using DST. I will conclude with an alternative dialogical interpretation for Gray's wry observation about men looking at her boobs.

DIALOGICAL SELF THEORY

I begin with an overview of DST and consider some specific extensions of the theory that are a part of the research approach taken here. Drawing originally on James (1890), Bakhtin (1981, 1929/1984), and Mead (1934), Hermans (2001; Hermans & Kempen, 1993) has defined the dialogical self as a dynamic multiplicity of several 'I-positions' in the landscape of the mind, each position voicing a different view of the self in an ongoing dialogue with the world. I think several key principles underpin this theoretical linkage of self with dialogue, summarized here in point form:

(i)   First there is really no transcendental, core, or super-ordinate self in a dialogical approach. The theory posits different voices *positioned* in the person as well as between persons. The self emerges in this field of dialogue (Raggatt, 2010).

(ii)   Second, different I-positions are emergent 'in' and 'over' time (the synchronic and diachronic dimensions are both important). I-positions, thus constituted, have both local specific action patterns and extended historical/narrative coherence and continuity (see Raggatt, 2006).

(iii) A corollary of (ii) is that positioning implies change, but also continuity. I-positions suggest oscillations of the self in time, but the concept of 'storied voice' implies continuity through time as well.

(iv)   Finally, I-positions are frequently described by individuals in terms of paired opposites (see e.g., Raggatt, 2000, 2002, 2006). I have argued that the coordinates of these oppositions can be explained by both intra-personal (reflexive) and inter-personal (social) positioning (Raggatt, 2007).

In the present approach the way persons construe conflict is viewed as crucial to positioning and hence to the formation of the self. It follows then that a theory of positioning will require further elaboration in the future if a dialogical approach to the self is to prosper. In the next section I address this topic briefly, before turning to a discussion of gender and embodiment in relation to positioning.

POSITIONING THEORY

Looking 'inside' individuals, positioning implies oppositions and tensions between voiced locations. Here I focus on the task of analysing opposed I-positions in a person's *narrative* accounts of self, as distinct from a positioning analysis of specific micro-social happenings. This distinction suggests that positioning theory has a range of different applications and proponents. The social constructionists have focussed on the flux of positioning in settings ranging from micro-social dyadic encounters to diplomatic exchanges between nation states (e.g., Harré & van Langenhove, 1991, 1999; Harré & Moghaddam, 2003; Hollway, 1984; Gergen, 1991). Constructivist and narrative-based approaches, on the other hand, began by focussing on positioning processes in personality and in individual development across time (e.g., Hermans, 2001; Hermans & Hermans-Konopka, 2010; Hermans & Kempen, 1993; Raggatt, 2006, 2007). The concept of positioning therefore has a wide range of convenience. It can be applied to what happens in conversations; it is constructed in relationships; it shapes the stories we tell; and it is often imposed by the political and social order (Raggatt, 2007). With this scope and flexibility in mind the approach taken here acknowledges the necessity to understand positioning in terms of both individual and social coordinates.

The approach that I use to code positioning processes is derived from a classificatory scheme developed in earlier work (Raggatt, 2007). In that work positioning was classified in three domains: (i) mode of expression, (ii) reflexive (or personal) forms, and (iii) socially constituted forms (Raggatt, 2007). Table 1 summarizes this classificatory scheme. No claims are made that the scheme is universal or comprehensive. It should be considered a 'work-in-progress' model. Referring to Table 1, in panel (a) under modes of expression are included the *Narrative/Discursive*, which is the medium of storytelling (Bruner & Kalmar, 1998; Freeman, 1993; Raggatt, 2010); the *Performative/Expressive*, which incorporates role play, stagecraft, and scripting; and the *Embodied*, which incorporates body image, non-verbal expression, and body adornment. Aspects of these elements can be coded in life history data (discussed later). The codes for reflexive positioning, shown in panel (b), were derived from the broad literature on 'intra-psychic' conflict in the person: *Esteem* – to maximize positive self-evaluations and minimize negative ones[1]; *Affective* - to maximize pleasure and minimize pain; *Agentic* – to act in the world as an independent being; and *Communion-Oriented* - to find intimacy, attachment and connection in the world (Bakan, 1966; McAdams, 1993)[2]. Socially constituted positioning (the last panel of Table 1) may take many forms. I have focussed here on the effects of power in social settings involving hierarchies. At least three forms meet this criterion: occupational/status conflict, gender conflict, and social class conflict. Their inclusion recognizes that social positioning is sanctioned by power differences which give rise to uncertainties and to tensions in various social settings[3]. Gender conflicts are, of course, one important arena for these tensions, and it is to this topic that I now turn. In the next section I address the question of how differences between the sexes might be expressed within a positioning framework.

---

[1] Modern notions of self esteem are linked to the much older idea of 'moral career' and to the problem of how to lead a good life (McIntyre, 1981). These concerns are reflected culturally in Campbell's (1956) monomyth of the hero fighting dark forces (on the inside as well as outside), and in Propp's (1928/1968) classic analysis of folk tales, in which plot resolves down to a confrontation between a hero and a villain. Hence, from the perspective of reflexive positioning of the self, we may each be the containers for internalized heroes and villains.

[2] The dynamic force behind agency is an existential need: By what consuming project or set of projects can my life take on special meaning (Sartre, 1965)? How is power to be exercised? Communion, on the other hand, addresses the problem of how to find love and companionship in the world. Who can one care for and who can one trust? The dialectical tension between agency and communion is widely recognized in the psychological literature. For example, the psycho-analytic (Bakan, 1966; Freud, 1920/1955), personological (Hermans & Kempen, 1993; McAdams, 1985) and social psychological traditions have all been concerned with agency and communion as sources of psychological conflict (Wiggins, 2003).

[3] See Raggatt (2007) for an extended discussion of all these positioning forms. Space restrictions do not allow further treatment here.

Table 1. Forms of positioning in the dialogical self

(a) Medium of Expression	
Narrative/Discursive	storied self; autobiography; narrative voice
Performative/Expressive	role play; scripts; rituals
Embodied	body image, costume
(b) Reflexive	
Esteem Conflict	good self vs. bad self
Agency Conflict	strong self vs. weak self
Communion Conflict	intimacy vs. separation
Affect	happy self vs. sad self
(c) Social	
Occupation/status Conflict	boss vs. subordinate
Social Class Conflict	higher vs. lower
Cross-Gender Conflict	patriarchy; masculinity vs. femininity

Note: Criteria for coding forms of positioning based on this classification system are:

1. Narrative — presence of narrative accounts linking opposed positions;
2. Performative — presence of role play (e.g., work roles) linking opposed positions;
3. Embodied — presence of body image links among opposed positions;
4. Esteem — presence of good self/bad self positions;
5. Agency — presence of strong self/weak self positions;
6. Communion — presence of intimacy vs. separation-related positions;
7. Affect — presence of happy self/sad self positions;
8. Occupation — presence of power differential arising from work/status conflict;
9. Cross-Gender — presence of power differential arising from cross-gender conflict ;
10. Social Class — presence of power differential arising from social class conflict.

POSITIONING, GENDER, AND EMBODIMENT

There has been little systematic empirical inquiry into positioning as a feature of the dialogical self in individuals, let alone a consideration of how important social categories such as gender might interact with these processes (Raggatt, 2008). Concerning the interface between gender and positioning, there is an extensive empirical literature inquiring into gender differences from which to draw some direction. It is not my intention to review that literature here. Instead, we can draw from it some pointers to gender differences in positioning. For example, in a real-world event-sampling study conducted in a large organization, Moskowitz, Jung Suh & Desaulniers (1994) found that females were more attuned to intimacy and affiliation needs in randomly sampled work situations *regardless* of status-relevant context (interactions with supervisors versus co-workers). Males, on the other hand, were more sensitive to the status-relevant context. These findings were significant because the researchers sampled everyday events as they happened, rather than relying on retrospective recall or on reports of attitudes and beliefs. More generally in research on social motives the literature suggests that females are typically more attuned to verbal communication and intimacy concerns, while males are more individualistic and concerned with status (e.g., Bakan, 1966; McAdams, 1989, 1993; McAdams et al., 1988; Stewart & Chester, 1982).

Assuming that these differences between the sexes are real[4], they can be evaluated by examining positioning in the context of how males and females construe the dialogical self. First, in the domain of reflexive positioning (Table 1), if females have more 'relational' selves (Josselson, 1994) they should prioritize intimacy and connection vs. its absence in opposing I-positions. Hence we would predict gender differences in communion-oriented positioning with this being more apparent in the self-positioning of women. On the other hand, if males are more concerned with social dominance (or its lack), then we would expect them to construe more agency concerns in their positioning conflicts. Second, from the perspective of social positioning (see Table 1), if females are positioned as less dominant and more "compliant", it could be predicted that gender-related interpersonal conflicts will be more salient for women.

Another domain in which differences have featured strongly in research findings involving gender is body image. The object relations theorists have used a broad definition for body image which is closest to the usage intended here. Feldman (1975) defines body image as "the sum of the attitudes, feelings, memories and experiences an individual has towards his own body – both as an integrated whole, and in respect of its component parts" (p. 317). Hence, 'body image' can be unpacked so that it is not in the ordinary sense a singular image so much as a collection of images[5]. Previous research suggests that women experience greater body image distortions than men, and they have repeatedly been found to have lower body image satisfaction (e.g., Cash & Henry, 1995; Penkal & Kirdek, 2007; Sondhaus, Kurtz & Strube, 2001; Tiggemann, 2004). How might such body image differences be reflected in gendered positioning? Since the method of evaluating the DS to be described here includes body image measures, and since the conceptualization of positioning used here includes 'embodiment' as one mode of expression, we can address this question here.

In terms of existing theory linking gender, embodiment, and positioning, Frederickson and Roberts (1997) have attempted to explain gender-specific body image differences using 'objectification theory'. The theory holds that women, more than do men, learn to assess their own value as a function of how they believe their bodies are viewed by others, particularly men – in other words, they 'self-objectify'. Hence, the body becomes the sight of imperfections imagined to be on display for others. Frederickson and Roberts propose that Western women in particular, when compared to men, learn to assess their own value as a function of body image (dis)satisfaction. The result is a heightened focus on grooming and other (body) image-enhancing behaviours for women relative to men, greater anxiety about appearance in women, and, some theorists argue, a diminished confidence in other evaluative contexts unrelated to appearance (e.g., Davis, Dionne and Shuster, 2001).

Assuming that female self-objectification is widespread in Western cultures one might expect greater salience for body image in the positioning conflicts of women compared to men. For example, one might predict that for females esteem conflicts (reflexive positioning)

---

[4] I will not address at this point the question of whether these differences can be explained by gender stereotypes.

[5] For example, the eyes can symbolize or represent friendliness, openness or sociability, the shoulders may represent 'strength of character', while the belly may stand for more negative attributes, such as laziness. It is a short step from there to conceptualize body image constituents as an important potential source of self-representations.

will interact with body image concerns (embodied positioning), and that women would generally hold more negative perceptions of their bodies.

In what follows, interactions between gender, positioning and body image are explored empirically. Two general propositions will be examined: (i) that there will be gender differences in positioning, and (ii) that measures of body image, gender and positioning will show interactions.

A SURVEY OF THE DIALOGICAL SELF: METHODS

The findings to be reported here form part of a larger ongoing project that examines the DS using life narrative methods. The data comes from 109 adults who were enrolled as mature age students in undergraduate courses at James Cook University in Australia (mean age was 31 years). They were predominantly white and middle class, and females were over-represented relative to males (33 males, 76 females). To investigate the dialogical self I use a life narrative-based assessment method (or more correctly, set of methods) that is designed to 'map' I-positions in the individual. The assessment procedure is called the Personality Web Protocol (PWP). It has been described in detail elsewhere (Raggatt, 2000, 2006) and so here I will confine my description to an abbreviated synopsis. The method can be combined with in depth semi-structured interviewing to yield detailed case studies (e.g., Raggatt, 2000, 2002, 2006). Alternatively, it can be adapted, as in the approach described here, to a pen and paper version in the form of a battery of instruments eliciting both quantitative and qualitative data. The procedure can be summarized as follows:

1. Informants list and describe 24 life history constituents or 'attachments'. The list must include 6 significant people, 6 life events, 8 objects and places, and 4 body part constituents. Liked and disliked, or positive and negative exemplars of each component type are elicited[6].
2. Informants sort their constituents into typically between 2 and 4 associated groups or clusters that define different self-relevant life themes and narratives.
3. Informants label each cluster with a self-relevant identifier (e.g., creative self, spiritual self, victim).
4. Informants are interviewed about their life history constituents and thematic clusters, or alternatively, they write commentaries on them.

For present purposes, as noted the data analyzed comes from a survey battery version of the PWP in which participants listed, sorted thematically, and labelled life history constituents and then wrote commentaries on the product of this exercise. Figure 1 shows a conceptual model for examining 'oppositions' in the life history thematic clusters derived using the PWP methodology. In Figure 1, the data collection and analytic process is summarized in the form of a flowchart. Life history constituents (people, events, etc.) are listed first. They are then

---

[6] The list of material generated included: two liked associates, two disliked associates, and a liked and disliked public figure; peak (happy) and nadir (sad) experiences described from childhood, adolescence, and adulthood; valued possessions, important places, and influential books or works of art; and four body part constituents (e.g., the eyes) that were respectively 'liked', 'disliked', 'strong', and 'weak'.

sorted into associated groupings as defined by the informant (using the broad criterion of "self-relevant themes in thinking, feeling and experiencing"). The informant then provides a self-relevant label for each cluster. It is these clusters, their formation and particularly their opposition, that are the focus here. In the final phase of the analytic process, opposing clusters in the informants' protocols are coded for positioning. For this analysis the positioning classification system outlined previously and shown in Table 1 was used.

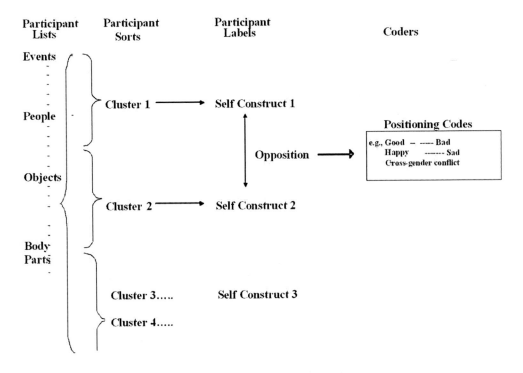

Figure 1. Conceptual model for coding positioning in the dialogical self.

Coding the Protocols for Positioning

Two independent judges with postgraduate training were used to code for positioning. The task required the judges to indicate the presence vs. absence of the expressive, reflexive, and social forms of positioning listed in Table 1. The coders were instructed to read synopses of the data provided by each informant. Table 2 shows a sample protocol from a 29 year old female participant. The protocol is typical of the sample in key respects. There is a pair of opposing I-positions she has called simply a "positive self" and a "negative self", and two other positions defined as "artistic" and "feminine". Note that the embodied mode of expression is important to both the "negative" and "feminine" positions. It was these protocols that were used to code for positioning.

The coders made judgments in two phases. In the first phase, the presence of opposing I-positions in the protocols was coded. It emerged that for 95 (86%) of the sample there was at least one pair of opposing I-positions. The coefficient of inter-judge reliability for this task was 0.94. In the second phase of coding, the pairs of opposing I-positions were marked, separately, for the presence/absence of first the expressive, then the reflexive, and finally the social forms of positioning. The mean co-efficient of inter-judge reliability for the second phase of the coding procedure was 0.88, and disagreements were resolved or the code entry was not scored.

Table 2. Sample protocol: I-position clusters, descriptions and commentary from a female participant, aged 29

1. Positive Self	"Brings together the positive, good and inspiring things in my life"
Mother	"she has always supported me in regard to traveling and learning".
First plane flight	(aged 8) "with my mother"; (excitement, joy)
Joining RAAF	"I learnt lots of good things about myself" (excitement, pride)
Travel to Europe	With partner; "a dream come true"; (happiness)
Going to Uni.	"I feel more confident"; (happiness, eagerness)
2. Negative Self	"I have a negative self …my childhood experiences with my father have been a dominating factor."
Father	"put-downs coupled with drunken behavior and emotional abuse." (anger)
Dispute - father	"father was drunk and was trying to load a gun. Mum took the gun". (fear)
Lost bicycle	"my father abused me and told me how bad it was and that I deserved it."
End Relationship	"huge self-doubt and lack of self-worth. I felt that I couldn't trust anyone."
My thighs	"I have cellulite, surface veins ands stretch marks." (insecurity)
Sweaty hands/feet	"I have hyperhydrosis (a medical condition) which is where there is an over-reaction of sweat glands. It worsens with anxiety." (embarrassed)
3. Artistic Self	"I have always loved theatre, art and creativity. I feel that even though I haven't pursued theatre, it really is my calling."
Cate Blanchett	"I like the roles she plays. I admire her devotion to her husband and life."
Sir Peter Ustinov	"I enjoy watching his character and the distinct sound of his voice."
Fancy dress	"I have fun when I portray a character and watch people's reaction."
Painting	"Special because it is old…fine and delicate"; (creativity)
4. Feminine Self	"I love being a woman – an equal woman. I accept the differences with men and I enjoy these differences. I love being a feminine shape."
Tailored suit	"It makes me feel professional and important, as well smart and beautiful."
Sexy dress	"I enjoy wearing this dress. It shows my womanly curves."
My calves	"I have always liked my calves as they look strong, athletic, and sexy."
My body	"My body is all intact and I have 'normal functioning'"..

Computation of Body Image Indices

In order to analyze the body image data in relation to positioning and gender, a series of body zone indices were constructed from the body part constituents reported on the PWP[7]. This was necessary because the frequencies for individual body part references on the PWP, e.g., to the legs, nose, or hands, were relatively low (a notable exception was the eyes). To address this problem, indices based on body zones or regions were compiled. Four zones were identified from the PWP data: the *face* (e.g., eyes, nose, mouth, hair), *torso* (shoulders, chest, stomach, back), *lower body* (butt, legs, thighs, calves, etc.) and *body organs* (brain, heart). Separate indices for positive references ('liked' and 'strong' body parts), and negative references ('disliked' and 'weak' body parts) were computed for each of these four body zones. Thus, for interpretation purposes, dichotomous (presence-absence) variables were created depending on whether participants had reported *any one* of the body constituents comprising each zone, and both positively and negatively loaded indices were created.

SURVEY FINDINGS: INTERACTIONS OF GENDER WITH POSITIONING AND EMBODIMENT

Table 3 shows frequencies (in %) broken down by gender, for the positioning codes [panel (a)] and the body image measures [panel (b)]. Since both the positioning codes and the embodiment measures were dichotomous, χ^2 (Chi-Squared) tests were computed to look at patterns of association with gender, and these are also reported in Table 3. With regard first to frequencies for the positioning codes in the sample as whole, frequencies for two of the codes -- the Narrative/Discursive and the Social Class Conflict codes -- were severely skewed and so no meaningful χ^2 comparisons on gender could be reported for these measures. Among the reflexive positioning codes, Communion and Esteem conflicts were the most frequently coded (45% and 38% of the total sample respectively). Among the social positioning codes, Cross-Gender Conflict was coded most frequently (39% of the sample). In the embodiment data, references to parts of the face (71% of the sample) and the torso (58% of the sample) were the most frequently reported.

Looking now at the frequencies broken down by gender and at the χ^2 tests for sex differences on the positioning codes [panel (a) of Table 3], first, there were no differences between the sexes on the *expressive* positioning codes. Notably, embodied expression was coded as frequently in the opposed I-positions of males as females (about 42% of protocols for both sexes). Hence the prediction of greater embodied conflict for females was not supported. However, there were marked gender differences in the results for both the *reflexive* and *social* forms of positioning, and these were largely in accord with predictions. Female protocols were coded for both Communion and Cross-Gender conflicts at significantly higher frequencies than for males, as had been predicted. Female protocols were also coded for Esteem conflicts (Good Self/Bad Self I-positions) at twice the frequency of males, and this was also statistically significant. Males, on the other hand, were nearly twice as likely to represent internal conflicts in terms of Agency themes, a difference that was also statistically

---

[7] Recall that informants were required to list and comment on a 'liked', 'disliked', 'strong', and 'weak' body part.

significant. With the possible exception of the differences on the code for Esteem, these gender effects are consistent with the research literature on social motives reviewed earlier. Further, the differences in reporting Cross-Gender conflicts may reflect real gender-based power differentials in the community sampled. This finding reinforces the importance of social positioning factors for identity conflicts, factors that may be outside individual agency or control.

Panel (b) of Table 3 shows the results of tests for gender differences on the body image indices. Here there are some intriguing interactions. The χ^2 tests reveal gender differences on the face, torso, and lower body indices. Females in the sample made significantly more *positive* references to the face on the PWP-Q (59% of females), and this was at nearly twice the rate of males (31%). Males, on the other hand, made significantly more *negative* references to the face (35%), at more than twice the rate of females (13%). For this sample then, it would appear that *positive* I-positions are signified in facial features for females only, while the males did the reverse, signifying *negative* I-positions in facial features. As expected, females were more negative than males in construing their torsos and lower bodies. Males produced significantly more positive references to their torsos in the protocols ($\chi^2 = 3.56$, p>0.05), while females made significantly more negative references to their lower bodies ($\chi^2 = 4.05$, p>0.05).

In summary the females in the sample construed their faces positively and their lower bodies negatively in the context of their I-positions, while the males construed their faces negatively and their torsos positively. These findings suggest that there are different processes of embodying the self in men and women. More light may be shed on this by looking at higher-order (three-way) interactions between gender, the positioning codes, and the body image measures. Since gender co-varies with both the positioning and body image data, the possibility of higher-order interactions can be explored. For example, since there were strong gender differences in the way the face was represented (positively by females, negatively by males) we might explore whether such patterns of difference interact with positioning. To address this question Log-Linear Analyses (based on χ^2) were performed to search for three-way interactions between gender, the positioning codes and the body zone indices. Two contrasting effects were detected. First, there was a significant three-way interaction between gender (being female), Esteem conflicts, and the positive Face index ($\chi^2 = 5.08$, p>0.05). Second, there was a significant three-way interaction between gender (being male), Esteem conflicts, and the positive Torso index ($\chi^2 = 3.44$, p>0.05). I think we can interpret these interactions within the framework of dialogical self theory in terms of two distinct patterns.

The women *embodied* healthy esteem through their faces while the men did this through their torsos. In short, in females conflicts involving esteem, communion, and cross-gender conflicts were more important than for males, the face was the sight of positive I-positions, and 'disliked' and 'weak' body parts were focussed in the lower body. In males, conflicts over agency (strong-weak I-positions) were more salient, the face was construed negatively rather than positively, and positive I-positions were given embodied expression through the torso.

Table 3. Gender comparisons on the positioning and body image measures

		Frequency (%)		df	Phi	χ^2
		Males	Females			
(a) Gender x Positioning						
Narrative		85.2	88.4			
Performative		27.3	17.1	1	-.12	1.48
Embodied		42.4	42.1	1	.01	0.01
Esteem		21.2	**40.8**	1	.19	**3.88***
Agency		**39.4**	22.4	1	-.18	**3.34***
Communion		24.2	**48.7**	1	.23	**5.67****
Affect		21.2	26.3	1	.05	0.32
Occupation/Status Conflict		21.2	11.8	1	-.12	1.61
Cross-Gender Interpersonal Conflict		21.2	**46.1**	1	.24	**5.99****
Social Class Conflict		10.1	11.7			
(b) Gender x Body Image Indices						
Face Index	positive	31.0	**59.4**	1	.26	**6.74****
	negative	**34.5**	13.5	1	-.24	**5.85****
Torso Index	positive	**37.9**	20.2	1	-.19	**3.64***
	negative	37.9	31.0	1	-.07	0.44
Lower Body Index	positive	21.0	20.8	1	-.01	0.01
	negative	6.9	**24.3**	1	.20	**4.05***
Body Organ Index	positive	20.6	30.0	1	.09	0.86
	negative	6.9	16.2	1	.12	1.54

N = 109.
* p<0.05, ** p<0.01.

IMPLICATIONS: DO MEN AND WOMEN SEE EYE TO EYE?

Here I want to make some observations about embodied communication, particularly keeping in mind the quotes from Jefferson and Gray with which I began this chapter. We might ask for example whether any new understandings about embodied processes of positioning can be gleaned from the findings described here. First, it needs to be reiterated that there will always be *uncertainty* about our own embodied expression in the world. This is because of a fundamental disengagement from the other's view. As Jefferson (1989, p. 154) observes, the image we see of ourselves in the mirror is but one "disparate fragment, dangling on the string of [our] inner sensation". Perhaps this fundamental uncertainty is implicated in the disengagement between the genders over issues of embodiment, even when accounting for the effects of patriarchy and gendered oppression? Certainly, a feminist interpretation can not be discounted because the findings presented here are in some respects consistent with Frederickson and Roberts (1997) 'objectification theory'. The females in the sample were more negative about their lower bodies than were the males. One possible resolution is to read the conflicts between the sexes over the body as arising out of *two* positioning processes, one based on the 'objectification' of women through *social* positioning, and the other arising out of uncertainties about self-embodied expression that we all share, but which the sexes perhaps handle differently (reflexive positioning). To put this another way, differences between the sexes in self-embodied representations arise not just out of conditions of patriarchy and gendered oppression, but also out of our fundamental blind-sightedness to the other's view of our bodies. Males and females may handle this problem quite differently.

Returning now to Melissa Madden Gray's (2008) wry observation that "No matter how much you think you're making sense, they're still looking at your boobs" (p. 7) -- notice that the gendered disjunction observed in the present findings is captured nicely in this jibe. That is to say, while Gray is 'speaking her mind' (and thinking she is making sense) her interlocutors are staring at her breasts. Putting aside for the moment the allusions to male lust and sexual aggression, on the one hand, and female 'honour' and opprobrium directed at men, on the other – the sub-texts in the joke – perhaps we can re-interpret the disengagement here in terms of fractured dialogues and failures of embodied communication across gender boundaries? That is to say, perhaps there is a deep *disengagement* between the sexes with respect to the way the body maps onto conceptions of the self? A disengagement that can not be fully explained in terms of gender wars over the 'objectification' of female bodies. Hence, while the male gaze may drop to a girl's torso and lower body, as it does in the joke, the male can be positioned as 'looking out' - *speaking* - from his own torso. That is, he *prefers* to speak with his good self from a site with an embodied focus in his own torso (not his head or face). Women, on the other hand, resist this kind of 'objectification' because they are looking out – *speaking* – from their faces. The female preference is for embodying desired selves in the face, not parts of the lower body. The findings reported here suggest that males do not share this preference. In consequence this dialogical disjunction becomes grist for the mill of sexual confusions, sexual politics, and feminist jokes.

Is there any evidence in the literature on body image that is congruent with the findings here? Several studies describe a similar pattern of findings. When Sondhaus, Kurtz and Strube (2001) examined body satisfaction in relation to self-esteem in a large sample of college students, they found that academic success was positively related to body satisfaction only in males. In the females, academic success was related to body *dissatisfaction*. It is not clear that this result can be explained fully in terms of patriarchy or Objectification Theory. When Feldman (1975) asked anorexic women to rate satisfaction with a range of body parts (including the face, hands, breasts, belly, and buttocks), the pattern of findings matched the present ones for females, but in an amplified way. That is, the anorexic women expressed an intense dislike for their lower body parts, but liked their faces a great deal. Since the beauty of a woman's face might also be the subject of objectification, it is not clear that objectification theory can account for the way females embody esteem through the face.

Perhaps the focus on *communion* themes in the positioning efforts of the women in this study is salient here? In the females, positive I-positions were linked to the face *as the focus for social interaction*. For example, many women in the sample described their eyes as embodying strength and honesty in the context of esteem concerns and relationship conflicts. The males in the sample positioned themselves very differently in embodied terms. As we have seen, they construed esteem through their torsos. Thus, when the pattern of embodied disengagement between the sexes is coupled with the more communion-oriented focus on conflict in the women, compared to the more individual (agentic) concerns of the men, a picture emerges of female sociality with positive I-positions embodied in the face, and male physicality, with positive I-positions embodied in the torso. Embodied positioning in men and women, therefore, is a source of important differences not just because of female objectification (social positioning), but because the dialogical self is embodied differently by men and women (reflexive positioning). Problems emerge, then, because males and females use quite different modes of embodying self-expression.

So, do men and women have trouble seeing eye to eye, as Gray (2008) asserts in her joke? The present analysis seems to confirm that a problem exists! Perhaps differences in embodying the self across the sexes are a natural concomitant of differences in the way conflict is construed by men and women. Should we accept then the canonical narrative of male lust and so blame the man for his wandering gaze? – the message behind Gray's joke. It is possible that males just can't help it; it being a curious outgrowth and consequence of the way men position *themselves* in embodied terms.

CONCLUSION

With reference finally to the development of positioning theory more generally, I have tried to illustrate how the approach taken here has the potential to provide a generative framework for studying the dialogical self in its social and cultural context. A principle purpose here was to demonstrate how the approach can account for the complexity of the self's constitution, *both* in individual-reflexive and social terms. The model of positioning used here assumes that both agentic/reflexive and socially constituted influences operate together in the formation of psychic conflict. In terms of dialogical self theory, it is noteworthy that the kinds of sex differences illustrated here may only become visible by conceptualising the self as a multiplicity of conflicting positions. Using this strategy, a picture of underlying tensions in the organisation of the self becomes apparent, and these tensions can be interpreted for specific individuals or for groups, in harness with positioning theory.

REFERENCES

Bakan, D. (1966). *The duality of human existence: Isolation and communion in western man.* Boston: Beacon.

Bakhtin, M. M. (1981). *The dialogic imagination* (M. Holquist Ed. & M. Holquist and C. Emerson, Trans.). Austin, Texas: University of Texas Press.

Bakhtin, M. M. (1929/1984). *Problems of Dostoevsky's poetics* (C. Emerson Ed. & Trans.). Minneapolis, MN: University of Minnesota Press.

Bruner, J., & Kalmar, D. A. (1998). Narrative and metanarrative in the construction of self. In M. Ferrari & R. J. Sternberg (Eds.), *Self-awareness: Its nature and development* (pp. 308-331). New York: Guilford Press.

Campbell, J. (1956). *The hero with a thousand faces.* New York: Meridian.

Cash, T. F., & Henry, P. E. (1995). Women's body images: The results of a national survey in the USA. *Sex Roles, 33*, 19 – 28.

Davis, C., Dionne, M., & Schuster, B. (2001). Physical and psychological correlates of appearance orientation. *Personality and Individual Differences, 30*, 21 – 30.

Feldman, M. M. (1975). The body image and object relations: Exploration of a method utilizing repertory grid techniques. *British Journal of Medical Psychology, 48*, 317 – 332.

Frederickson, B. L., & Roberts, T. A. (1997). Objectification theory: Towards understanding women's lived experiences and mental health risks. *Psychology of Women Quarterly, 21,* 206-273.

Freeman, M. (1993). *Rewriting the self: History, memory, narrative.* London: Routledge.

Freud, S. (1920/1955). Beyond the pleasure principle. In J. Strachey (Ed.), *The standard edition of the complete psychological works of Sigmund Freud (Vol. 18)* (pp.7 - 64). London: Hogarth.

Gergen, K. J. (1991). *The saturated self.* Oxford: Basil Blackwell.

Gray, M. M. (April 19-20, 2008). Profile: Melissa Madden Gray. In *Weekend Australian Review* (p. 17 - 18). Sydney: News Limited Press.

Harré, R., & Moghaddam, F. (2003). The self and others in traditional psychology and in positioning theory. In R. Harré and F. Moghaddam (Eds.), *The self and others: Positioning individuals and groups in personal, political and cultural contexts* (pp. 1 – 12). Westport, CO: Praeger.

Harré. R., & Van Langenhove, L. (1991). Varieties of positioning. *Journal for the Theory of Social Behaviour, 21,* 393-407.

Harré. R., & Van Langenhove, L. (Eds.) (1999). *Positioning theory.* Oxford: Blackwell.

Hermans, H. J. M. (2001). The dialogical self: Toward a theory of personal and cultural positioning. *Culture & Psychology, 7,* 243-81.

Hermans, H. J. M., & Hermans-Konopka, A. (2010). *Dialogical self theory: Positioning and counter-positioning in a globalizing society.* Cambridge, UK: Cambridge University Press.

Hermans, H. J. M., & Kempen, H. J. (1993). *The dialogical self: Meaning as movement.* San Diego: Academic Press.

Hollway, W. (1984). Gender differences and the production of subjectivity. In J. Henricks, W. Hollway, C. Urwin, L. Venn & V. Walkerdine (Eds*.), Changing the subject: Psychology, social regulation and subjectivity* (pp. 227-263). London: Methuen.

James, W. (1890). *The principles of psychology. Vol. 1.* London: MacMillan.

Jefferson, A. (1989). Bodymatters: Self and other in Bakhtin, Sartre, and Barthes. In K. Hirshkop & D. Sheperd (Eds.), *Bakhtin and cultural theory* (pp. 152-179), Manchester: Manchester University Press.

Josselson, R. (1994). Identity and relatedness in the life cycle. In H. A. Bosma, T. L. G. Graafsma, H. G. Grotevant, & D. J. de Levita (Eds.), *Identity and development: An interdisciplinary approach* (pp. 81 – 101). Thousand Oaks: Sage.

McAdams, D. P. (1985). *Power, intimacy and the life story: Personological inquiries into identity.* New York: The Guilford Press.

McAdams, D. P. (1989). *Intimacy: The need to be close.* New York: Doubleday.

McAdams, D. P. (1993). *The stories we live by: Personal myths and the making of identity.* New York: William Morrow.

McAdams, D. P., Lester, R., Brand, P., McNamara, W., & Lensky, D. B. (1988). Sex and the TAT: Are women more intimate than men? Do men fear intimacy? *Journal of Personality Assessment, 52,* 397 – 409.

McIntyre, A. (1984). *After virtue.* Notre Dame, Indiana: University of Notre Dame Press.

Mead, G. H. (1934). *Mind, self and society.* Chicago: University of Chicago Press.

Moskowitz, D. S., Suh, E. J., & Desaulniers, J. (1994). Situational influences on gender differences in agency and communion. *Journal of Personality and Social Psychology, 66,* 753 – 761.

Penkal, J. L., & Kerdek, L. A. (2007). Gender and race differences in young adults' body dissatisfaction. *Personality and Individual Differences, 43,* 2270-2281.

Propp, V. (1928/1968). *The morphology of the folktale* (L. Scott, Trans.). Austin, TX: University of Texas Press.

Raggatt, P. T. F. (2000). Mapping the dialogical self: Towards a rationale and method of assessment. *European Journal of Personality, 14,* 65 - 90.

Raggatt, P. T. F. (2002). The landscape of narrative and the plural self: Exploring identity using the Personality Web Protocol. *Narrative Inquiry, 12,* 290-318.

Raggatt, P. T. F. (2006). Multiplicity and conflict in the dialogical self: A life-narrative approach. In D. P. McAdams, R. Josselson & A. Lieblich (Eds.), *Identity and story: The narrative construction of the self* (pp. 15 – 35). Washington, DC: American Psychological Association Press.

Raggatt, P. T. F. (2007). Forms of positioning in the dialogical self: A system of classification and the strange case of Dame Edna Everage. *Theory & Psychology, 17,* 355-383.

Raggatt, P. T. F. (2008). Interaction of personal and social positioning in the formation of the dialogical self: A study of Australian adults. *Psychological Studies, 8,* 149-174.

Raggatt, P. T. F. (2010). The dialogical self and thirdness: A semiotic approach to positioning using dialogical triads. *Theory & Psychology, 20* (3), 400-419.

Sartre, J.-P. (1965). *Essays in existentialism.* Secaucus, NJ: Citadel Press.

Sondhaus, E. L., Kurtz, R. M., & Strube, M. J. (2001). Body attitude, gender and self-concept: A 30-year perspective. *Journal of Psychology, 135,* 413 – 429.

Stewart, A. J., & Chester, N. L. (1982). Sex differences in human social motives: Achievement, affiliation and power. In A. J. Stewart (Ed.), *Motivation and society* (pp. 172 – 218), San Francisco: Jossey-Bass.

Tiggemann, M. (2004). Body image across the adult life span: Stability and change *Body Image: An International Journal of Research, 1,* 29 – 41.

Wiggins, J. S. (2003). *Paradigms of personality assessment.* NY: Guilford Press.

In: Dialogicality in Focus
Editors: M. Märtsin, B. Wagoner, E.-L. Aveling et al.

ISBN: 978-1-61122-817-5
© 2011 Nova Science Publishers, Inc.

Chapter 11

DIALOGICALITY AND THE (DE)SECURITISATION OF SELF: GLOBALISATION, MIGRATION AND MULTICULTURAL POLITICS

Catarina Kinnvall and Sarah Scuzzarello

INTRODUCTION

The idea that multiculturalism is in crisis is a predominant feature of the 21st century. In the aftermath of the terrorist attacks in New York, Madrid, and London this idea has become a pronounced aspect of public debate across Western Europe. Glazer's optimistic statement that "We're All Multiculturalists Now!" (1997, book title) seems to have lost its resonance among both politicians and the public at large. A commonly shared narrative of crisis has emerged among the public and policy makers who perceive previous policies, which emphasised difference over communality and cultural particularity over social cohesion, as a kind of failed experimentation.

Several academic studies have demonstrated a 'retreat' of multiculturalism in Europe and their replacement by policies of civic integration (Joppke, 2004). By way of example, several countries traditionally labelled 'multicultural' (e.g., Britain, Sweden, and the Netherlands) have introduced citizenship rituals, while others have made language and national culture tests a precondition for naturalisation (e.g., Britain and Denmark). Furthermore, politicians and policy-makers increasingly use a rhetoric which emphasises the need to develop a sense of belonging and identity (Home Office, 2002). A number of studies have argued that migration is increasingly being presented as a danger to the public order and a threat to European society. Drawing upon critical security studies, Weaver et al. (1993) argue, for instance, that migration has increasingly become constructed as a threat to cultural, economic but also physical security (see also den Boer, 1995; Huysmans, 1995, 2000; Kinnvall, 2004; Kinnvall & Nesbitt-Larking, 2011)[1].

---

[1] For a critique and a development of this approach, see Boswell (2007).

In this context Tariq Modood (2005, 2007), among others, has argued that Muslims in Europe have become the main scapegoats of the critics of multiculturalism. Young male Muslims are often depicted as increasingly radicalized and urban areas, densely populated by Muslims, are often seen as a fertile breeding ground for Islamic fundamentalism. Women and the veiling issue in particular, has also become an easy target well beyond France, where the debate started in the late 1980s. The veil, in all its shapes and lengths, often stands for the most visible illustration of patriarchal, religious oppression of Muslim women[2]. In this context several European countries have decided to ban (or attempted to do so) the use of headscarves in the public domain. Sceptical voices concerning the possibilities to live in a multicultural, non-antagonistic society have also been augmented among minorities. Research shows that events like rallies in support of the terrorist attacks of September 11, 2001 could be the expression of sceptical voices among minority groups regarding the possibilities of living in a multicultural society (Akthar, 2005).

In this chapter we argue that in an increasingly globalised and culturally diverse world, majority and minority communities may perceive migration and increased diversity as threats in relation to the survival of the community and the preservation of culture and heritage. They are securitised, i.e., presented as an existential threat[3], thus justifying actions outside the common bounds of political procedure (Buzan et al., 1998). These perceived threats are likely to lead to 'monological closures', to use Bakhtin's terminology (1979/1986), which refers to the attempts made by a single authority to monopolise meaning to the exclusion of all competing voices[4]. A range of threats to identity and beliefs prompt communities to seek socio-cultural and religious refuge in a series of 'born again' adoptions of religious, national, ethno-racial, or gendered signifiers (Kinnvall & Nesbitt-Larking, 2011). This resort to essentialism is what we label the 'securitisation of subjectivity' (Kinnvall, 2004, 2006), as discussed later. As Akhtar (2005) demonstrates, young Muslims' increased adherence to religion can be explained not only in structural terms (e.g., their economic and social exclusion) but also in psychological terms. The "return to religion" is a phenomenon "that offers individuals who feel in some ways constrained by their circumstances an alternative ideology, a sense of belonging, solidarity and a means of political mobilization" (Akhtar, 2005, p. 165).

Yet globalisation and diversity need not only prompt closure and securitisation. The late-modern world also brings with it an empowering and transformative potential as people have the possibility of organising themselves against different kinds of oppression (Nesbitt-Larking, 2009). The multitude of daily encounters at work, in schools, or through associations, for instance, provide several opportunities for challenging one's mores and traditions, for questioning those taken-for-granted narratives about society, its members and their "proper" behaviour (i.e., desecuritisation). We argue that the processes of securitisation and desecuritisation can be better understood and analyzed by reference to dialogical approaches to research in social psychology. In the field of international relations (IR), where the concept of 'securitisation' was originally developed, there is a tendency to focus on social

---

[2] For recent works on the veiling issue see, among others Mahmood (2005), Scott (2007), Roy (2007), Joppke (2009).

[3] Here we rely on Anthony Giddens' (1991) discussion of existential as being concerned with existence itself, the external world and human life, the existence of the other, and what self-identity actually is. An existential threat is perceived as a threat against all these aspects of being.

[4] See also Gillespie (2008) for a similar argument.

and cognitive relations at the macro level, while devoting less attention to how securitisation processes affect people's lives. Coming from a research tradition in IR, we see a need to complement this body of work with analytical tools borrowed from social psychology to better understand how macro phenomena, such as the construction of social representations, impact on the micro level of individual identification.

We argue that a dialogical conceptualisation of the self as proposed by, among others, Hermans and associates (1992) contributes significantly to the understanding of the dynamics of identity construction in the context of globalised and diverse societies. We identify two reasons for this. First, it provides a perspective on the self that enables researchers to better understand the mechanisms that may lead to monological closures and the securitisation of subjectivity. At the same time, a dialogical understanding of the self challenges the practices and discourses which tend to portray identity as static and reified. Second, a dialogical approach provides a number of critical theoretical and analytical tools for challenging the consequences of monological closures. As Hermans and Dimaggio emphasize "one of the central features of dialogical relationships is that they have the potential of innovating the self" (2007, p. 53). In the context of globalisation and increased migration flows a person could develop new personal stories which create new affiliations and forms of identification with the 'other'. In this way she could change her antagonistic psychological orientations towards the 'other' and thus promote social courage, pro-social behaviour, tolerance and care in a global world.

We proceed by presenting the work on dialogical self (Hermans et al., 1992; Hermans, 2001; Hermans & Dimaggio, 2007) and clarify the theoretical linkages between this body of literature and critical security studies as developed in IR (Buzan et al., 1998). Second, in addressing some of the shortcomings of dialogical self theory we demonstrate how positioning theories (Harré & van Langenhove, 1991) can strengthen a conception of dialogical self. Here we draw upon Marková's (2003a; 2003b; 2006) concept of dialogicality, i.e., "the capacity of the human mind to conceive, create and communicate about social realities in terms of the 'Alter'" (i.e., of otherness) (2003b, p. 249) as well as Raggatt's understanding of positioning (2007; 2010; 2011) and argue that both examine personal and social constructions of self and that they therefore force us to think of self and identity in terms of both change and continuity. Finally, we present some of the implications of dialogicality, positioning and the (de)securitisation of subjectivity for ethics and politics in the context of globalisation and increased migration flows. In conclusion, we argue in favour of a dialogically constituted critical self that is capable of distancing itself from other symbolic orders. This can lead to a heightened degree of reflexivity.

DIALOGICAL SELF, POSITIONING AND GLOBALISATION

The Russian literary theorist and critic Mikhail Bakhtin (1979/1986; 1994) stressed that the characters in Dostoevsky's works were created in a dialogue of intersecting voices. Bakhtin called this sort of novel polyphonic. The concept of polyphony has implications for how the self is re-conceptualized in terms of continuous interpersonal and intrapersonal dialogues and has recently inspired social psychologists and personality psychologists. One of the strands of literature inspired by a Bakhtinian understanding of the self as polyphonic is dialogical self theory (Hermans et al. 1992; Hermans, 2001; Hermans & Dimaggio, 2007).

Hermans and colleagues define the dialogical self as "a dynamic of multiplicity of relatively autonomous I-positions in an imaginal landscape" (1992, p. 28). The self is constituted by a polyphony of voices in constant dialogue with each other and with the outer world. One voice is emphasized over others in accordance with changes in time and space. These voices are not necessarily harmonious, but can rather express different and even opposed narratives about the self (Hermans et al., 1992; Hermans, 2001)[5]. The metaphor of voices within the self is commonly translated in terms of "a dynamic multiplicity of positions" (Hermans, 2001, p. 258), in which the individual is involved in an active process of positioning depending on the particular situation at hand. Thus conceived, the dialogical self is dynamic in that the 'I' can occupy different positions depending on the context in which it acts. It is 'social', not so much in the sense that a self-contained individual enters into social interactions with others, but in the sense that the self is constituted by a multiplicity of internal and external positions (Hermans, 2001). Internal positions refer to those conceived of as parts of one's self (e.g., I as a mother), while external positions are used to describe people and objects that are part of the external environment and relevant from the perspective of one or more of the internal positions (e.g., my child) (Hermans, 2001). These positions interact with each other, and also with a third zone, the outside world. Hermans (2001) argues that a person is not necessarily aware of all aspects of these positions (e.g., a person may be positioned as a migrant despite the fact that he or she may be a citizen in a country and not feel like a migrant), but they may become part of their internal and external positions later in life (for instance when entering the job market, he or she may be unable to get a job because of their particular migrant positioning). The distinction between the 'outside world' and 'external/internal positions' is problematic, however, if the relation between them, i.e., the dynamics of positioning[6], is not studied and understood. Taking the work of Hermans and colleagues as a case in point, it remains unclear how broader social positions affect the development of the self unless we also take seriously the discursive and structural aspects of positioning. This is particularly important as we discuss how a dialogical approach can actually be helpful for changing the often marginalized positions of migrants in Western societies.

In contrast to dialogical self scholars, Harré and van Langenhove (1991; 1999), in their original definition of positioning theory, emphasize the social and discursive aspects of positioning at the cost of the personal. Positioning, according to Harré and van Langenhove, indicates the relational cluster of generic personal attributes which impinges on the possibilities of interpersonal, intergroup and even intrapersonal action. Positioning takes place within a moral order as people are positioned in various ways; dominant or submissive, dependent or independent, masculine or feminine, and so on. Such dichotomies reflect current power relationships and have consequences for how others are conceived. Outsiders

---

[5] Valsiner (2005) argues that Hermans' and associates' conception of different I-positions as alternating between internal and external positions, is an implementation of George Herbert Mead's original view of the ongoing relation between I and ME. This line of thinking is not new, he argues. Rather, psychological theorising has long been concerned with counter-positioning, such as: ego and non-ego, narrative and counter-narrative, voice and non-voice, etc.

[6] Positioning was originally defined by Harré and van Langenhove as "the discursive construction of personal stories that make a person's actions intelligible and relatively determinate as social acts and within which the members of the conversation have specific locations" (1992, p. 395).

(immigrants, minorities, strangers) are commonly perceived as a homogenous category of others even when being insiders to a social, economic and political system. However, the level of 'foreignhood', or 'strangeness', given to the other is contextual. It is dependent upon the type of situation in which the other is observed as well as the hierarchical position of the other (Oommen, 1994).

This line of reasoning can be illustrated by looking at the situation in Italy, while recognizing that these developments are not limited to Italy alone. Since the early 1990s, Italian immigration policies have defined migrants as extracomunitari (extra-communitarians), which denotes their origins outside the European Community, now the European Union. In public discourse, the term also positions them in a permanent status of non-belonging to the Italian nation and it underlines not only an ethno-cultural distance, but also a material one. The extracomunitario is a person who has emigrated because she/he is poor (Schmidt, 2004; Scuzzarello, 2010). Interestingly, while the definition of migrants as extracomunitari is unavoidably homogenizing, the national groups that have been included in this definition by the media and the public have varied depending on a range of socio-political processes that have affected the country. In the 1990s, when Italy was experiencing significant migration flows from Albania, people coming from that part of the world were not positioned mainly as extracomunitari, but rather as Albanesi. This image depicted Albanian migrants as particularly prone to criminality and violence (Mai, 2002). Since the increased migration flows from Eastern Europe during the early 2000s, the public's attention has turned away from Albanians, who are now usually labelled extracomunitari. Romanians have instead become the new target of public attention and have recently been positioned by the media and in the political debates as violent and criminals[7].

The psychological impact of such positioning on migrants may be difficult to grasp, however, unless we move towards a more complex approach to positioning. Raggatt (2007), in criticizing Harré's and Langenhove's definition of positioning for prioritizing the discursive aspects of positioning at the cost of the personal, suggests that the relation between the social and the personal cannot be conceived of as independent processes: "the self embodies the personal and the social simultaneously, just as it also embodies change and permanence" (Raggatt, 2007, p. 359). Positioning, he argues, captures the dynamics (movement) in polyphonic conceptions of the self from both a personal-dynamic perspective and a social-discursive perspective. The classification he suggests is based on three distinctions: (1) indicating medium or mode of expression of positioning (narrative/discursive, performative/expressive and embodied), (2) personal positioning identifying conflict within a person, and (3) social positioning involving social and cultural constructions (conversational/discursive, institutional roles/rituals, political/hierarchical). The advantage of Raggatt's classification, which is explored further in the concluding section of this chapter, lies in its focus on both personal and social constructions of self which implies that self and identity are understood in terms of both change and continuity. In this sense, as Raggatt points out, self is embodied and biological as well as social and cultural and must, as a consequence, be examined in both senses to understand of it.

---

[7] This depiction of Romanians has become increasingly vicious following the sexual assault and murder of an Italian woman in Rome by a Romanian man at the end of October 2007 and a series of other assaults and crimes allegedly conducted by Romanians (*La Repubblica* 31 October, 2007)

The conceptualisation of the self presented thus far, i.e., as constituted by a dynamic multiplicity of interrelated personal and social positions, highlights the processual and relational character of the processes of self and collective identity formations. Our examples of young Muslims in Western Europe can illustrate this further. The fact that Islam, in response to legacies of colonialisation, modernity, globalisation and current discourses on terror, has become increasingly politicized and is depicted by some members of the majority societies as a security threat, has sharpened identity issues among many young Muslims. This entails that they may experience the need to constantly negotiate with the rest of the society what it means to be a Muslim. As young Muslims inhabiting societies where Islam is continuously being discussed and questioned, not least in media, they see themselves as being stereotypically defined in religious terms. Despite the fact that these young European Muslims are often legal citizens of the societies in which they reside, they find themselves under strong pressures to take a stand in the perceived conflict between various notions of European secularism and Islamic religion (Kinnvall & Nesbitt-Larking, 2011).

In an increasingly globalised world, individuals become subject to meetings with other forms of identifications expressed in ethnic, cultural and religious terms. Dialogical self theory, with its emphasis on dialogues, turns the researcher's attention to the dynamics of positioning among voices, and enables us to understand the self as processual, multiple and relational. In fact, the interactions between social and personal positions and the meetings with actual others affect one's sense of the self. The other "questions, challenges and changes existing positions in the self, and is able to introduce new ones" (Hermans, 2001, p. 255, emphasis added). To conceive of the dialogical self as being open to an ambiguous other and in flux toward a future that is largely unknown therefore leaves space for creativity and innovation. At the same time, Hermans and Dimaggio (2007) contend that there are both biological and social limits to this intrinsic openness and fluidity. People are apparently in need of an environment stable enough to feel at home and to experience a feeling of security and safety in a rapidly changing world. This is similar to Valsiner's (2003) discussion of 'enabling constraints' in response to macro-level cultural restrictions. Such 'constraints' consist of a set of semiotic mediators to cope with bounded indeterminacy which allow the person to transcend the here-and-now setting through intra-psychological distancing. Increasing interconnections between cultural groups may pose pressures on the dialogical capacity of the self to integrate an increasing number of voices. As a result, negative feelings of uncertainty caused by growing complexity, ambiguity, deficit knowledge and unpredictability could be released and evoke defensive strategies such as the "monological domination by only one voice (e.g., nationalism, fundamentalism, sexism, or terrorism)" (Hermans & Dimaggio, 2007, p. 50). In the following two sections we address first the issue of closure and uncertainty by linking it to theories of securitisation (Buzan et al., 1998). Second, drawing from Ivana Marková's understanding of dialogue and dialogicality (2003a, 2003b), we explore the opportunities for change in psychological orientations of self and other.

DIALOGICAL SELF AND DESECURITISATION

We agree with Hermans and Dimaggio (2007) as far as the problematic aspects and effects of globalisation are concerned, i.e., feelings of uncertainty and the increased risk for monological closure. However, their attempt to bring together neurobiological and socio-emotional factors to explain monological closure (2007) could benefit from further clarification and from the insights of discursive and narrative approaches to security, thus addressing the structural and psychological mechanisms that lead to monologue. Proceeding from work in international relations (Buzan et al., 1998), we understand 'security' as being about survival (of the state, the community, the culture, and/or the sense of self). It is a discursive move that takes politics beyond the established rules of the game and frames the issue either as a special kind of politics or as above politics. Thus 'securitisation' refers to the politicization of certain phenomena that enables the use of extraordinary means in the name of security. Securitisation studies aims to understand "who securitizes, on what issues (threats), for whom (referent object), why, with what results, and not least, under what conditions" (Buzan et al., 1998, p. 32). It can therefore be interpreted as the process of labelling a particular referent object (e.g., migration or cultural and religious change) as an existential threat, which implies that an individual's or a collective's sense of the self is perceived as threatened (Buzan el al., 1998)[8]. Securitisation is important for conceptualizing the dynamics of positioning in terms of reducing the heterogeneity of positions and silencing other personal and social positions. Indeed, a process of innovation of the individual and collective self that is able to move away from confrontational self-other relations can be promoted only when people are made aware of the dynamics resulting in closure and antagonism and when the discursive and material structures change to become inclusive rather than exclusive. This latter process is referred to as desecuritisation, i.e., the shifting of issues out of emergency mode into an area of accommodation and dialogical understanding that reduce feelings of insecurity.

Hermans and Dimaggio (2007) argue that the uncertainties and instabilities caused by increased globalisation trigger individuals' desire for stability and satisfaction of basic biological needs. When these needs for a stable enough environment are threatened, the authors argue, people tend to respond with anxiety, hate and anger. The explanations they provide for increased anxiety in response to threatened universal biological needs are both biological and emotional. Their conclusion is worth mentioning at length.

"Evolutionary-based motives that grant survival and fitness and the need for safety, protection, and stability lead to establishing a set of positions that create a split between in-group and out-group in the service of confirming the identities of individuals and groups. The neurologically based tendency to return to ordinary and familiar positions [...] have the advantage that people can use an economical set of stereotypical or abbreviated dialogues (Lyra, 1999), but they do not permit the individual to move easily beyond the constraints of traditional or familiar interactions. The socially based emotion rules, on the other hand, help individuals and groups to interact in ways that are shared and appreciated by the community

---

[8] Not everything can become a security issue. Securitisation theory presents a list of three necessary steps - the completion of which guarantees a successful securitisation. These are: (1) identification of existential threats; (2) emergency action; and (3) effects on inter-unit relations by breaking free of rules (Buzan et al. 1998, p. 6).

to which they belong, but they restrict the range of positions and limit the openness of dialogical relationships with people outside the community." (2007, p. 47-48)

We find their conclusion problematic in two ways. First, the biological explanation they provide whereby a specific part of the brain "favors emotionally based monological responses" (2007, p. 44), reduces closures and their effects (e.g., stereotypes, exclusion, devaluation) to biological deficiencies rather than knowledge structures that contain beliefs and expectations about social groups. Second, while we are not questioning the existence of basic human needs (see Winnicot, 1965; Staub, 2003), we argue that Hermans and Dimaggio overlook the interaction between the social and the personal, focusing mainly on the latter. Their attention to emotions as the main expressions of the social and the societal is certainly interesting. However, it is insufficient to explain the social mechanisms that lead to monological closures in some cases, while not in others, and to the perception of certain needs as being more important than others, and therefore more important to protect if threatened. What, in other words, is the role of social norms in changing the significance of those positions in the self that are constructed as "exclusively important" (Hermans & Dimaggio, 2007, p. 43)? And how can "emotion rules" (p. 47), understood as the collective and individual ethic and morality, be changed to become more inclusive and open to other groups and individuals? While the psychological mechanisms underlying a need for stability can be seen as essential to human beings, their focus on evolutionary-based motives and personal positions at the expense of a contextual interrogation of what is needed to feel secure, weaken their general conclusions. As a result we prefer to interpret threatened needs and the search for solutions, not only as an individual process, but also as an outcome of social processes. In this way we emphasise the dialogical relation between the social and the personal, as discussed previously in the chapter. In particular, we maintain that the social process of presenting an issue as a threat to one's sense of the individual and/or collective self, i.e., securitising it, affects the personal positioning of an individual.

Securitisation theory was originally formulated within international relations theory, as noted above (see Buzan et al., 1998). Of importance is how security issues are produced by actors who interpret a problem as an existential threat and therefore claim the right to use extraordinary measures to defend (and defeat) that problem. The perspective entails a shift from regarding security, and the lack thereof, as a fact, to see it as the outcome of a specific speech act, i.e., the process of securitisation (Waever, 1995). As Sheehan (2005) has noted:

"European politicians in the early 1990s allowed migration to come to be seen as an issue that could threaten domestic social and political cohesion, and subsequent political developments such as the Gulf wars and Al-Qaida terrorist attacks made it comparatively easy to manipulate sentiments and securitize the migration issue in a negative manner." (p. 95)

This conceptualisation of security as an outcome of a speech act is not only a political statement. Scholars should understand securitisation as having political as well as ontological and emotional implications in order to understand that the definition of a security issue is not just a fact, but also a discursive construction that taps on people's feelings (Kinnvall, 2004).

Securitising subjectivity may be manifested in forms of totalistic modes of reasoning, black and white thinking, religious or secular fundamentalism, and other manifestations of psychic rigidity, such as intolerance of ambiguity, or a rejection of the artistic or the expressive. Securitising subjectivity thus secures coherence in a world that is otherwise fragmented and threatening. Familiar symbols and tropes, such as those of nation, gender, and religion, are used to anchor the self, often through a retreat to a mythical past. In the process, identity becomes essentialised as meaning is appropriated in the establishment of a privileged interpretation of certain discourses and texts, preventing further explorations of meaning. This process is likely to take place regardless of the multiple and instable character of subjectivity (Giddens, 1991; Bauman, 2001; Kinnvall, 2004, 2006; Kinnvall & Nesbitt-Larking, 2011). This can be illustrated by reference to multicultural Western European societies. As local cultures are challenged and changed as a result of globalisation, some people find themselves adrift: at home neither in the local context nor in the global situation. As vividly expressed by Janusz Bakrawi in an interview shown in the documentary; Mit Danmark ("My Denmark", Final Cut Film Production, DR 1, February 4, 2007):

> "I was born in Denmark, here in Virum. [...]. My mother is Polish and my father Palestinian. As a child and a teenager I never saw myself as being different. I was Danish and my friends were called Mikael and Jakob. Slowly I discovered however, that people saw something different. A stranger, an immigrant – somebody allowed visiting. The only immigrants I had known were my mother and father. I didn't even know that they were immigrants. It is strange to discover that you are suddenly a guest."

During a walk through the city Bakrawi talks about the anger and frustration of not belonging. He talks about how he has tried to fit in; tried to be a "real" Arab, tried to laugh with the Danes when they made jokes about immigrants, but all this just made him angrier. In response he finds himself asking questions about his identity: Who am I? How do I define myself? Where do I belong? Am I an Arab, a Pole or Danish? Who do you think I am?

In response to such questions, young (first or second-generation) migrants may search for alternative answers in mythologized traditions, fundamentalist religions or far-away nationalisms (Brubaker, 2002; Vertovec 2000). These answers are often provided by so-called hegemonic traditionalists (Hansson & Kinnvall, 2004), who tend to construct a range of essentialist readings of past, present, and future in which Islamic authority is made prominent. For instance, in 2006 nearly 30 British Islamic groups, including the Muslim Council of Britain which is one of the largest Muslim organizations in the country, issued a statement on the use of the veil by Muslim women. The statement urged:

> "All members of the Muslim community to show solidarity against criticising the veil or any other Islamic practice as this might prove to be a stepping-stone towards further restrictions. Today the veil, tomorrow it could be the beard, jilbab and thereafter the head-scarf! Such a strategy, unfortunately, has been widely used by many European countries."

It called on the "Muslim community" [sic!] to "remain united regardless of its differences and opinions about the veil" because:

> "The unexpected and ruthless reaction of the media over the past few weeks on this issue gives an indication that there is a political agenda behind this campaign. [...] This becomes

more apparent when observing the already tense climate facing Muslims, which is contributing towards creating hostility in the wider society against the Muslim community[9]."

These quotes construct a particular notion of crisis, by depicting Muslims as ruthlessly and disrespectfully treated by segments of the majority society. Statements like these, even if not shared by the vast majority of Muslims, are likely to resonate with feelings of structural exclusion and psychological vulnerability. Hence, they may trigger the development of what Jovchelovitch (2008) calls 'non-dialogical encounters', i.e., encounters characterized by the lack of mutual recognition and by the attempt to impose one system of meaning and knowledge to the least powerful group. They may thus affect some young Muslims in their search for an embracing identity.

These young Muslims' condition is clearly existential in a dialogical sense, related to their youth, context and the way they are perceived by parts of the majority society – structurally as well as psychologically. In the words of Ivana Marková (2003a), their identities are 'co-authored' by the other, i.e., the society in which they live and the people whom they meet. This implies that the solution to their situation cannot be focused on these young people alone, but must involve the majority society as well, including the norms and values that inform and shape it. Here the advantages of adopting a dialogical approach which incorporates the insights of securitisation theory in understanding monological closures are evident. On the one hand this approach acknowledges the deeply rooted need for safety and stability in life circumstances, strongly emphasised by object relation theorists (e.g., Winnicott, 1965; 1975). On the other hand it provides the analytical tools for understanding the contextual and socially constructed character of those phenomena that may threaten one's sense of safety and stability. Referring to the example above, this approach provides scholars with the theoretical tools for understanding young Muslims' search for a stable and "true" sense of the self. At the same time it emphasizes the importance of investigating how young Muslims are positioned as security threats by parts of the majority society as well as by hegemonic traditionalists who use monological closure to depict the West as a threat to Muslims. When the dialogue between personal and social positions, as well as between imposed and adopted ones is well understood, scholars will be able to suggest ways to introduce changes in psychological orientations that challenge antagonistic relations.

DIALOGICALITY AND CHANGE IN PSYCHOLOGICAL ORIENTATIONS

So far we have argued that a dialogical understanding of the self coupled with an approach that sees threats as socially constructed, thus affecting individuals' personal sense of security, provide interesting insights for understanding the emergence of "monological domination by only one voice" (Hermans & Dimaggio, 2007, p. 50) in increasingly globalised and diverse societies. In this section we want to argue for a second important advantage in adopting a dialogical understanding of the self. A direct consequence deriving from a dialogical approach is that it conceives of the self in non-static terms and is therefore

---

[9] The quotes come from the statement "Important advice to the Muslim community in light of the debate over the veil". Issued on October 15, 2006. Available at http://www.islam21c.com/index.php?option=com_content&task=view&id=18282&Itemid=18 . Accessed on March 14, 2010.

able to account for change (Hermans & Dimaggio, 2007). This does not mean that the self is constantly in flux because individuals tend to search for a sense of continuity of their identities. Rather, it entails a challenge to monological and antagonistic group relations and non-dialogical encounters (Jovchelovitch, 2008) as it provides the opportunity for the development of a transformative multicultural theory.

In Marková's interpretation (e.g., 2003b), dialogue is not only important at the intrapersonal level (between different I positions), but also at the interpersonal one – between the self and the other, the 'Ego' and the 'Alter'. In Marková's work, dialogicality, i.e., the capacity of the human mind to conceive, create and communicate about social realities (2003b), sets the foundations for a conception of ontology which sees the self and the other not only as interrelated but as equally engaged in an interdependent relation (Marková, 2006). This means that the "dialogicality of the Ego-Alter is of ontological nature. In and through communication the Ego-Alter intersubjectively co-constitutes one another: one does not exist without the other" (Marková, 2006, p. 126). A dialogical understanding of self-other relations is important in the context of multiculturalism as it challenges the assumptions that group relations are only antagonistic in nature (self versus other). The other, be it an individual or a collective, is fundamental to the self's identity and vice-versa. The self has to struggle and come to terms with the strangeness of the other not by fusing him or herself with the other but by recognizing the strangeness of the other (Marková, 2003a). Total consensus is impossible to achieve in the dialogue between self and other (Marková, 2003a). Given the impossibility of reaching total consensus, the dialogical principle cannot be reduced to intersubjectivity, reciprocity and mutuality, but must be open to difference and conflict that allow for innovation and creativity. Hence, if we accept that the dialogical relation is an existential relation then, according to Marková, our social psychological questions will be different than those asked in non-dialogical approaches. They should not involve individuals and groups as separate entities. Instead, they should involve varieties of Ego-Alter relations which cannot be anything but communicative (Markova 2003; for an extended discussion see Kinnvall & Lindén, 2010). Thus, when investigating minorities, for example, they should be viewed as mutually interdependent with majorities. The interdependence of Ego-Alter thus constitutes a point of departure in social inquiry.

What are the practical implications of a dialogical understanding of self-other relations in the context of multiculturalism? By what means can we attempt to innovate the self in order to desecuritise subjectivity and transform antagonistic relationships between groups to relationships that acknowledge the dialogicality of the Ego-Alter? Hermans and Dimaggio suggest that the most straightforward way in which the self can be innovated is when new forms of identification and new positions (I as a mother; I as a worker; I as a Muslim; I as a Briton) are introduced "that lead to the reorganization of the repertoire in such a way that the self becomes more adaptive and flexible in a variety of circumstances" (2007, p. 53). The concept of 'transformative dialogue' (Gergen et al., 2001; McNamee & Gergen, 1999) is useful to understand this.

TRANSFORMATIVE DIALOGUE IN A MULTICULTURAL CONTEXT

The aim of transformative dialogue is to develop dialogues with members of allegedly antagonistic groups (e.g., pro-life activists with supporters of abortion rights; members of the majority society with migrants). Some may want to draw parallels to the idea of intercultural dialogue introduced by several multicultural theorists (e.g., Taylor, 1994; Parekh, 2000). While we agree on the importance of dialogue for the development of diverse societies, we read intercultural dialogue to be based on certain antagonisms between two parties where one party disapproves of the other's practices[10]. As a result, intercultural dialogue tends to construct the other as an object (sometimes even an object of contempt) and is therefore likely to lead to alienation. Indeed if intercultural dialogue is not successful, "incomprehension, intransigence, irreconcilable differences" (Parekh, 2000, p. 272), will arise.

In contrast, transformative dialogue emerges when the speaker and the respondent recognize the perspective of the other and, further, when they are able and willing to revise and change their initial standpoints by taking the preceding utterances of the other into account (Gergen et al., 2001; Jovchelovitch, 2008; Scuzzarello, 2010). Gergen et al. (2001) argue that in engaging in a transformative dialogue with others, and by acknowledging our relatedness to them, we are not necessarily aiming at consensus. Rather, we aim at opening up the possibility for the development of new forms of self and collective identification. Given the impossibility of total consensus, as Marková suggests, it is therefore necessary for all concerned – minorities as well as majorities – to avoid a reduction of dialogical principle to intersubjectivity, reciprocity and mutuality and, instead, strive to secure openness to difference and conflict that allows for innovation and creativity (see also Jovchelovitch, 2008).

This is different from Parekh's notion of intercultural dialogue which does not necessarily aim at developing a new sense of community and loyalty. In contrast, a transformative dialogue leads to an understanding of what it means to belong to a community and therefore goes beyond a formal contract between the state and its citizens. This is important for the establishment of a multicultural society devoid of tension and conflict, as a transformative dialogue recognises the emotional bonds embedded in the construction of a citizen. Thus, in the context of multicultural citizenship debates, we would argue that while it is important to guarantee minorities' equal access to rights, a dialogue should be established between the recipient society and minority communities in order to develop psychological and emotional bonds that can provide a deeper meaning to societal membership. In this way, minority communities can be provided with the tools for experiencing a stronger commitment and responsibility to their country of settlement.

How can a transformative dialogue be achieved? This type of dialogue requires that we are attentive to the viewpoints of others and to their needs. This means that in the course of the dialogue ample opportunity is given to self-expression, that each part can make its voice heard (Gergen et al., 2001). Transformative dialogue also requires that we are responsive to the other part in the dialogue. This does not mean that we should try to put ourselves in the situation of the other. As Young (1997) points out this would obscure the social positions of

---

[10] Intercultural dialogue proceeds in three stages (Parekh 2000). The minority defends the practice in question in terms of its cultural authority; its community-sustaining role; and by looking for moral similarities in the majority society's culture.

the parties, thus neglecting the different positions in the distributions of power. Instead we should retain an asymmetrical understanding of reciprocity through a communicative interaction that acknowledges the specificity of positions of those involved and their unique life histories and psychological constitution.

Scuzzarello (2008), for instance, notes that projects aimed at integration (e.g., Britain or Sweden) or assimilation (e.g., France or Denmark) of immigrants into the host society often focus on the need to help these immigrants out of oppressive traditions. Many people engaged in these policies are clearly doing this out of a sense of moral responsibility. However, the wish to help immigrants to integrate into the recipient society is related to conceptions of what is held to be morally right and normal to do. Hence despite good intentions, the normative boundaries of the majority are often reproduced and strengthened in relation to representations of the other as socially less apt. The way immigrants are perceived and dealt with becomes, in other words, a matter of performing within the parameters of cultural and structural conditions. Integration policies are not created in a vacuum but are conceptualized, implicitly or explicitly, through a relationship with those to whom they are directed: the immigrants. Similarly, cultural closing down or the securitisation of subjectivity among many migrants and members of minority populations is performed in relation to such policies as well as in relation to the social world which they have left behind and now wish to recreate.

A transformative dialogue intends to move away from such one-dimensional strategies. Hence, to engage in a transformative dialogue entails that both parties manage to move beyond the rhetoric of group blame and begin to assume the responsibility for each other's identified needs and claims. For instance, if two cultural groups were to engage in a transformative dialogue, they would try to understand what has caused the other group's defensive position rather than blaming one another for destroying cultures and traditions as blame only deepens antagonisms. In line with transformative dialogue, Hermans and Dimaggio (2007) demonstrate that in clinical experimental studies, communication with real others and engagement with other people's narratives supply means for overcoming the fears and uncertainties of contemporary Western societies. Although important as a first step, one should note that the presupposition that greater knowledge of the other is enough to prevent discrimination, conflict or violent acts, is not entirely consistent with empirical research (Todorov, 1982; Kinnvall, 2006). Rather than being a reality, greater knowledge, mutual respect and tolerance often remain moral ideals. Instead the contextual relationship between groups that are perceived as different from each other is frequently characterised by prejudice, xenophobia, and ethnocentrism.

Hence, looking at the reality of many communities in Europe, majority and minority societies tend to live parallel lives. Real others are not always easily accessible. This is characteristic for many major cities in Europe. Birmingham in the UK, for instance, has long been characterized by strong urban segregation. Areas such as Handsworth, Soho and Sparkbrook have a residential concentration of black and minority ethnic communities of more than 66 percent with a strong domination of one or a few ethnic groups in each neighbourhood (Cangiano, 2007). Similar patterns of urban segregation along ethnic lines can be found across Europe. Many of the areas densely populated by migrant minorities are also affected by high levels of social deprivation and low educational levels. Such areas often constitute zones of exclusion, heavily policed and frequently characterized by violence as a way of ruling by provocation. As most members of the majority society never visit these areas, they are indeed alien communities (Kinnvall & Nesbitt-Larking, 2011). Thus, instead of being based on real encounters, people's fears are often dominated by rumours, media images, and meta-narratives dividing worlds into neat essentialised categories. How can these images and narratives be countered through the use of real or imaginary others?

Gergen's work does not provide a clear answer to this. Hermans and Dimaggio (2007; Hermans, 1996), in contrast, describe a number of clinical experiments conducted by them and others that are aimed towards establishing a dialogue with an imagined other. In the context of globalisation, they argue, experiments could be run with participants instructed to believe that they communicate with people from groups of diverse cultural origins. According to Hermans and Dimaggio, such experiments could examine under which conditions participants, positioned as members of a particular cultural group, would learn from interlocutors positioned as members of another cultural group. A particularly relevant question, they maintain, would be whether participants are able or willing to modify their selves, taking the strangeness of the interlocutor into account. Hermans and Dimaggio do not provide explicit examples of actually conducted experiments with members of particular groups but, based on experiments with student populations instructed to take different positions (in their case as laymen or experts) which, they argue, influenced their ways of behaving and conceptions of the other, this could plausibly be a useful methodology.

Yet these studies do not deal specifically with how we can overcome stereotypical conceptions of other individuals or groups in increasingly multicultural societies. Furthermore, Hermans and Dimaggio's approach has significant problems in addressing real structural inequalities. Being able to envision yourself using alternative narratives, real or imagined, is only a temporary solution to structural discrimination. At the end of the day those who experience themselves as disadvantaged will return to their real material reality and structural inclusion or exclusion. As their lives run parallel to that of the majority society, it matters little how much they understand others' life worlds as their life chances are still inhibited compared to those who share the majority narrative (Kinnvall & Lindén, 2010). If a transformative dialogue aims at opening up the possibility for the development of new forms of self and collective identification, then it should appeal to a potential sense of belonging to the physical space in which individuals live. Local communities may be particularly suitable for this scope. They constitute the main sites where immigrants and recipient society meet and confront one another; where the questions of how to come to terms with diversity are concretely felt; and where people's stereotypes and fears for each other are played out (Penninx & Martiniello, 2004). If local communities can be re-imagined to be devoid of segregated spaces, they are plausibly the best places where dialogues with real others can be established. Such communities may provide an important basis on which to construct a new sense of belonging devoid of negative images and stereotypical representations of the other[11] (Marshall, 1950/1992; Amin, 2006).

---

[11] It is important to acknowledge however that not all migrants intend to stay in the recipient country for an extended period of time. This is particularly true of migrant workers whose patterns of migration are significantly different from, for example, asylum seekers and refugees. Indeed, a recent report issued by the West Midlands Regional Observatory (2007) shows that the median duration of stay for migrant workers in the UK was 17 months. This has important, but often unexplored, consequences for the debates on cohesion and belonging.

SEARCHING FOR DESECURITISING SOLUTIONS
TO INSECURITY IN A GLOBAL WORLD

Building on work by Kinnvall and Lindén (2010) and by Kinnvall et al. (2009), we envisage a number of ways in which negative images and narratives of real or imaginary others can be countered. Changing negative images of the other requires that we address the structural and psychological order in which these images are formed. This, in turn, means revisiting the construction of this order at all three levels of analysis as suggested by Raggatt (2007, 2010, 2011): mode of expression, personal positioning and social positioning. At the first level it involves changing the narratives that shape our performance as social and embodied actors. This requires a change in strategies at the leadership level to avoid the promotion of scapegoating and divisive ideologies. Instead, in order to create a shared understanding of future life, leaders must engender a vision of the future and realistic plans that are able to include all groups (Staub & Bar-Tal, 2003). Changing narratives affect personal positioning, as value positions are embodied in countless forms, according to our personal histories, the social context and our collections of personal constructs. Reorienting moral space in the direction of transformative dialogue and inclusion is thus a fundamental task for practitioners involved in changing hostile attitudes and images between majority and minority populations.

This is particularly relevant for the post-migration generation of young Muslims in Europe as many of them have become increasingly dissatisfied with low status, social exclusion, and discrimination. Both in France and the Netherlands, for instance, Muslim youth have been particularly vocal in demanding broader public support for their new-found Muslim demands. In the Netherlands, as in other European countries, many Moroccan and Turkish youth living segregated lives do not feel empowered to affect the Dutch society and thus feel inhibited from developing a Dutch identity. The relatively low economic status of many Moroccan and Turkish youth has further contributed to their search for secure religious identities (Kinnvall & Nesbitt-Larking, 2011)[12]. However, it is important to stress that Moroccan youth has also played an important role in countering the current polarization in societal climate by engaging in activities that promote dialogue. As a result of the need for young Muslims to respond to hostility or prejudice at school or at work, Islamic youth organizations have initiated public discussion meetings (e.g. the foundation "Ben je bang voor mij?" [are you afraid of me?]), in order to raise awareness of Islam and the positions of Muslim youth (ter Val, 2005).

Addressing change in narratives and structural positioning is not enough, however; we also need to take structural change into account. Creating narrative change in moral conceptions of self and others thus requires that structural change is initiated, such as changes in the economic situation of a particular group. As both Ferguson (2009) and Lowe, Muldoon and Schmid (2009) show in the case of Northern Ireland, greater economic opportunities and the greater material well-being of the Catholic minority has contributed to the possibilities of peace. Improving the life of less-privileged groups in society, as well as reducing inequalities, is thus a critical, albeit practically complex, aspect of reducing conflict. However, changes in

---

[12] Young Muslims throughout Europe experience a higher level of unemployment than other groups (Pêdziwiatr, 2007).

structural positioning must occur at all three dimensions outlined by Raggatt: the conversational/discursive form, which involves the micro encounters of daily life, whether at work, in the home or in the street; the positioning in terms of institutional roles involving prevailing stereotypes, such as gender roles, parental roles, age roles, class behaviour etc., and the positioning arising from the effects of power in various social and political hierarchies. This is obviously difficult in practice as such changes involve both structural mechanisms (legal and institutional changes) and psychological reorientations (changes in beliefs, perceptions and values). However, some steps in this direction can be suggested.

Political programs need to be designed in ways that address all these dimensions. Education is crucial in this regard, as it involves fostering an understanding of the roots of structural, psychological and physical violence among both youth and adults (Staub & Bar-Tal, 2003). It is also dialogical as it requires participation of all involved (majorities, minorities, perpetrator, victims, and bystanders) in order to promote positive attitudes toward people in general and towards other groups in society (migrants, strangers, enemies). Organized in such a way, these programs embrace a dialogical understanding of self-other relations, as discussed by Ivana Marková (2003a; 2003b). Both the 'Ego' and the 'Alter' must be aware of the importance of the other part in 'co-authoring' life.

In conclusion, a dialogical approach emphasizes the need to understand that we are not autonomous, independent individuals (as often presumed in liberal accounts), but are rather ontologically related to one another. This affects the ways in which we understand relations with those whom we identify as others. As a result a dialogically constituted critical self must be envisioned. Although always situated and positioned, this critical self is nonetheless capable of distanciating itself from other symbolic orders. This can lead to a heightened degree of reflexivity. This self is neither a fully conscious self understanding a transparent background nor a self run by forces beyond the conscious control of the individual (e.g., being, language or power structures) (Kinnvall & Lindén, 2010). One important consequence of this approach is evident. This perspective calls for the preservation of the other within the interpretation. This can be helpful for individuals but also for institutions in avoiding the danger of ethnocentrism and of being locked in either the epistemic overpowering of the other, or in historicism, individualization and concealment of power structures and practices.

REFERENCES

Akhtar, P. (2005). '(Re)turn to religion' and radical Islam. In T. Abbas (Ed.), *Muslim in Britain. Communities under pressure* (pp. 164-175). London & New York: Zed books.

Amin, A. (2006). The good city. *Urban Studies, 43*, 1009-1023.

Bakhtin, M. (1979/1986). *Speech genres and other late essays*. (V. W. McGee, Trans.) Austin: University of Texas Press.

Bakhtin, M. (1994). *The Bakhtin reader: Selected writings of Bakhtin, Medvedev and Voloshinov*. (P. Morris, Ed.). London: Arnold.

Bauman, Z. (2001). *Community: Seeking safety in an insecure world*. Cambridge: Polity Press.

Boswell, C. (2007). Migration control in Europe after 9/11: explaining the absence of securitization. *Journal of Common Market Studies, 45*, 589-610.

Brubaker, R. (2002). Ethnicity without groups. *Archives Européennes de Sociologie, 43*, 163-189.

Buzan B., Waever O., & de Wilde J. (1998). *Security: A new framework for analysis.* Boulder: Lynne Rienner.

Cangiano, A. (2007). Mapping of race and poverty in Birmingham. Report for the Barrow Cadbury Trust. http://www.bctrust.org.uk/pdf/Mapping-Birmingham-Report.pdf Accessed 11th July 2010.

den Boer, M. (1995). Moving between bogus and bona fide: The policing of inclusion and exclusion in Europe. In R. Miles, and D. Thränhardt (Eds.), *Migration and European integration. The dynamics of inclusion and exclusion* (pp. 92-111). London: Pinter.

Ferguson, N. (2009). Political conflict and moral reasoning in Northern Ireland. In S. Scuzzarello, C. Kinnvall & K. Monroe (Eds.). *On behalf of others: The psychology of care in a global world* (pp. 233-254). Oxford and New York: Oxford University Press.

Glazer, N. (1997). *We're all multiculturalists now!* Harvard: Harvard University Press.

Gergen, K., McNamee, S., & Barrett, F. (2001). *Toward a vocabulary of transformative dialogue.* www.dlka.com Accessed October 27, 2008.

Giddens, A. (1991). *Modernity and self-identity: Self and society in the late modern age.* Cambridge: Polity Press.

Gillespie, A. (2008). Social representations, alternative representations and semantic barriers. *Journal for the Theory of Social Behaviour, 38*, 375-391.

Hansson, S., & Kinnvall, C. (2004). Women as symbols in religious discourses: Feminist perspectives on gender and Indian religions, *Chakra, 1*, 1-26.

Harré, R., & Van Langenhove, L. (1991). Varieties of positioning. *Journal for the Theory of Social Behaviour, 21*, 393-407.

Harré, R., & van Langenhove, L. (1999). The dynamics of social episodes. In R. Harré and L. van Langenhove (Eds.), *Positioning theory* (pp. 1-13). Oxford: Blackwell.

Hermans, H., Kempen, H. & van Loon, R. (1992). The dialogical self. Beyond individualism and rationalism. *American psychologist, 47*, 23-33.

Hermans, H. (1996).Voicing the self: From information processing to dialogical interchange. *Psychological Bulletin, 119*, 31–50.

Hermans, H. (2001). The dialogical self: Toward a theory of personal and cultural positioning. *Culture & Psychology, 7*, 243-281.

Hermans, H., & Dimaggio, G. (2007). Self, identity, and globalisation in times of uncertainty: A dialogical analysis. *Review of General Psychology, 11*, 31-61.

Hermans, H., Kempen, H., & van Loon, R. (1992). The dialogical self. Beyond individualism and rationalism. *American Psychologist, 47*, 23-33.

Home Office. (2002). *Secure Borders, Safe Haven: integration with diversity in modern Britain.* London: The Stationery Office.

Huysmans, J. (1995). Migrants as a security problem: Dangers of 'securitising' societal issues. In R. Miles and D. Thränhardt (Eds.), *Migration and European integration. The dynamics of inclusion and exclusion* (pp. 53-72). London: Pinter.

Huysmans, J. (2000). The European Union and the securitization of migration. *Journal of Common Market Studies, 38*, 751–77.

Joppke, C. (2004). The retreat of multiculturalism in the liberal state: theory and policy. *The British Journal of Sociology, 55*, 237-257.

Joppke, C. (2009). *Veil: Mirror of identity.* Cambridge: Polity Press.

Jovchelovitch, S. (2008). "Reflections on the diversity of knowledge: power and dialogue in representational fields. In T. Sugiman, K.J. Gergen, W. Wagner & Y. Yamada (Eds), *Meaning in action. Construction, narratives and representations* (pp. 23-38). Shinano: Springer.

Kinnvall, C., & Lindén, J. (in press). Dialogical selves between security and insecurity: Migration, multiculturalism and the challenge of the global. *Theory & Psychology*.

Kinnvall, C., & Nesbitt-Larking P. (2010). *The political psychology of globalisation: Muslims in the West*. Oxford and New York: Oxford University Press.

Kinnvall, C., Renwick Monroe K. & Scuzzarello, S. (2009). Care and the transformative potential of ethics. In Scuzzarello, S., C. Kinnvall, C., & K. Renwick Monroe (Eds.), *On behalf of others: The psychology of care in a global world* (pp. 279-291). Oxford and New York: Oxford University Press.

Kinnvall, C. (2004). Globalisation and religious nationalism: self, identity and the search for ontological security. *Political Psychology, 25,* 741-767.

Kinnvall, C. (2006). *Globalisation and religious nationalism in India: The search for ontological security*. London: Routledge.

Lowe, R., Muldoon, O., & Schmid K. (2009). Expected and unexpected identity combinations in Northern Ireland: Consequences for identifications, threat and attitudes. In S. Scuzzarello, C. Kinnvall & K. Monroe (Eds.), *On behalf of others: The psychology of care in a global world* (pp. 255-276). Oxford and New York: Oxford University Press.

Lyra, M. C. D. P. (1999). An excursion into the dynamics of dialogue: Elaborations upon the dialogical self. *Culture & Psychology, 5,* 477–489.

Mahmood, S. (2005). *Politics of piety*. Princeton, NJ: Princeton University Press.

Mai, N. (2002). Myths and moral panics: Italian identity and the media representation of Albanian immigration. In R. Grillo & J. Pratt (Eds.), *The politics of recognizing difference. Multiculturalism Italian-style* (pp. 77-95). Aldershot: Ashgate.

Marshall, T. H. (1950/1992). *Citizenship and social class*. London: Pluto Books.

Marková, I. (2003a). Constitution of the self: Intersubjectivity and dialogicality. *Culture & Psychology, 9,* 249-259.

Marková, I. (2003b). *Dialogicality and social representations: The dynamics of mind*. New York: Cambridge University Press.

Marková, I. (2006). On the 'inner-alter' in dialogue. *International Journal of Dialogical Science 1,* 125-147.

McNamee, S., & Gergen K. (1999). *Relational responsibility: Resources for sustainable dialogue*. Thousand Oaks: Sage.

Modood, T. (2005). *Multicultural politics: Racism, ethnicity, and Muslims in Britain*. Edinburgh: Edinburgh University Press.

Modood, T. (2007). *Multiculturalism: A civic idea*. Cambridge: Polity Press.

Nesbitt-Larking, P. (2009). Terrible beauty: globalisation, consciousness, and ethics. In Scuzzarello, S, C. Kinnvall & K. Monroe (Eds.), *On behalf of others: The psychology of care in a global world* (pp. 15-34). Oxford and New York: Oxford University Press.

Oommen, T.K. (1994). The changing trajectory of constructing the other: West Europe and South Asia. *Sociological Bulletin, 43.*

Parekh, B. (2000). *Rethinking multiculturalism. Cultural diversity and political theory*. Houndmills: Palgrave Macmillian.

Pedziwiatr, K. (2007). Public Mobilisation of Islam in Europe: Possible Outcomes of the Activism Within Student Islamic Societies. In C. Timmerman, D. Hutsebaut, S. Mels, W. Nonneman, & W. Van Herck (Eds.), *Faith-based radicalism - Christianity, Islam and Judaism between constructive activism and destructive fanaticism* (pp. 293-306). Brussels: P.I.E. Peter Lang.

Penninx, R., & Martiniello, M. (2004). Integration policies and policies: state of the art and lessons. In R. Penninx, K. Kraal, M. Martiniello & S. Vertovec (Eds.), *Citizenship in European cities. Immigrants, local politics and integration policies* (pp. 139-164). Aldershot: Ashgate.

Raggatt, P. T. F. (2007). Forms of positioning in the dialogical self. A system of classification and the strange case of dame Edna Everage. *Theory & Psychology, 17*, 355-382.

Raggatt, P. T. F. (2011). Gender, embodiment, and positioning in the dialogical self: do males and females see eye to eye? In M. Märtsin, B. Wagoner, L. Whittaker, E. L. Aveling & I. Kadianaki (Eds.), *Dialogicality in focus: Challenges to theory, method and application* (pp. 300-320). New York: Nova Science Publishers.

Roy, O. (2007). *Secularism confronts Islam*. New York: Colombia University Press.

Schmidt, D. (2004). Introduzione: esiste un modello italiano verso la differenza? In D. Schmidt, & A. Marazzi (Eds.), *Tre paesi, un progetto. Percorsi formativi con donne migranti* (pp. 4-55). Padova, Italy: Unipress.

Scott, W. (2007). *The politics of the veil*. Princeton: Princeton University Press.

Scuzzarello, S. (2010). *Caring multiculturalism and local immigrant policies. Narrating integration in Birmingham, Bologna and Malmö*. Lund: Lund University Press.

Scuzzarello, S. (2008). National security versus moral responsibility: An analysis of integration programs in Malmö, Sweden. Social Politics. *International Studies in Gender, State & Society, 15*, 5-31.

Sheehan M. (2005). *International security: An analytical survey*. Boulder: Lynne Rienner.

Staub, E. (2003). Notes on cultures of violence, cultures of caring and peace, and the fulfilment of basic human needs. *Political Psychology, 24*, 1-21.

Staub, E., & Bar-Tal, D. (2003). Genocide, mass killing and intractable conflict: Roots, evolution, prevention, and reconciliation. In D. Sears, L. Huddy & R. Jervis (Eds.), *Oxford handbook of political psychology* (pp. 710-753). Oxford: Oxford University Press.

Taylor, C. (1994). *Multiculturalism and "the politics of recognition"*. Princeton: Princeton University Press.

Ter Val, J. (2005) *Active civic participation of immigrants in the Netherlands*. Country report prepared for the European research project POLITIS, Oldenburg 2005. www.uni-oldenburg.de/politis-europe. Accessed January 18, 2009.

Todorov, T. (1982). *The Conquest of America*. New York: Harper.

Valsiner, J. (2003). Beyond social representations: A theory of enablement. *Papers on Social Representations, 12*, 7-16.

Valsiner, J. (2005). Scaffolding within the structure of Dialogical Self: Hierarchical dynamics of semiotic mediation. *New Ideas in Psychology, 23*, 197–206.

Vertovec, S. (2000). *The Hindu diaspora: Comparative patterns*. London and New York: Routledge.

Waever, O., Buzan, B., Kelstrup, M., & Lemaitre P. (1993). Introduction. In O. B. Waever, M. Buzan, Kelstrup & P. Lemaitre (Eds.), *Identity, migration and the new security agenda in Europe* (pp. 1-18). London: Pinter.

West Midlands Regional Observatory. (2007). *The economic impact of migrant workers in the West Midlands.* http://www.wmro.org. Accessed February 25, 2009.

Winnicott, D. W. (1965). *The maturational process and the facilitating environment.* New York: International Universities Press.

Winnicott, D.W. (1975). *Through paediatrics to psycho-analysis.* New York: Basic Books.

Young, I.M. (1997). *Intersecting voices. Dilemmas of gender, political philosophy and policy.* Princeton: Princeton University Press.

In: Dialogicality in Focus   ISBN: 978-1-61122-817-5
Editors: M. Märtsin, B. Wagoner, E.-L. Aveling et al.   © 2011 Nova Science Publishers, Inc.

COMMENTARY TO PART III: COORDINATING POSITIONS TO ARRIVE AT CHANGE: CREATIVE TENSIONS WITHIN THE DIALOGICAL SELF FRAMEWORK

Jaan Valsiner

The chapters in this section do not form a coherent whole – which is precisely what is needed for a dialogically open discourse about the dialogical self. They thus reflect the status of the dialogical self research field – a sufficiently open field with variety of ideas and no theoretical monologisation anywhere in sight. This is crucial for keeping the research direction open for innovation – especially as interdisciplinary cooperation is the name of the game. The critical orientations visible among the four contributions, is a fitting testimony to the rapid development of ideas. While Kinnvall and Scuzzarello (2011) criticise Hermans' original version of the Dialogical Self Theory (DST) for overlooking the implications of the social power that creates the ambience for the self (mostly relying upon as recent a text as Hermans & Dimaggio, 2007), Hermans himself has developed his theoretical ideas in a new direction (Gieser & Hermans, 2011; Hermans & Hermans-Konopka, 2010). Gieser and Hermans take their advancement of the DST, in this volume, in a direction opposite to what Kinnvall and Scuzzarello would want to see developed. Yet it is not their role to fill in all the existing gaps in DST – it is precisely the role of the critiques to transcend the existing theoretical system and transform it into a more thorough version. In my view this transformation has not (yet) happened – the social power context of DST and its implications for the dynamic functioning of the dialogical self remains without sufficient theoretical elaboration. The problem is sighted – but its solution is not created.

FROM DECONSTRUCTION TO RECONSTRUCTION

The latter problem – critique without constructive innovation – is of course a wider issue in the social sciences at large. The deconstructionist fashion – building on the easy opportunity to look smart in the post-modern era by fighting all kinds of dualism, or positivism, or any other '–ism' (behaviourism, cognitivism, etc.) – has left a profound mark on the thinking of new generations of social scientists who often even label their perspectives 'critical X' ('critical psychology' is but one example). The discourses around DST are about to – but have not yet – overcome the confines of the deconstructionist ethos and move into the reconstruction path. This is partly due to the researcher's closeness to the phenomena (self dialogues, inside the mind or between them), and to the connection with one particular area where these phenomena are especially accentuated. This area is the study of psychotherapy processes – as discussed by two of the four contributions in this section (Gieser & Hermans, 2011; Gonçalves et al., 2011). Psychotherapy is a context of human activity that is particularly suited for DST as it entails the slowed-down (or temporarily arrested) flow of the operation of the dialogical self. The client – as well as the therapist – spend many sessions having intense dialogues in order to arrive at a single – and often reversible – innovative moment in the course of their thinking (and feeling – see Gonçalves et al., 2011). Hence the phenomena of new, emerging forms within the dialogical self are more discernible and accessible than in the flow of ordinary dialogues. Psychotherapy is a kind of a microscope for the purposes of DST. The 'father of microbiology' Antoni van Leeuwenhoek and the 'father of DST' Hubert Hermans thus have something in common – besides being Dutch – that is of relevance for biology and psychology – the means for how to look and the directions in which to look.

RECONSTRUCTION NEEDS THEORETICAL CREATIVITY: TENSIONS AND TRANSITIONS

However, sciences do not develop by data. They develop by ideas. Psychology at large has accumulated empirical evidence on almost every possible common-sense problem of the mind. Yet it fails to produce coherent knowledge that is elegant in its abstract form and applicable in the myriads of social contexts.

The four chapters in this section of the book point to three themes – the need to view the dialogical self within its social power context *(structured environment)*, recognition of the affective dynamics of the I-positions *(dynamic change)*, and the *coordination* of the networks of I-positions and their structured contexts. While widening the scope of the study of the self by turning the concept from unitary self to multiple I-positions, the dialogical self perspective has reached a state in which these issues cannot be ignored. The contributions to this section offer fresh recipes for theoretical innovation: linking empathy with the DST as Gieser and Hermans (2011) do; looking at the moments of breakthrough in the self-negotiation processes, using the notion of re-conceptualisation as Gonçalves and his colleagues (2011) propose in their chapter; and pointing to the real social power structures that guide the dialogical selves of immigrants as Kinnvall and Scuzzarello (2011) show in their chapter. Raggatt's (2011) focus on the dialogical self creating different arenas of embodiment for men and women allows the reader to see the immediacy of the starting point of dialogical encounters. We can outline a number of tensions the reader might feel while encountering discourses in the social sciences.

Tension in the Methods<>Theory Relations

It is usual in the social sciences that there are discrepancies between the theories and methods used in empirical work. Or – theories may be fitted to the methods, rather than the other way around. On the side of empirical research techniques in DST we do not see the kind of heterogeneity that is evident in the theoretical ideas in the four chapters in this section. The use of statistical inference based on accumulating coded units still continues to be a part of the researchers' empirical strategies. To borrow Kinnvall and Scuzzarello's (2011) notion of *securitising* from the domain of social regulation of immigrants' conduct, we could think of the demands of the social sciences as an institution for limiting the creativity of methods construction in the past decades (Toomela & Valsiner, 2010). This is a form of securitisation – ensuring that whatever the social scientists may talk about, their actual empirical data pass the phenomena under consideration by. The result has been a conceptual confusion (Wittgenstein, 1958, p. 232).

A newly conceptually liberated field, such as the dialogical self perspective, needs a corresponding liberating focus in methods. Here we see different directions – Gieser and Hermans (2011) move in the direction of dynamic analysis of processes in their look at empathy, and Gonçalves and his colleagues (2011) demonstrate the unique events of Innovat*ing* Moments in their meticulous analysis of psychotherapy processes. At the same time, Raggatt (2011) investigates the dialogical self by way of a life narrative-based *assessment* method, designed to 'map' I-positions within the individual (Personality Web Protocol). Theoretically Raggatt emphasises that I-positions – which are frequently described by individuals in terms of paired opposites – can be explained by both intra-personal (reflexive) and inter-personal (social) positioning. The relatedness of these positions is implicated – but not studied. The results that are reported do not show how the different I-positions are being coordinated – but merely end in a claim about a basic gender difference in what constitutes the "embodiment arena" for males (torso) and females (face). This evidence is undoubtedly useful – but not directly relevant for the development of DST.

The very notion of *assessment* may guide researchers towards overlooking the coordinative dynamics of the relations between I-positions – thus securitizing the empirical domain of dialogical self research for the purposes of social desirability of the normal science of psychology. Such *monological closure of methodology* is a social constraint on the path of an innovative set of ideas becoming productive in arriving at new knowledge. To live up to the focus on coordination – as a process – the methods of the study of dialogical self need to go beyond repertoires of static representations of I-positions and – after locating such positions in space and time – make their mutual interweaving explicit.

Tension between Monologising Institutions and Dialogical Selves

Kinnvall and Scuzzarello (2011) criticise the DST for overlooking the moves by social institutions to guide human selves towards 'monological closures' – attempts made by a single authority to monopolise meaning to the exclusion of all competing voices. It is true that from its outset the different versions of the DST have prioritised the self in amidst other selves. After all, the revolution in understanding the self that Hermans introduced – seeing the double system of unity of A and its opposite (counter-A) in the same whole – has been the main focus of enquiry. While the social context of the self has not been denied – it has also not been the target of specific attention. The important step in DST is to examine personal (dialogical) and social (monologizing) constructions of the self – so the tension in the self/other relation should lead the field to think of self and identity in terms of *both* change and continuity. This amounts to assuming the developmental perspective and moving the DST out of its original birthplace (personality theory) to the wide and tumultuous waters of developmental science (Cairns, Elder & Costello, 1996). Again the need to study the dynamics of positioning becomes evident:

> "...a dialogically constituted critical self must be envisioned. Although always situated and positioned, this critical self is nonetheless capable of distanciating itself from other symbolic orders. This can lead to a heightened degree of reflexivity. This self is neither a fully conscious self understanding a transparent background nor a self run by forces beyond the conscious control of the individual (e.g., being, language or power structures)." (Kinnvall & Scuzzarello, 2011, p. 236)

This theoretical direction needs to lead to a developmental research programme where the coordination of uniform demands and multiform versions of dialogical self is being studied. The unifying loyalty demands ("you must be X") are targets of dialogical resistance (I-position of X <> I-position of non-X) that is further coordinated with the role of others ("my mother insists I should be X... I am X but I am happier as non-X"). It is here that the notion of empathy enters (Gieser & Hermans, 2011). Yet merely importing the notion of empathy – feeling into the other – to the dialogical self is no solution. The empathic process needs to be located within the transforming kaleidoscope of I-positions – which are guided by monologising social imperatives. The impact of the 'ten commandments' for one's dialogical relating with oneself is not to be overlooked in the European Reformation/Counter-Reformation era, just as the Kali/Durga myth may be the social guide for understanding gender relations in the Indian context.

Tension between Myself-oriented-to-the-other and Myself-oriented-towards-Myself

All external dialogues are *de facto* trialogues – aside from the interlocutor *out there,* there exists a basic duality within the self right in the very act of speaking. As Gieser and Hermans emphasise,

> "Whenever we have a conversation, we hear our own voice and the voice of the other. Moreover, in a friendly conversation we also tend to adjust our use of words or phrases, pronunciation and intonation to our fellow conversant. This enables us to feel into the experience of another person's voice because of its similarity to our own voice. What further contributes to this empathy is that, in the course of a conversation, we experience a continual switching of attentional focus, between our voice either in the background or in focus and the other's voice either in the background (e.g., when both of us speak simultaneously) or in focus. In either case, our voices become linked in one experiential *Gestalt* and hence we may feel into another person's narratives *as if they were our own*." (Gieser & Hermans, 2011, p. 200, original emphasis)

The point of *feeling as-if-the other* is crucial here – without such feeling-in no relating between the interacting I-positions – be those interacting persons or interacting I-positions within the dialogical self – would be possible.

The innovative moment here is the notion of *experiential Gestalt* – a term that needs further elaboration. *Gestalt* is of course a term well known for psychologists from their usually monologised education about the history of their discipline. It is a whole – but here the problems begin. Which kind of whole? A static one? A dynamic field? How do "voices become linked" in a whole? By simple merging, or by mutual resonating? These are questions that the new direction charted out by Gieser and Hermans needs to address.

Tension between *Distancing* and *Feeling-in*: The Basis for Re-Conceptualisation

Of all the four in this section, the chapter by the Minho Group (Gonçalves et al., 2011) addresses these issues of development most directly. The key is the notion of the transition from *mutual in-feeding* processes to re-conceptualisation (and further to irreversible change). As they remark,

"...re-conceptualisation implies the contrast between past and present, and aggregates the old self with the transformed self, it achieves a new sense of unity in the dialogical self, surpassing the former dualities and ambivalence usually inherent to a mutual in-feeding process between opposing voices." (Goncalves et al., 2011, p. 189)

The focus on re-conceptualisation brings the process orientation of the DST to the need to conceptualise dialectical synthesis. Psychology has had an ambivalent history of relations with the notion of dialectics – striving towards it, yet dismissing it near the point of new solutions to old problems. It is here where the focus on feeling-in (*Einfühlung*) fits as a process mechanism. As Gieser and Hermans point out, the process of psychotherapy is

"...a dynamic process of distancing and feeling into, of emotional reflection and emotional immersion. But we would also like to take it a step further and argue that empathy, broadly conceived, is more than a complex psychological phenomenon; it is the ontological basis of dialogue and dialogical relationships as such. Too often we tend to narrow down the notion of dialogue to an interplay of words." (Gieser & Hermans, 2011, p. 203)

Thus, distancing *together with* simultaneous feeling-in is the mechanism that leads to re-conceptualisation and change. In order to arrive at change the person needs to empathise with oneself – at first moving part of the self to a distance from where the given I-position can feel in with the other one. As described by Gonçalves et al. (2011),

"...preliminary findings indicate that mutual in-feeding tend to persist during therapy when the therapist respond to it by understanding predominantly the innovative voice (by amplifying it), instead of understanding the problematic voice (trying to explore what it is in the client's experience that prevents change)." (p. 188)

Amplification of the innovative voice – 'pushing' the psychological system beyond its limits (and preventing the return to the previous equilibrium) – seems to be the pathway to qualitative breakthrough. If we consider the therapist to be one of the social monologisation agents – after all, the role of the therapist is that of a social power – we can consider amplification of monologisation by the therapist as a distancing device (for example, client: "I feel X and non-X"→ therapist: "but it seems X is *really* what you feel"→ client: "oh yes, I *really* feel X… thank you… and I suddenly feel confused as I now feel Y and non-Y"). *By suggesting a monologised moment the therapist attempts – basically forces – the client to overcome the previous dialogical state.* This move on the therapist's behalf is possible through emulating – feeling into, but not becoming identical with – the client's current dialogical state. The suggested monologised moment is distanced from the previous (hyper)dialogical state of the client – and thanks to that distance makes it possible to develop into a new dialogical state. In general – the dialogical self works through constant efforts towards monologisation that – when it succeeds – may lead to a qualitatively new state of the dialogical self. If this is so – it is not Mikhail Bakhtin's but Georg Friedrich Wilhelm Hegel's forgotten and retrospectively distorted theoretical legacy that the DST might need. Time will tell.

CONCLUSION: THE IMPORTANCE OF BEING OPEN

Theoretical innovations go through a set of phases where at first they open the thinking of researchers to new possibilities of enquiry, then constitute the arena for such enquiry in practice, and – finally – reach a plateau where no new exciting issues seem possible. DST opened the field of self/personality research in the 1990s to the possibility of enquiring the processes behind categorical statements about the self. The contributions to this book as a whole – and the four contributions that have been the focus of this commentary – show that the DST discourses are in the intermediate state of active but somewhat parallel lines of enquiry. Such multivoicedness – if maintained both in theoretical and empirical efforts – should save the field from reaching the final state of monologised 'expertise' status. Coordination – rather than assimilation – of perspectives remains the key to such intellectual longevity.

ACKNOWLEDGMENT

This commentary benefited from the conditions that the David Parkin Visiting Professorship at University of Bath, and discussions with members of the CSAT research centre, made possible in 2009-2010.

REFERENCES

Cairns, R. B., Elder, G., & Costello, E. J. (Eds.) (1996). *Developmental science*. New York: Cambridge University Press.

Hermans, H. J. M., & Dimaggio, G. (2007). Self, identity, and globalisation in times of uncertainty: A dialogical analysis. *Review of General Psychology, 11,* 31-61.

Hermans, H. J. M., & Hermans-Konopka, A. (2010). *Dialogical self theory: Positioning and counter-positioning in a globalizing society*. Cambridge, UK: Cambridge University Press

Gieser, T., & Hermans, H. J. M. (2011). Empathy and emotion from the perspective of Dialogical Self Theory. In M. Märtsin, B. Wagoner, E. L. Aveling, I. Kadianaki, & L. Whittaker (Eds.). *Dialogicality in focus. Challenges to theory, method and application,* (pp. 193-204). New York: Nova Science Publishers.

Gonçalves, M., Cunha, C, Ribeiro, A. P., Mendes, I., Santos, A., Matos, M., & Salgado, J. (2011). Innovative moments in psychotherapy: Dialogical processes in developing narratives. In M. Märtsin, B. Wagoner, E. L. Aveling, I. Kadianaki, & L. Whittaker (Eds.). *Dialogicality in focus. Challenges to theory, method and application,* (pp. 173-192). New York: Nova Science Publishers.

Kinnvall, C., & Scuzzarello, S (2011). *Dialogicality and the (de)securitisation of self:* Globalisation, migration and multicultural politics. In M. Märtsin, B. Wagoner, E. L. Aveling, I. Kadianaki, & L. Whittaker (Eds.). *Dialogicality in focus. Challenges to theory, method and application,* (pp. 221-240). New York: Nova Science Publishers.

Raggatt, P. (2011). Gender, embodiment, and positioning in the dialogical self: Do men and women see eye to eye? In M. Märtsin, B. Wagoner, E. L. Aveling, I. Kadianaki, & L. Whittaker (Eds.). *Dialogicality in focus. Challenges to theory, method and application,* (pp. 205-220). New York: Nova Science Publishers.

Toomela, A., & Valsiner, J. (Eds.) (2010). *Methodological thinking in psychology*. Charlotte, NC: Information Age Publishers.

Wittgenstein, L. (1958). *Philosophical investigations*. Oxford: Blackwell.

IN PLACE OF A CONCLUSION

IN SEARCH OF AN ALTERNATIVE

This book has placed dialogicality at the centre of understanding human mind and interaction. In their sometimes complimentary, sometimes divergent ways all the chapters in this volume have been concerned with the maintenance of a dialogical conceptualisation in unpacking the complexities of human sense-making, communication and inter-group relations. The contributions by Haye and Larrain, by Raggatt, and by Lonchuk and Rosa have all engaged with the question, how to best conceptualise and analyse our dialogical engagement with the world through which our knowledge – including the knowledge about ourselves – becomes constructed. Likewise, Joerchel's contribution, in forcing us to start our investigations by looking at the resonance of two individuals (instead of one), deals with the question of how intersubjectivity and the possibility for communication emerges. Moving from the abstract to the concrete, the chapters by the Minho group and by Gieser and Hermans consider what this dialogical engagement means for the organisation and development of the individual self. Moving beyond the individual level, Kinnvall and Scuzzarello tackle the issue of dialogicality in the society, trying to explore how and why people sometimes do and sometimes do not want to dialogue with each other.

Importantly though, this book has also placed dialogicality at the centre of understanding the phenomenon of 'research'. Many of the authors in this book have touched upon the issue of maintaining and encouraging dialogue in the conduct and presentation of research, and reflected upon the pressures and constraints in the research world that close down possible dialogues and avenues for discussion. The authors have been concerned with how commonly employed methods may lose the phenomenon in movement and thus eclipse its dialogicality (*inter alia* Valsiner, Shotter, Akkerman & Niessen, Murakami). Others have talked about ways of resisting reification and monologisation in writing (e.g., Billig), about encouraging multivocality in analysis, in the presentation of research and in academic collaboration (e.g., Wagoner et al.), and raised concerns about the lack of dialogue between researchers and research participants (e.g., Hviid & Beckstead). In response, this book attempts to promote dialogue between authors through adopting the format of target articles and commentaries, thus focusing not on the monologues of individual authors, but on dialogues between several authors. In this way, it endeavours to foreground the responsive nature of acts of discourse, as highlighted by Haye and Larrain: the chapters represent active responses both to pre-existing and anticipated acts of discourse by others. We can thus only hope that the book will be read as an invitation to continue the dialogue presented in these pages.

It is obvious that some of these concerns about the conduct and presentation of research are related to the need to be 'true' to the underlying assumptions of the dialogical perspective. That is, to take ideas about orientation to the other, contextualism, interactionalism and the emphasis on semiotic mediation (Linell, 2009) seriously when doing research. They thus bring to mind the old dilemma of the turtle and Achilles, with Achilles as practice never really catching up with the theory-turtle. Yet the convergence of these diverse voices in raising the need to leave behind conventional ways of conceptualising, conducting and presenting academic research and welcoming a new, dialogical alternative seems to work also as an identity project for dialogists. It functions as an effort to create a 'we' in relation to 'they' – the monologists – where 'we' is distinctly different, but also (and importantly) better than 'they'. Yet is it better?

DIALOGUE AND TRANSFORMATION

In their contribution, Gieser and Hermans suggest that difference and distance are essential to dialogue. Likewise, Marková (2011) notes in her commentary: "The fundamental feature of dialogue is a clash of ideas, their tension and transformation through their confrontation" (p. 67). However, as authors in this volume emphasise, dialogue – or dialogical engagement with the other – does not necessarily lead to transformation, change or innovation of the self or 'ideas'. Nor does it necessarily lead to a 'resolution of discord', as Marková asserts. Assuming this would be to impose a normative interpretation on the meaning of dialogue or dialogical, as Linell (2009) has highlighted (see also Akkerman and Niessen in this book). It is in this sense then, as Gillespie points out in his foreword, that a dialogical perspective allows us to understand human interaction as intersubjective, symbolic, cultural, but importantly also conflictual *and* potentially transformative.

While the clash of divergent perspectives is fundamental, dialogue or encounters with the other that lead to some kind of transformation – a 'transformative' dialogue[1] – also require the effort to overcome distance and difference. We may think of Gieser and Hermans' discussion of 'feeling into' the other, or Bakhtin's notion of 'active empathising' (1986/1993; as quoted by Marková, 2003, p. 103) for describing this kind of dialogical engagement. It is an ongoing struggle of relating to the other which is the starting point for transformation, rather than the retention of distance or 'pure emphasising' (ibid.) that eliminates or submerges the strangeness of the other. It leads to the creation of a new perspective, which moves beyond the ones out of which it has emerged.

Yet how can we achieve such transformation in research? How can different voices, meanings or ideas come together in a new configuration that goes beyond their differences? How can dialogism become a 'better' science than monologism that makes sense and, dare we say, makes a difference, to others? This is an age old question that concerns us not only as a community of researchers, but as members of a heterogeneous society.

---

[1] In our discussion about 'transformative dialogue' we draw on Freire's (2003/1973) notion of 'critical dialogue' and Jovchelovitch's (2007) discussion about 'dialogical encounters'. See also Aveling (2010) for further discussion.

By asking this question we refer, on the one hand, to the situation where both parties consider their own points of views too precious to let go of. This is the A *versus* B situation that Kinnvall and Scuzzarello tackle in their discussion about 'securitization' in the face of existential threat; a situation where tensions between perspectives are too substantial for dialogue to occur. In the research context, this might refer to the impossibility of having a transformative dialogue between dialogists and monologists, to use Billig's language. Yet we also, on the other hand, refer to the situation that Gonçalves and his colleagues refer to as mutual in-feeding: a process of continuing dialogue between mutually re-affirming ideas A_1, A_2, A_3 etc., which does not lead to any productive outcome or significant change. This latter situation seems to be characterised by abundance of dialogue, yet with equally fruitless results. These then are the friendly dialogues between like-minded dialogists, where the 'problem is sighted, but its solution is not created', as Valsiner explains in his commentary (p. 241). The question thus remains – how do we surpass the unproductive mutual in-feeding within the dialogical perspective?

In our attempt to answer this question we return to Billig's call in the opening chapter of this book. Billig reminds us that arguing, including academic debate, is contextual and relational. That is, in order to understand an argument and maintain its relevance, we need to know what it is argued against and need to continuously renew that relationship to the outside context. In Billig's version then, dialogism needs to encourage transformative dialogue not only amongst the like-minded dialogical researchers, but also continuously re-negotiate its relation to the other 'external' perspectives in contemporary social sciences, such as mainstream cognitive psychology.

Paying attention to the ground to better define and develop the figure – in this case dialogism – is obviously in accordance with the principles and assumptions of dialogical science. Having an idea how the ground is moving and evolving, in order to continuously re-define and refine the figure is important for maintaining the relevance of the dialogue. However, leaving the dialogical aspirations aside, it is not immediately clear how a return to mutual in-feeding – that neither surpasses essential differences nor fuels innovation – is to be avoided. Because at the end of the day it is not about dialogical dreams, but about the 'real stuff' that matters in research, such as publications, grant funding, jobs, acknowledgment, recognition etc., which preferably should be given to 'us' and not to 'them'.

We agree with Billig that in order to break out of such mutual in-feeding within research a little help from others, who can function as catalysts of change, is needed. However, we would suggest that rival theoretical perspectives are not the only significant others who need to be (implicitly or explicitly) invited to take part in the dialogue. We would suggest that the invitation to participate should be extended also to those who are researched – that is, to the members of communities, organisations and groups of people that we do research with and, some would argue, do it for.

CHANGING PRACTICES

Who is social research meant for? Who should benefit from it? These questions about the purpose of social research are difficult and complex, with no easy and obvious answers. The impact of social research cannot be efficiently measured through the number of published articles, conference presentations and other dissemination activities. As Gillespie points out in his foreward, an alternative measure of the 'health' of a field might be to ask the pragmatist question. Yet, as the current wealth of academic and political interest in 'closing the gap' between research and practice would indicate, translating research into policies and practices which make immediate and direct differences to people's lives is difficult to achieve. The pragmatist's 'So what?' question is thus an important, albeit difficult one to answer and engage with.

In their chapter, Hviid and Beckstead (2011) call for "a solution based on the establishment of communities of researchers and research-participants, where the objectives and the direction of the research as well as the intervention in practice outside the empirical 'zone of research' is constituted and created as a shared agenda with importance to both parties" (p. 160). On a more abstract level, Shotter (2011) too calls for research that *works from within*, with the aim "of resolving specific confusions, disquiets, bewilderments, perplexities, etc., within [practices]" (p. 98). We find these calls to be important ones. If taken seriously and turned into research practice they have the potential to make dialogical research conceptually solid, academically competitive and socially relevant.

Together with these and other authors (see for example Hedegaard & Chaiklin, 2005) we envisage a research practice where researchers move away from their tradition of thinking through their theoretical position, deciding about the research questions and choosing the methodologies *before* engaging with the research participants. Instead we suggest proposing researcher projects, which are not only open-ended, but where also the starting point is approximate and up for negotiation. Again building on Shotter's ideas, we imagine research where researchers let go of their ordinary practice of knowing their way about, and instead are willing to take on a journey and find their way together with others, in an unfolding activity in which they are equally immersed as participants. For as Shotter (2011) argues in this book, only by allowing oneself to resonate with the others in the unfolding activity, only by listening to one's own ambiguities, doubts and hesitations can one become aware of the 'determining surroundings' (p. 78) and thus be able to exhibit 'the responsive understandings [the others] expect' (p. 98).

Yet there is more at stake than just our ability to understand things in the making, which can only happen if we work from within. Drawing on Levinas's ideas, Marková in her commentary reminds us that our engagement with the world is above all engagement with others. Thus our being is fundamentally ethical, for by being part of the social world we have a responsibility to the other. She writes: "The self has no right to question what the other requires from him: his obligations and generosity to others is unlimited" (Marková, 2011, p. 68). Similarly, Ellis and Stam (2010), drawing this time on Ricoeur, argue: "an I is *accountable* for its actions in front of an other, as the other is *counting on* the I to perform them" (p. 429, original emphasis). The responsibility to the other is thus central to the dialogical conceptualisation of human interaction, and our responsibility as researchers in "aiming at the 'good life', with and for others, in just institutions" (Ricoeur, 1990/1992, p. 172; as quoted by Ellis & Stam, 2010, p. 429) is central to our practices.

It is through such a conceptualisation that the approach we envision is also essentially transformative. It is about difference between the viewpoints of researchers and participants; yet equally it is about emergence, about coming together in another way, for another reason. As Jovchelovitch (2007) has argued in the context of relations between intervention practitioners and the beneficiaries of intervention, what is required is an approach characterised by the effort to take into account the perspective of the other and recognise it as legitimate. But beyond an ethical imperative, what reason could motivate the struggle to recognise the other – a struggle that has historically proven so difficult to overcome (Foucault, 1980)? The lack of a 'reason' or mutually relevant common goal may be the main difficulty of working within and between the different schools of thought. It is difficult to envisage a significant change, a move away from mutual in-feeding, without an external common goal. That is, it is not immediately obvious, how C can suddenly emerge from a friendly dialogue between A_1, A_2, A_3 etc. Likewise, it is difficult to envisage finding a common goal that goes beyond the rivalry for scarce resources between different schools of thought, without it coming from somewhere else. That is, it is difficult to imagine how the fight between A and B can suddenly turn into a striving towards C, unless the common goal is introduced by those who do not necessarily care about the inter- and intra-disciplinary power struggles and simply want their lives to be improved.

However, in envisioning this alternative we do not want to emphasise the importance of community engagement at the expense of theoretical innovation and conceptual development. On the contrary. Theory is the contribution of the researchers to the common activity of doing research. It is the tool that moves beyond the common-sense language, opening up solutions and ways of seeing the world that turns the everyday particular matters into generalized knowledge where what was previously tacit, becomes visible and intelligible. It is the researchers' task to make it usable (Valsiner, 2009) for the common project, just as it is the research-participants' task to 'show' the researchers where their concepts and methods fail and new tools need to be invented. In Freire's (2003/1973) sense, researchers and participants should be *co-agents*. And as noted before, as humans living in the social world we have a responsibility to each other. Ideally then novelty emerges for the lived practices of the research participants and equally for the practices of researchers.

Doing things differently is difficult. It takes time and energy and requires us to abandon our comfort zone for something unpredictable. Yet the 'So what?' questions do matter. And perhaps the unpredictable will not be that uncomfortable after all. Perhaps it will even turn out to be rewarding.

REFERENCES

Aveling, E. L. (2010). *Partnership in whose interests? The impact of partnership-working in Cambodian HIV prevention program.* Unpublished PhD thesis. University of Cambridge.

Bakhtin, M. M. (1986/1993). *Towards a philosophy of the act.* (V. Liapunov Trans. and notes). Austin: University of Texas Press.

Ellis, B. D., & Stam, H. J. (2010). Addressing the other in dialogue: Ricoeur and the ethical dimensions of the dialogical self. *Theory & Psychology, 20*(3), 420-435.

Foucault, M. (1980). *Power/knowledge: Selected interviews and other writings, 1972-1977.* Brighton: Harvester.

Freire, P. (2003/1973). *Education for critical consciousness.* New York: Continuum Publishing Company.

Hedegaard, M., & Chaiklin, S. (2005). *Radical-local teaching and learning. A cultural-historical approach.* Aarhus: Aarhus University Press.

Hviid, P. & Beckstead, Z. (2011). Dialogues about research. In M. Märtsin, B. Wagoner, E. Aveling, I. Kadianaki & L. Whittaker (Eds.), *Dialogicality in focus: Challenges to theory, method and application* (pp. 147-162). New York: Nova Science Publishers.

Jovchelovitch, S. (2007). *Knowledge in context: Representation, community and culture.* London: Routledge.

Linell, P. (2009). *Rethinking language, mind, and world dialogically. Interactional and contextual theories of human sense-making.* Charlotte, NC: Information Age Publishing.

Marková, I. (2003). *Dialogicality and social representations.* The dynamics of mind. Cambridge: Cambridge University Press.

Marková, I. (2011). Challenges to dialogical science. In M. Märtsin, B. Wagoner, E. Aveling, I. Kadianaki & L. Whittaker (Eds.), *Dialogicality in focus: Challenges to theory, method and application* (pp. 65-76). New York: Nova Science Publishers.

Ricoeur, P. (1992). *Oneself as another.* (K. Blamey, Trans.). Chicago, IL: University of Chicago Press. (Original work published 1990).

Shotter, J. (2011). From 'already made things' to 'things in their making': Inquiring 'from within' the dialogic. In M. Märtsin, B. Wagoner, E. Aveling, I. Kadianaki & L. Whittaker (Eds.), *Dialogicality in focus: Challenges to theory, method and application* (pp. 77-102). New York: Nova Science Publishers.

Valsiner, J. (2009). Rethinking dialogicality. Solidity of theory amidst of the flow of dialogues. In P. Linell *Rethinking language, mind, and world dialogically. Interactional and contextual theories of human sense-making* (pp. xxi-xxv). Charlotte, NC: Information Age Publishing.

Valsiner, J. (2011). Coordinating positions to arrive at change: Creative tensions within the dialogical self framework. In M. Märtsin, B. Wagoner, E. Aveling, I. Kadianaki & L. Whittaker (Eds.), *Dialogicality in focus: Challenges to theory, method and application* (pp. 241-248). New York: Nova Science Publishers.

ABOUT THE AUTHORS

Sanne Akkerman, Ph.D., is associate professor at the Institute of Education and Freudenthal Institute at Utrecht University. For many years she has been studying social interaction and collaboration of professionals and students. Her Ph.D. *Strangers in Dialogue* focused on inter-organizational and inter-cultural academic collaboration. Her main concern has been how diversity, multi-membership and instances of ambiguity can function as resources for development not only within collaborative groups, but also with respect to identity development of individual agents. She has focused on the notion of boundaries as a central issue in group negotiations, considering how these take place simultaneously on identity level, group level and institutional level. She recently conducted a literature review on boundary crossing and boundary objects, and studies learning processes of vocational students in apprenticeships as being on the boundary between school and work. In her research she draws on socio-cultural theories and uses a dialogical approach towards identity, cognition and learning. EMAIL: s.f.akkerman@uu.nl.

Emma-Louise Aveling is a researcher in social science applied to health at the University of Leicester. She completed her Ph.D. in social psychology at the University of Cambridge, supported by the Economic and Social Research Council. Her main research focus is the conceptual and empirical exploration of psychosocial processes shaping health and development interventions. Her Ph.D. research used a dialogical social representations approach to study the construction and impact of partnership-working in a Cambodian HIV prevention program. She is particularly interested in how a dialogical epistemology can illuminate our understanding of the relations between knowledge, communication, context and action. She has published in the *Journal of Constructivist Psychology*, the *Journal of Special Education*, the *Journal of Community Psychology* and *AIDS Care*, as well as contributing chapters to *Symbolic transformation: The mind in movement through culture and society* (Routledge, 2010), *Meaning in action: Construction, narrative and representation* (Springer, 2008) and *Cultural dynamics of women's lives: Personal cultures at critical transitions of the life course* (Information Age Publishing, 2010). EMAIL: emmilie_may@yahoo.co.uk

Zachary Beckstead is currently working on his doctoral degree at Clark University in Worcester, USA. His general theoretical and research interest has been oriented to developing a psychology of pilgrimages or how people relate to the holistic structure of shrines, memorials, and other symbolic places and objects. His work has explored how pilgrimage experiences become woven into one's life course and modify a persons' value system; how the holistic organization of memorial or shrine complexes (e.g., both material and social organization of these places) relates to meaning-making processes; and how the episodic moments of affective relevance evoked in these visits become generated and generalized by the person. He is also interested in the history and philosophy underlying the theoretical foundations and praxis of psychology and investigating the relationship between the researcher and research-participant. EMAIL: zbeckstead@gmail.com

Michael Billig is professor of social sciences at Loughborough University and a member of the Discourse and Rhetoric Group at Loughborough. His background is in social psychology, originally having studied under Henri Tajfel at Bristol University. He has written books on a number of different topics, including the extreme right-wing, psycho-analysis, rhetoric, nationalism and the history of rock'n'roll. His most recent books are *Laughter and Ridicule: Towards a Social Critique of Humour* (Sage, 2005) and *The Hidden Roots of Critical Psychology: Understanding the Impact of Locke, Shaftesbury and Reid* (Sage, 2008). He is currently interested in the academic style of writing. EMAIL: M.G.Billig@lboro.ac.uk.

Carla Cunha, M.A., is currently completing her Ph.D. studies in the School of Psychology at the University of Minho (Braga, Portugal) with support from the Portuguese Foundation for Science and Technology. She is also a researcher on the project *Narrative Processes in Psychotherapy* headed by Miguel M. Gonçalves at the University of Minho. Additionally, she is a teaching assistant at the Department of Psychology at ISMAI (Instituto Superior da Maia, Maia, Portugal) and a researcher at GEDI (Group of Studies in Dialogicality and Identity), Unidep, at ISMAI. Her current research interests are focused on identity and change processes following a narrative and dialogical approach, applied to the fields of psychotherapy and human development. EMAIL: ccunha@ismai.pt.

Thorsten Gieser, M.A. in social anthropology and religious studies (University of Heidelberg, Germany) and Ph.D. in social anthropology (University of Aberdeen, UK), is an independent scholar with a particular interest in the cultural phenomenology of intersubjective experience, perception, embodiment and empathy. He has been contributing to the development of dialogical self theory for more than five years. In a *Culture & Psychology* article on ritual shapeshifting practices in Sierra Leone he explored the transgression of boundaries between internal and external positions. In a later *Studia Psychologica* article he made an elaborate case for the embodiment of I-positions in the composition of the self by examining mimetic hunting practices of the Siberian Yukaghir people. He is currently editing (with Hubert Hermans) the upcoming *A Handbook on the Dialogical Self Theory* (Cambridge University Press). EMAIL: thgieser@freenet.de.

Alex Gillespie is a senior lecturer at the University of Stirling in the UK. His main interests are the formation of intersubjectivity, the self, and self-reflection in social interaction. This line of enquiry follows the work of James, Mead, Vygotsky and Bakhtin. He has published a book on this theoretical and empirical work entitled *Becoming Other: From Social Interaction to Self-Reflection* (Information Age Publishing, 2006). He is co-editor, with Ivana Marková, of a forthcoming volume entitled *Trust and Conflict: Representation, Culture and Dialogue* (Routledge). EMAIL: alex.gillespie@stir.ac.uk.

Miguel M. Gonçalves, Ph.D., is professor at the School of Psychology in the University of Minho (Braga, Portugal). He is interested in dialogical and narrative studies of the self and in narrative psychotherapy. He is presently developing a research project to investigate the role of narrative innovations in the promotion of psychotherapeutic change. He and his research team have published several articles and chapters in the last few years on this topic. EMAIL: mgoncalves@psi.uminho.pt.

Andrés Haye is assistant professor at the School of Psychology, Pontificia Universidad Católica de Chile. He has a Ph.D. in psychology from the University of Sheffield. His areas of interest are social psychology, philosophical psychology, and social theory. His research has been focused on the bond of mind and society, for instance, exploring the social basis of memory, involving historical memory of political events; the physiological, cognitive, and cultural aspects of inter-group and political attitudes, comparing generations; and the nature of language operations in biographical discourse both among youth and older people. His current research, with Antonia Larraín, is focused on a dialogical reconstruction of basic psychological concepts, such as memory, representation, thinking, learning, feeling and emotion. The contribution to this book, elaborating on a dialogical approach to language, is part of this effort to understand basic psychological phenomena on the grounds of discursive activity. EMAIL: ahaye@uc.cl.

Hubert J. M. Hermans is emeritus professor of psychology at the Radboud University of Nijmegen. His dissertation (1967) was on *Motivation and Achievement* and resulted in two psychological tests: *The Achievement Motivation Test for Adults* (1968) and *The Achievement Motivation Test for Children* (1971). As a reaction to the static and impersonal nature of psychological tests, he developed a *Self-Confrontation Method* (SCM; 1974; book published in English in 1995). Application of this method in practice led to the establishment of the *Dutch Association for SCM Consultants* that counted 300 members in 2010. In the 1990s he developed a *Dialogical Self Theory*, inspired by the American pragmatism of William James and the dialogical school of the Russian literary scholar Mikhail Bakhtin. Since 2002 he is the president of the *International Society for Dialogical Science* (ISDS) and since 2006 editor-in-chief of the *International Journal for Dialogical Science* (IJDS). Together with Agnieska Hermans-Konopka, he has recently published the book *Dialogical Self Theory: Positioning and Counter-Positioning in a Globalizing Society* (Cambridge University Press, 2010). For his scientific merits to society, he was decorated as Knight in the Order of the Netherlands Lion in 2002. Website: www.huberthermans.com. EMAIL: hhermans@psych.ru.nl.

Pernille Hviid was educated as a preschool teacher, and is now associate professor of psychology at the University of Copenhagen, Denmark. She works on developmental psychology with a special focus on children's own experience of their everyday lives, their institutional arrangements and their development. She has recently published in *European Journal of Psychology of Education*, and contributed a chapter to the book *Studying Children – A Cultural Historical Approach* (Open University Press, 2008, edited by Hedegaard and Fleer). At present she is conducting an ecological experiment on developing alternative strategies to New Public Management in the day-care sector, in cooperation with children, parents, pedagogues, administrators and politicians. She has been a member of the National Council of Children's Rights in Denmark for eight years. EMAIL: Pernille.Hviid@psy.ku.dk.

Amrei Joerchel has received her B.A., majoring in psychology, from Clark University, USA, in 2003 and her M.Sc. in 2004 from the London School of Economics and Political Science in social psychology. She is currently working towards her Ph.D. at the University of Vienna, focusing on the formation of the self-concept in relation to social and cultural processes. Parallel to her Ph.D. studies she has started her training program to become a psychotherapist and is a founding member of the Institute for Cultural Psychology and

Qualitative Social Research (*Institut für Kulturpsychologie und Qualitative Sozialforschung*) based in Vienna. EMAIL: amreijoerchel@hotmail.com.

Irini Kadianaki has recently received her Ph.D. in social psychology from the University of Cambridge, with the support of Alexander S. Onassis Public Benefit Foundation and Cambridge European Trust. Her work is on the topic of immigration from a cultural-psychological perspective. She has examined the ways that immigrant employ cultural elements as symbolic resources to cope with psychological challenges of relocation; the ways they negotiate perceptions of self and other in their discourse and the structures of meaning they employ to protect the self from stigma; the function of immigrant communities and the ways they mediate the experience of immigrants in a new social context. Her publications appear in *Culture & Psychology*, and in the books *Oxford Handbook of Culture and Psychology* (Oxford University Press, forthcoming), *Symbolic Transformation: The Mind in Movement through Culture and Society"* (Routlege, 2009) and *Dynamic Process Methodology in the Social and Developmental Sciences* (Springer, 2009). EMAIL: eirinikad@gmail.com.

Catarina Kinnvall is associate professor at the Department of Political Science, Lund University, Sweden. She is the former vice-president of the International Society of Political Psychology (ISPP). She was program chair and local organizer for the ISSP Annual Conference in Lund, July 2004. She is the author of a number of books and articles. Some of her publications include: *The Political Psychology of Globalisation: Muslims in the West* (Oxford University Press, 2010, with P. Nesbitt-Larking); *On Behalf of Others: The Psychology of Care in a Global World* (Oxford University Press, 2009, co-ed.); *Globalisation and Religious Nationalism in India: The Search for Ontological Security* (Routledge, 2006); and *Globalisation and Democratization in Asia: The Construction of Identity* (Routledge, 2002, co-ed.). EMAIL: Catarina.Kinnvall@svet.lu.se.

Antonia Larrain is assistant professor at the Faculty of Psychology, Universidad Alberto Hurtado, Chile. She has a Ph.D. in psychology from Pontificia Universidad Católica de Chile. Her current research is on the relationship between discourse and thinking. From a theoretical point of view, she has been engaged in re-conceptualising key psychological notions from a dialogical and discursive approach, particularly influenced by the works of Vygotsky, Bakhtin and Voloshinov. Her empirical research has been focused on the effect of particular kinds of discursive activities in thinking development among preschool and school aged children. During 2010 she carried out postdoctoral research in the Faculty of Education, Cambridge University, UK, which aimed at describing the uses of argumentative discourse in science teaching and learning in secondary Chilean education. EMAIL: alarrain@uahurtado.cl.

Marcela Lonchuk is associate professor at the Universidad de Buenos Aires where she teaches semiotics. Her research focuses on the semiotic interpretation of graphic art images, discourse and communication. She has published on the application of semiotic models as didactic tools for understanding academic texts by university students. Currently she is interested in understanding how graphic art images and shapes that are available in the urban space can constitute arguments of national identity. EMAIL: marlonchuk@gmail.com.

Mariann Märtsin holds a Ph.D. from the University of Bath, where she was a member of the Centre for Sociocultural and Activity Theory Research. She is currently working at Cardiff University, as a researcher in the Wales Institute of Social & Economic Research, Data & Methods (WISERD). She is interested in exploring how young people make sense of their life-course transitions and how socio-cultural contexts and structures shape and are shaped by young people as they imagine themselves forward. She is also interested in using multi-modal methods in the investigation of sense-making. Her work is published in *Theory & Psychology* and in *Integrative Psychological & Behavioral Science*. She has also contributed to the forthcoming *Oxford Handbook of Culture and Psychology* (Oxford University Press) and to the journals *Culture & Psychology* and *Yearbook of Idiographic Science*. EMAIL: M.Martsin@gmail.com.

Marlene Matos, Ph.D., is assistant professor at the School of Psychology in the University of Minho (Braga, Portugal). She has been interested in studies about partner violence and psychotherapeutic change. She is presently developing a research project regarding group intervention with battered women (efficacy and change processes). EMAIL: mmatos@psi.uminho.pt.

Inês Mendes, B.A., is currently completing her Ph.D. studies in the School of Psychology at the University of Minho (Braga, Portugal) with support from the Portuguese Foundation for Science and Technology. Her current research interests are theoretically focused on the development of novel self-narratives and their application to change processes in psychotherapy. EMAIL: id1596@alunos.uminho.pt.

Kyoko Murakami is a lecturer in the Department of Education and a member of the Centre for Sociocultural and Activity Theory Research at the University of Bath, UK. Her research interests include social remembering, reconciliation, identities and social action, social shaping of technology and development of learning in intercultural and intergenerational encounters. Her research is informed by discourse analysis, discursive psychology and sociocultural theory. Her research publications include papers and book chapters on discourse analysis, Anglo-Japanese reconciliation initiatives, the narrative learning of students on work placements, and prosody in classroom discourse. EMAIL: k.murakami@bath.ac.uk

Theo Niessen, Ph.D., works as researcher and teacher of ethics in nursing at Fontys University of Applied Sciences. In his teaching he aims at stimulating movement and reflection on care, authenticity and passion. In his research he investigates how to stimulate development of practice and theory in nursing. He has a background in philosophy and has been mainly concerned with epistemologies in the context of education. His Ph.D. study *Emerging Epistemologies: Making Sense of Teaching Practice* addressed the experiences and struggles of teachers in the context of educational renewal. In contrast to common approaches of educational research that study isolated variables, he explicitly aims to preserve the complexity of teaching by staying close to the narratives and daily practice of teachers. In his research he takes an enactivist and hermeneutic approach. EMAIL: t.niessen@fontys.nl.

Peter Raggatt is a senior lecturer in the Department of Psychology at James Cook University, Townsville, Australia. He has broad interests in social and cultural theory, social psychology, personality, semiotics, and narrative psychology. He has made recent contributions to *Theory & Psychology* (2007, 2010), the *Journal of Personality* (2006), and the forthcoming *A Handbook on the Dialogical Self Theory* (Cambridge University Press). His book entitled *Dialogical Formations: Investigations into the Origins of the Dialogical Self* will appear in 2011. EMAIL: Peter.Raggatt@jcu.edu.au.

António P. Ribeiro, M.A., is currently completing his Ph.D. studies in the School of Psychology at the University of Minho (Braga, Portugal) with support from the Portuguese Foundation for Science and Technology. His current research interests are theoretically focused in narrative and dialogical perspectives and their application to change processes in psychotherapy. EMAIL: id2218@alunos.uminho.pt.

Alberto Rosa is professor of psychology at the Universidad Autónoma de Madrid, where he teaches courses on the history of psychology and cultural psychology. He is the co-author of *Methodology of History of Psychology* (Alianza Editorial, 1996, with J.A. Huertas and F. Blanco) and the co-editor of the *Cambridge Handbook of Sociocultural Psychology* (Cambridge University Press, 2007, with Jaan Valsiner). He has carried out research on developmental psychology of the physically challenged, co-authoring *Psychology of Blindness* (Alianza Editorial, 1993, with E. Ochaíta) and *The Child with Cerebral Palsy* (Ministerio de Educación y Ciencia, 1993, I.Montero and M.J. García-Lorente). Currently he is carrying out research to unpack how cultural and historical knowledge influences the shaping of identity. He has co-edited *Collective Memory and National Identity* (Biblioteca Nueva, 2000, with G. Bellelli and D. Bakhurst) and *Teaching of History and Collective Memory* (Paidós, 2006, with M. Carretero and F. González). EMAIL: alberto.rosa@uam.es.

João Salgado, Ph.D., is assistant professor and head of the Department of Psychology and Communication at ISMAI, Portugal. He is also a psychotherapist and the director of the counselling service of his university. His main research interests are associated with the theoretical and methodological developments of a dialogical perspective within psychology, and with the applications of this framework to the field of psychotherapy and clinical psychology. He is presently developing a research project on the role of the decentering processes in psychotherapeutic change. EMAIL: jsalgado@docentes.ismai.pt

Anita Santos, Ph.D., is a visiting assistant professor at ISMAI—Instituto Superior da Maia (Maia, Portugal). Her research interests are related to psychotherapy and change processes, within the theoretical framework of narrative therapy and dialogical self theory. She has been co-author of several papers in this scientific area, mainly utilising case studies and microgenetic analysis of psychotherapeutic processes. She has also been involved in research projects concerning therapeutic change. EMAIL: anitasantos@docentes.ismai.pt.

Sarah Scuzzarello, Ph.D., currently holds a lectureship in international relations at Lund University. Her field of research is multiculturalism, feminist ethics, and comparative narrative analysis. Her empirical areas of research have included Sweden, Italy and Britain. She has been a visiting fellow at the Centre for the Study of Ethnicity and Citizenship, at Bristol University and at the Centre for Narrative Research, University of East London. She has recently published in *Social Politics* and co-edited the book *On Behalf of Others: The Psychology of Care in a Global World* (Oxford University Press, 2009). EMAIL: Sarah.Scuzzarello@svet.lu.se.

John Shotter is emeritus professor of communication in the Department of Communication, University of New Hampshire and is now a tutor on a Professional Doctorate in Systemic Practice program in the University of Bedfordshire, Luton, England. He is the author of *Social Accountability and Selfhood* (Blackwell, 1984), *Cultural Politics of Everyday Life: Social Constructionism, Rhetoric, and Knowing of the Third Kind* (Open University, 1993), and *Conversational Realities: the Construction of Life through Language* (Sage, 1993). He has a new book in press: *Getting It: Withness-Thinking and the Dialogical... In Practice* (Hampton Press). EMAIL: jds@hypatia.unh.edu.

Lívia Mathias Simão is associate professor at the Institute of Psychology of the University of São Paulo, Brazil, where she has been professor since 1987, coordinating the Laboratory of Verbal Interaction and Knowledge Construction and lecturing courses on

History and Philosophy of Psychology, Processes of Knowledge Construction in I-Other and I-Self Relationships and Theoretical and Methodological Issues in Psychology. She is also a sponsored researcher of the National Council for Scientific and Technologic Development of Brazil. Her main research concerns issues embracing the ontological construction of human subjectivity in I–world, I–other and I–self relationships from the perspective of the semiotic-cultural constructivism in psychology and from the broader perspective of the philosophy of psychology. She has co-edited the book *Otherness in Question: Labyrinths of the Self* (Information Age Publishing, 2007, with Jaan Valsiner) and made contributions to the book *Striving for the Whole: Creating Theoretical Syntheses* (Transaction Publishers, 2008) and for the forthcoming *Oxford Handbook in Culture and Psychology* (Oxford University Press), as well as for the journals *Theory & Psychology*, *Culture & Psychology*. EMAIL: limsimao@usp.br

Jaan Valsiner is a cultural psychologist with a consistently developmental axiomatic base that is brought to analyses of any psychological or social phenomena. He is the founding editor (1995) of the Sage journal *Culture & Psychology*. He is currently professor of psychology at the Department of Psychology, Clark University, USA. He has published many books, the most pertinent of which are *The Guided Mind* (Harvard University Press, 1998) and *Culture in Minds and Societies* (Sage, 2007). He has edited the *Handbook of Developmental Psychology* (Sage, 2003, with Kevin Connolly) as well as the *Cambridge Handbook of Sociocultural Psychology* (Cambridge University Press, 2007, with Alberto Rosa). He is the editor-in-chief of *Integrative Psychological and Behavioral Science* (Springer, from 2007) and *History and Theory of Psychology* (Transaction Publishers, from 2008). In 1995 he was awarded the Alexander von Humboldt Prize in Germany for his interdisciplinary work on human development and in 1995-1997 the Senior Fulbright Lecturing Award in Brazil. He has been a visiting professor in Australia, Brazil, Estonia, Germany, Italy, Japan, the Netherlands and United Kingdom. EMAIL: jvalsiner@clarku.edu.

Brady Wagoner completed his Ph.D. at University of Cambridge and is now associate professor of psychology at Aalborg University, Denmark. His interests include the history and philosophy of psychology, cultural psychology, constructive memory, existentialism, pragmatism and the absurd pursuit of mountain summits. He is on the editorial board of *Culture & Psychology* and *Integrative Psychological and Behavioral Science*, and is co-founding editor of *Psychology & Society* [accessed at: www.psychologyandsociety.sps.cam.ac.uk]. Additionally, he is a co-creator of the *Sir Frederic Bartlett Internet Archive* [accessed at: www.ppsis.cam.ac.uk/bartlett/] and has recently published *Symbolic Transformation: The Mind in Movement through Culture and Society* (Routledge, 2010). EMAIL: wagoner@hum.aau.dk.

Lisa Whittaker is in the final stages of her PhD at the University of Stirling, Scotland, supported by the Economic and Social Research Council. Her research explores the identities of young people who are not in education, employment or training. She is particularly interested in the role recognition plays within identity construction. She has published in *Psychology & Society* and the *International Journal for Dialogical Science* as well as co-authoring a chapter in the forthcoming *Handbook on Dialogical Self Theory* (Cambridge University Press). In addition, Lisa has explored how young people present themselves on the social networking site Bebo and she sits on an Internet Safety Steering group with Central Scotland Police and other agencies. Lisa has recently taken up a post with The Prince's Trust,

Scotland a youth charity which supports young people into education, employment or training. EMAIL: sw25@stir.ac.uk

Tania Zittoun is a professor at the Institute of Psychology and Education at the University of Neuchâtel (Switzerland). With a background in socio-cognitive learning psychology, she has adopted a sociocultural perspective to understand lifelong developmental processes. She is particularly interested in the role of cultural experiences in daily life, and in the social and emotional conditions for processes of semiotic elaboration to occur and for new ideas to emerge. Her work has brought her to study ruptures and transitions in the life course, and how people might use cultural elements available to them as semiotic resources in times of change. She is associate editor of the Sage journal *Culture & Psychology*, the author of *Transitions: Development through Symbolic Resources* (Information Age Publishing, 2006) and a co-author of *Melodies of Living. Developmental Science of the Human Life Course* (Cambridge University Press, forthcoming, with J. Valsiner, D. Vedeler, J. Salgado, M. Gonçalves, & D. Ferring). EMAIL: tania.zittoun@unine.ch

INDEX

L

M

S